OLDBOY

volume 7

story by
GARON TSUCHIYA

art by
NOBUAKI MINEGISHI

translation
KUMAR SIVASUBRAMANIAN

lettering and retouch
MICHAEL DAVID THOMAS

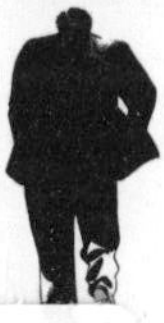

DARK HORSE MANGA™

CONTENTS

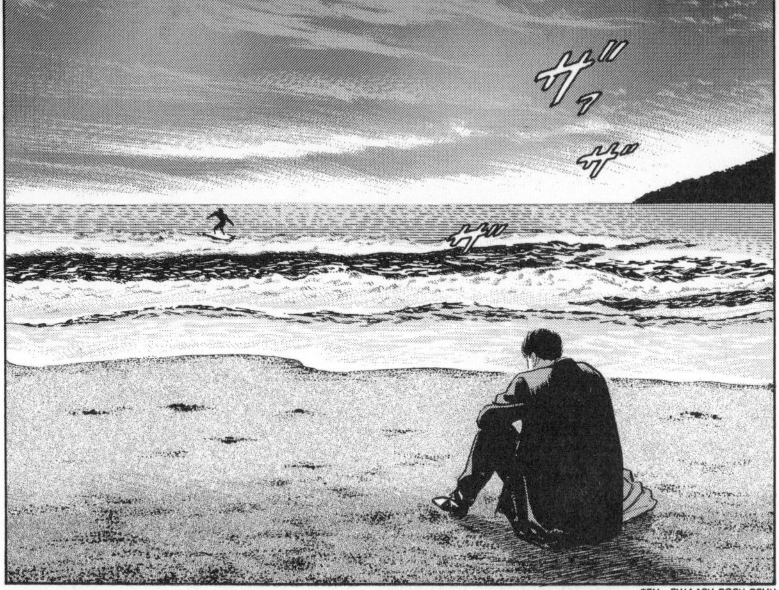

*FX: FWAASH FSSH FSHH

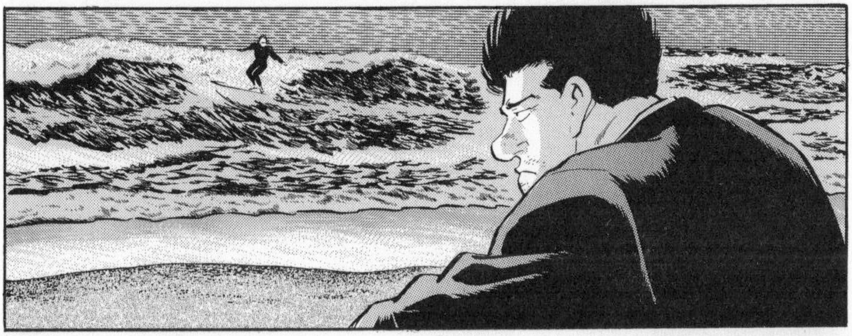

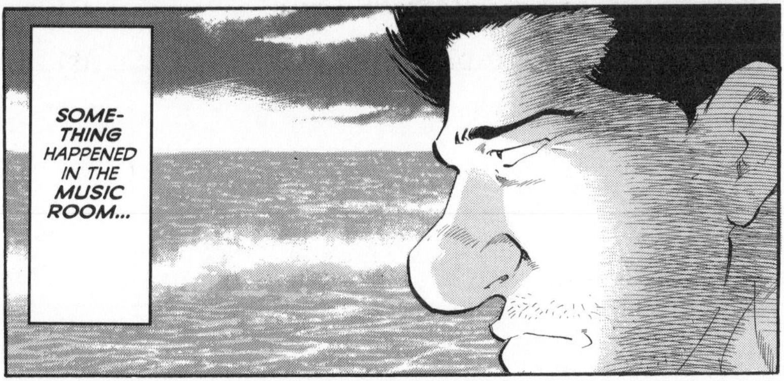
SOME-THING HAPPENED IN THE MUSIC ROOM...

Chapter 60
Shooting Star Epiphany

第60話◎流星の啓示

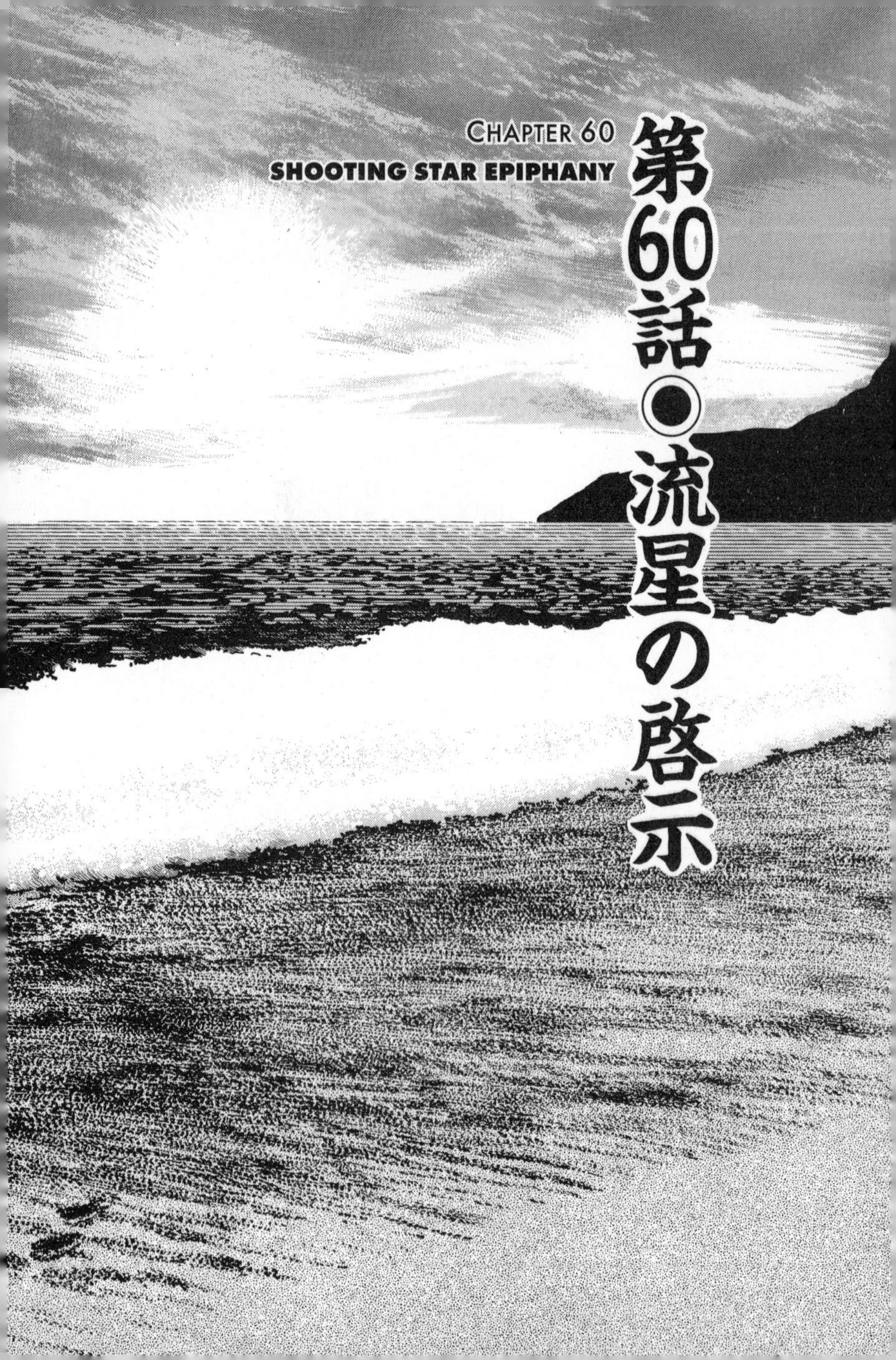

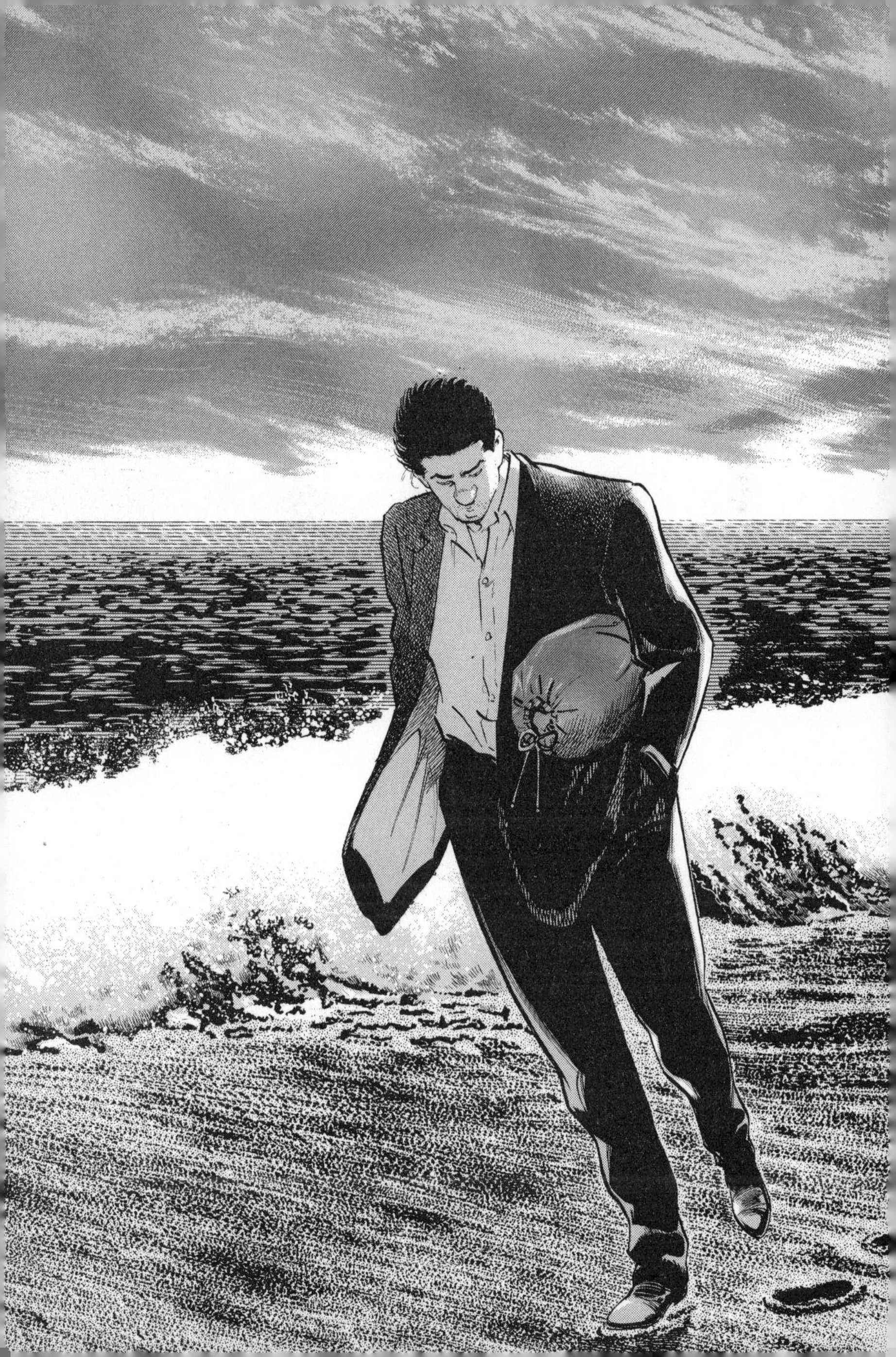

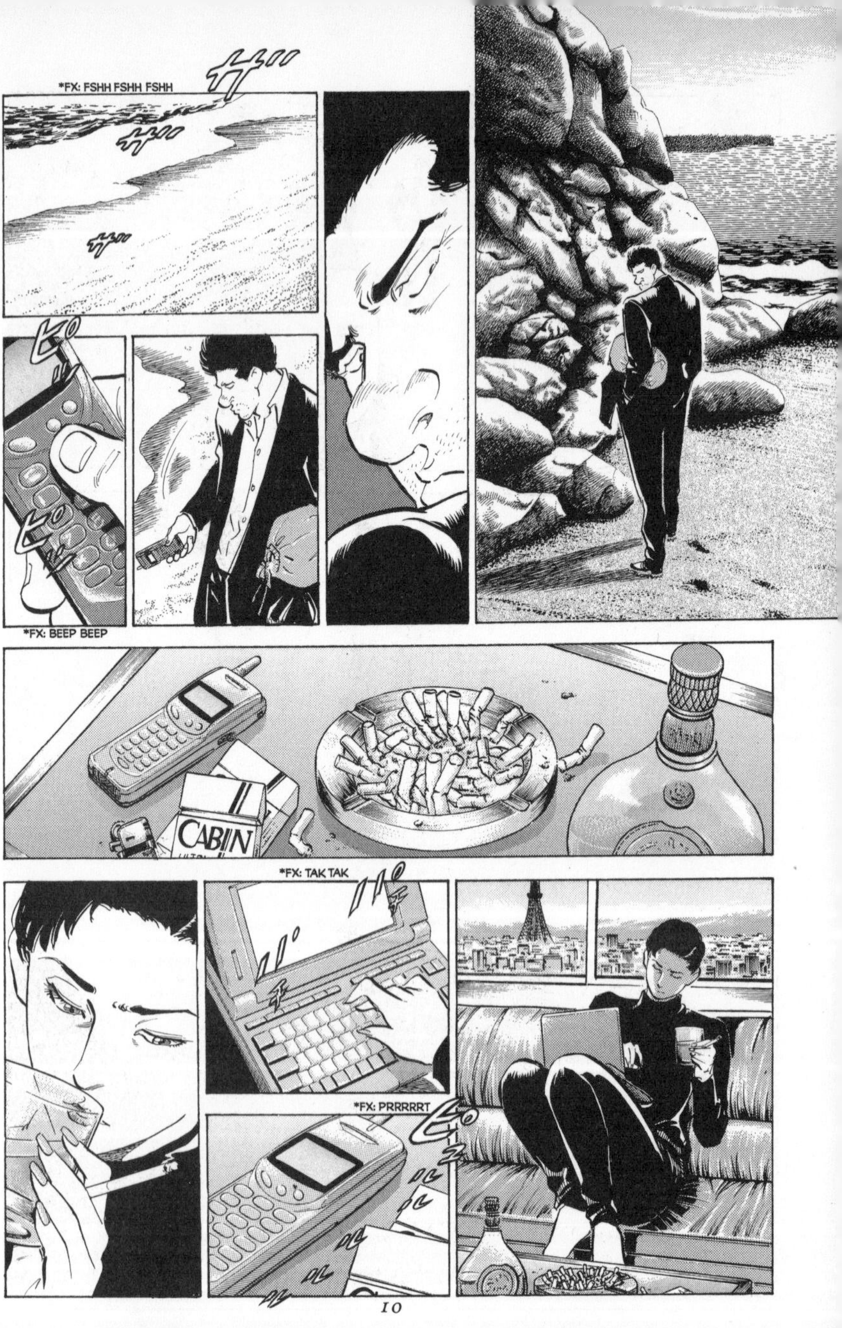
*FX: FSHH FSHH FSHH
*FX: BEEP BEEP
CABIN
*FX: TAK TAK
*FX: PRRRRRT

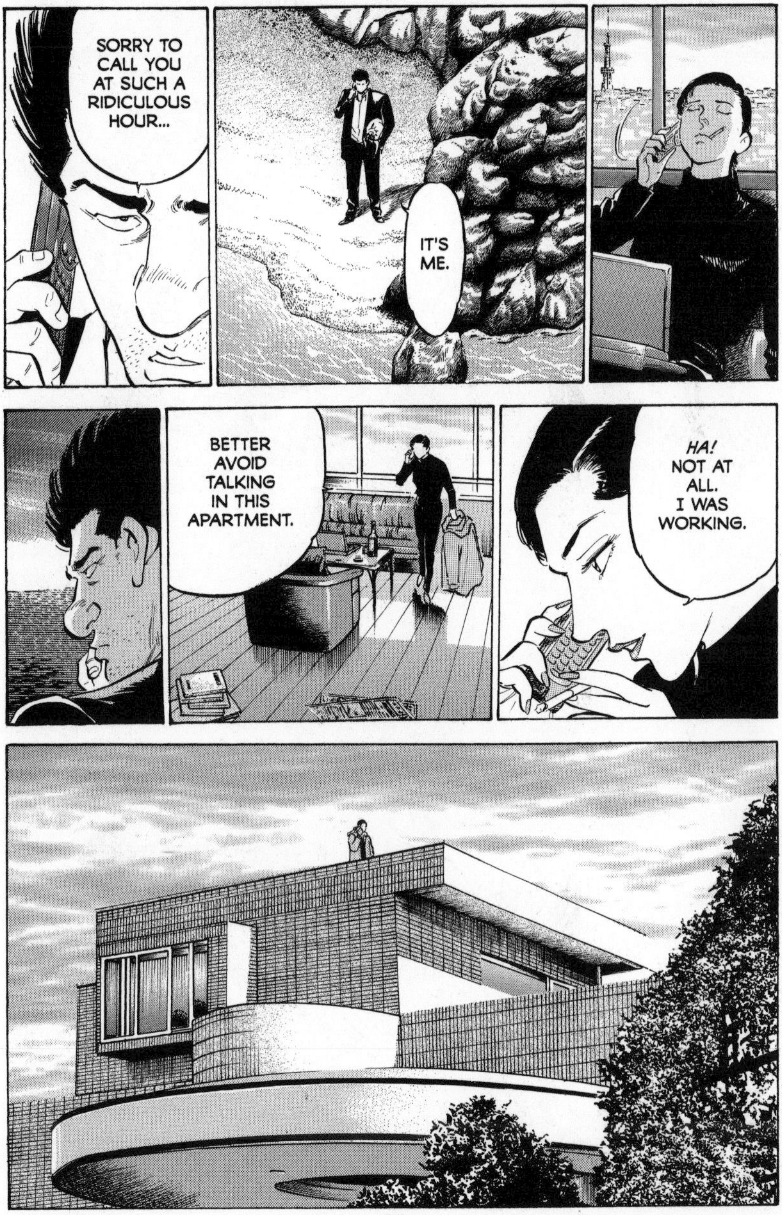
IT'S ME.
SORRY TO CALL YOU AT SUCH A RIDICULOUS HOUR...
HA! NOT AT ALL. I WAS WORKING.
BETTER AVOID TALKING IN THIS APARTMENT.

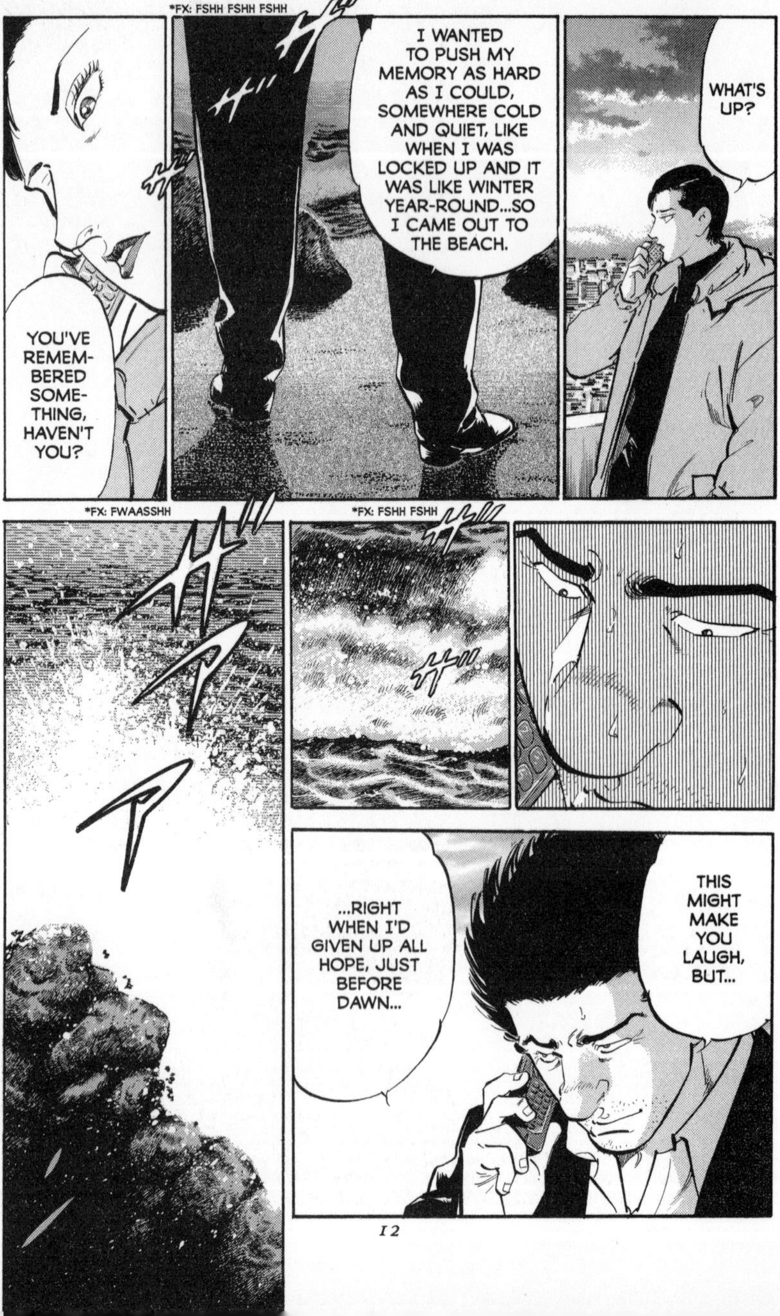
WHAT'S UP?
*FX: FSHH FSHH FSHH
I WANTED TO PUSH MY MEMORY AS HARD AS I COULD, SOMEWHERE COLD AND QUIET, LIKE WHEN I WAS LOCKED UP AND IT WAS LIKE WINTER YEAR-ROUND...SO I CAME OUT TO THE BEACH.
YOU'VE REMEMBERED SOMETHING, HAVEN'T YOU?
*FX: FSHH FSHH
THIS MIGHT MAKE YOU LAUGH, BUT...
...RIGHT WHEN I'D GIVEN UP ALL HOPE, JUST BEFORE DAWN...
*FX: FWAASSHH

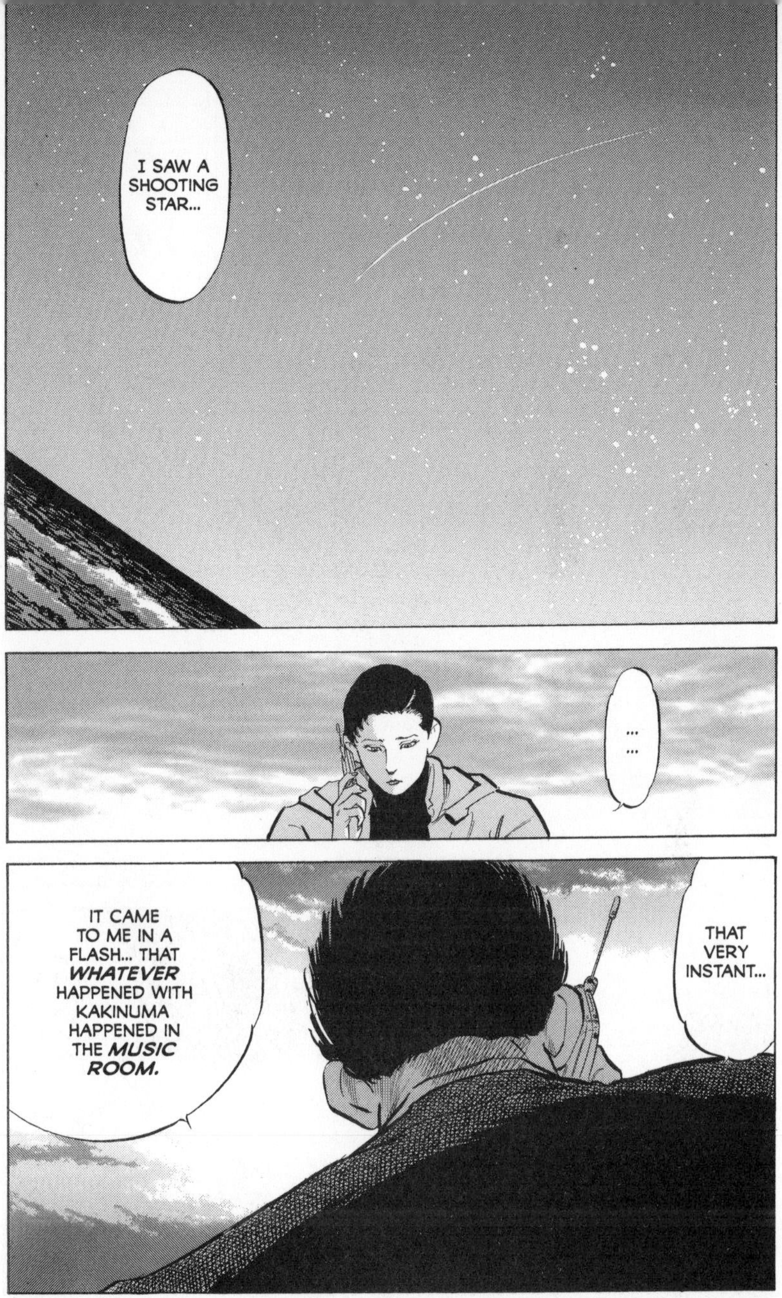
I SAW A SHOOTING STAR...
......
THAT VERY INSTANT...
IT CAME TO ME IN A FLASH... THAT ***WHATEVER*** HAPPENED WITH KAKINUMA HAPPENED IN THE ***MUSIC ROOM.***

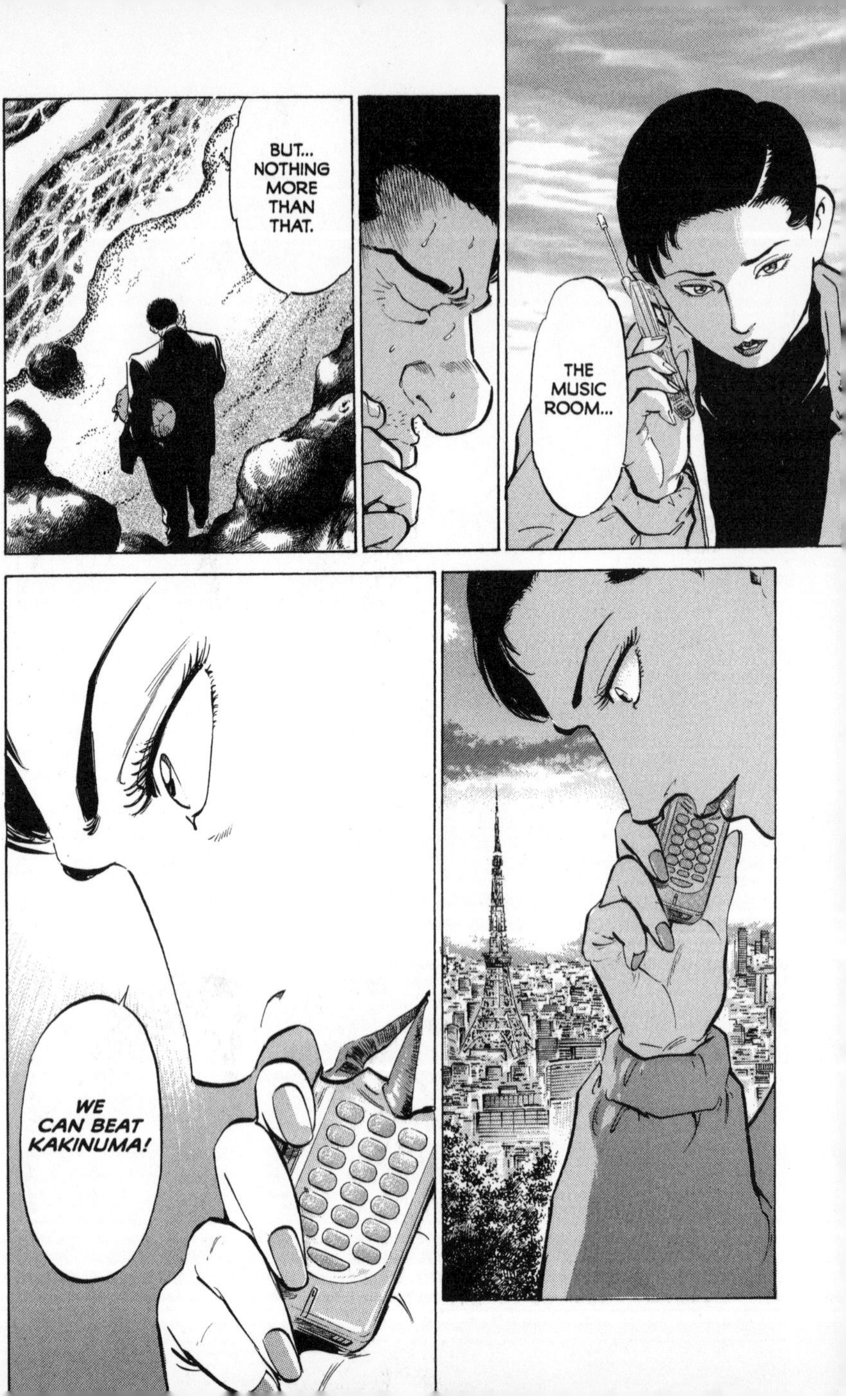
THE MUSIC ROOM...
BUT... NOTHING MORE THAN THAT.
WE CAN BEAT KAKINUMA!

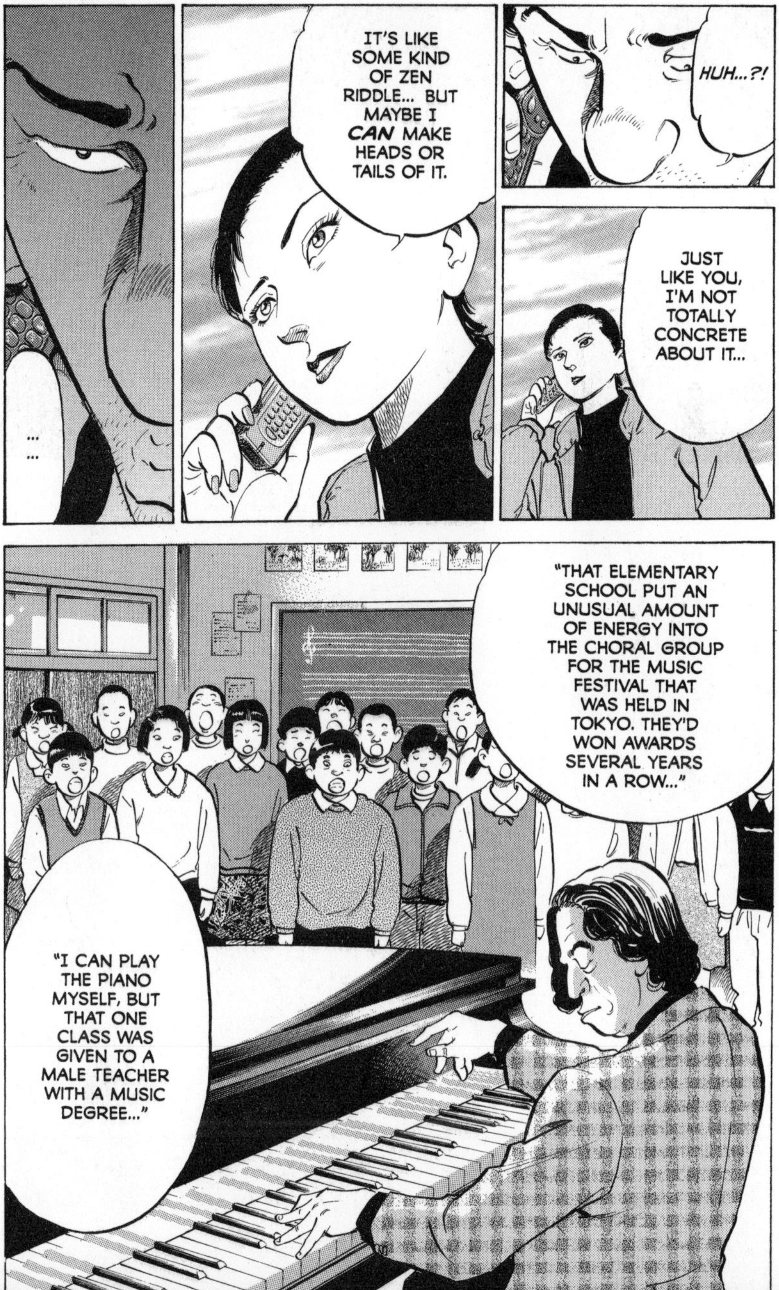
HUH...?!
JUST LIKE YOU, I'M NOT TOTALLY CONCRETE ABOUT IT...
IT'S LIKE SOME KIND OF ZEN RIDDLE... BUT MAYBE I *CAN* MAKE HEADS OR TAILS OF IT.
... ...
"THAT ELEMENTARY SCHOOL PUT AN UNUSUAL AMOUNT OF ENERGY INTO THE CHORAL GROUP FOR THE MUSIC FESTIVAL THAT WAS HELD IN TOKYO. THEY'D WON AWARDS SEVERAL YEARS IN A ROW..."
"I CAN PLAY THE PIANO MYSELF, BUT THAT ONE CLASS WAS GIVEN TO A MALE TEACHER WITH A MUSIC DEGREE..."

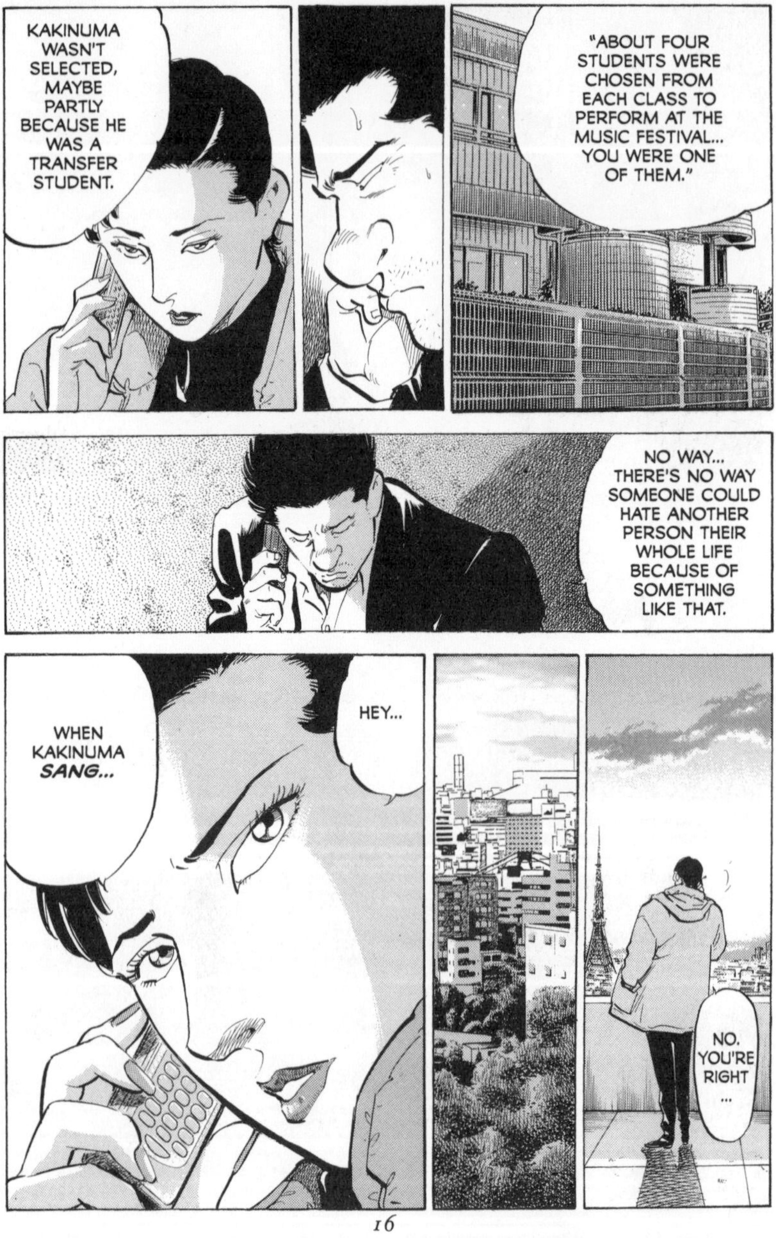
"ABOUT FOUR STUDENTS WERE CHOSEN FROM EACH CLASS TO PERFORM AT THE MUSIC FESTIVAL... YOU WERE ONE OF THEM."
KAKINUMA WASN'T SELECTED, MAYBE PARTLY BECAUSE HE WAS A TRANSFER STUDENT.
NO WAY... THERE'S NO WAY SOMEONE COULD HATE ANOTHER PERSON THEIR WHOLE LIFE BECAUSE OF SOMETHING LIKE THAT.
NO. YOU'RE RIGHT ...
HEY...
WHEN KAKINUMA *SANG...*

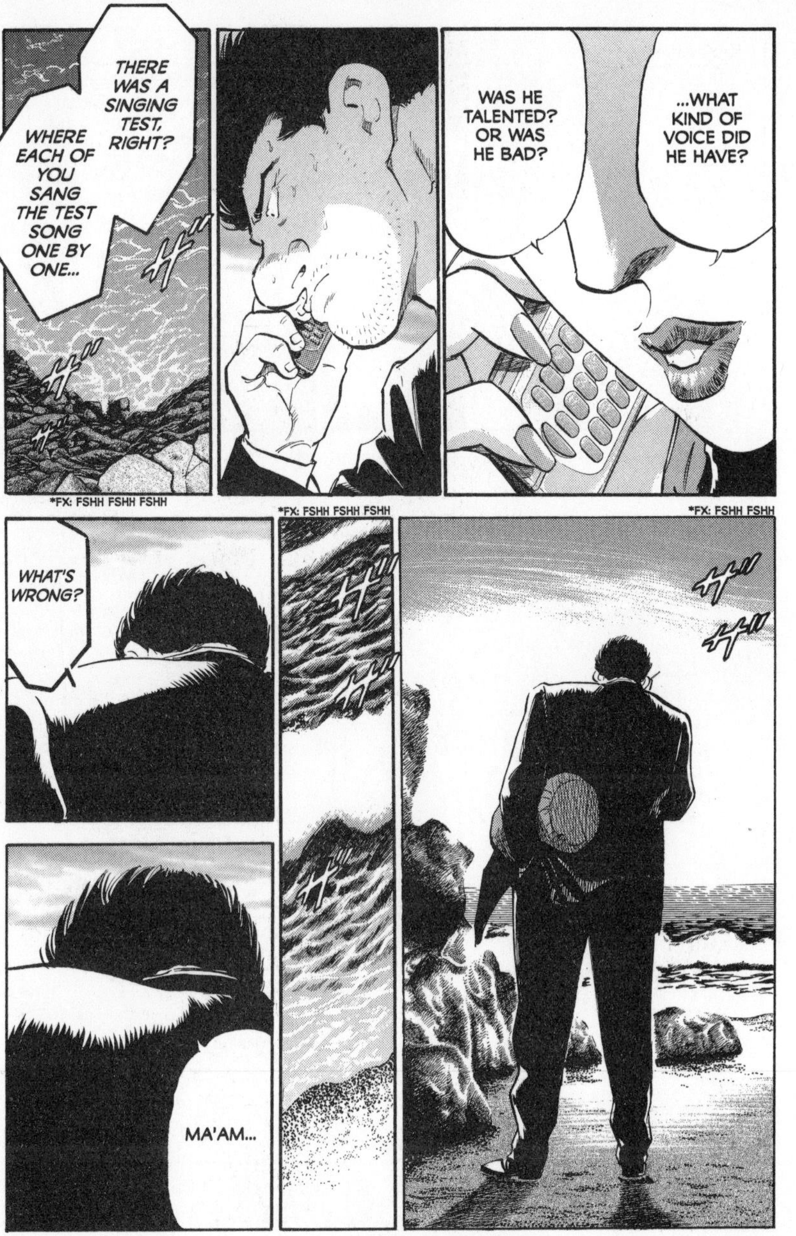

...WHAT KIND OF VOICE DID HE HAVE?
WAS HE TALENTED? OR WAS HE BAD?
*FX: FSHH FSHH
*FX: FSHH FSHH FSHH
THERE WAS A SINGING TEST, RIGHT?
WHERE EACH OF YOU SANG THE TEST SONG ONE BY ONE...
*FX: FSHH FSHH FSHH
WHAT'S WRONG?
MA'AM...

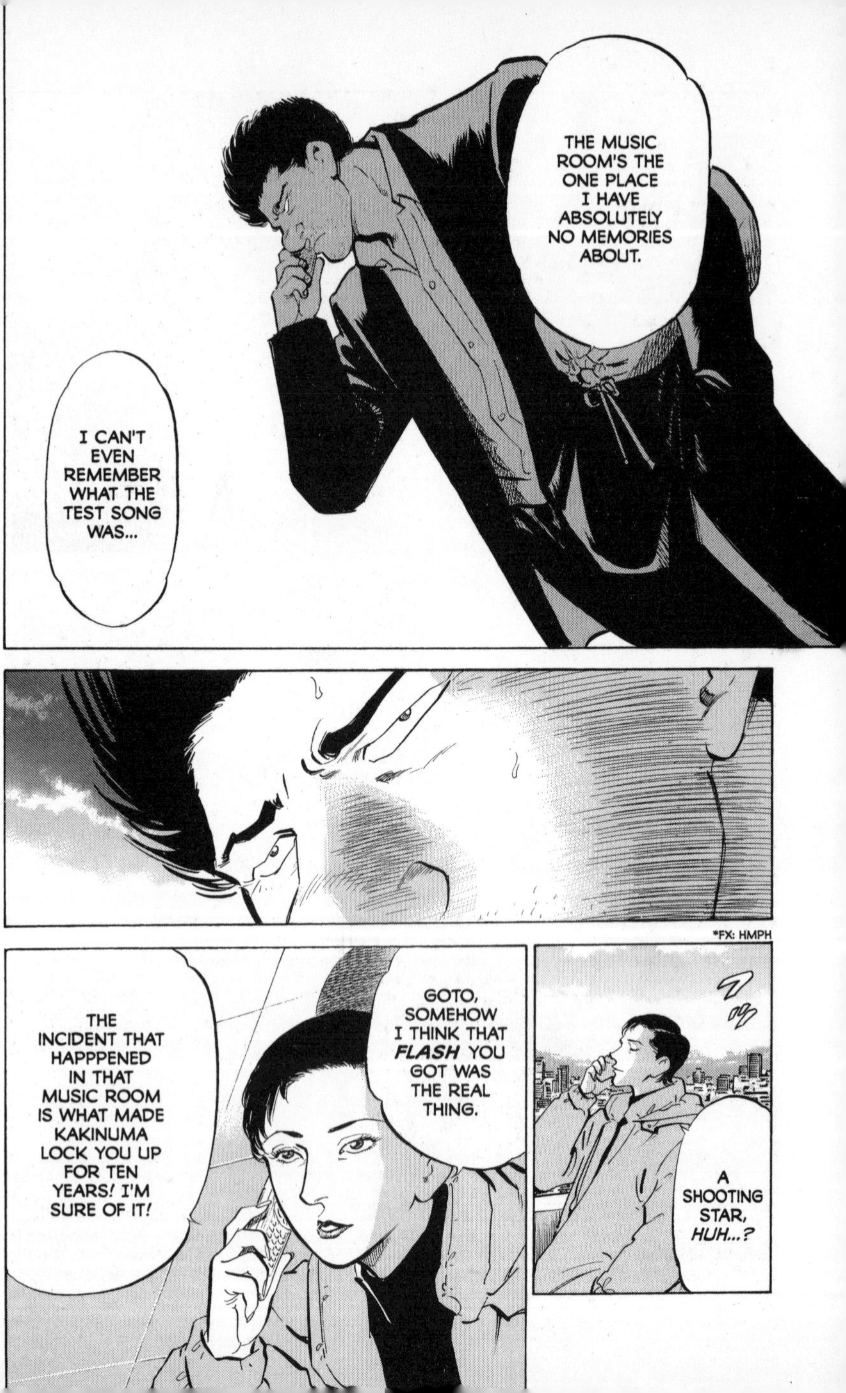
THE MUSIC ROOM'S THE ONE PLACE I HAVE ABSOLUTELY NO MEMORIES ABOUT.
I CAN'T EVEN REMEMBER WHAT THE TEST SONG WAS...
*FX: HMPH
A SHOOTING STAR, *HUH...?*
GOTO, SOMEHOW I THINK THAT ***FLASH*** YOU GOT WAS THE REAL THING.
THE INCIDENT THAT HAPPPENED IN THAT MUSIC ROOM IS WHAT MADE KAKINUMA LOCK YOU UP FOR TEN YEARS*!* I'M SURE OF IT*!*

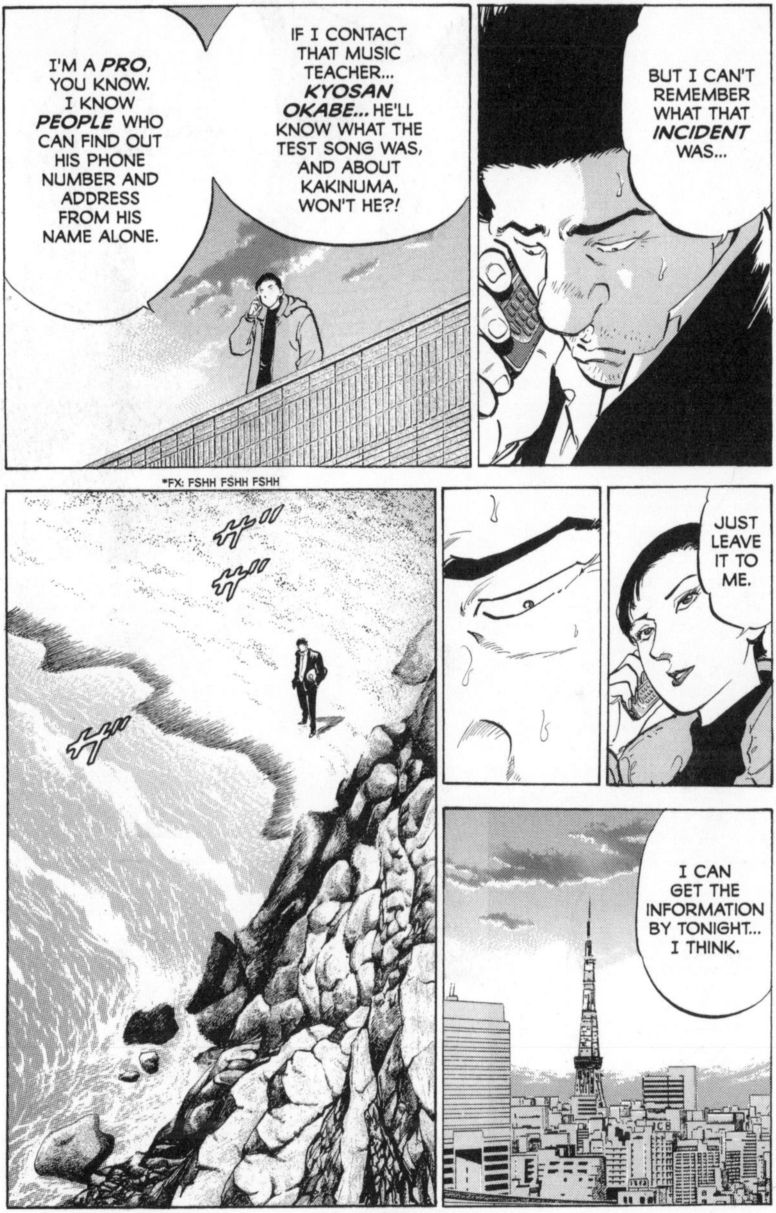
BUT I CAN'T REMEMBER WHAT THAT INCIDENT WAS...
IF I CONTACT THAT MUSIC TEACHER... KYOSAN OKABE... HE'LL KNOW WHAT THE TEST SONG WAS, AND ABOUT KAKINUMA, WON'T HE?!
I'M A PRO, YOU KNOW. I KNOW PEOPLE WHO CAN FIND OUT HIS PHONE NUMBER AND ADDRESS FROM HIS NAME ALONE.
JUST LEAVE IT TO ME.
I CAN GET THE INFORMATION BY TONIGHT... I THINK.
*FX: FSHH FSHH FSHH

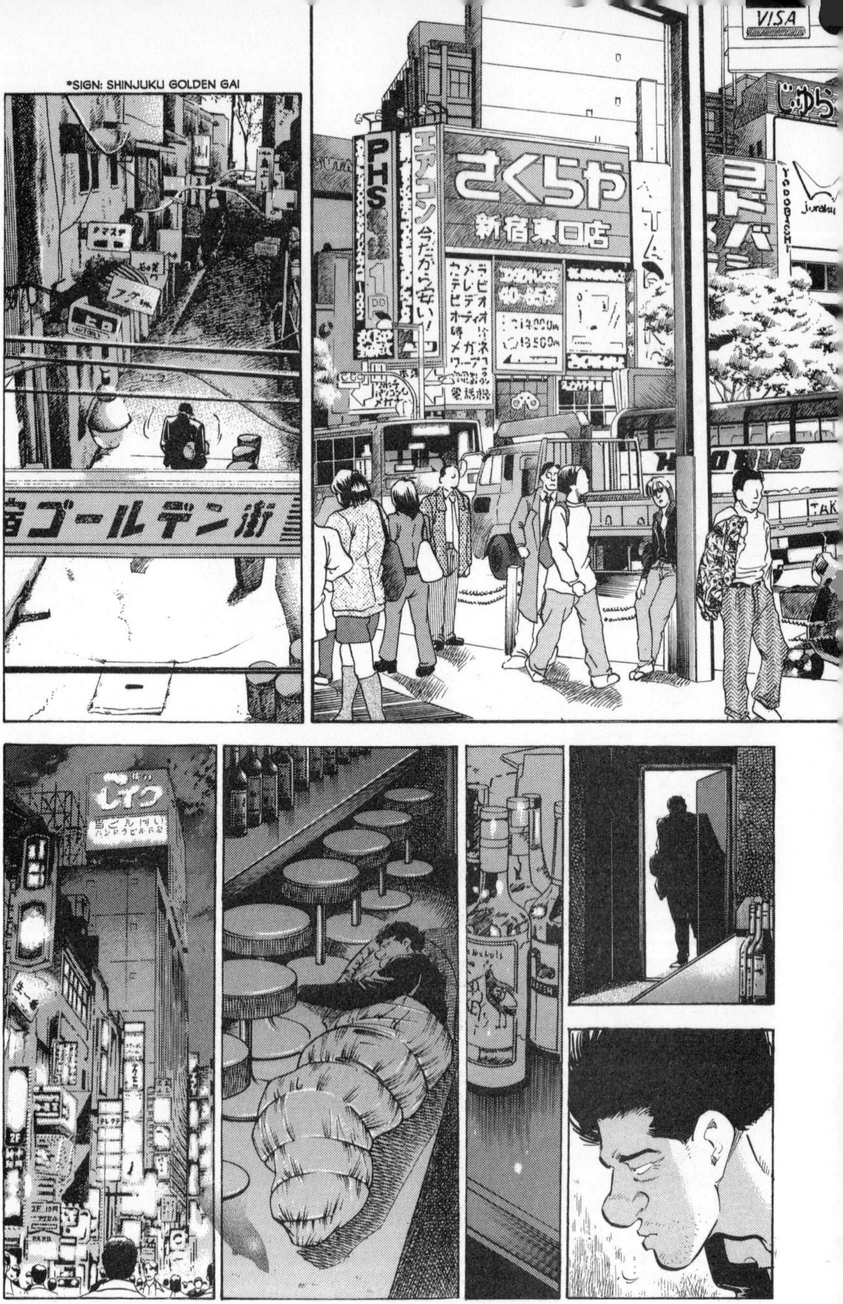
VISA
さくらや
新宿東口店
エアコン今だから安い!
PHS
YODOBASHI
*SIGN: SHINJUKU GOLDEN GAI
ゴールデン街

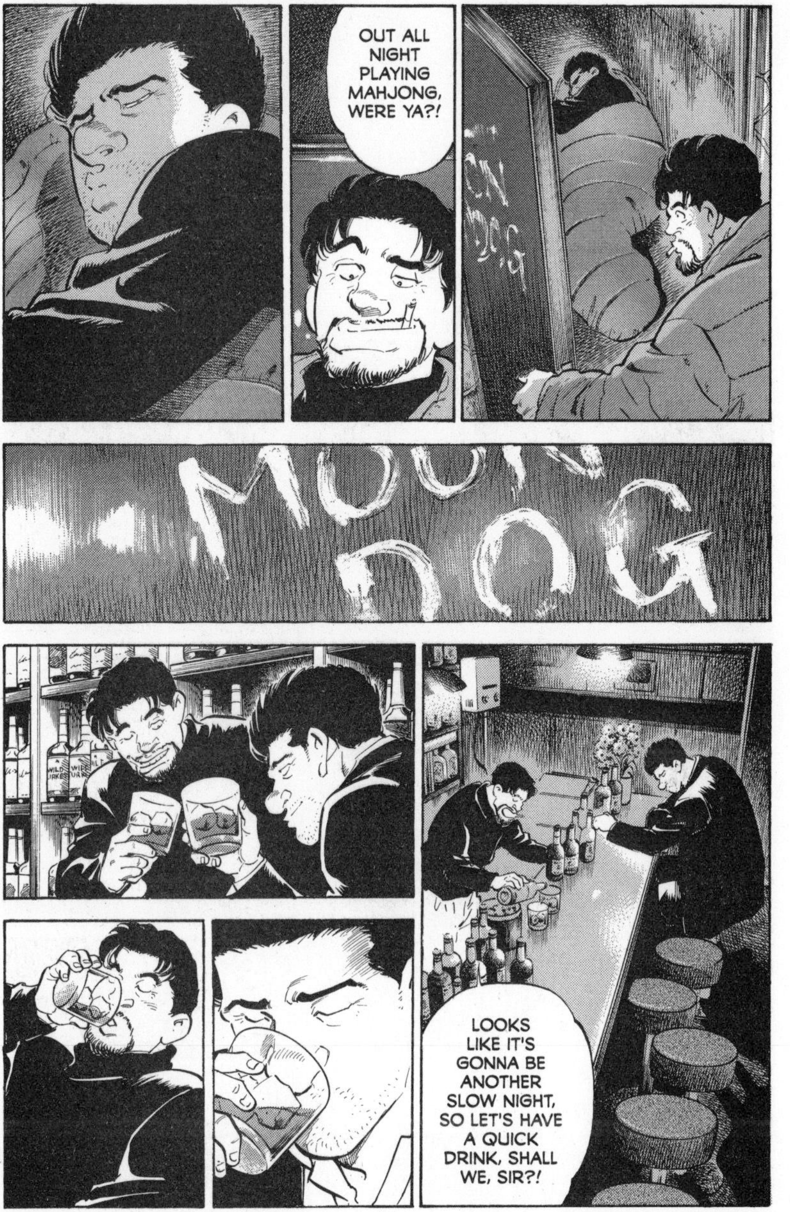
OUT ALL NIGHT PLAYING MAHJONG, WERE YA?!
MOON DOG
LOOKS LIKE IT'S GONNA BE ANOTHER SLOW NIGHT, SO LET'S HAVE A QUICK DRINK, SHALL WE, SIR?!

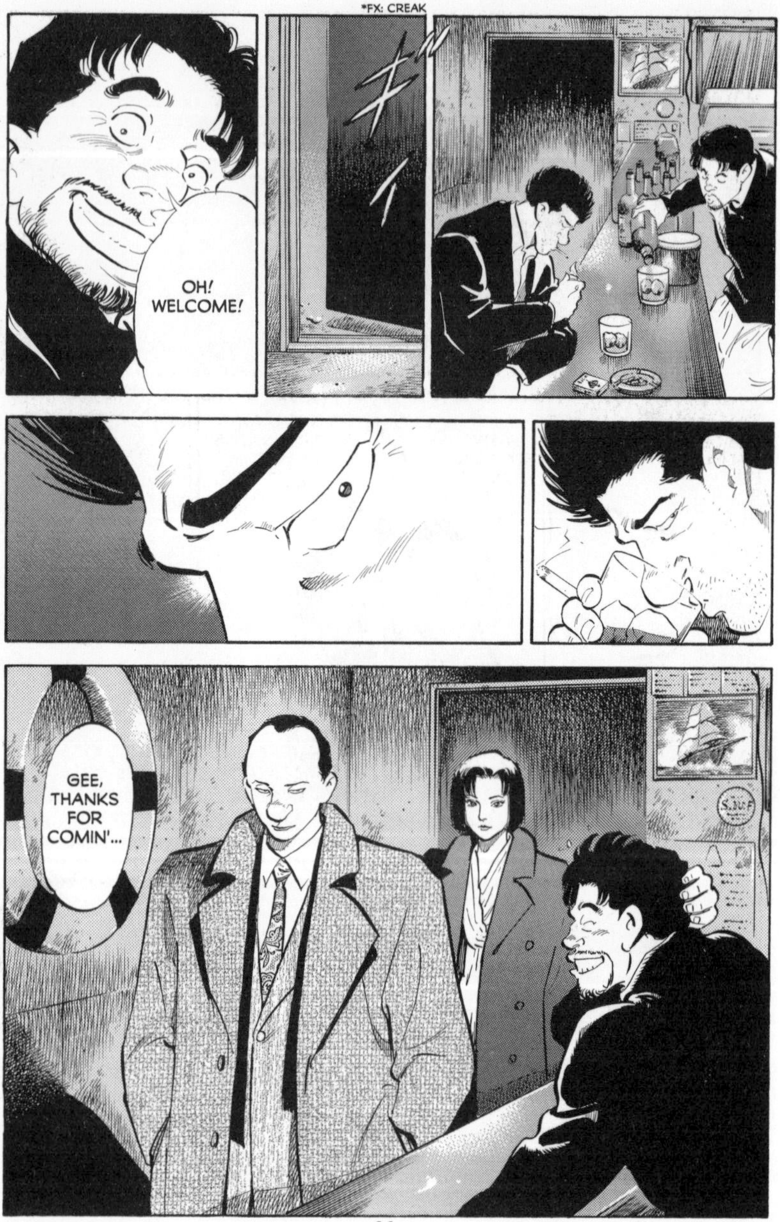
*FX: CREAK
OH! WELCOME!
GEE, THANKS FOR COMIN'...

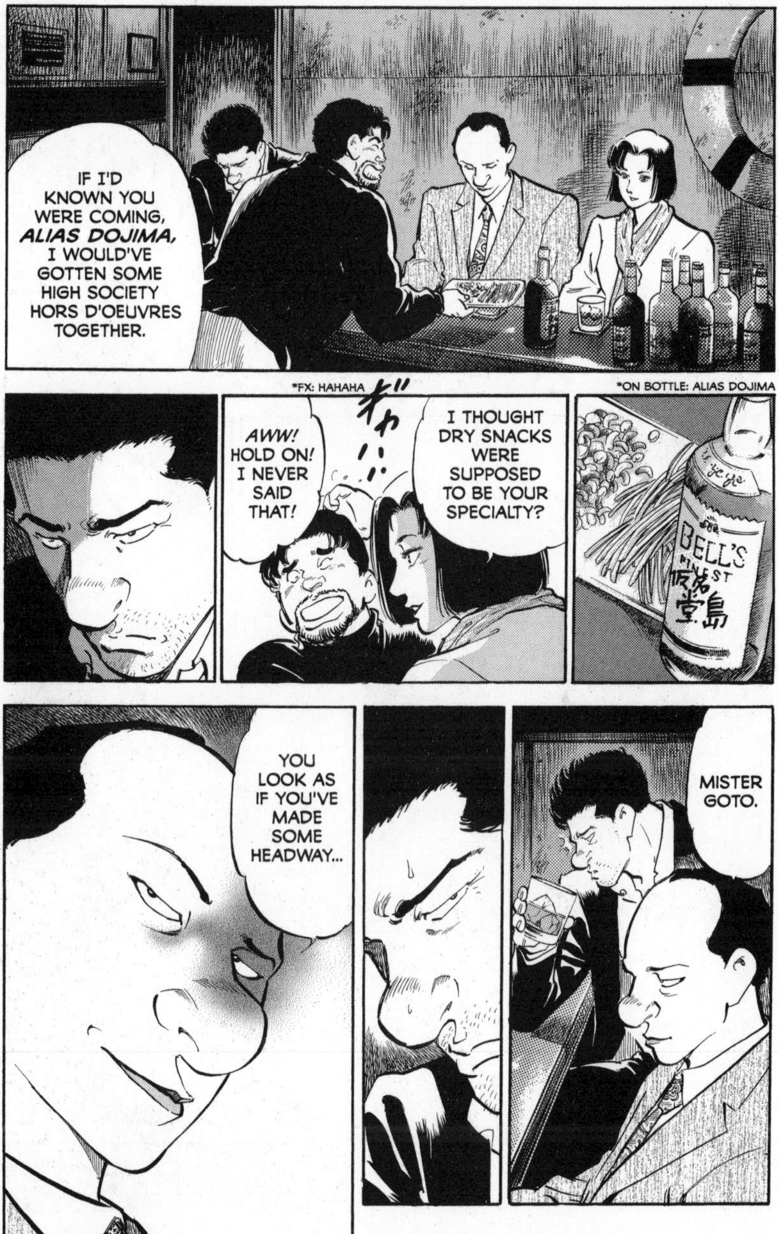
IF I'D KNOWN YOU WERE COMING, *ALIAS DOJIMA,* I WOULD'VE GOTTEN SOME HIGH SOCIETY HORS D'OEUVRES TOGETHER.
*ON BOTTLE: ALIAS DOJIMA
*FX: HAHAHA
BELL'S FINEST
仮名 堂島
I THOUGHT DRY SNACKS WERE SUPPOSED TO BE YOUR SPECIALTY?
AWW! HOLD ON! I NEVER SAID THAT!
MISTER GOTO.
YOU LOOK AS IF YOU'VE MADE SOME HEADWAY...

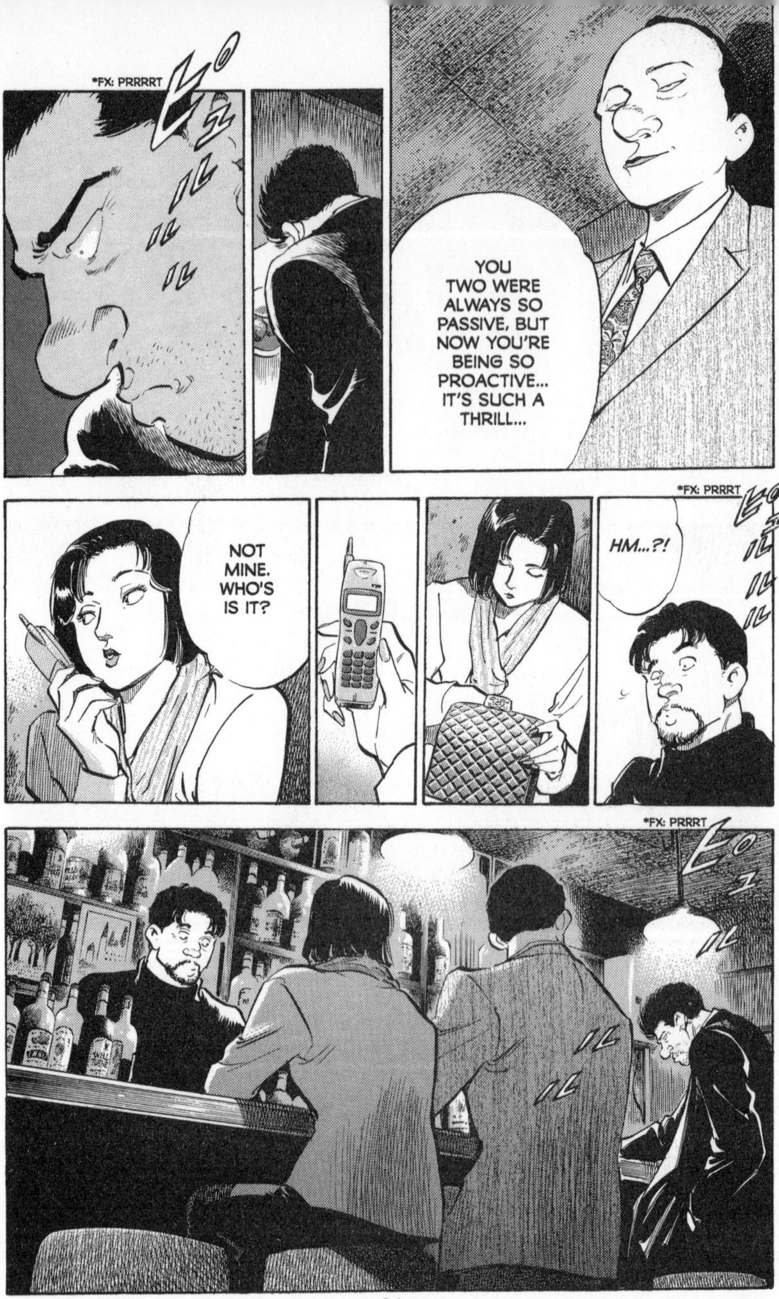
YOU TWO WERE ALWAYS SO PASSIVE, BUT NOW YOU'RE BEING SO PROACTIVE... IT'S SUCH A THRILL...
*FX: PRRRRT
*FX: PRRRT
HM...?!
NOT MINE. WHO'S IS IT?
*FX: PRRRT

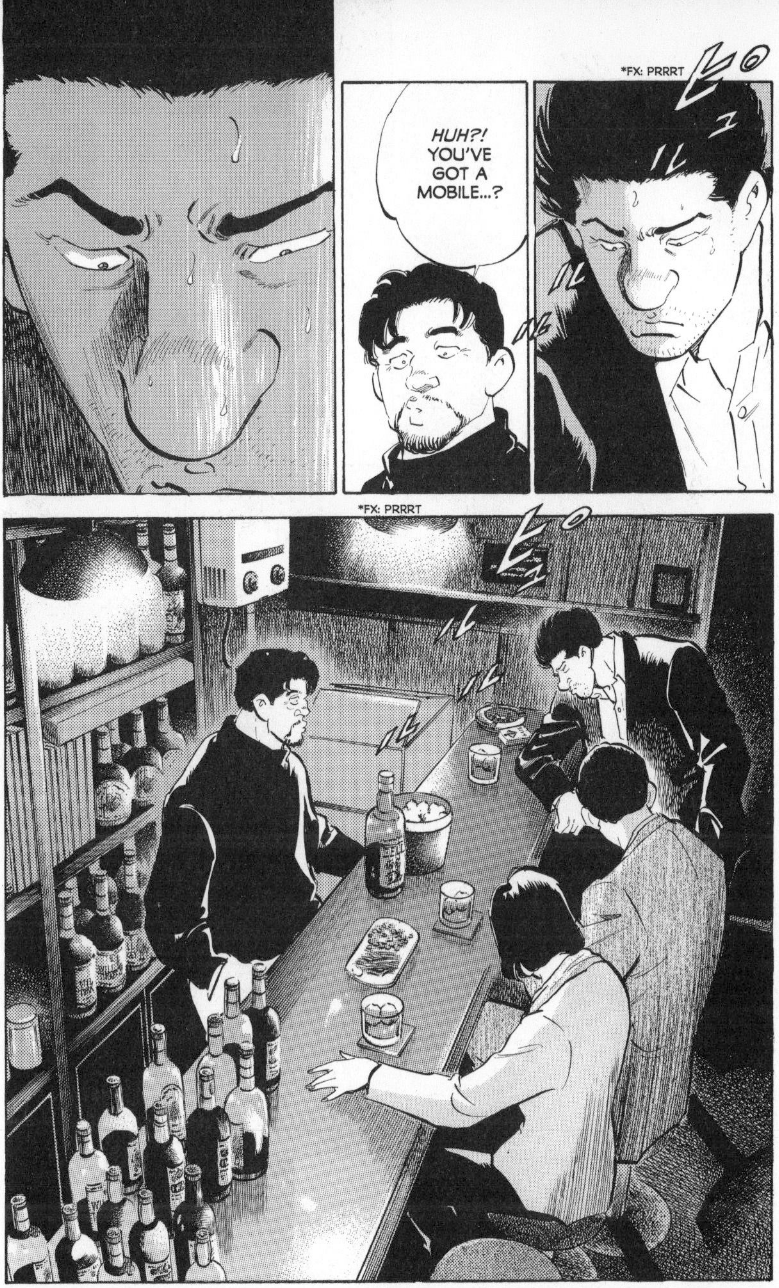
*FX: PRRRT
HUH?! YOU'VE GOT A MOBILE...?
*FX: PRRRT

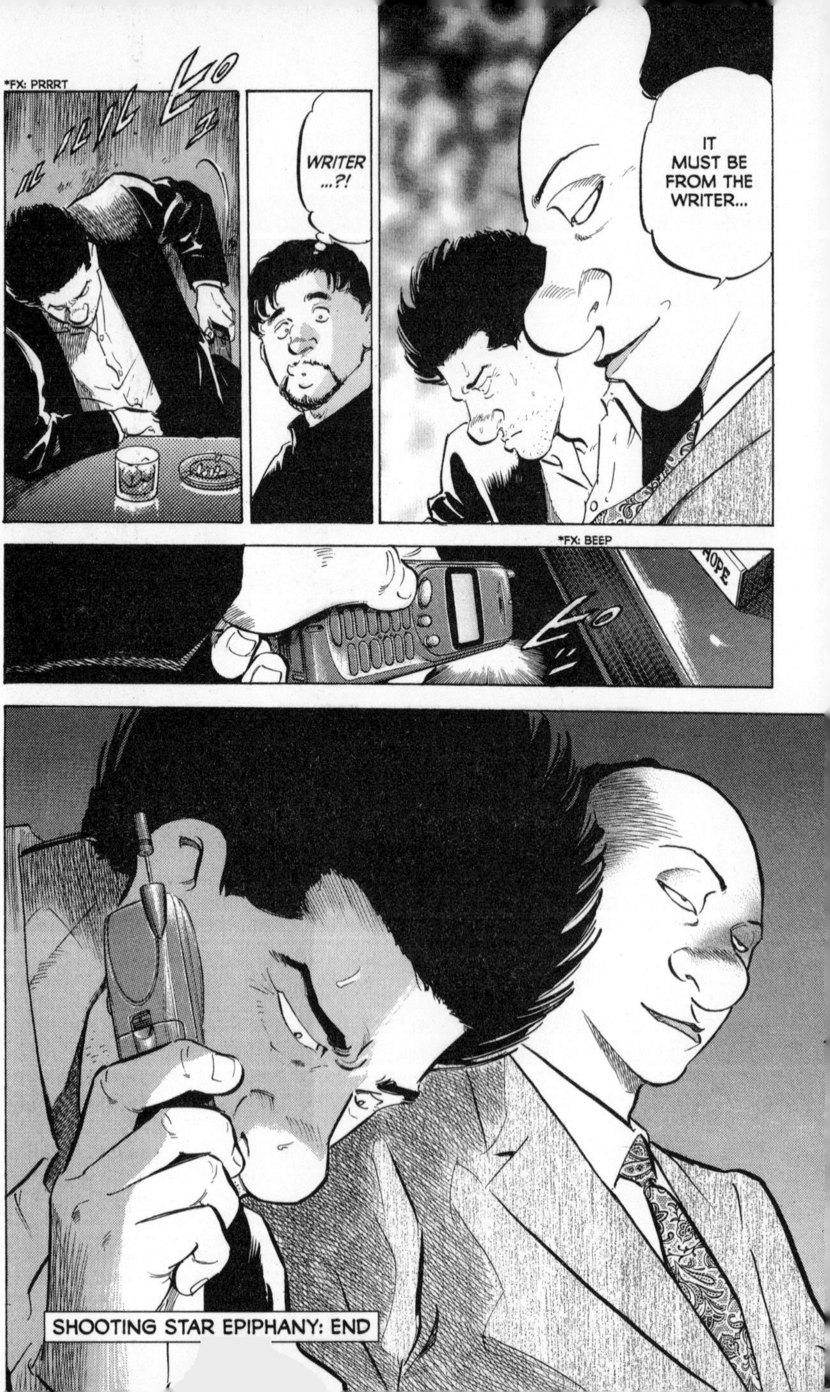
IT MUST BE FROM THE WRITER...
WRITER ...?!
*FX: PRRRT
*FX: BEEP
HOPE
SHOOTING STAR EPIPHANY: END

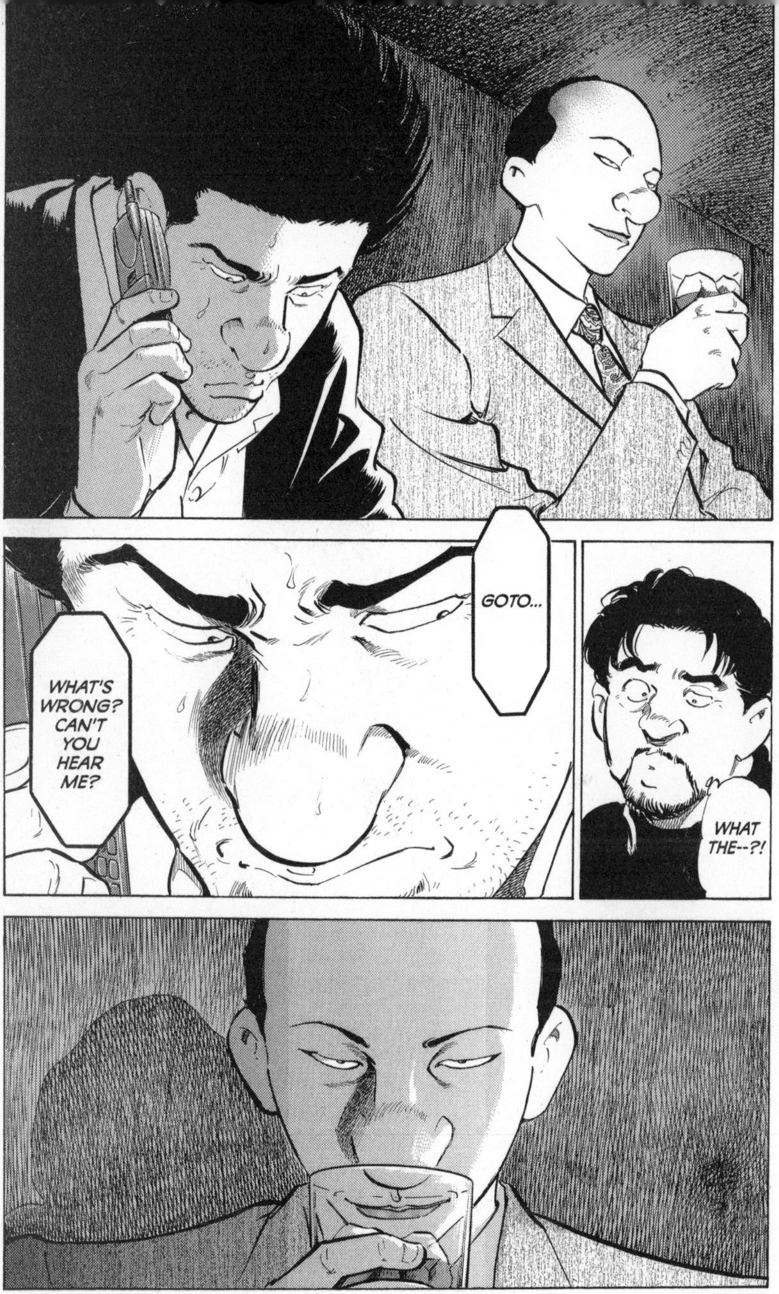
WHAT THE--?!
GOTO...
WHAT'S WRONG? CAN'T YOU HEAR ME?

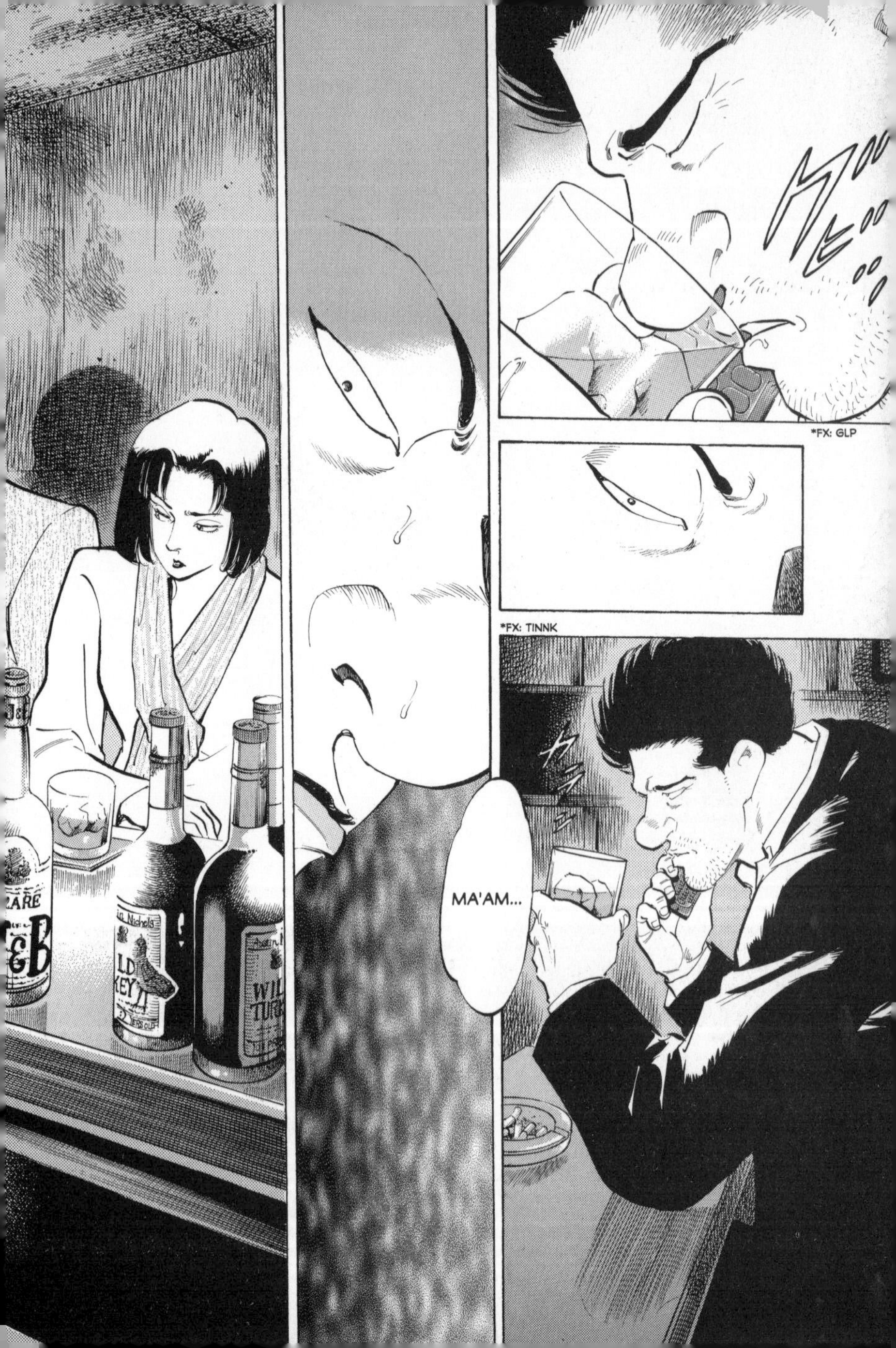
*FX: GLP
*FX: TINNK
MA'AM...

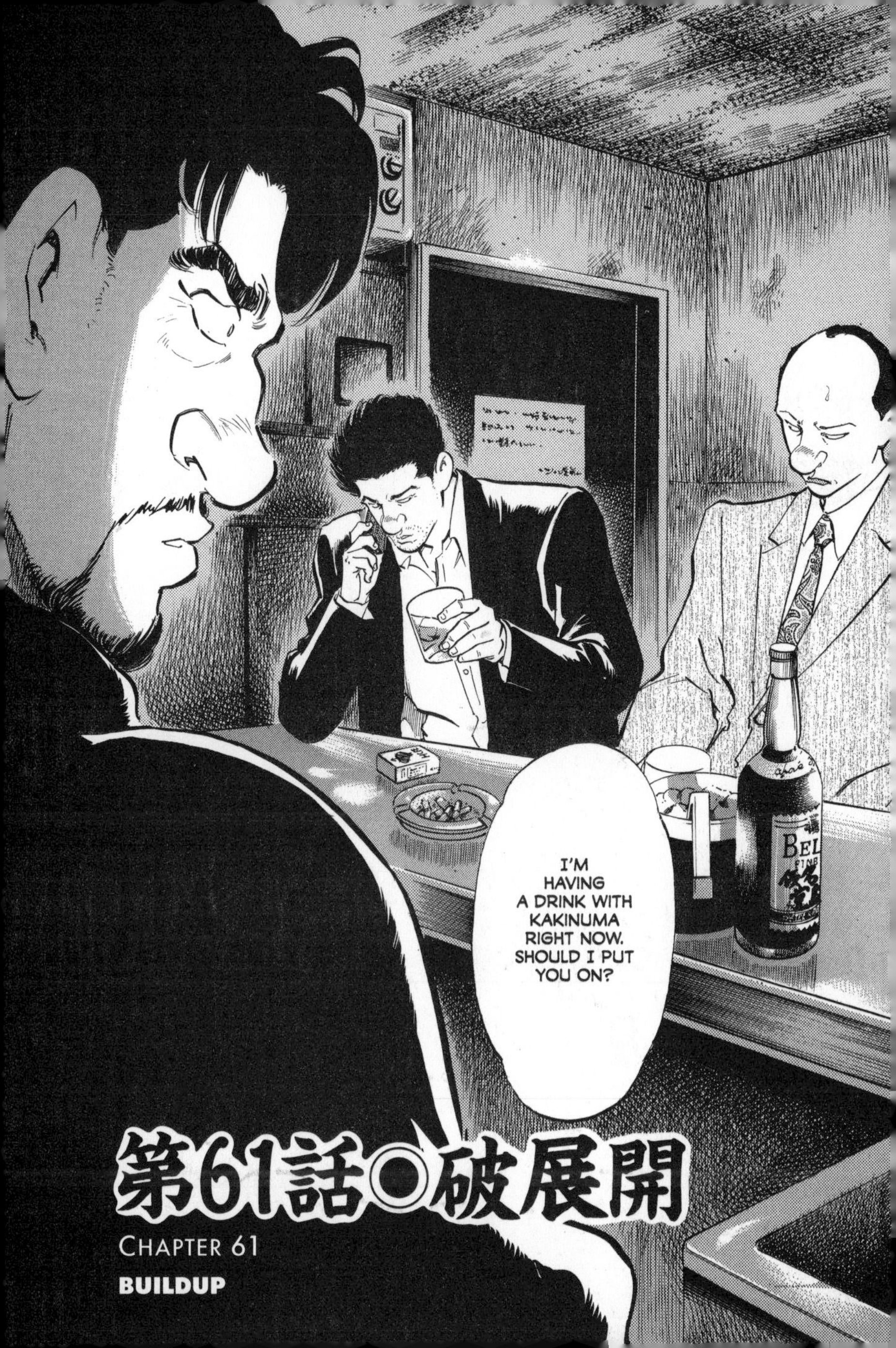
I'M HAVING A DRINK WITH KAKINUMA RIGHT NOW. SHOULD I PUT YOU ON?
第61話○破展開
CHAPTER 61
BUILDUP

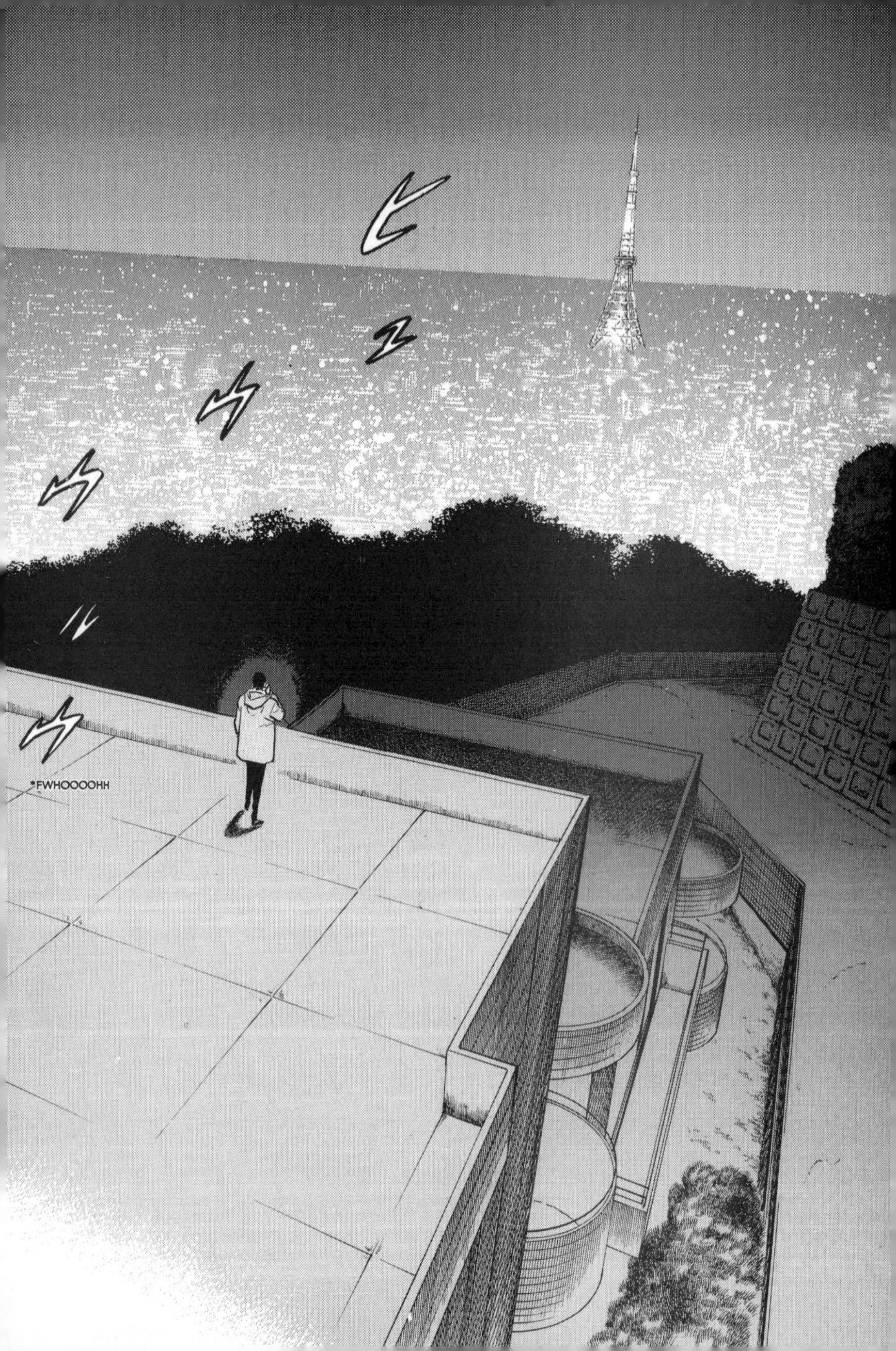
ヒュゥゥゥ
*FWHOOOOHH

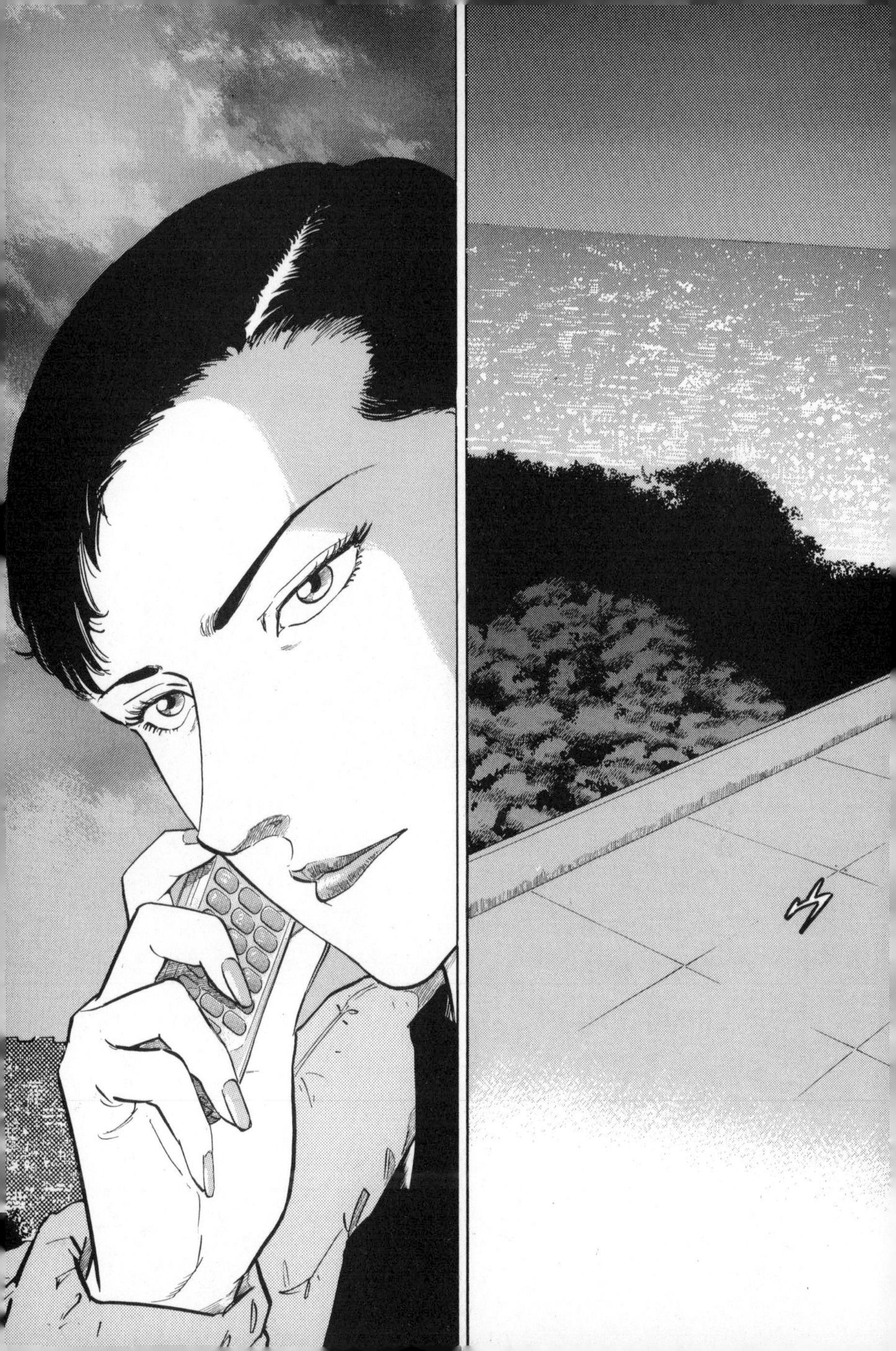

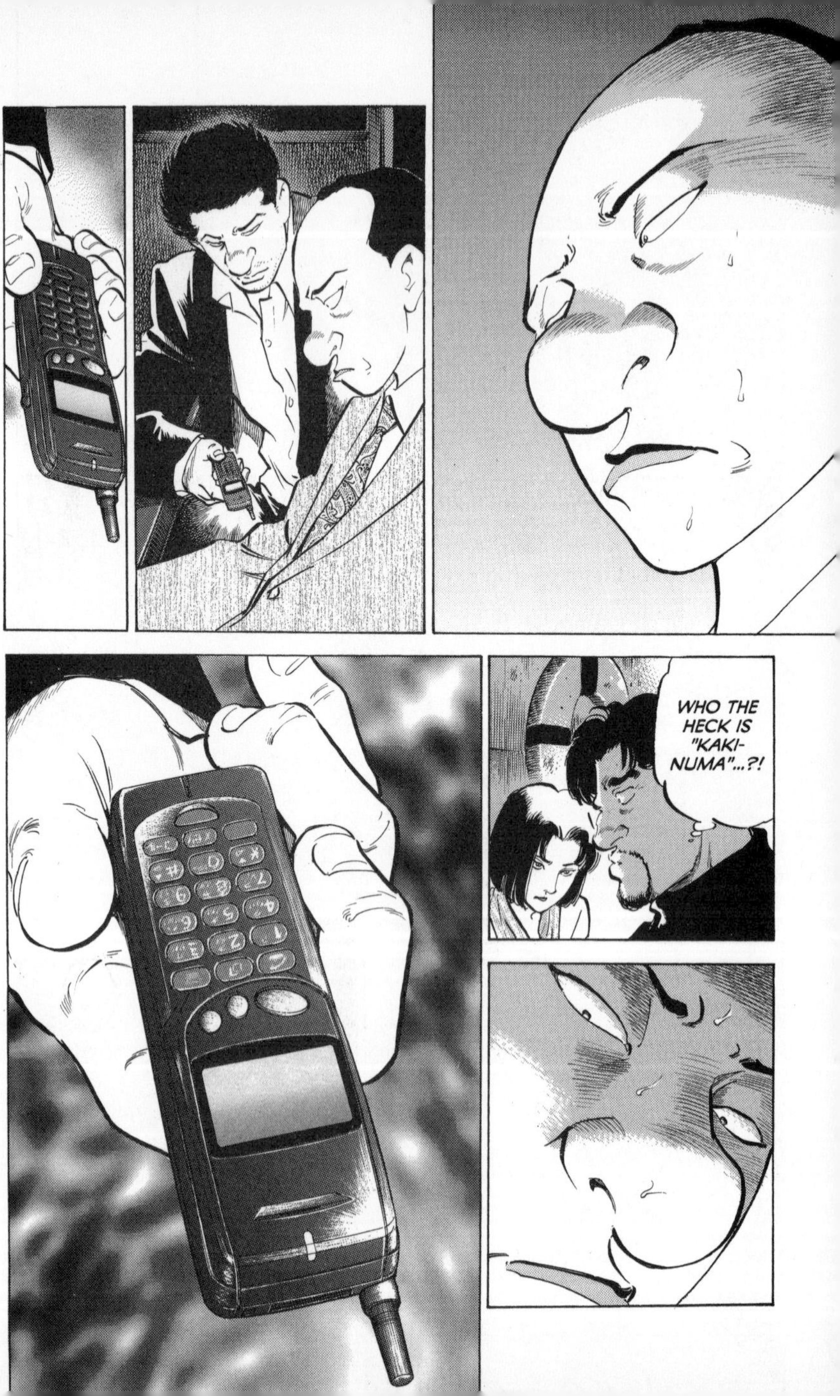
WHO THE HECK IS "KAKI-NUMA"...?!

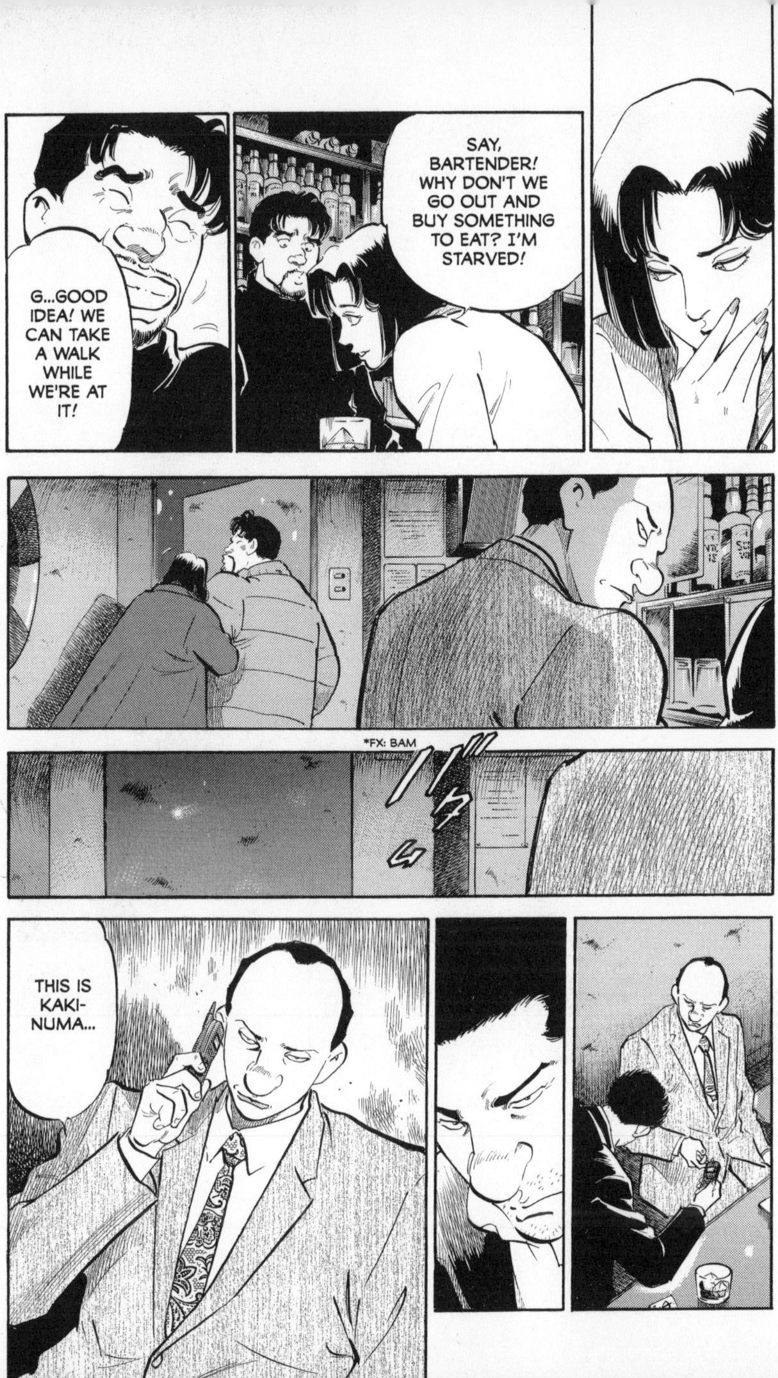
SAY, BARTENDER! WHY DON'T WE GO OUT AND BUY SOMETHING TO EAT? I'M STARVED!
G...GOOD IDEA! WE CAN TAKE A WALK WHILE WE'RE AT IT!
*FX: BAM
THIS IS KAKI-NUMA...

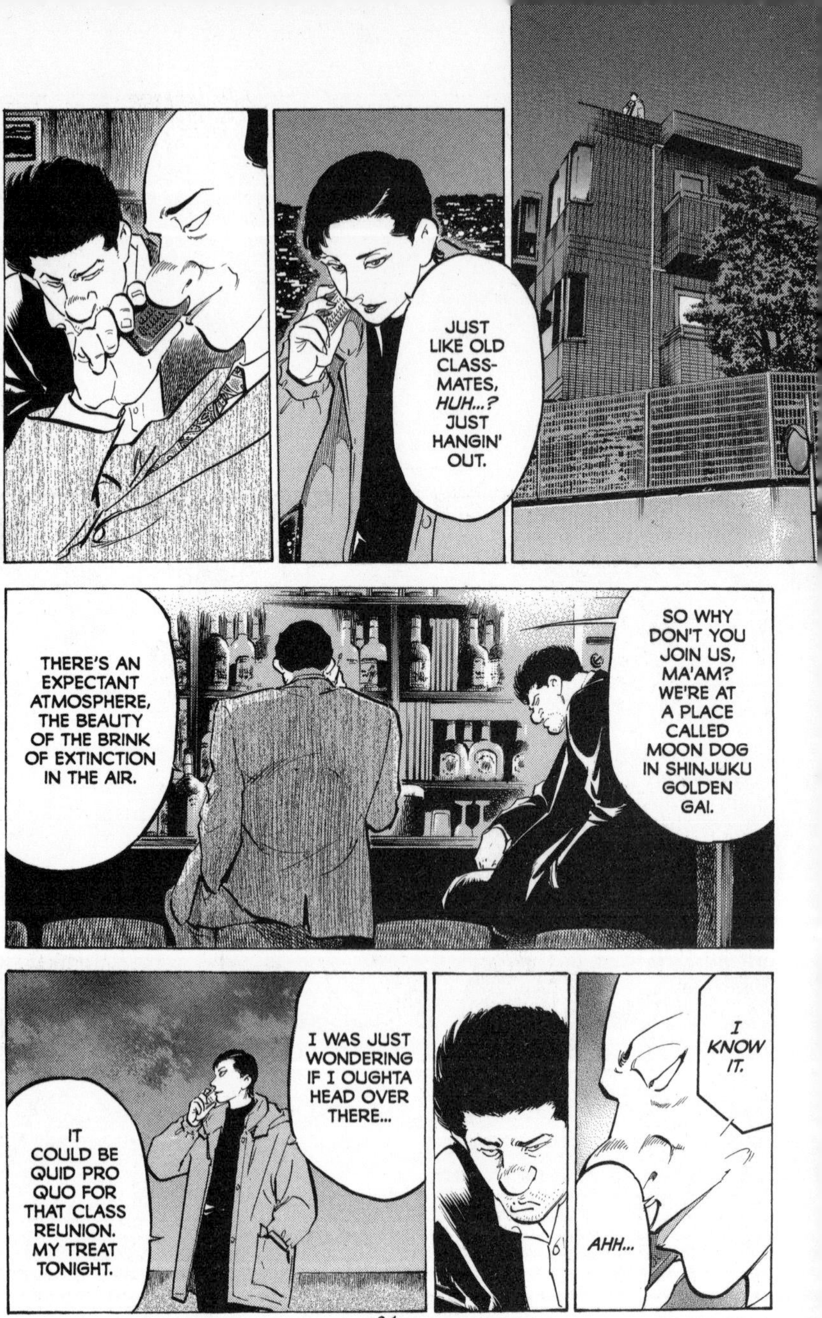
JUST LIKE OLD CLASSMATES, HUH...? JUST HANGIN' OUT.
SO WHY DON'T YOU JOIN US, MA'AM? WE'RE AT A PLACE CALLED MOON DOG IN SHINJUKU GOLDEN GAI.
THERE'S AN EXPECTANT ATMOSPHERE, THE BEAUTY OF THE BRINK OF EXTINCTION IN THE AIR.
I KNOW IT.
AHH...
I WAS JUST WONDERING IF I OUGHTA HEAD OVER THERE...
IT COULD BE QUID PRO QUO FOR THAT CLASS REUNION. MY TREAT TONIGHT.

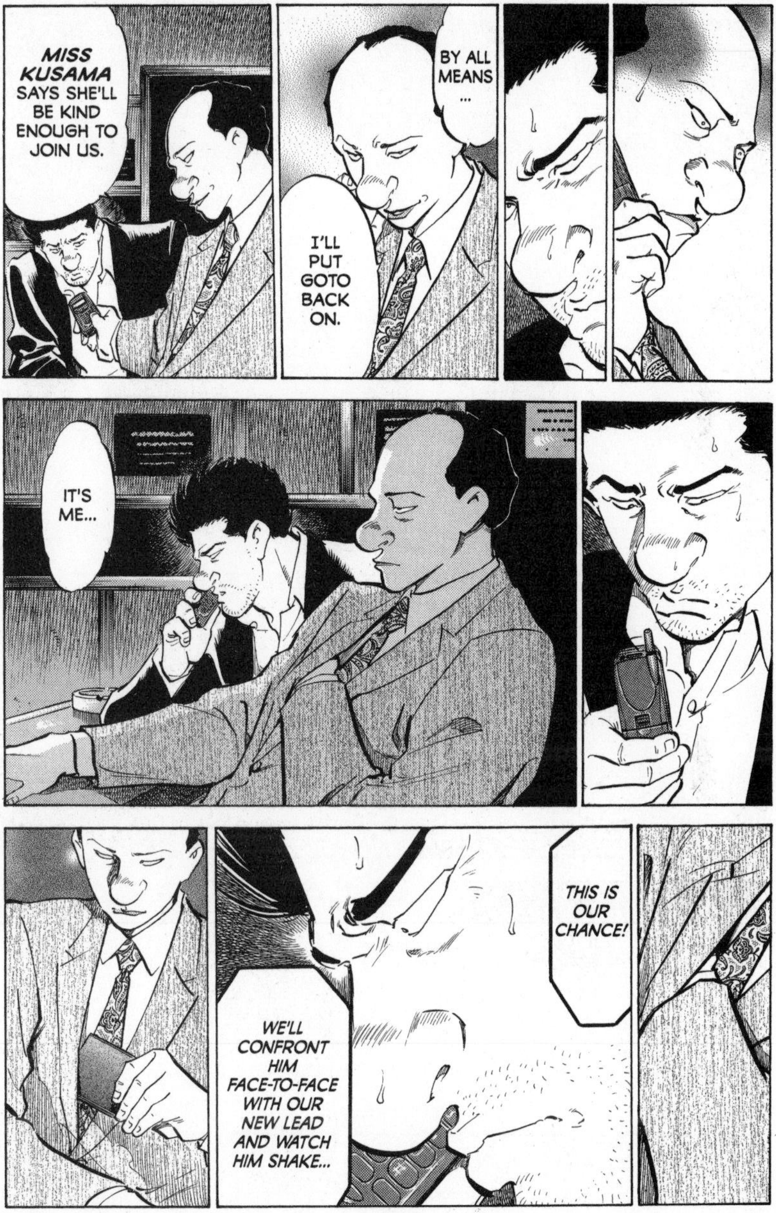
BY ALL MEANS ...
I'LL PUT GOTO BACK ON.
MISS KUSAMA SAYS SHE'LL BE KIND ENOUGH TO JOIN US.
IT'S ME...
THIS IS OUR CHANCE!
WE'LL CONFRONT HIM FACE-TO-FACE WITH OUR NEW LEAD AND WATCH HIM SHAKE...

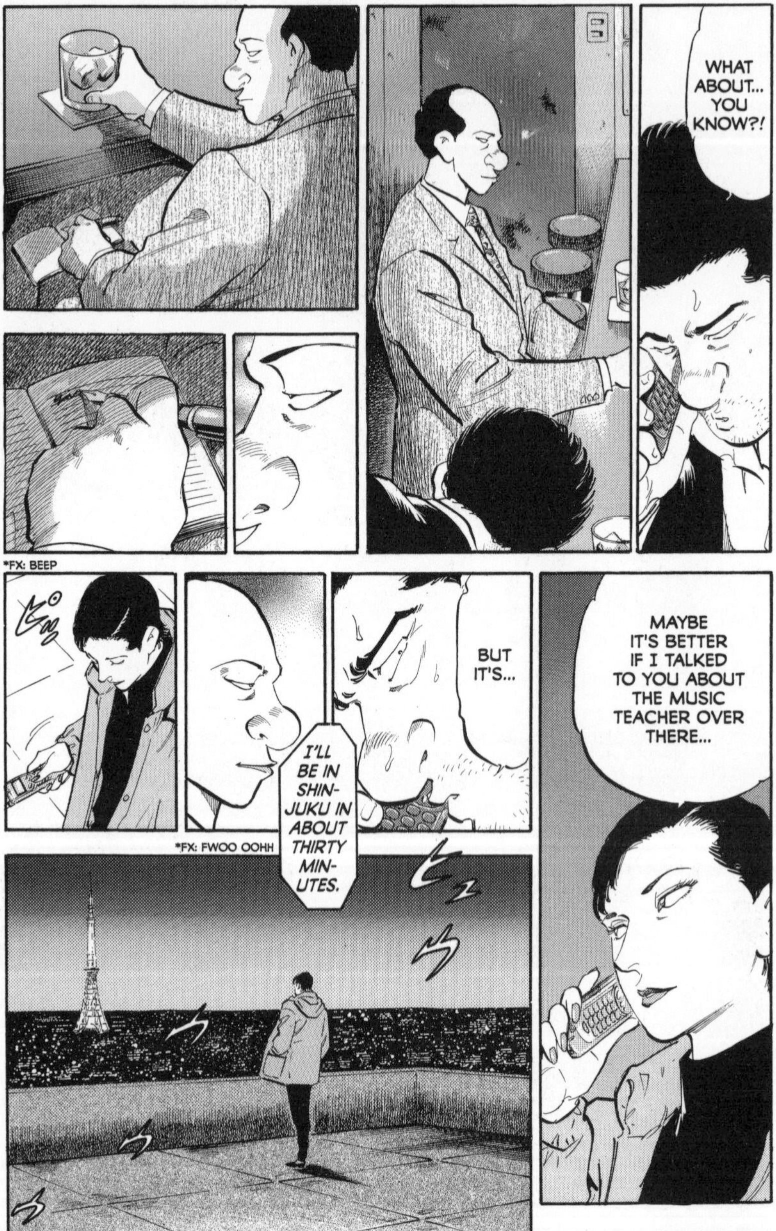
WHAT ABOUT... YOU KNOW?!
MAYBE IT'S BETTER IF I TALKED TO YOU ABOUT THE MUSIC TEACHER OVER THERE...
BUT IT'S...
I'LL BE IN SHIN-JUKU IN ABOUT THIRTY MIN-UTES.
*FX: BEEP
*FX: FWOO OOHH

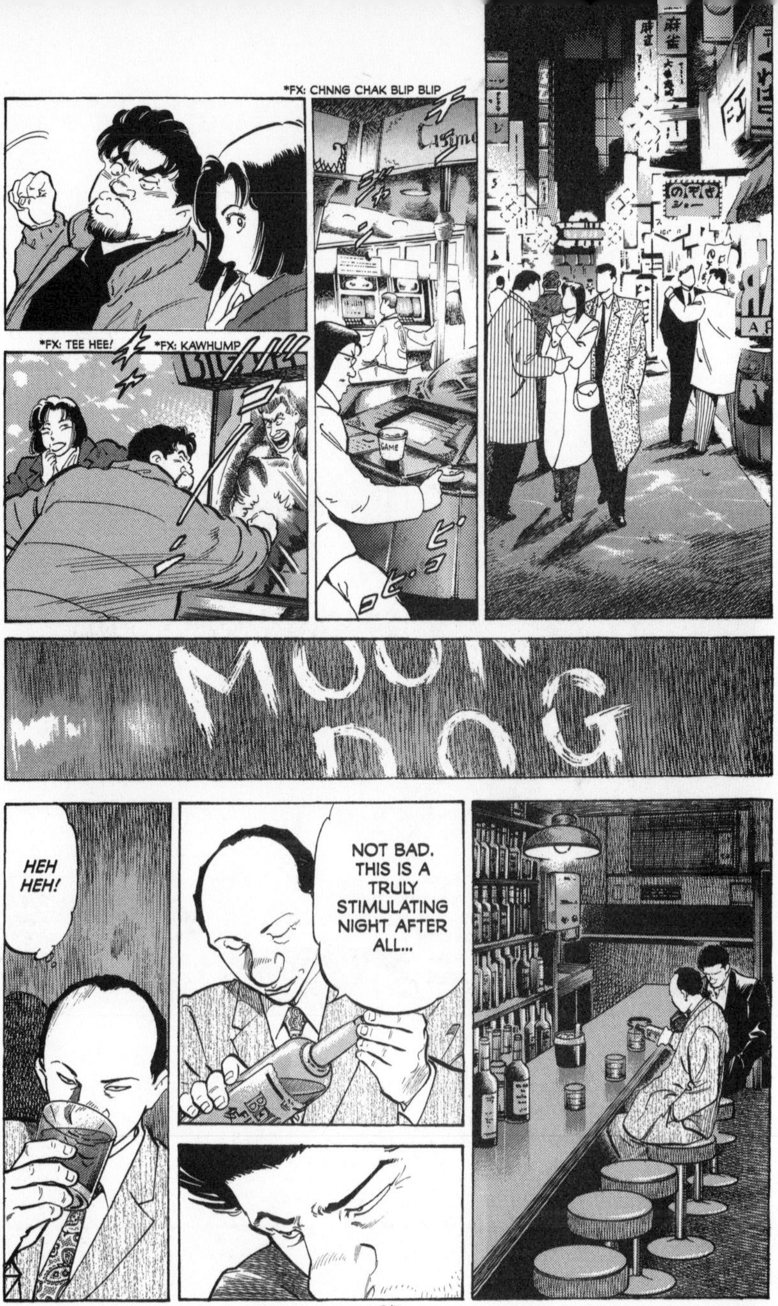
*FX: CHNNG CHAK BLIP BLIP
*FX: TEE HEE!
*FX: KAWHUMP
NOT BAD. THIS IS A TRULY STIMULATING NIGHT AFTER ALL...
HEH HEH!

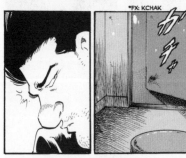

UHH...
'SIT COOL
IF WE
COME
IN?!

WE GOT
SOME
CHOICE HORS
D'OEUVRES
FROM A
TAIWANESE
STALL!

38

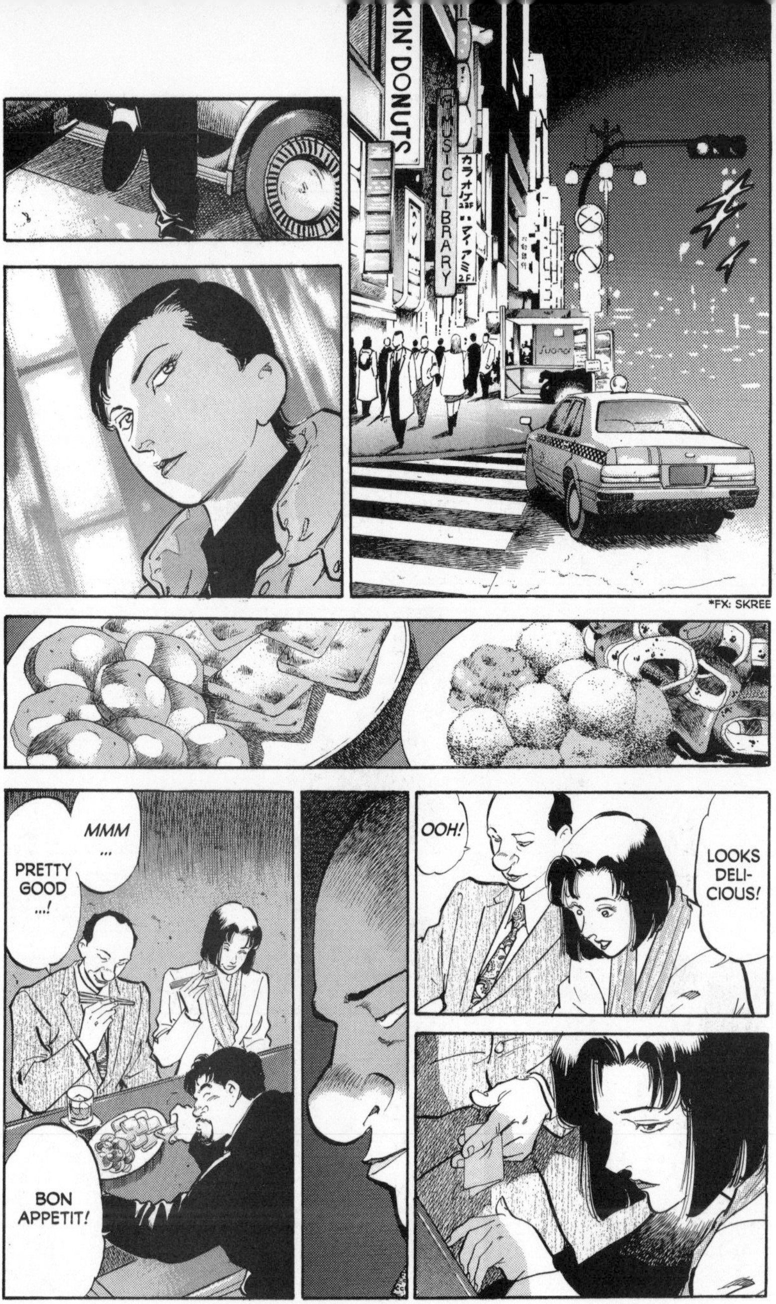
KIN' DONUTS
MUSIC LIBRARY
*FX: SKREE
OOH!
LOOKS DELICIOUS!
MMM ... PRETTY GOOD ...!
BON APPETIT!

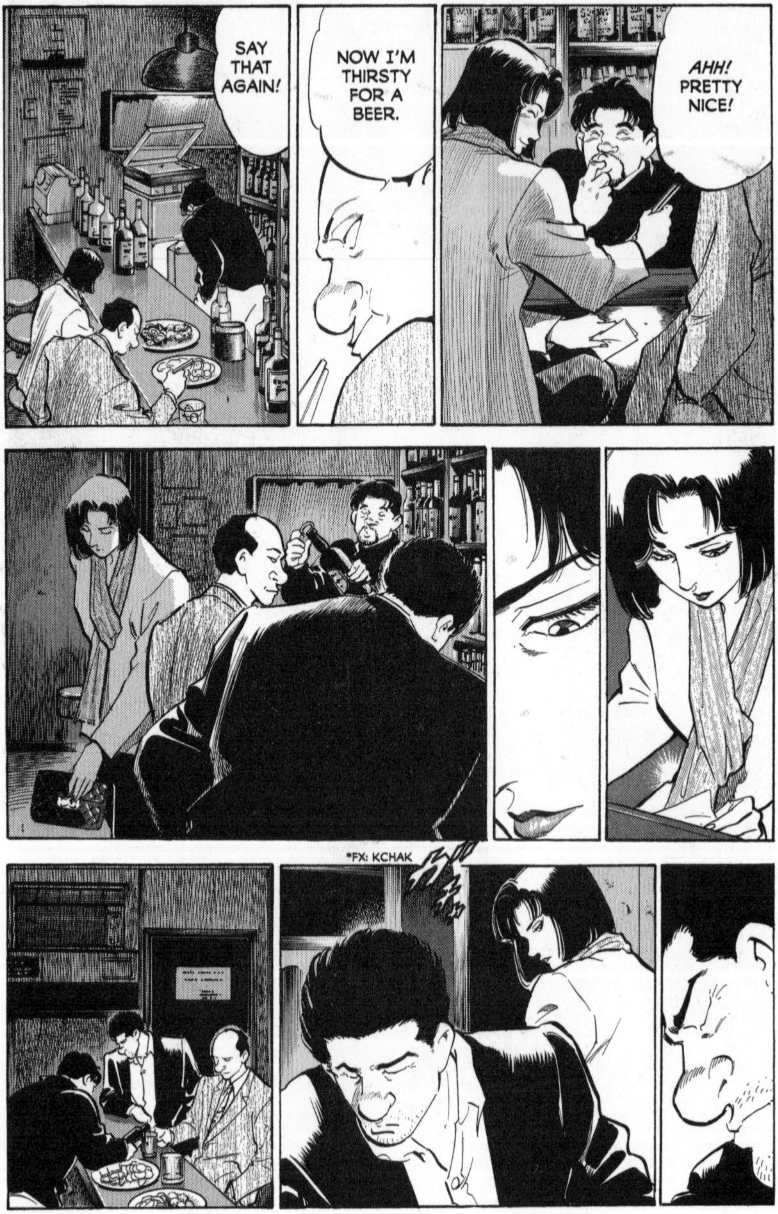
AHH! PRETTY NICE!
NOW I'M THIRSTY FOR A BEER.
SAY THAT AGAIN!
*FX: KCHAK

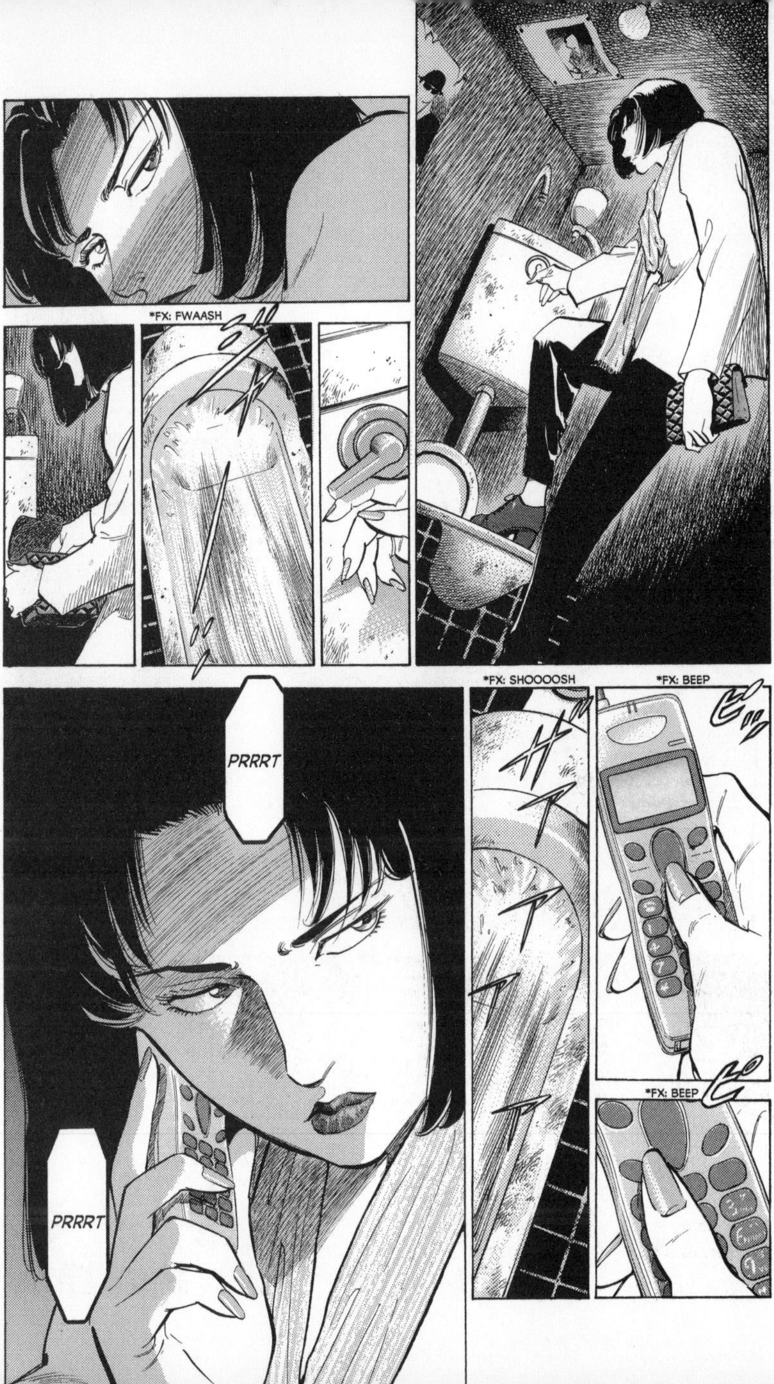
*FX: FWAASH
*FX: BEEP
*FX: BEEP
*FX: SHOOOOSH
PRRRT
PRRRT

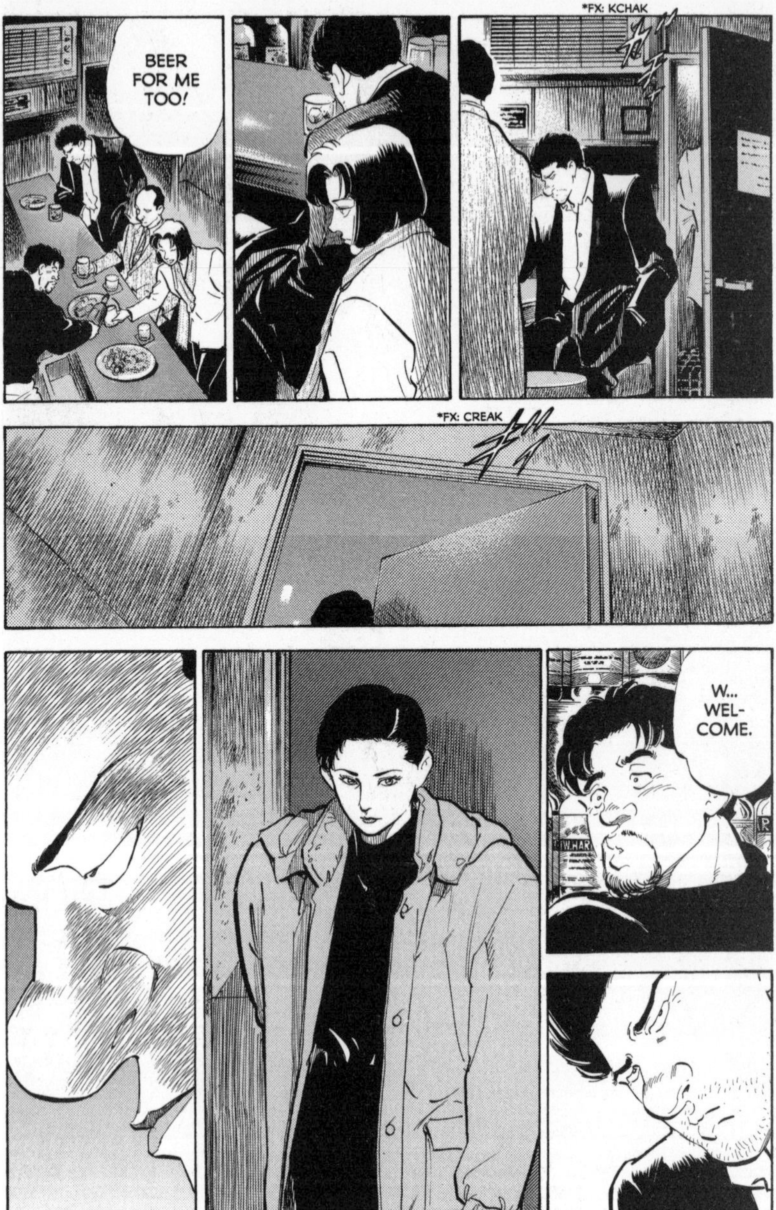
*FX: KCHAK
BEER FOR ME TOO!
*FX: CREAK
W... WEL-COME.

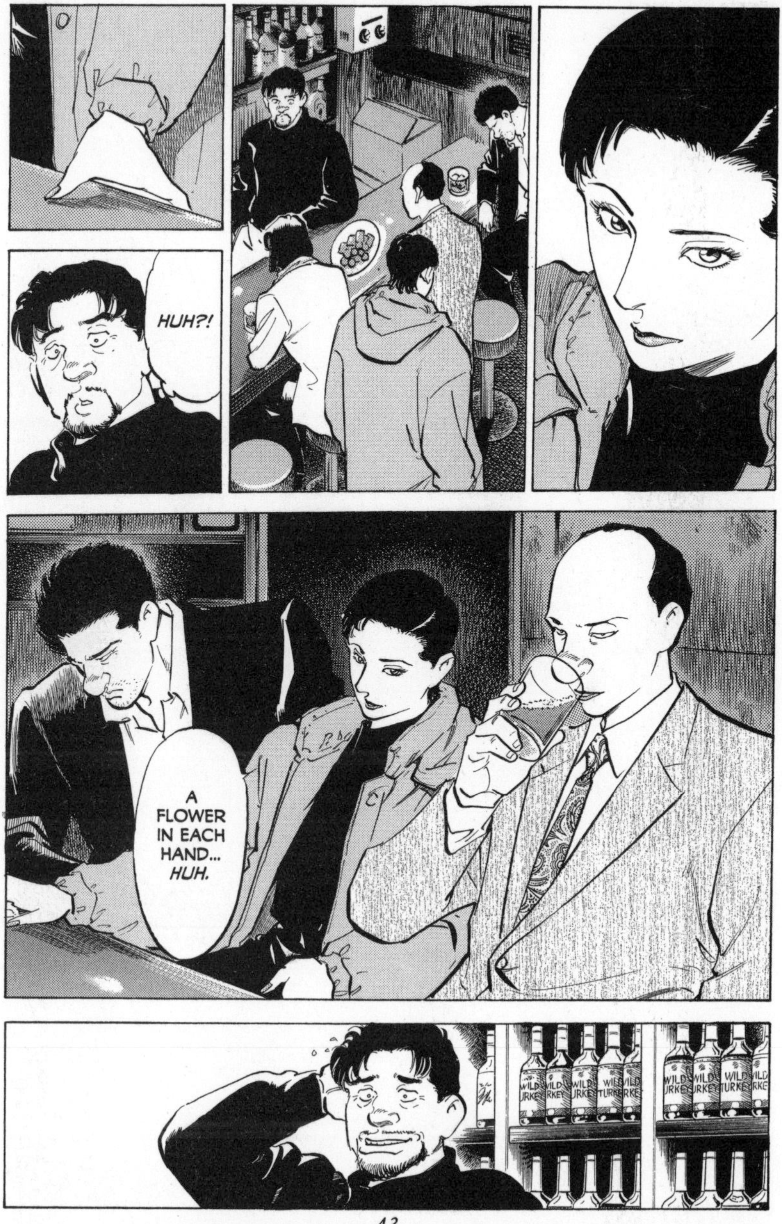

HUH?!
A FLOWER IN EACH HAND... *HUH.*

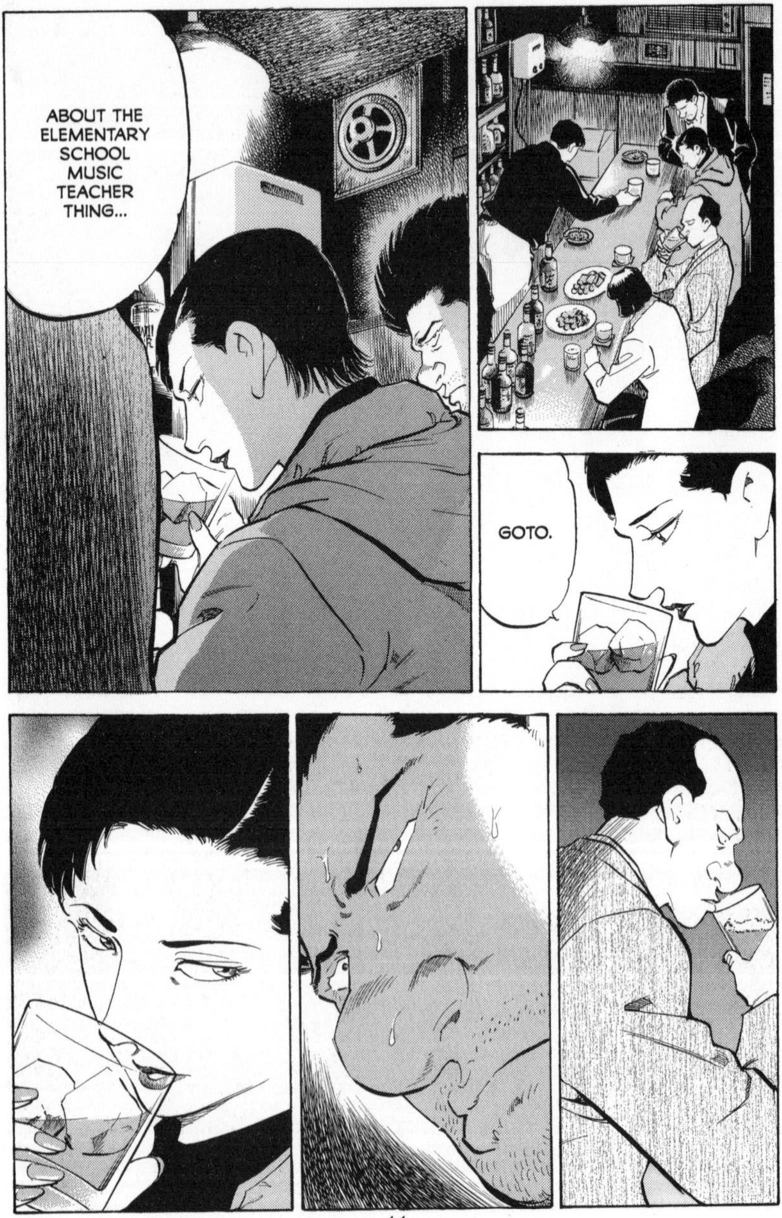
GOTO.
ABOUT THE ELEMENTARY SCHOOL MUSIC TEACHER THING...

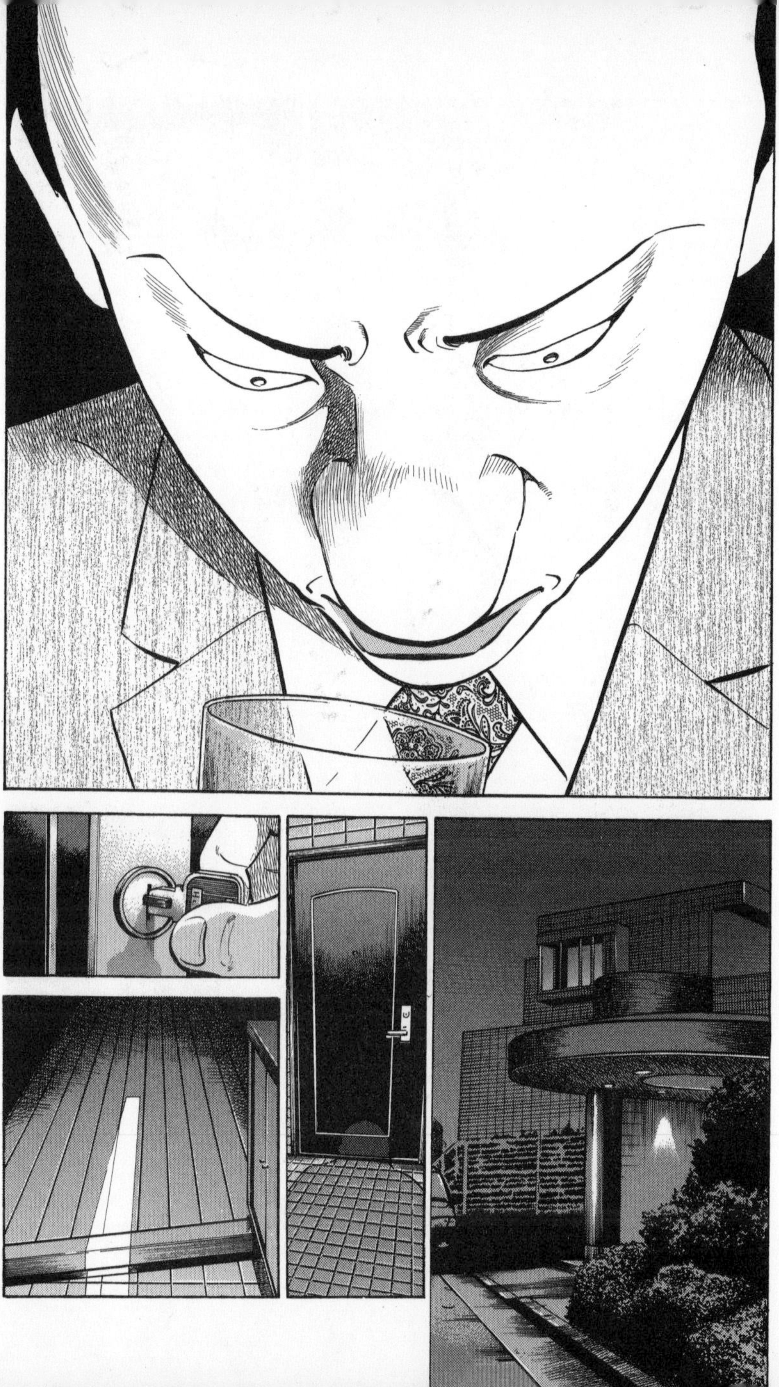

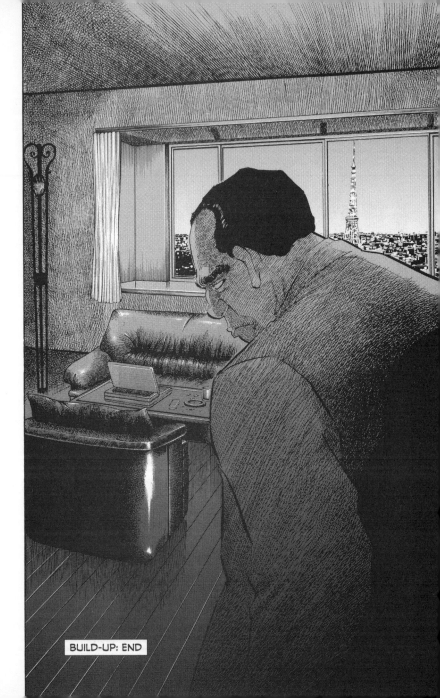

BUILD-UP: END

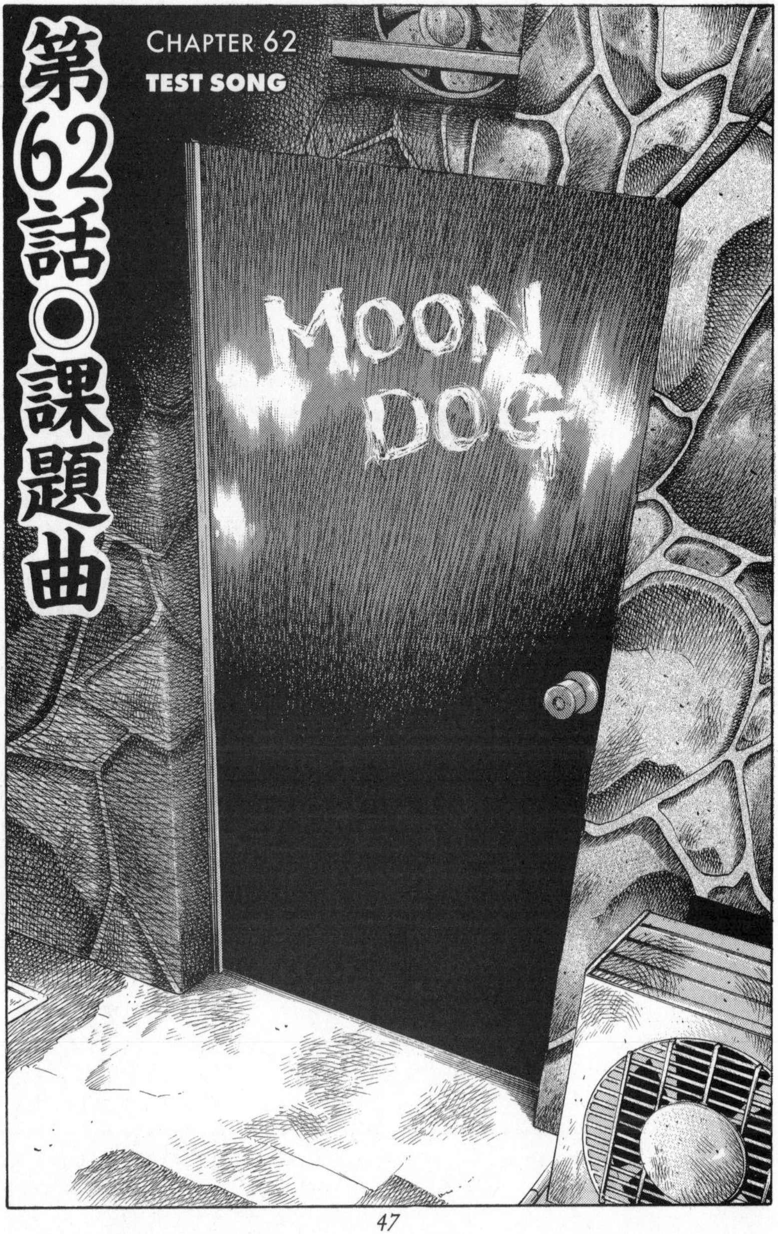
第62話◎課題曲
CHAPTER 62
TEST SONG
MOON DOG

UHH... I'M SURE YOU WERE HERE THE OTHER NIGHT TOO, RIGHT, MISS?!
COME ON! INTRODUCE ME, PLEASE!

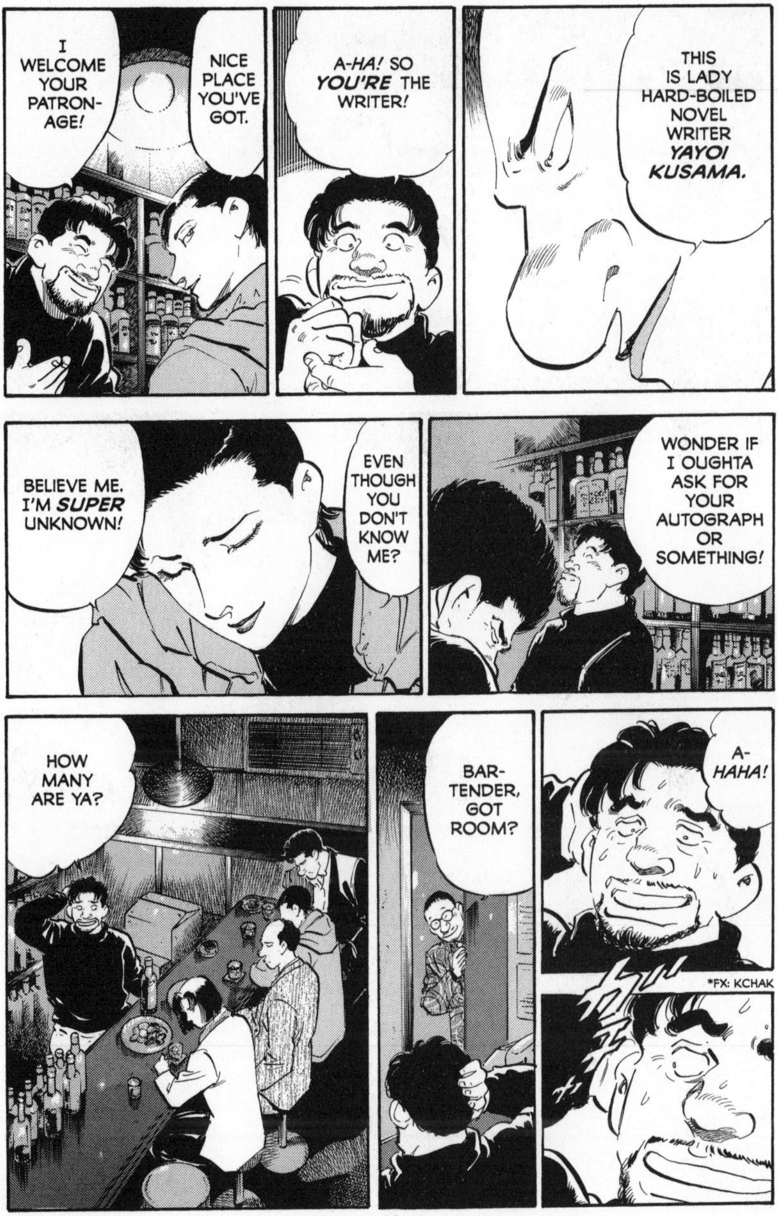
THIS IS LADY HARD-BOILED NOVEL WRITER *YAYOI KUSAMA.*
A-*HA!* SO *YOU'RE* THE WRITER!
NICE PLACE YOU'VE GOT.
I WELCOME YOUR PATRON-AGE!
WONDER IF I OUGHTA ASK FOR YOUR AUTOGRAPH OR SOMETHING!
EVEN THOUGH YOU DON'T KNOW ME?
BELIEVE ME. I'M *SUPER* UNKNOWN!
A-*HAHA!*
*FX: KCHAK
BAR-TENDER, GOT ROOM?
HOW MANY ARE YA?

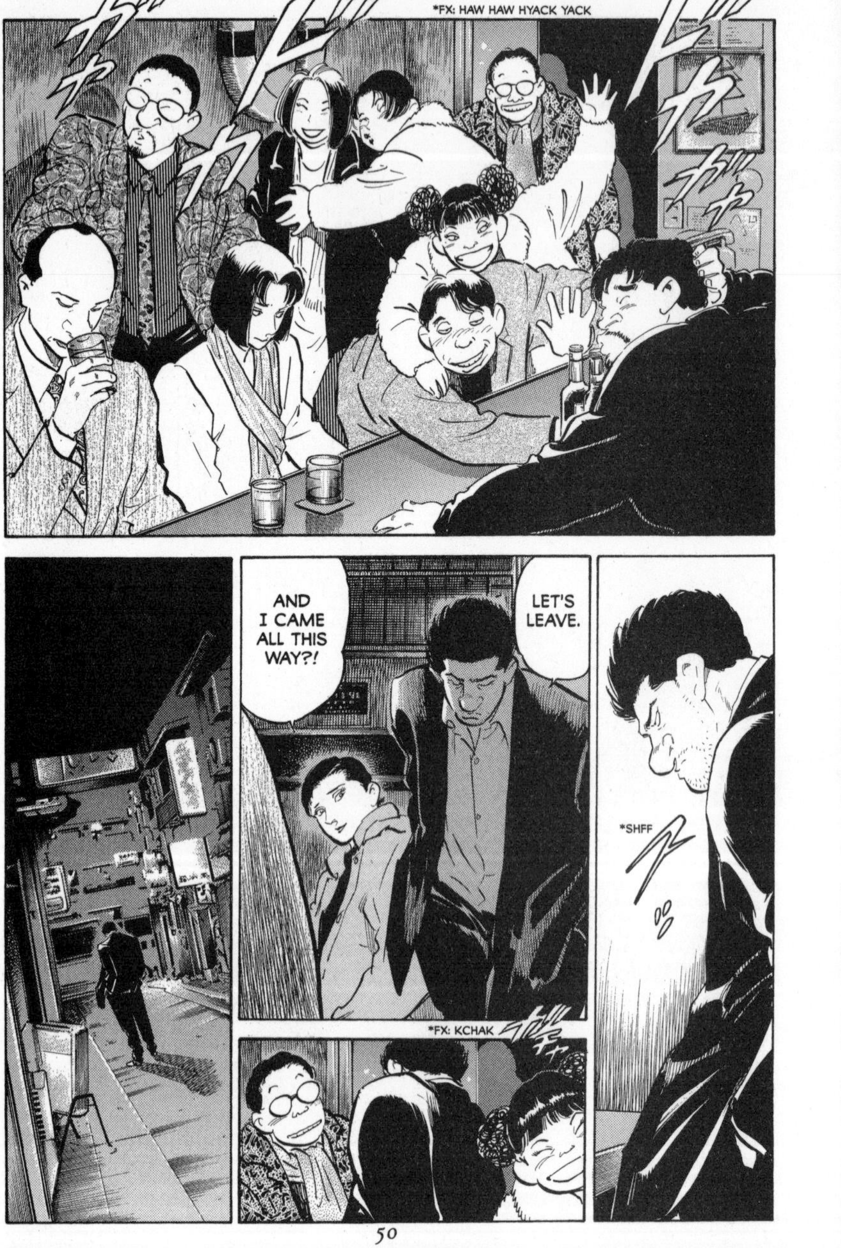
*FX: HAW HAW HYACK YACK
*SHFF
LET'S LEAVE.
AND I CAME ALL THIS WAY?!
*FX: KCHAK

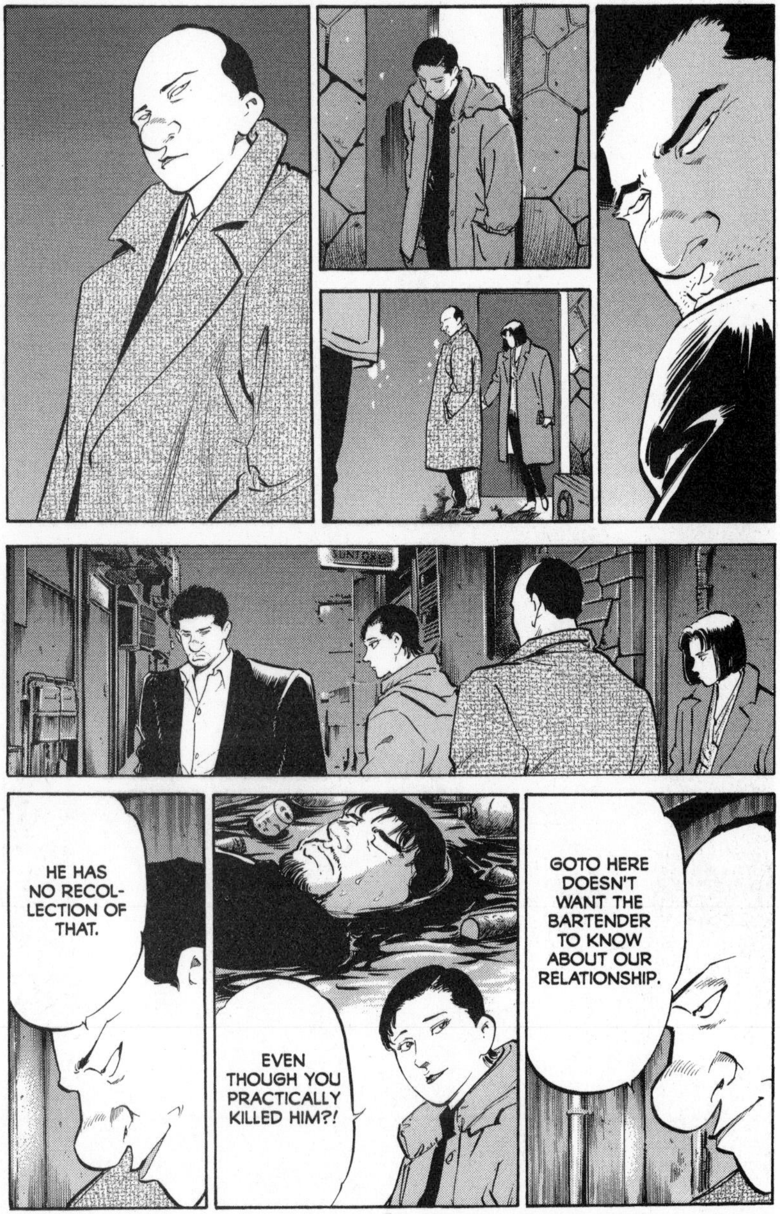
GOTO HERE DOESN'T WANT THE BARTENDER TO KNOW ABOUT OUR RELATIONSHIP.
EVEN THOUGH YOU PRACTICALLY KILLED HIM?!
HE HAS NO RECOL-LECTION OF THAT.

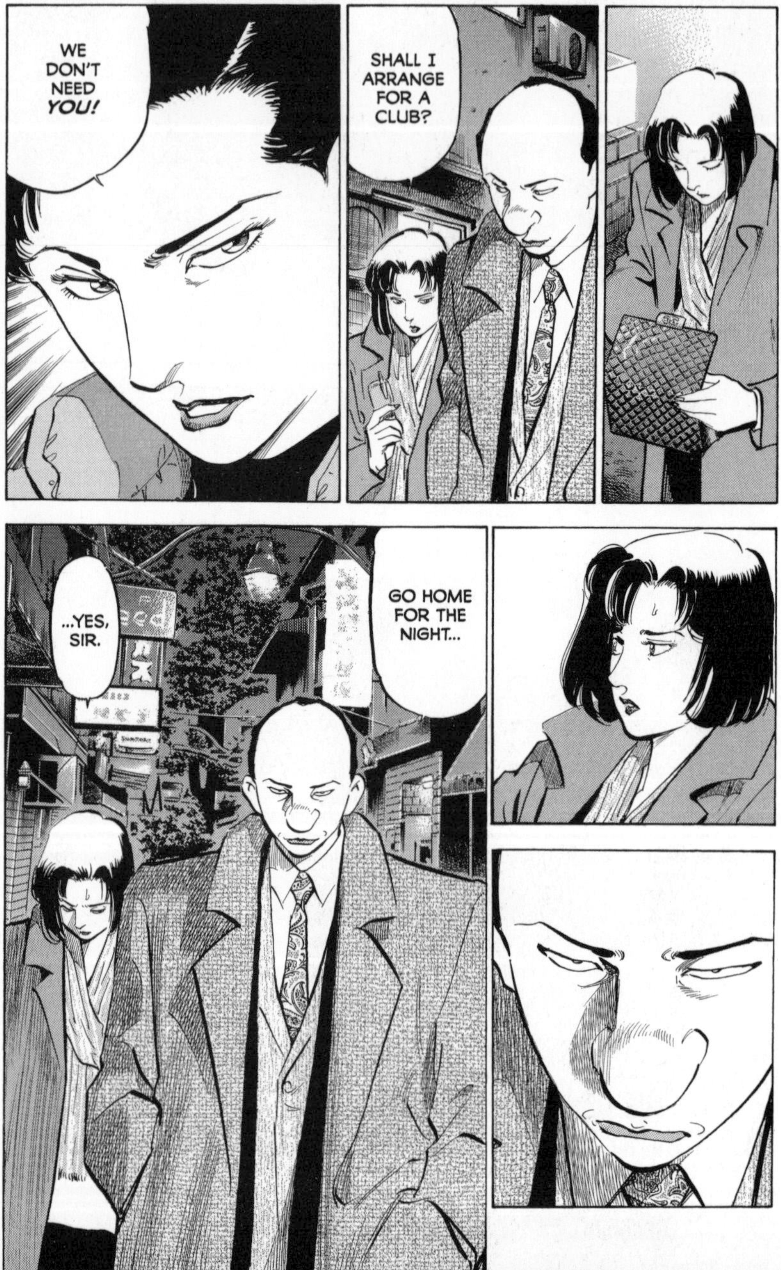
SHALL I ARRANGE FOR A CLUB?
WE DON'T NEED *YOU!*
GO HOME FOR THE NIGHT...
...YES, SIR.

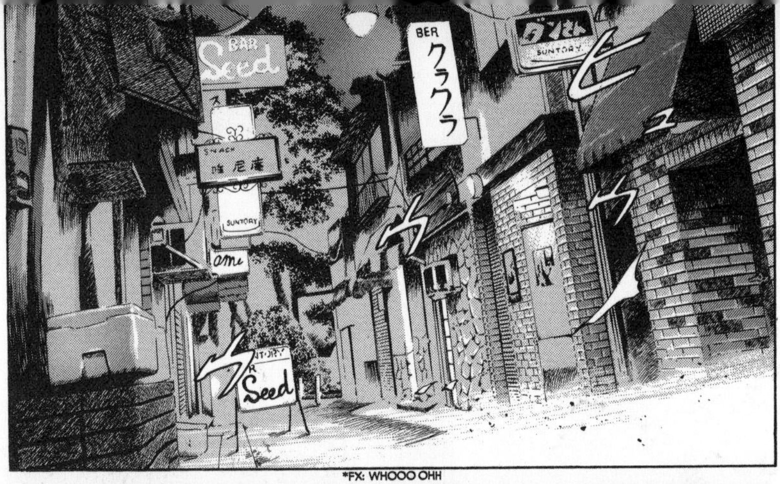
BAR
Seed
BER
クラクラ
SUNTORY
SUNTORY
Seed
*FX: WHOOO OHH

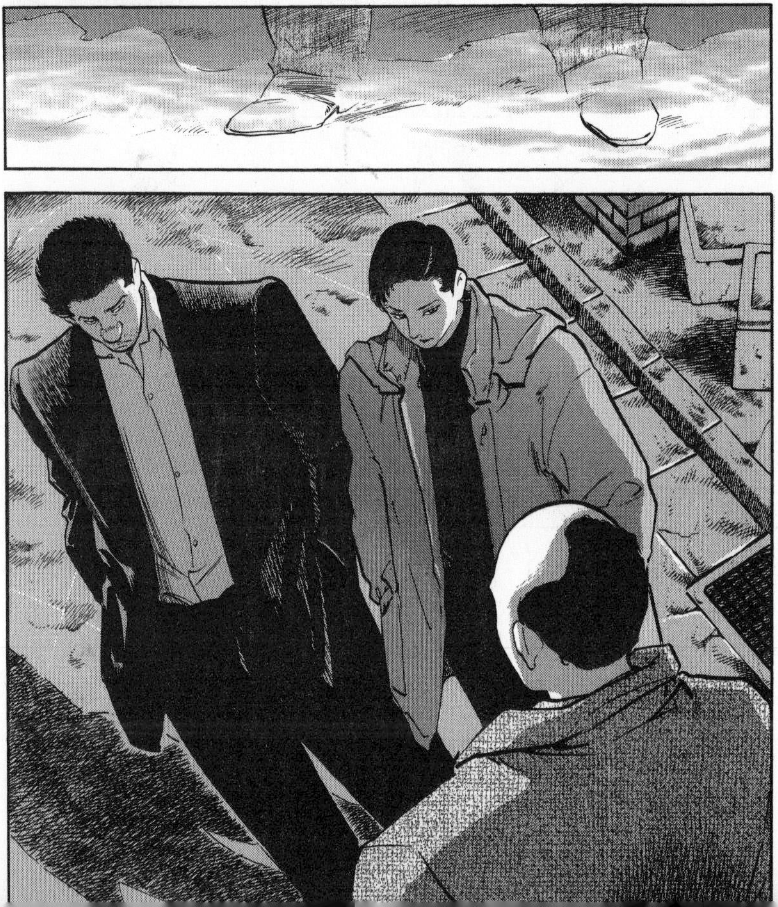

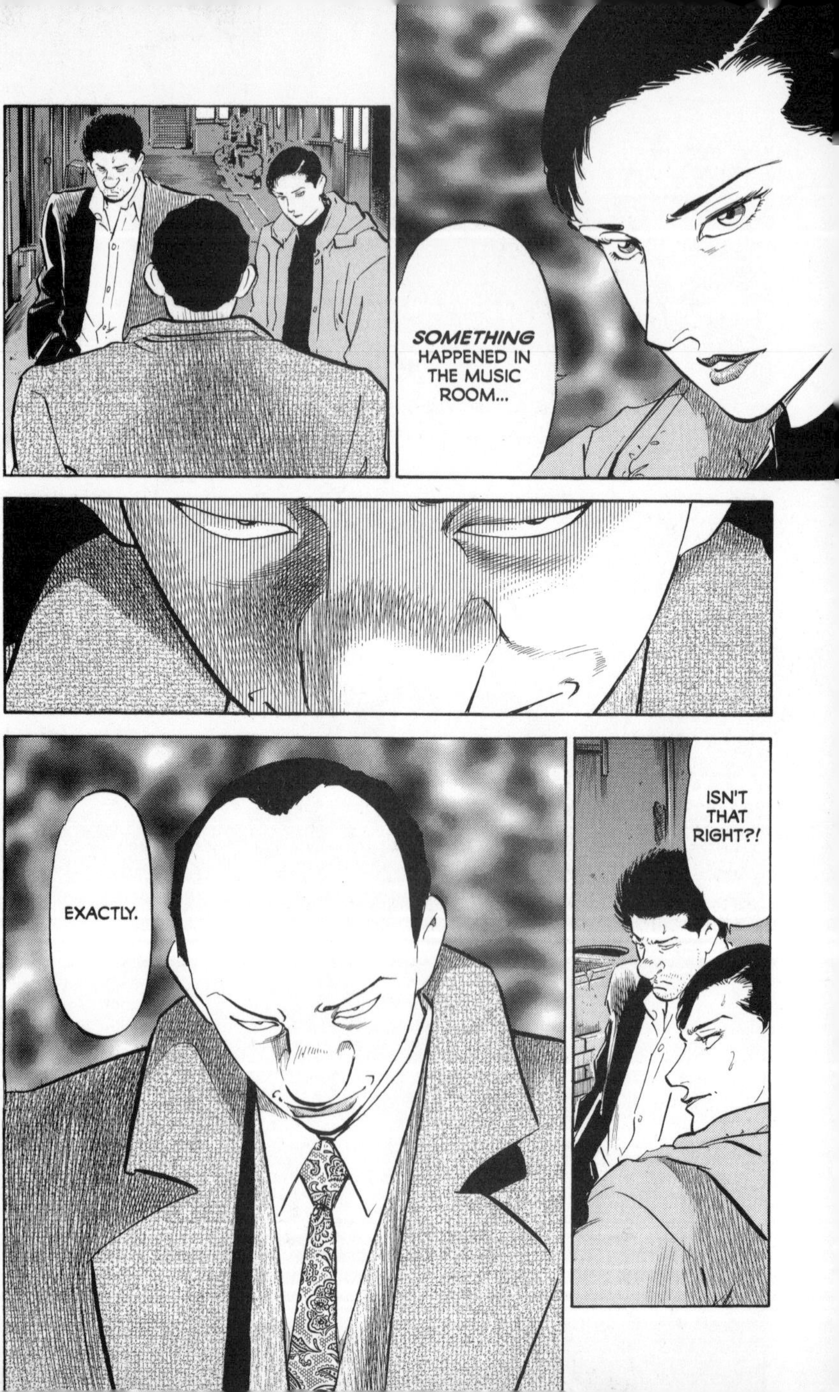
SOMETHING HAPPENED IN THE MUSIC ROOM...
ISN'T THAT RIGHT?!
EXACTLY.

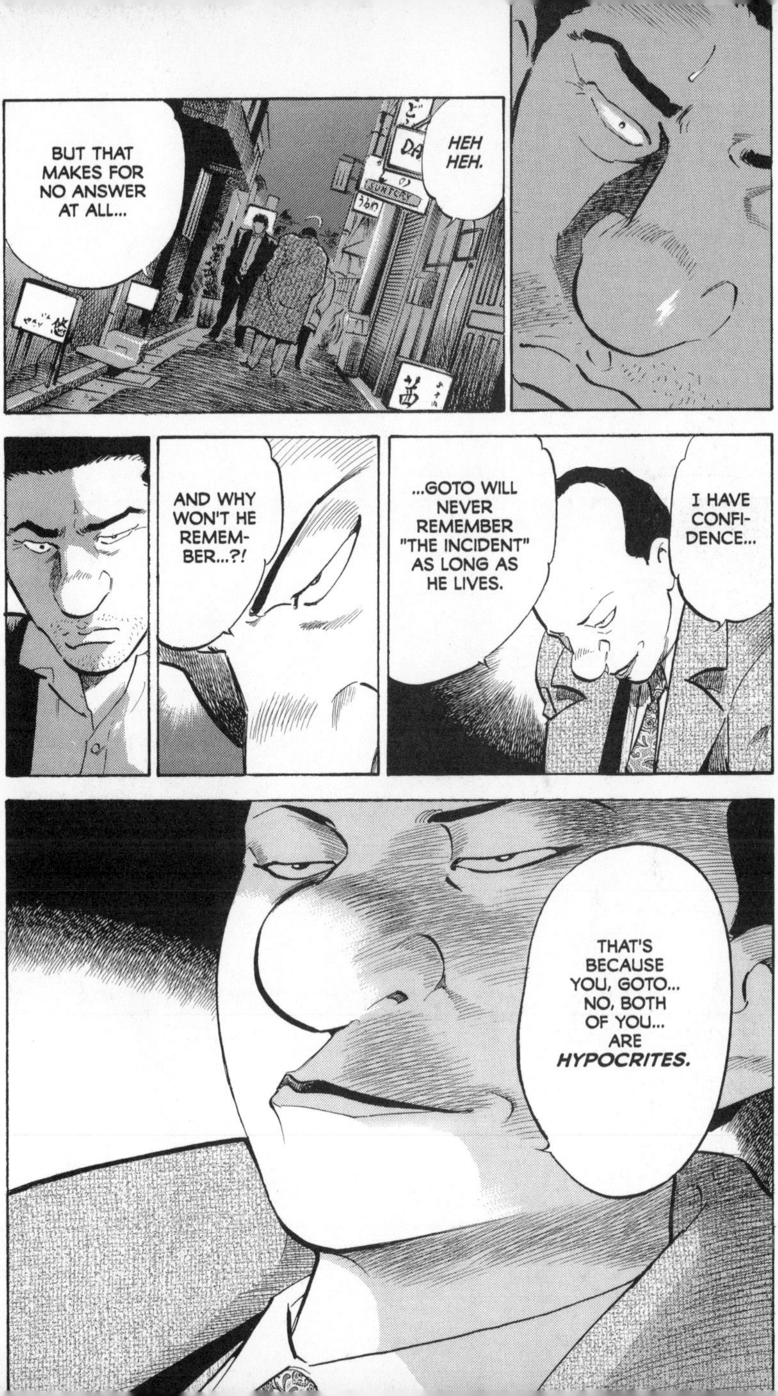
HEH HEH.
BUT THAT MAKES FOR NO ANSWER AT ALL...
I HAVE CONFI-DENCE...
...GOTO WILL NEVER REMEMBER "THE INCIDENT" AS LONG AS HE LIVES.
AND WHY WON'T HE REMEM-BER...?!
THAT'S BECAUSE YOU, GOTO... NO, BOTH OF YOU... ARE *HYPOCRITES.*

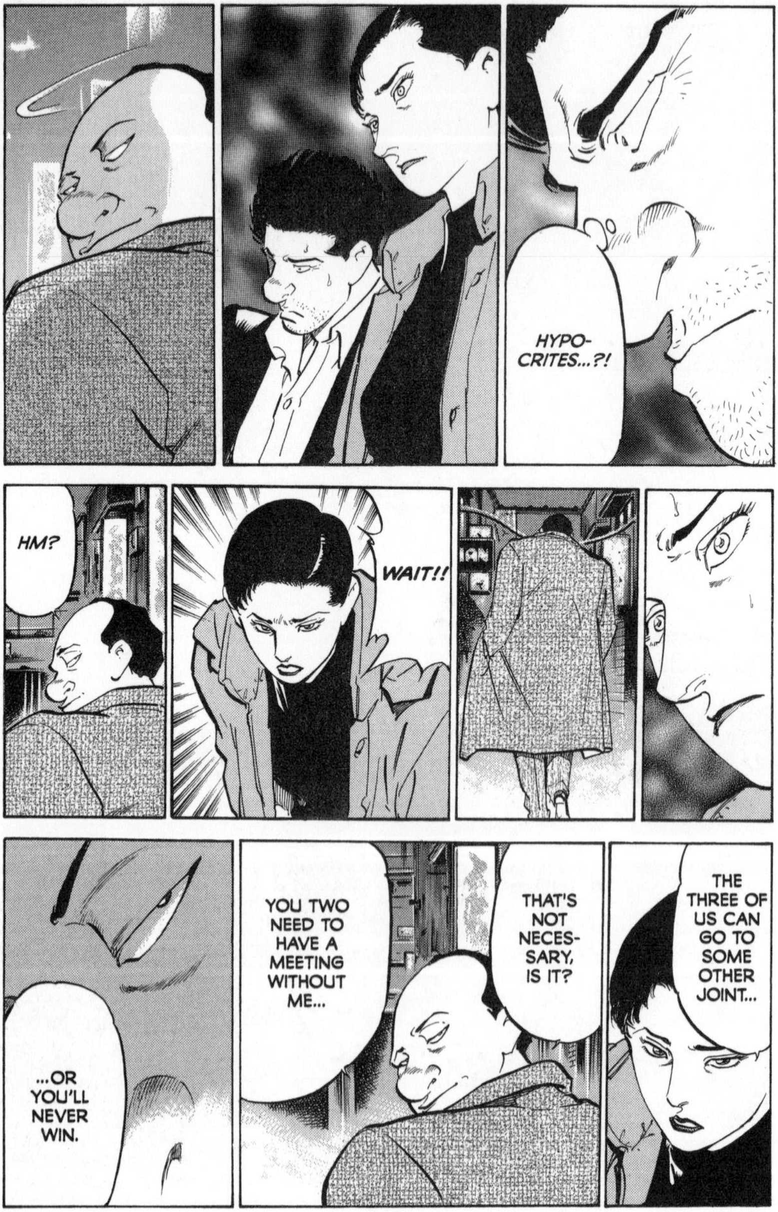
HYPO-CRITES...?!
WAIT!!
HM?
THE THREE OF US CAN GO TO SOME OTHER JOINT...
THAT'S NOT NECES-SARY, IS IT?
YOU TWO NEED TO HAVE A MEETING WITHOUT ME...
...OR YOU'LL NEVER WIN.

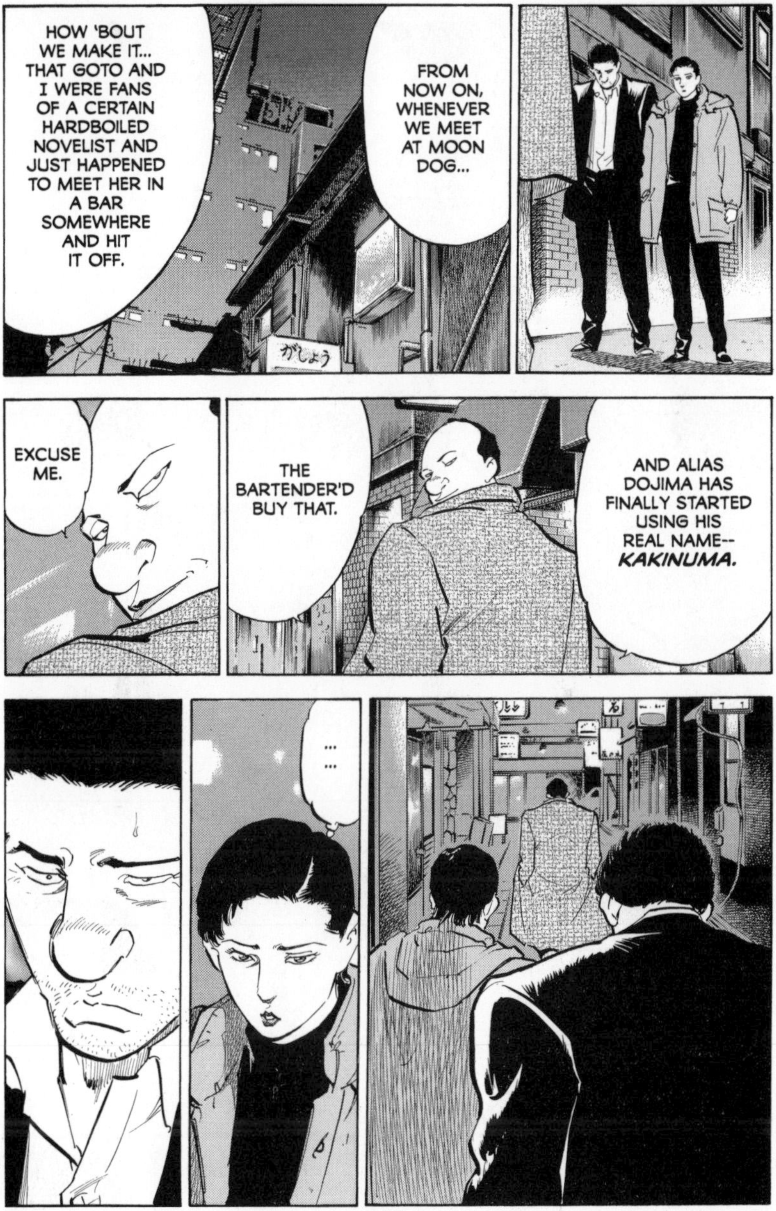
FROM NOW ON, WHENEVER WE MEET AT MOON DOG...
HOW 'BOUT WE MAKE IT... THAT GOTO AND I WERE FANS OF A CERTAIN HARDBOILED NOVELIST AND JUST HAPPENED TO MEET HER IN A BAR SOMEWHERE AND HIT IT OFF.
がしょう
AND ALIAS DOJIMA HAS FINALLY STARTED USING HIS REAL NAME-- ***KAKINUMA.***
THE BARTENDER'D BUY THAT.
EXCUSE ME.
... ...

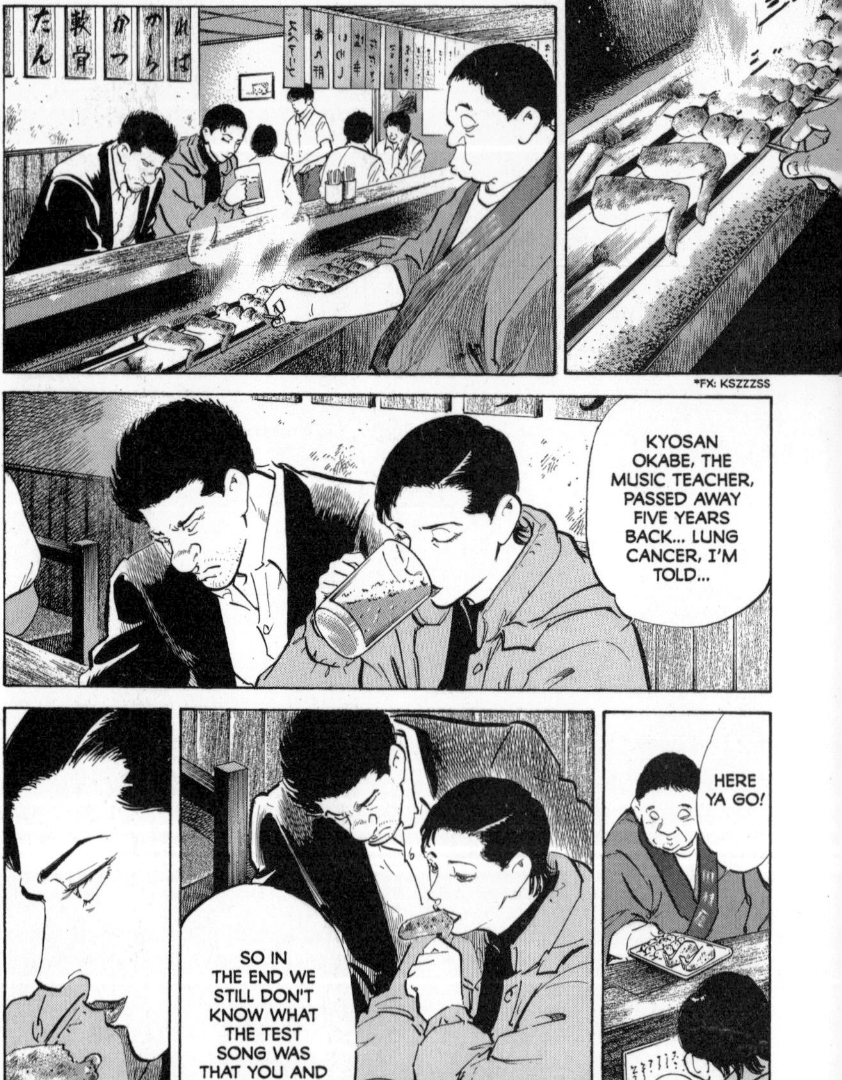
ジジジ
れば
かしら
かつ
軟骨
たん
KYOSAN OKABE, THE MUSIC TEACHER, PASSED AWAY FIVE YEARS BACK... LUNG CANCER, I'M TOLD...
HERE YA GO!
SO IN THE END WE STILL DON'T KNOW WHAT THE TEST SONG WAS THAT YOU AND KAKINUMA SANG IN THE MUSIC ROOM...

*FX: KSZZZSS

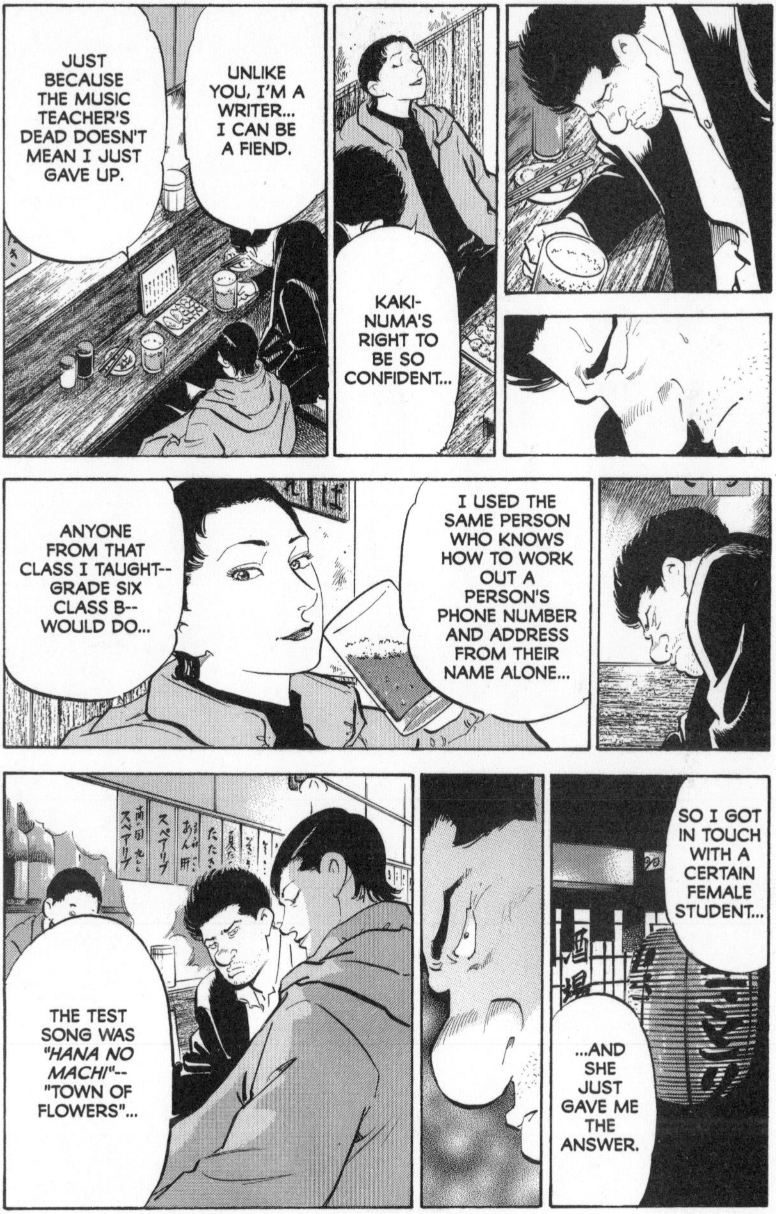
KAKI-NUMA'S RIGHT TO BE SO CONFIDENT...
UNLIKE YOU, I'M A WRITER... I CAN BE A FIEND.
JUST BECAUSE THE MUSIC TEACHER'S DEAD DOESN'T MEAN I JUST GAVE UP.
I USED THE SAME PERSON WHO KNOWS HOW TO WORK OUT A PERSON'S PHONE NUMBER AND ADDRESS FROM THEIR NAME ALONE...
ANYONE FROM THAT CLASS I TAUGHT-- GRADE SIX CLASS B-- WOULD DO...
SO I GOT IN TOUCH WITH A CERTAIN FEMALE STUDENT...
...AND SHE JUST GAVE ME THE ANSWER.
THE TEST SONG WAS "HANA NO MACHI"-- "TOWN OF FLOWERS"...

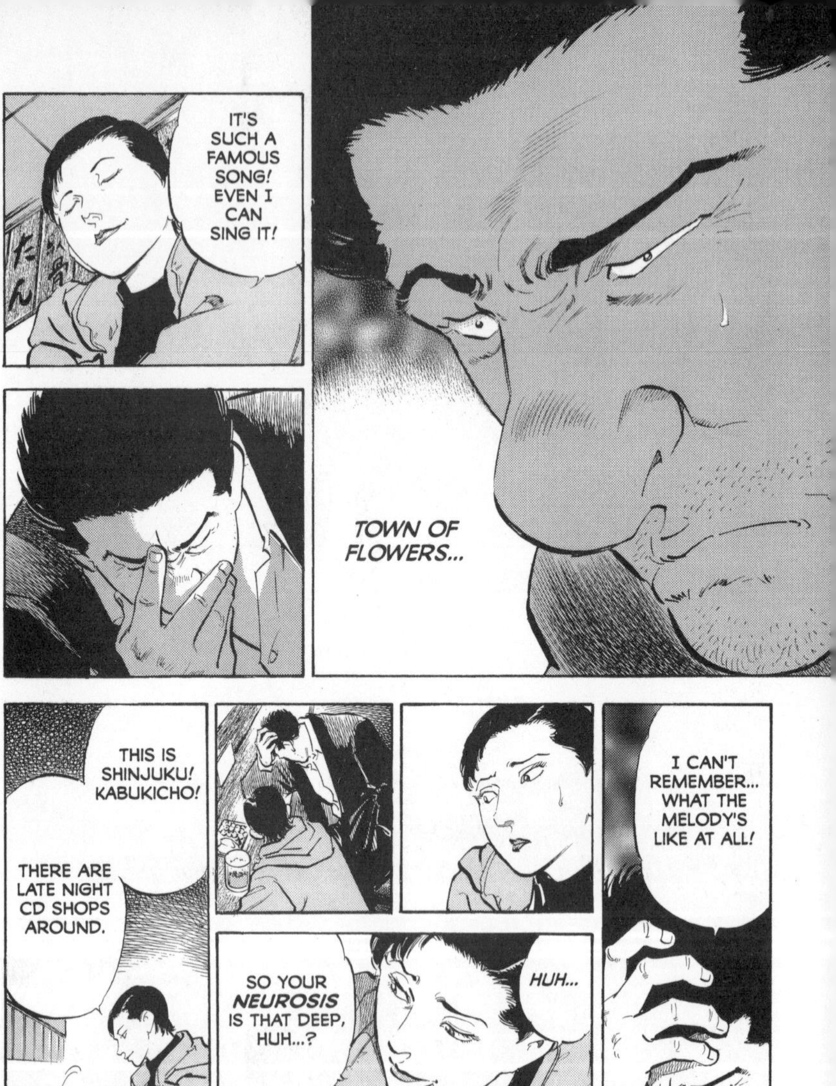
TOWN OF FLOWERS...
IT'S SUCH A FAMOUS SONG! EVEN I CAN SING IT!
I CAN'T REMEMBER... WHAT THE MELODY'S LIKE AT ALL!
HUH...
SO YOUR *NEUROSIS* IS THAT DEEP, HUH...?
THIS IS SHINJUKU! KABUKICHO!
THERE ARE LATE NIGHT CD SHOPS AROUND.

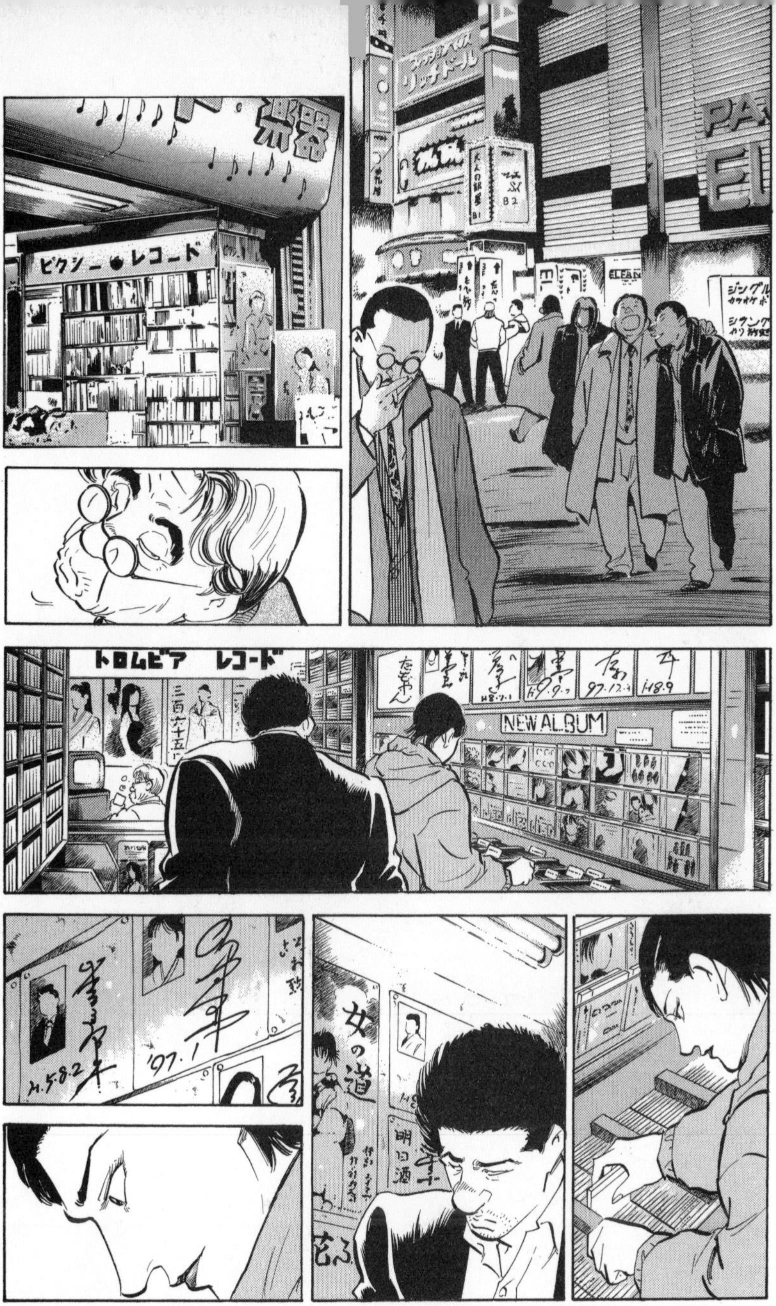
リッチドール
ジングル
楽器
ピクシー レコード
トロムビア レコード
NEW ALBUM
女の道
明日酒

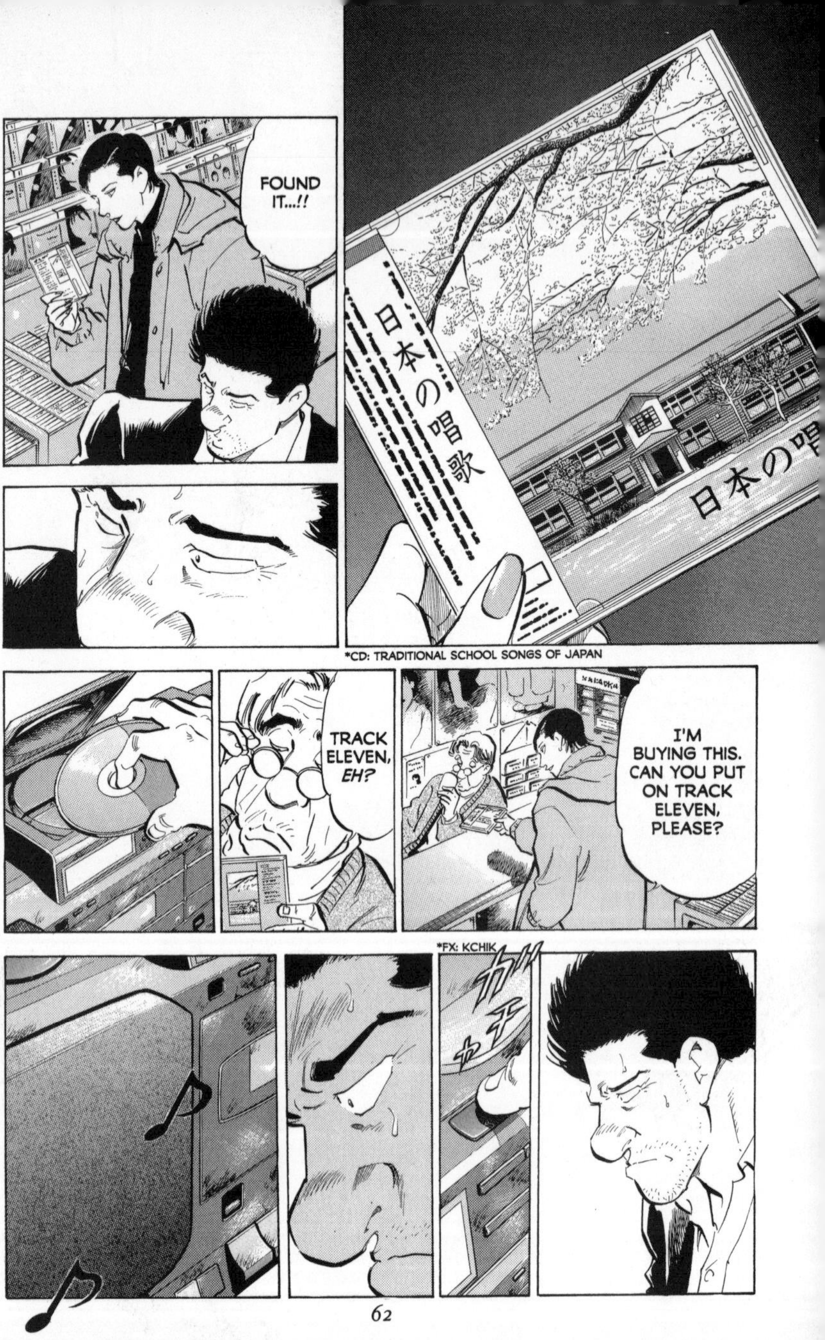

日本の唱歌
*CD: TRADITIONAL SCHOOL SONGS OF JAPAN
FOUND IT...!!
I'M BUYING THIS. CAN YOU PUT ON TRACK ELEVEN, PLEASE?
TRACK ELEVEN, *EH?*
*FX: KCHIK

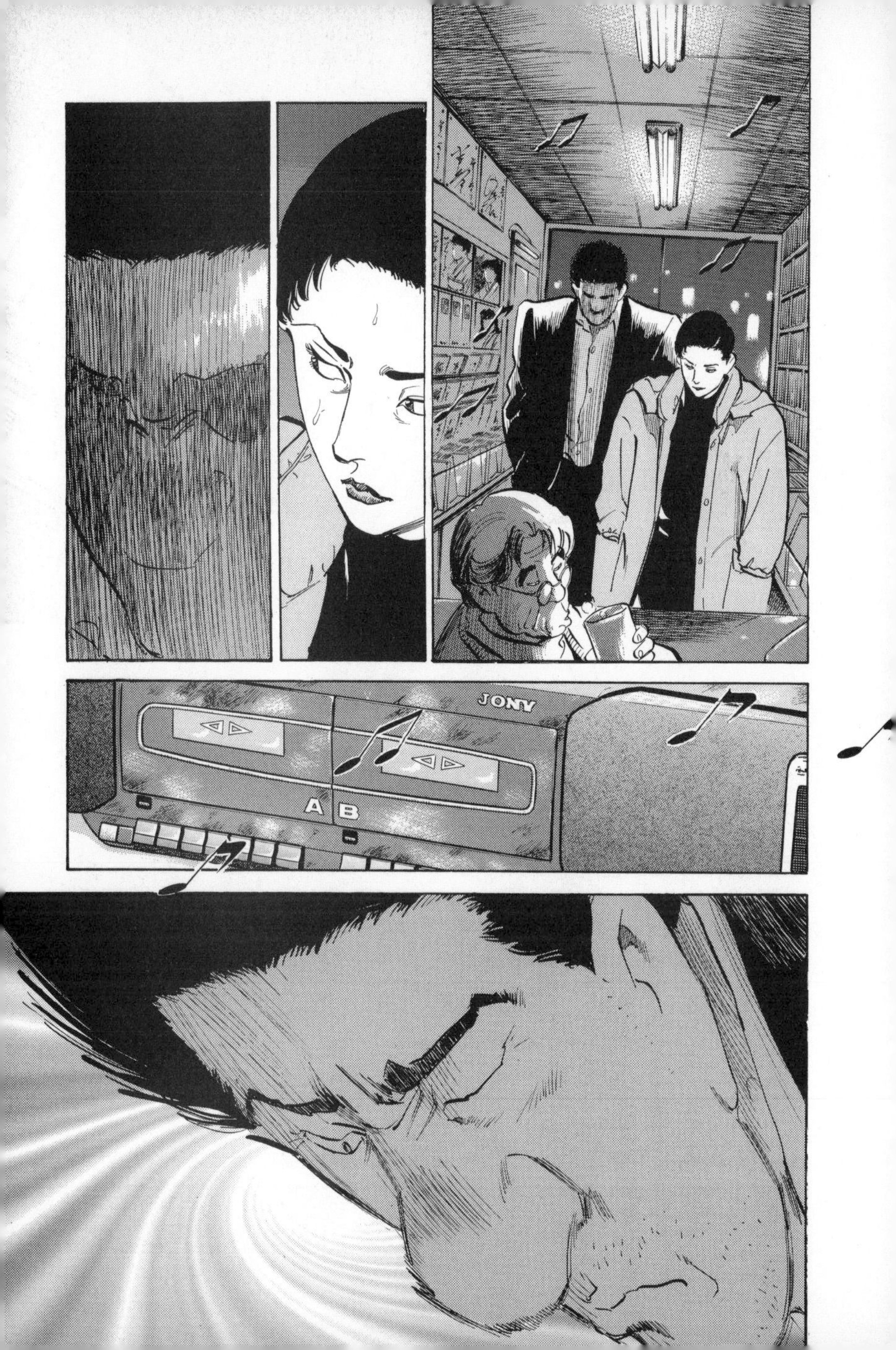
JONY
A B

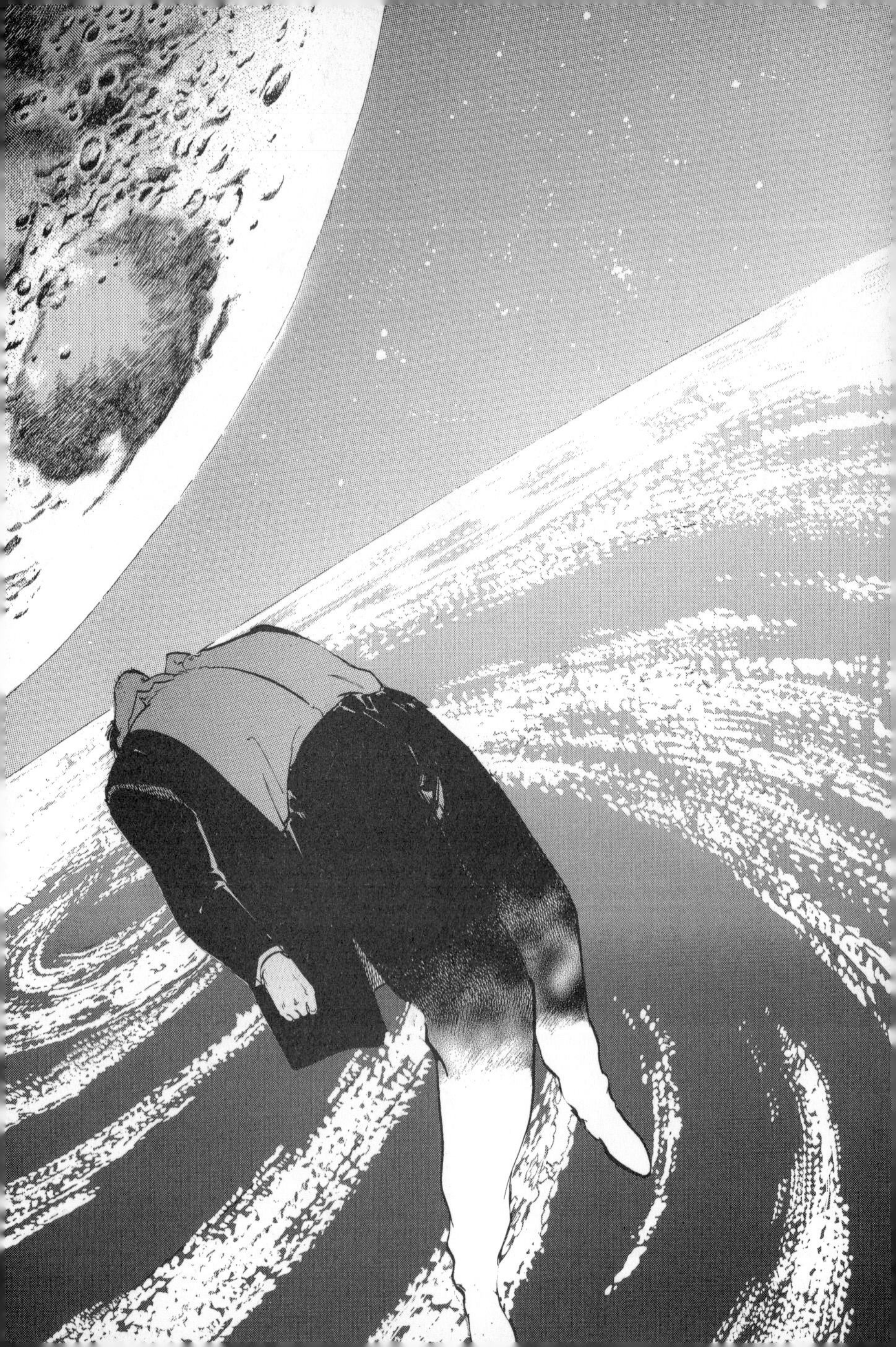

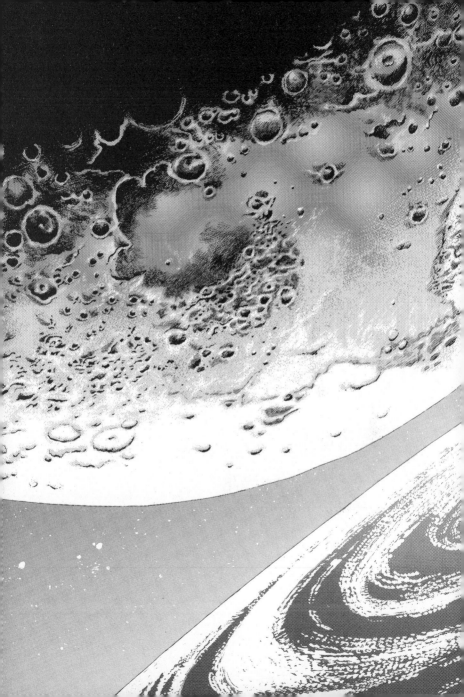

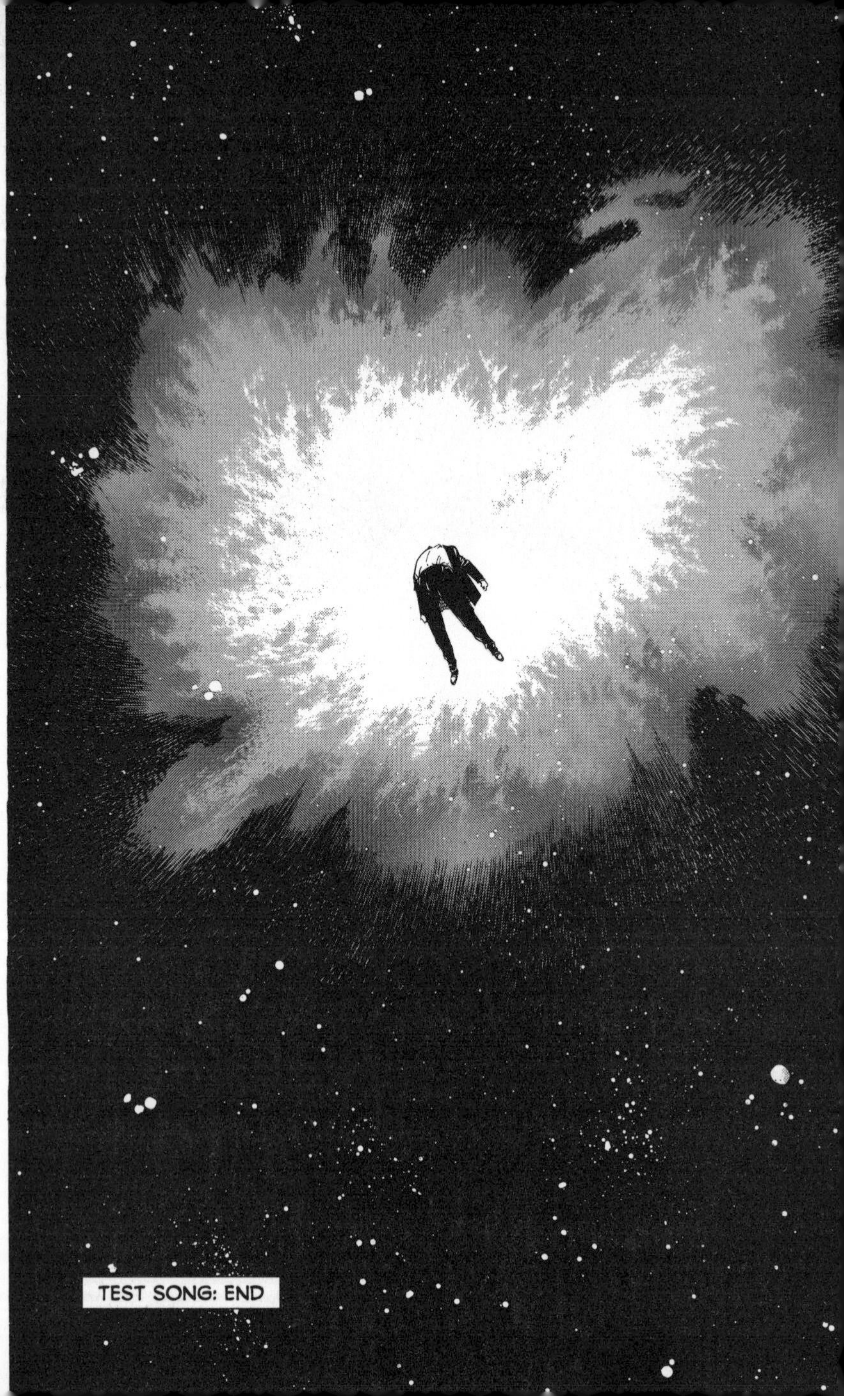
TEST SONG: END

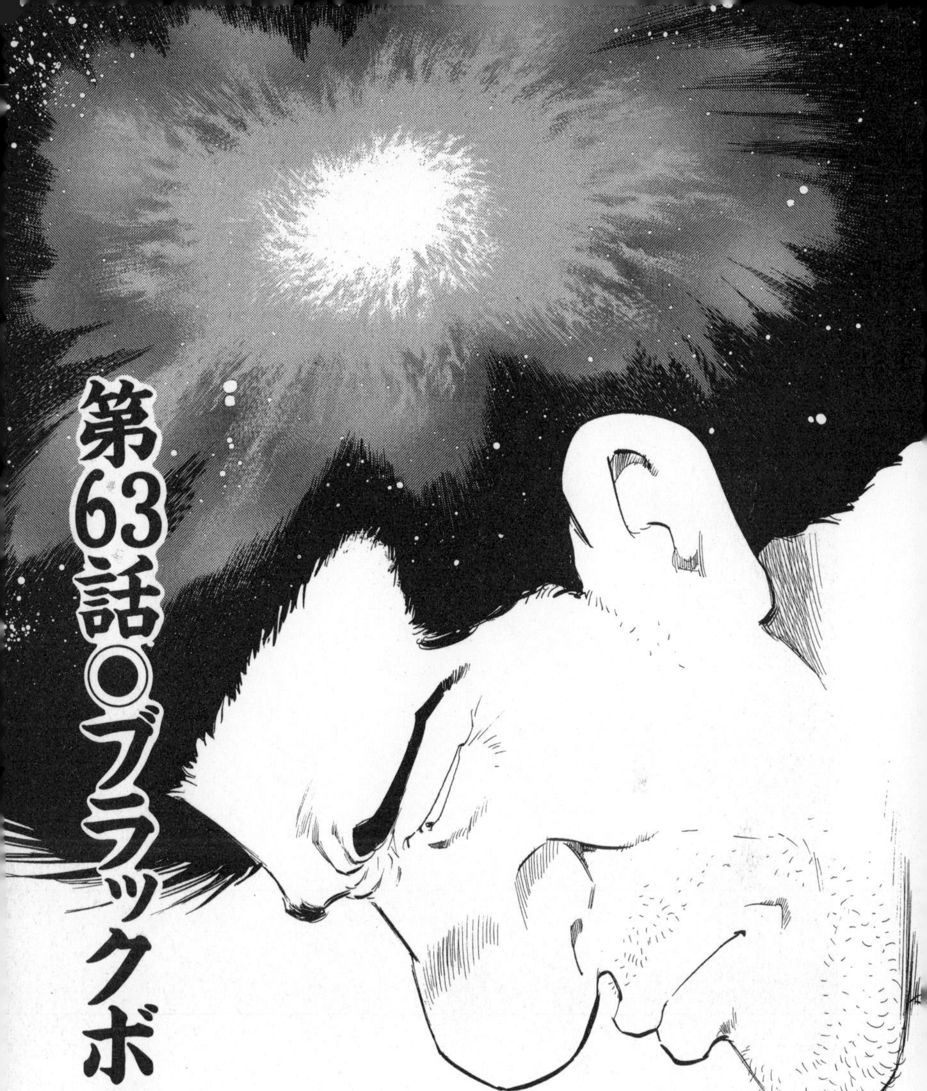

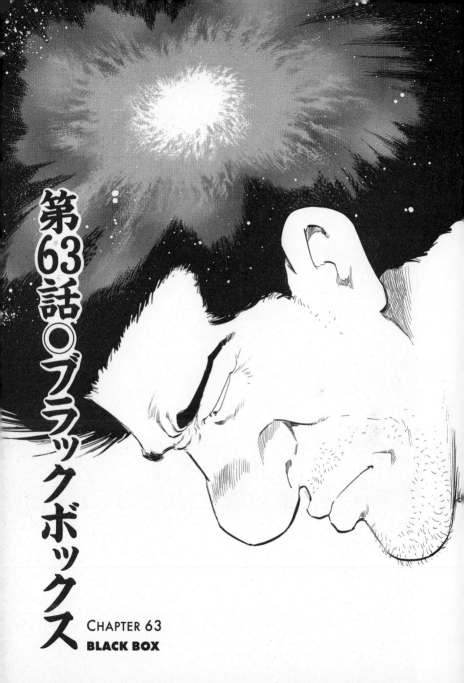

第63話◎ブラックボックス

CHAPTER 63
BLACK BOX

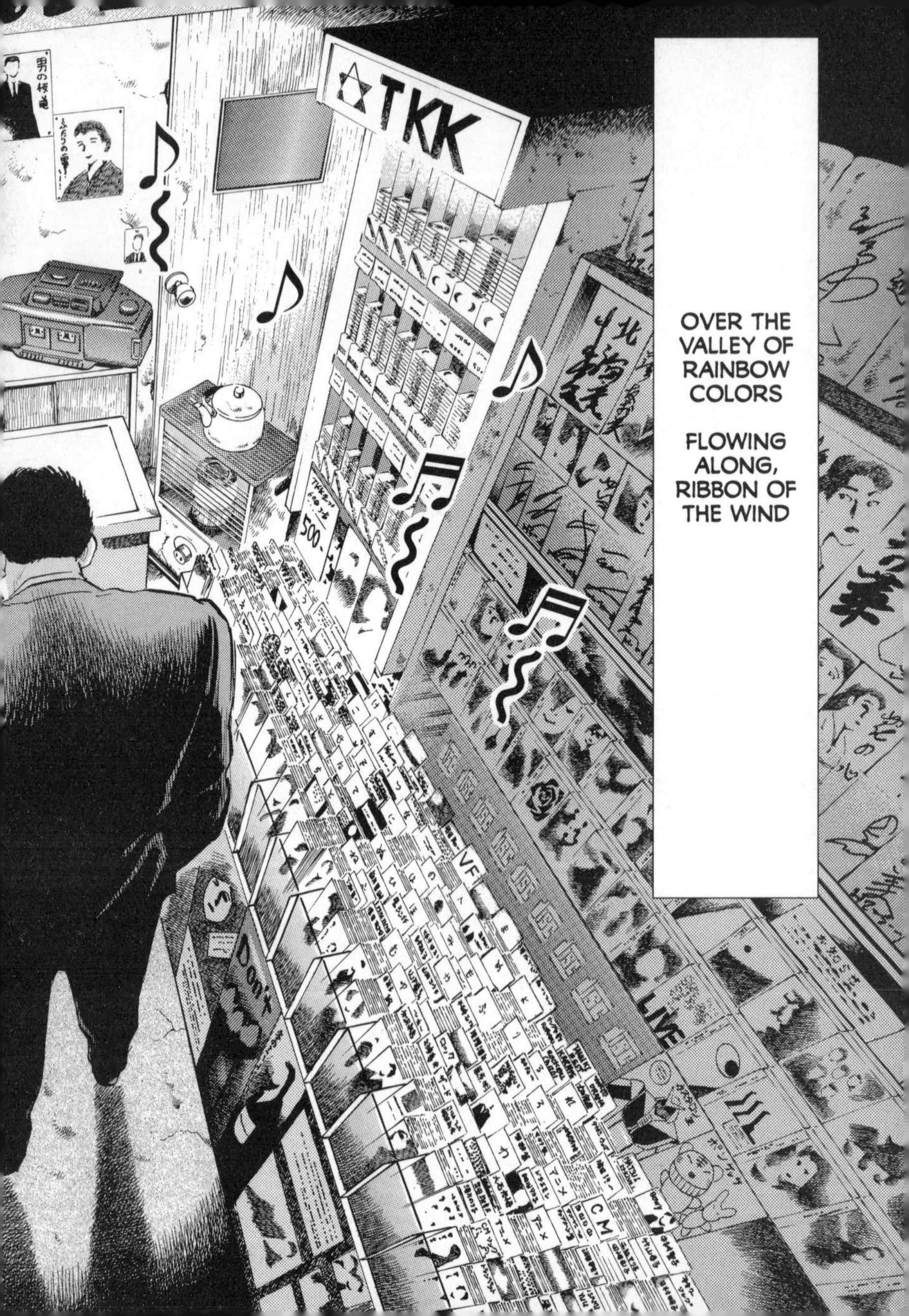
OVER THE VALLEY OF RAINBOW COLORS

FLOWING ALONG, RIBBON OF THE WIND
TKK
500
VF
LIVE
Don't

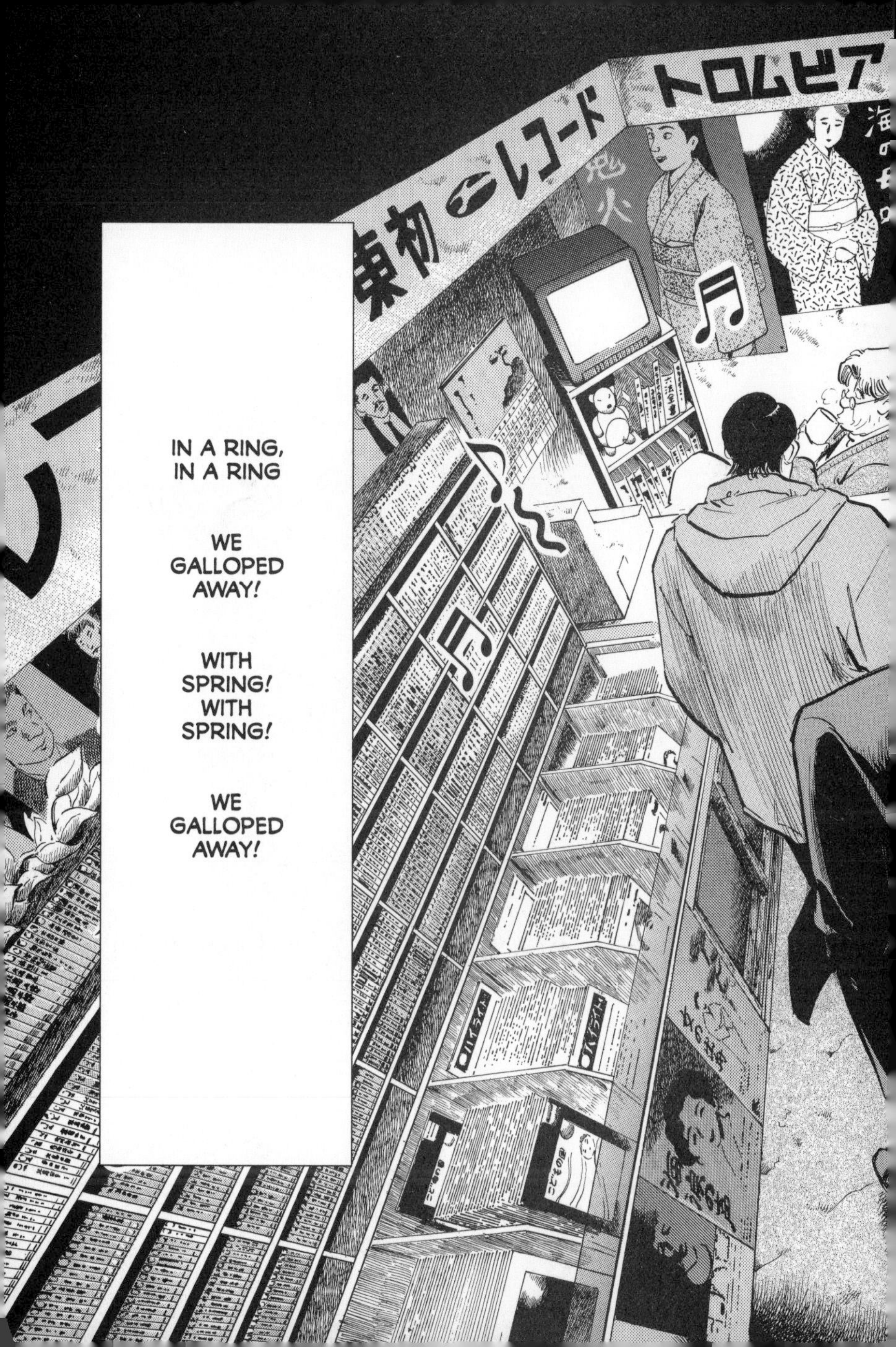

レコード
IN A RING, IN A RING
WE GALLOPED AWAY!
WITH SPRING! WITH SPRING!
WE GALLOPED AWAY!

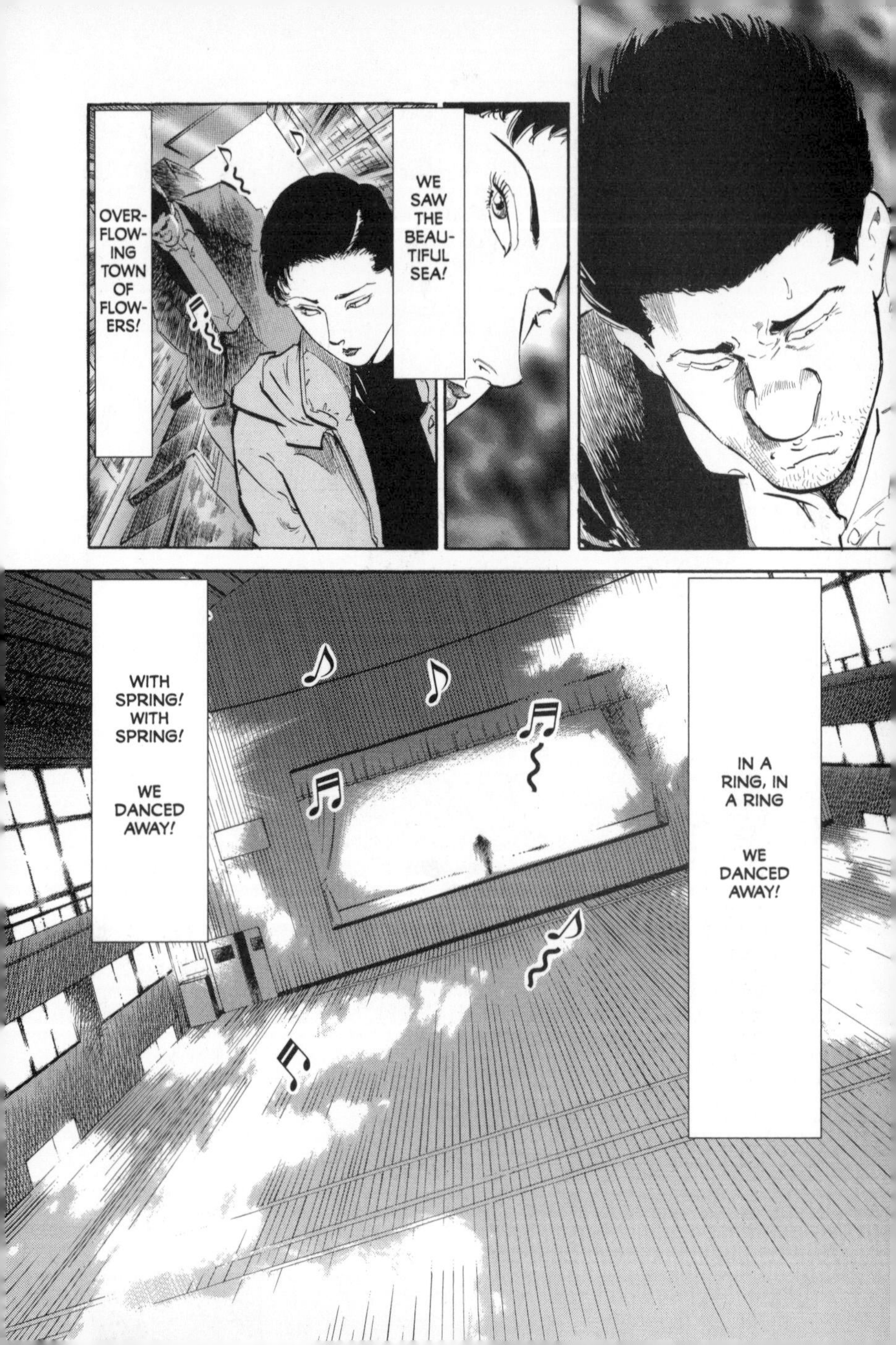
WE SAW THE BEAU-TIFUL SEA!
OVER-FLOW-ING TOWN OF FLOW-ERS!
IN A RING, IN A RING
WE DANCED AWAY!
WITH SPRING! WITH SPRING!
WE DANCED AWAY!

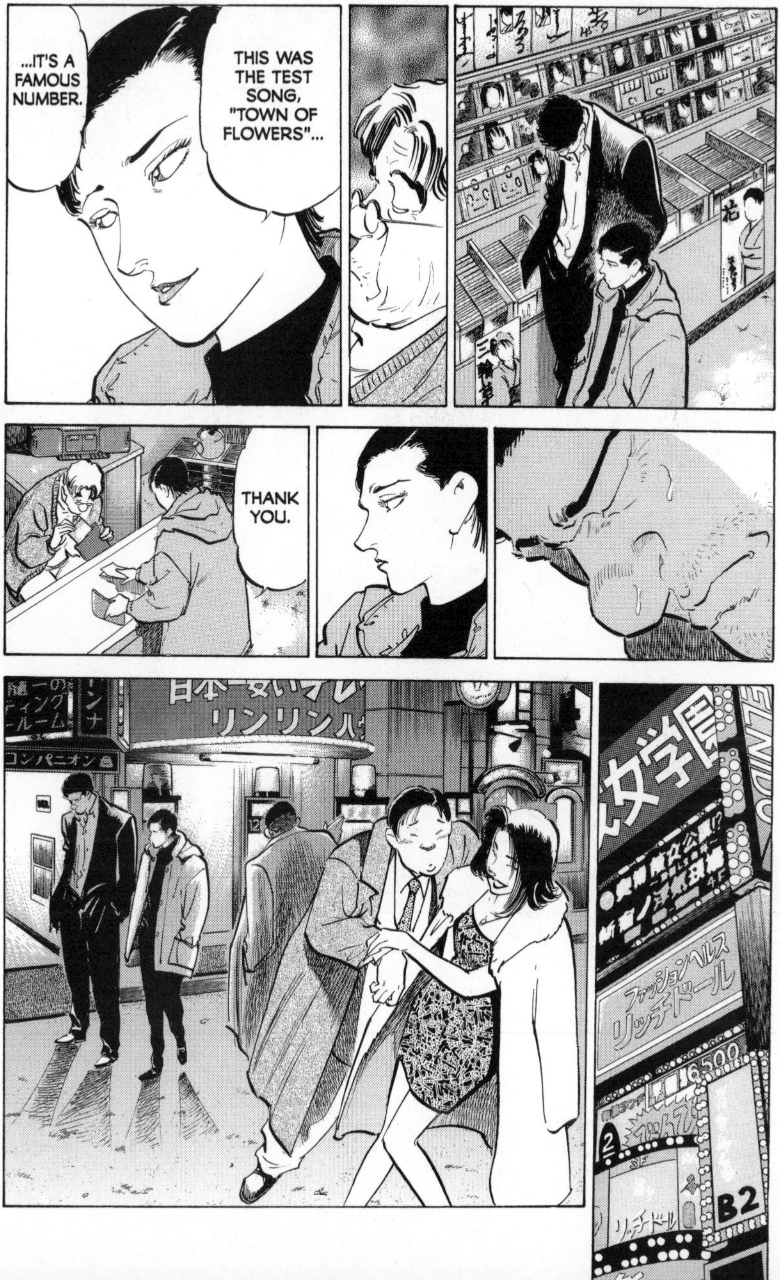
THIS WAS THE TEST SONG, "TOWN OF FLOWERS"...
...IT'S A FAMOUS NUMBER.
THANK YOU.
ファッションヘルス
リッチドール
B2
コンパニオン

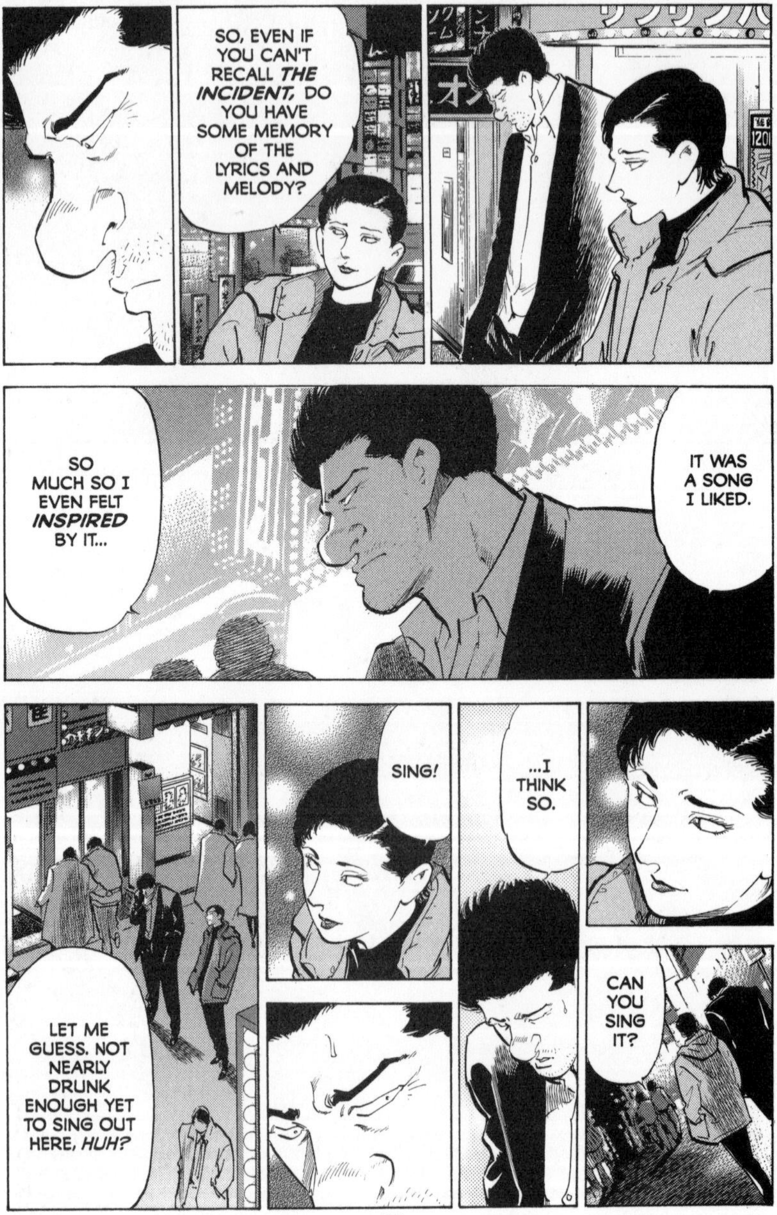
SO, EVEN IF YOU CAN'T RECALL *THE INCIDENT,* DO YOU HAVE SOME MEMORY OF THE LYRICS AND MELODY?
IT WAS A SONG I LIKED.
SO MUCH SO I EVEN FELT *INSPIRED* BY IT...
CAN YOU SING IT?
...I THINK SO.
SING!
LET ME GUESS. NOT NEARLY DRUNK ENOUGH YET TO SING OUT HERE, *HUH?*

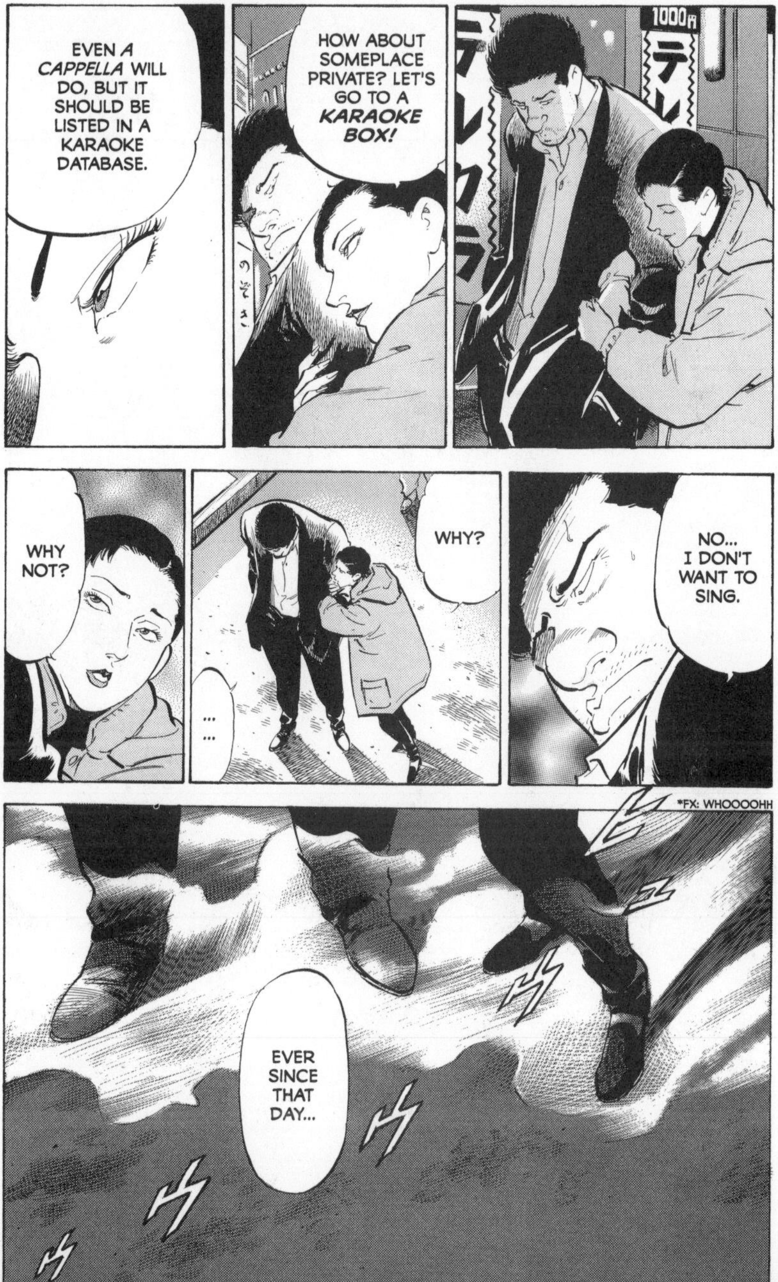
1000円
HOW ABOUT SOMEPLACE PRIVATE? LET'S GO TO A *KARAOKE BOX!*
EVEN *A CAPPELLA* WILL DO, BUT IT SHOULD BE LISTED IN A KARAOKE DATABASE.
NO... I DON'T WANT TO SING.
WHY?
... ...
WHY NOT?
*FX: WHOOOOHH
EVER SINCE THAT DAY...

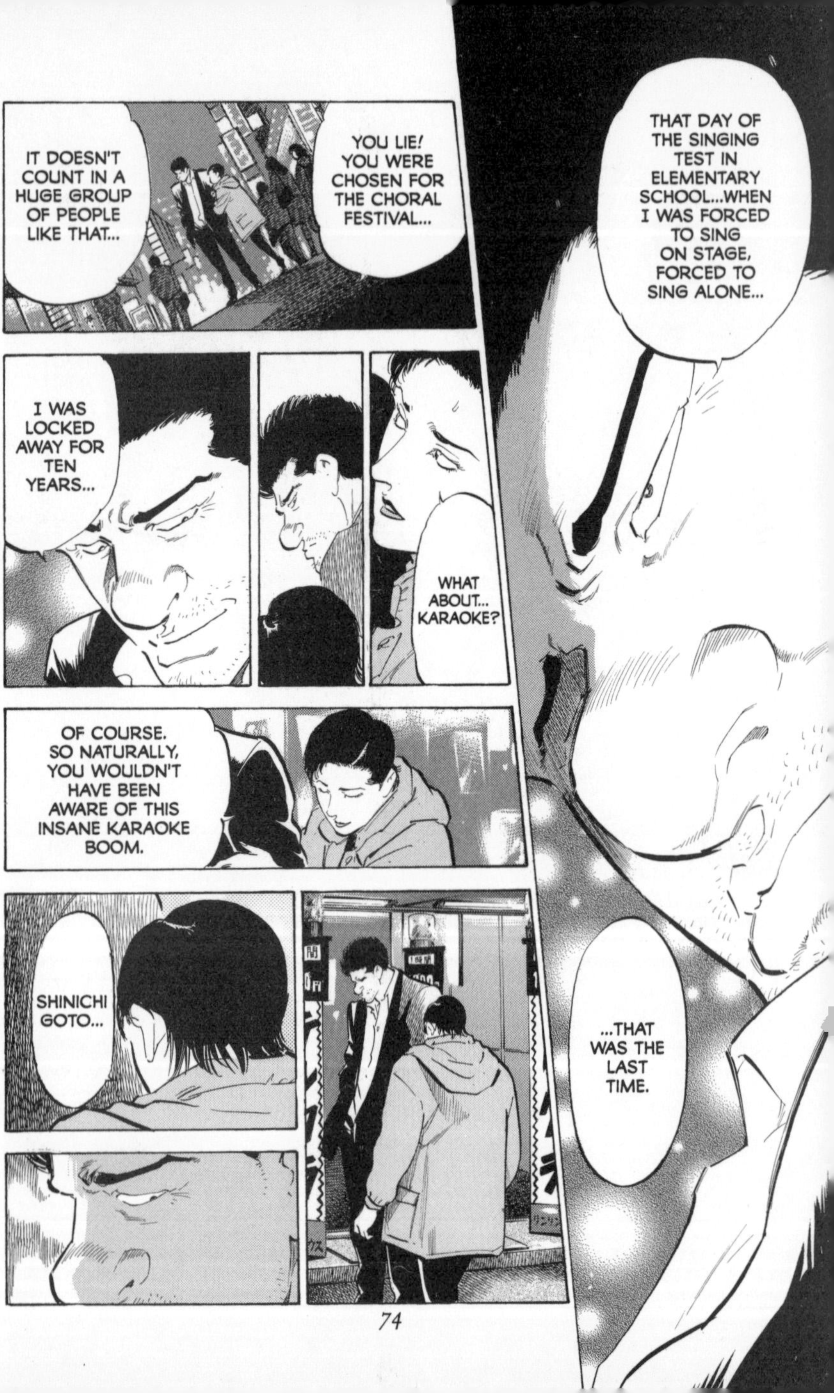
THAT DAY OF THE SINGING TEST IN ELEMENTARY SCHOOL...WHEN I WAS FORCED TO SING ON STAGE, FORCED TO SING ALONE...
...THAT WAS THE LAST TIME.
YOU LIE! YOU WERE CHOSEN FOR THE CHORAL FESTIVAL...
IT DOESN'T COUNT IN A HUGE GROUP OF PEOPLE LIKE THAT...
WHAT ABOUT... KARAOKE?
I WAS LOCKED AWAY FOR TEN YEARS...
OF COURSE. SO NATURALLY, YOU WOULDN'T HAVE BEEN AWARE OF THIS INSANE KARAOKE BOOM.
SHINICHI GOTO...

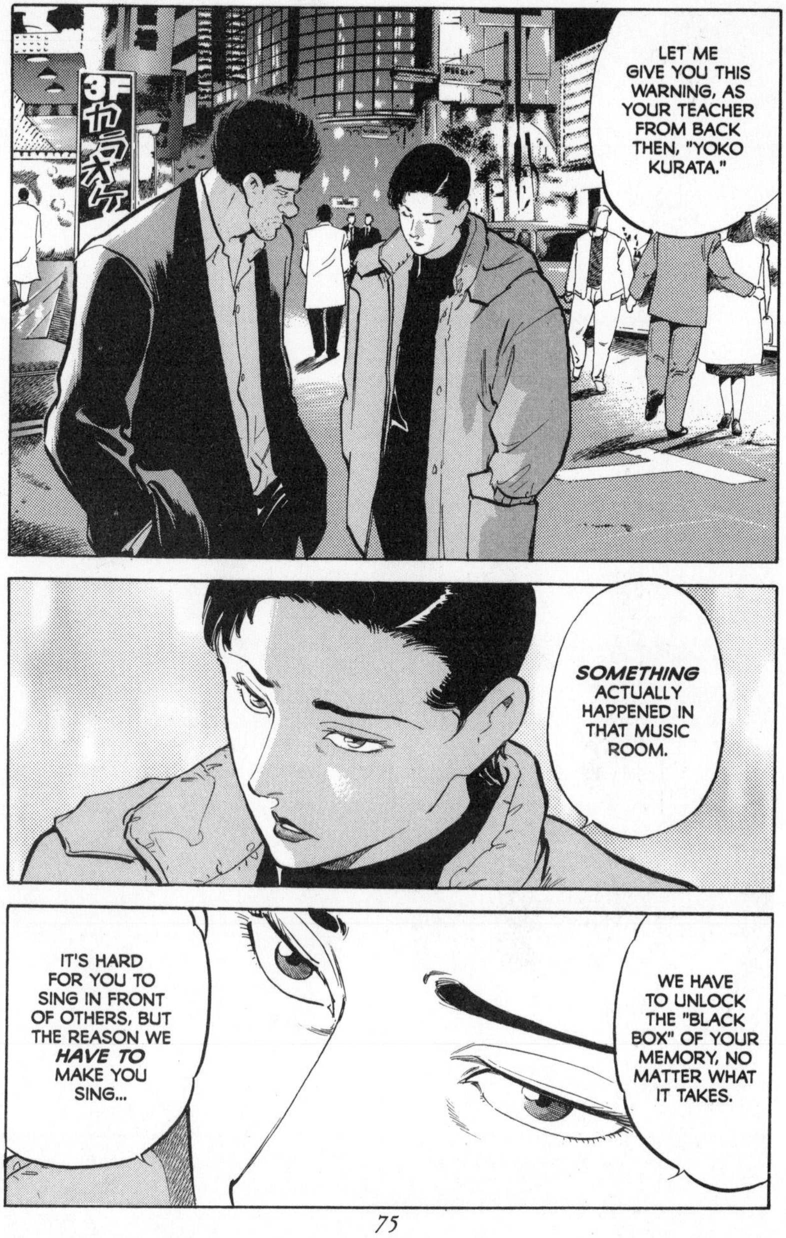
LET ME GIVE YOU THIS WARNING, AS YOUR TEACHER FROM BACK THEN, "YOKO KURATA."
3F
カラオケ
SOMETHING ACTUALLY HAPPENED IN THAT MUSIC ROOM.
WE HAVE TO UNLOCK THE "BLACK BOX" OF YOUR MEMORY, NO MATTER WHAT IT TAKES.
IT'S HARD FOR YOU TO SING IN FRONT OF OTHERS, BUT THE REASON WE *HAVE TO* MAKE YOU SING...

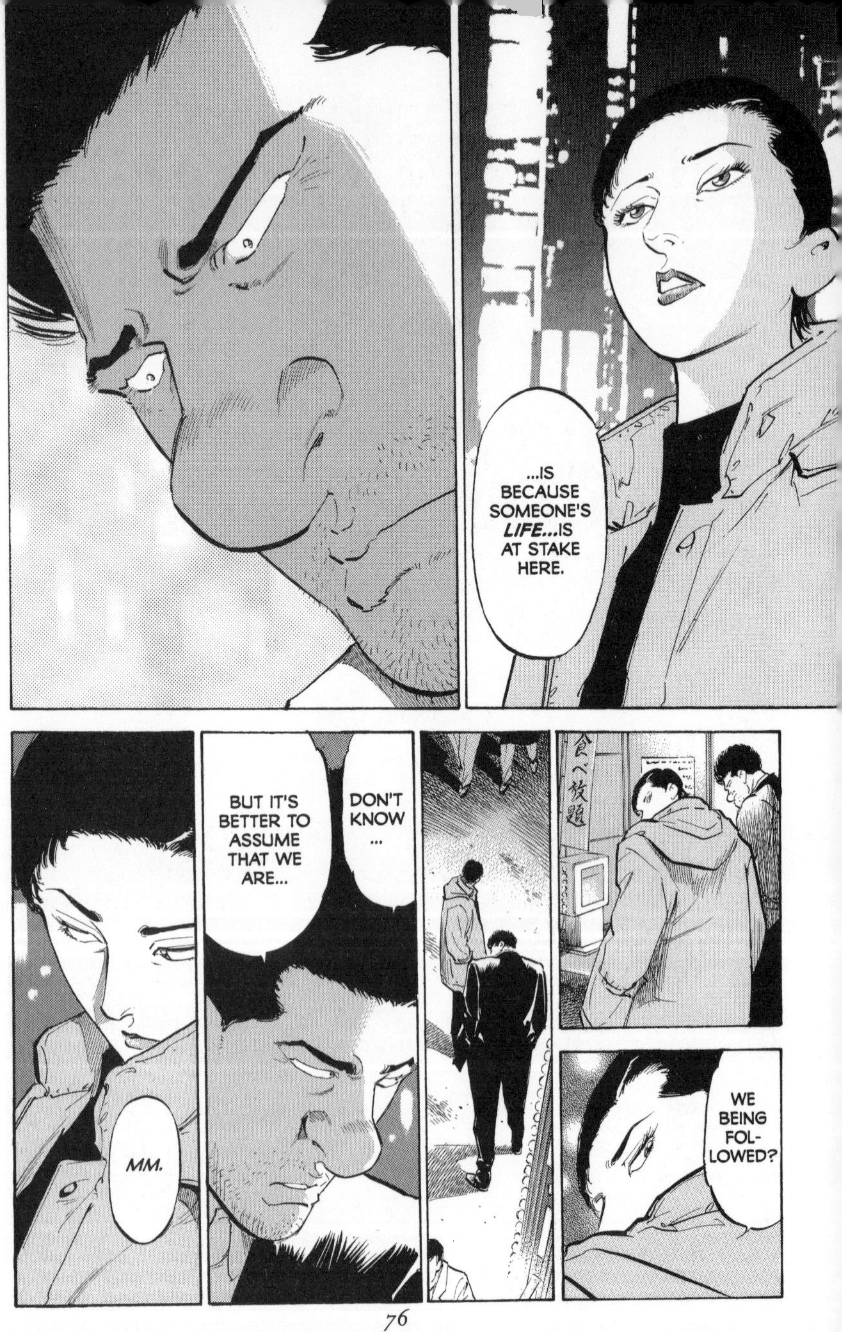
...IS BECAUSE SOMEONE'S *LIFE...*IS AT STAKE HERE.
食べ放題
WE BEING FOL-LOWED?
DON'T KNOW ...
BUT IT'S BETTER TO ASSUME THAT WE ARE...
MM.

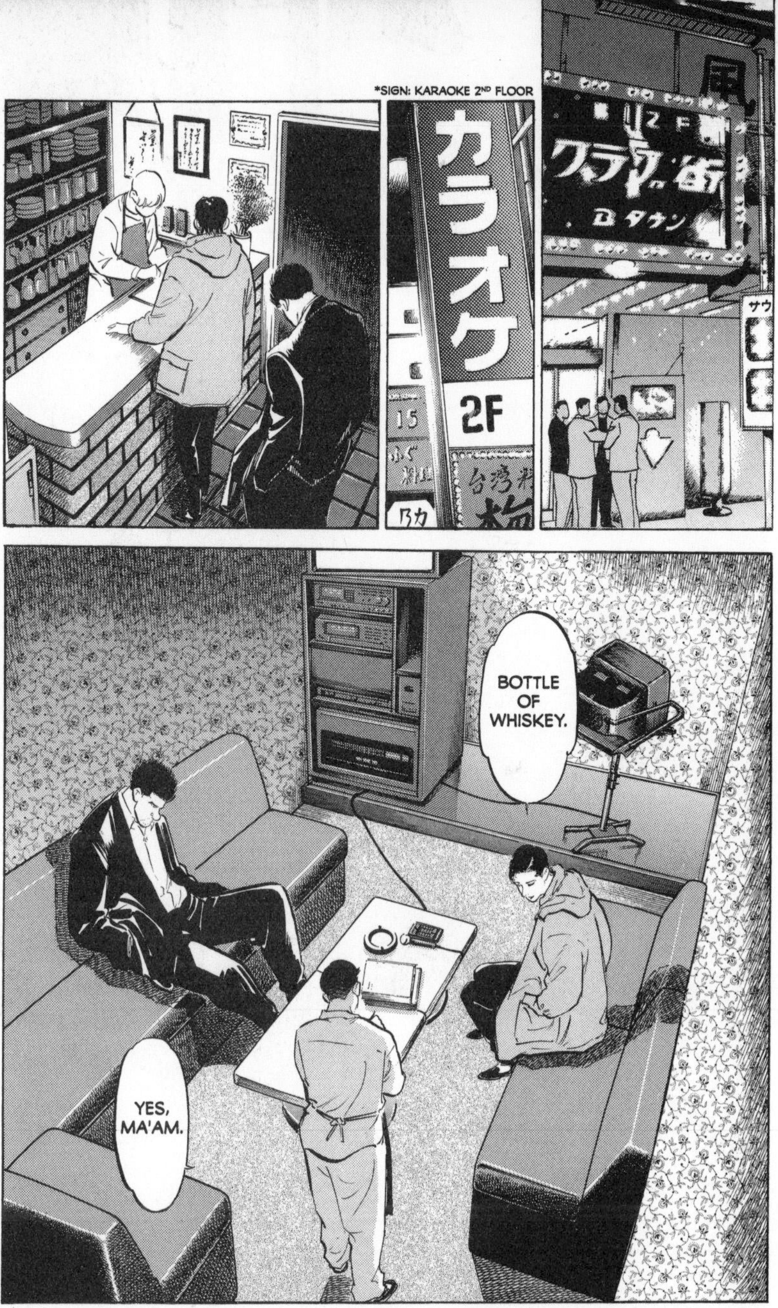
*SIGN: KARAOKE 2ND FLOOR
カラオケ
2F
BOTTLE OF WHISKEY.
YES, MA'AM.

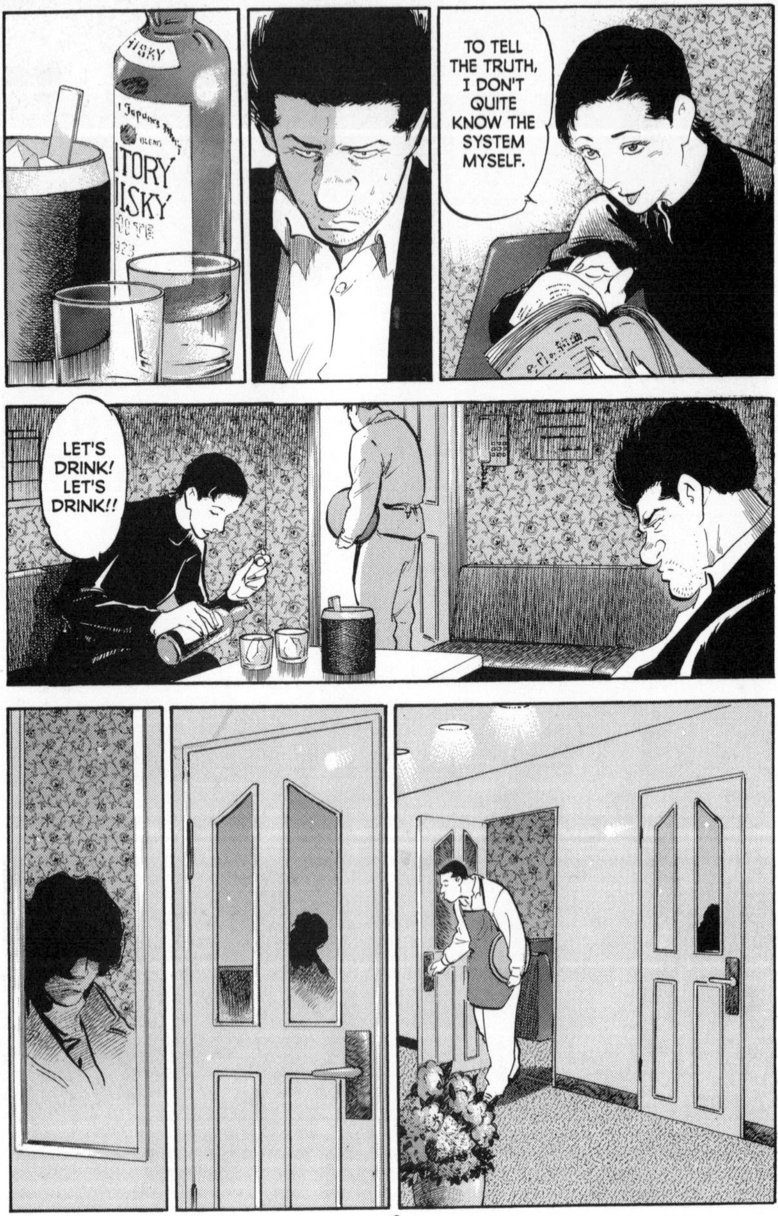
TO TELL THE TRUTH, I DON'T QUITE KNOW THE SYSTEM MYSELF.
LET'S DRINK! LET'S DRINK!!

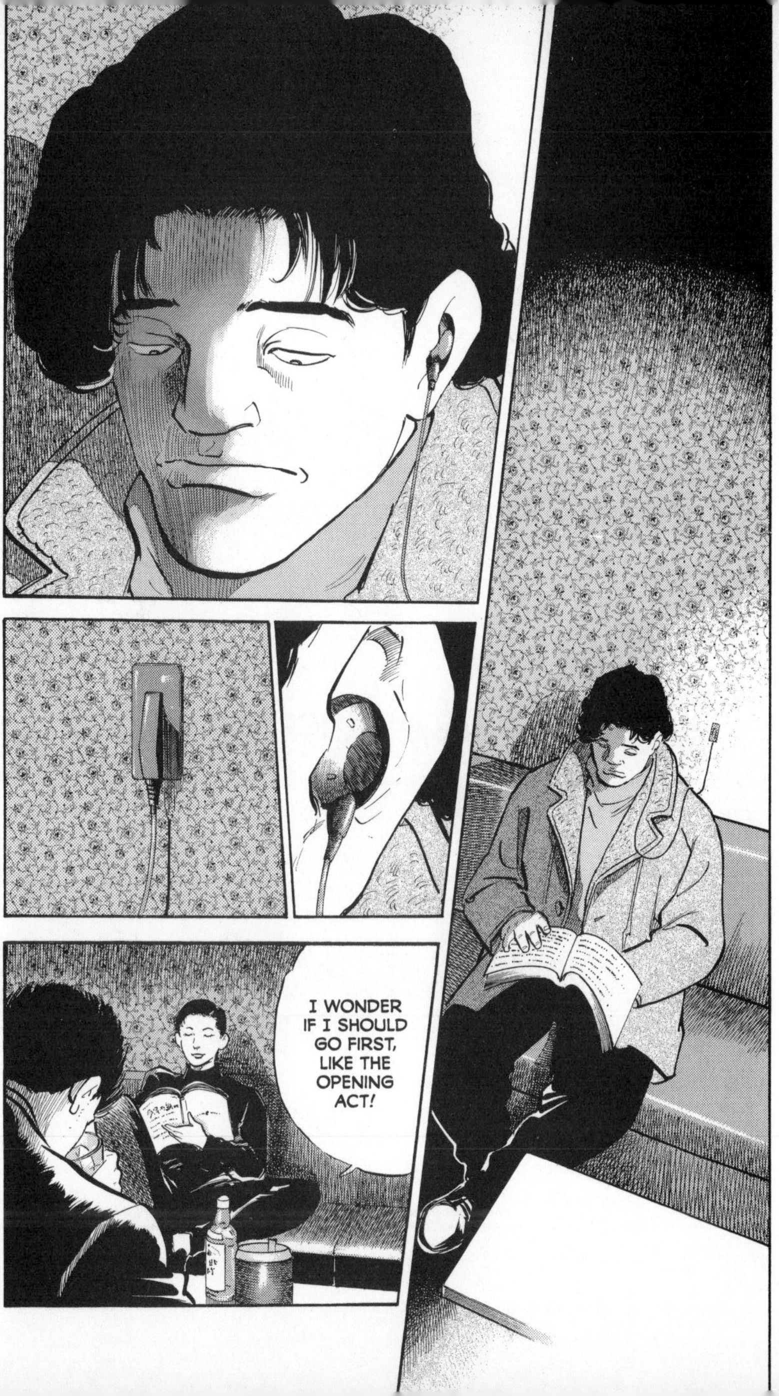
I WONDER IF I SHOULD GO FIRST, LIKE THE OPENING ACT!

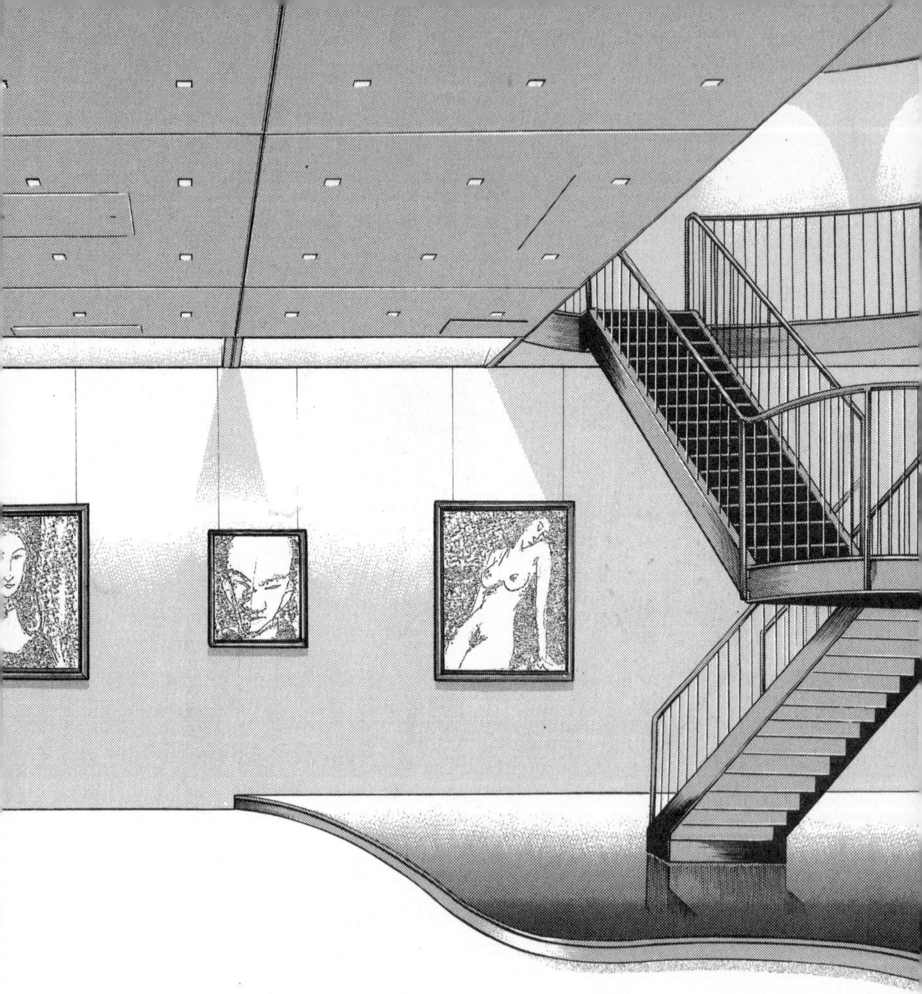

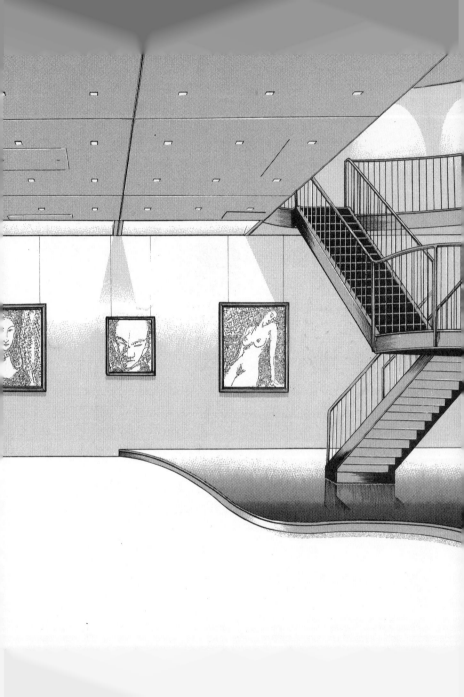

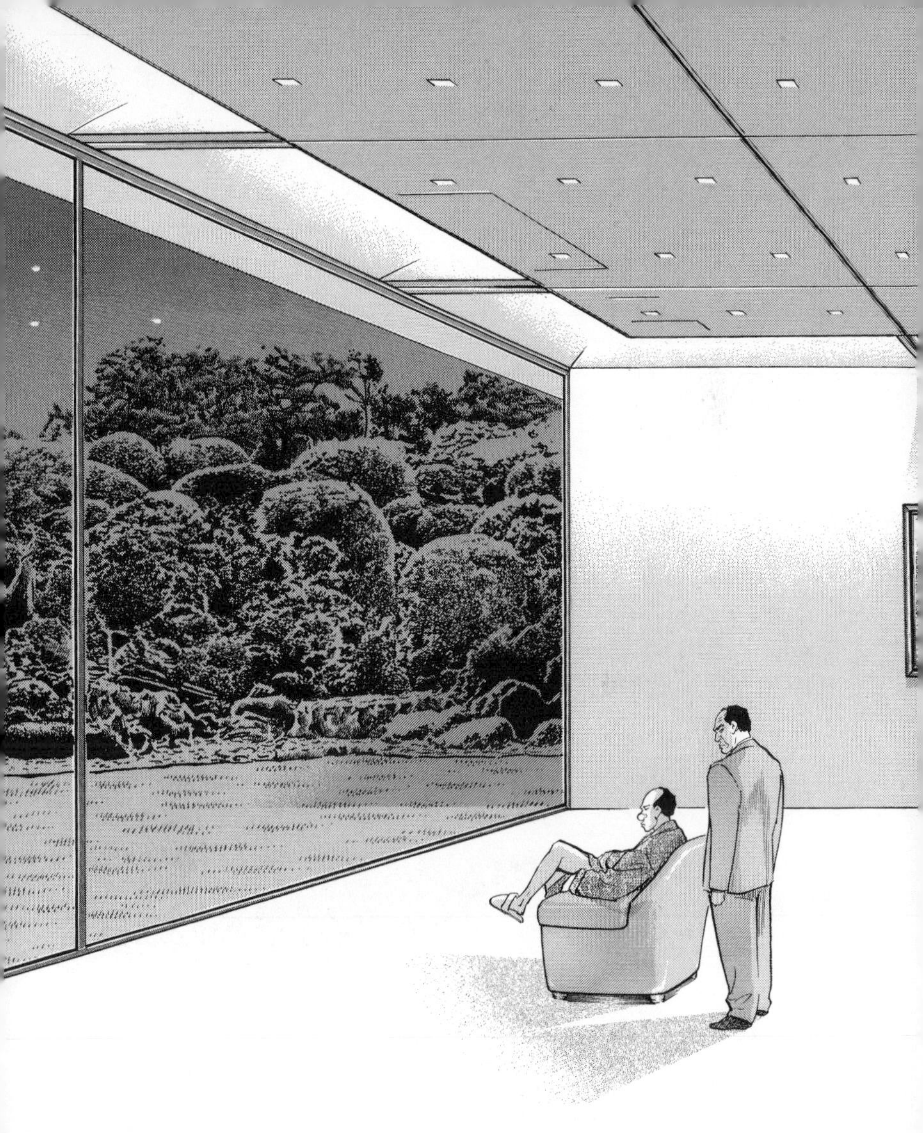

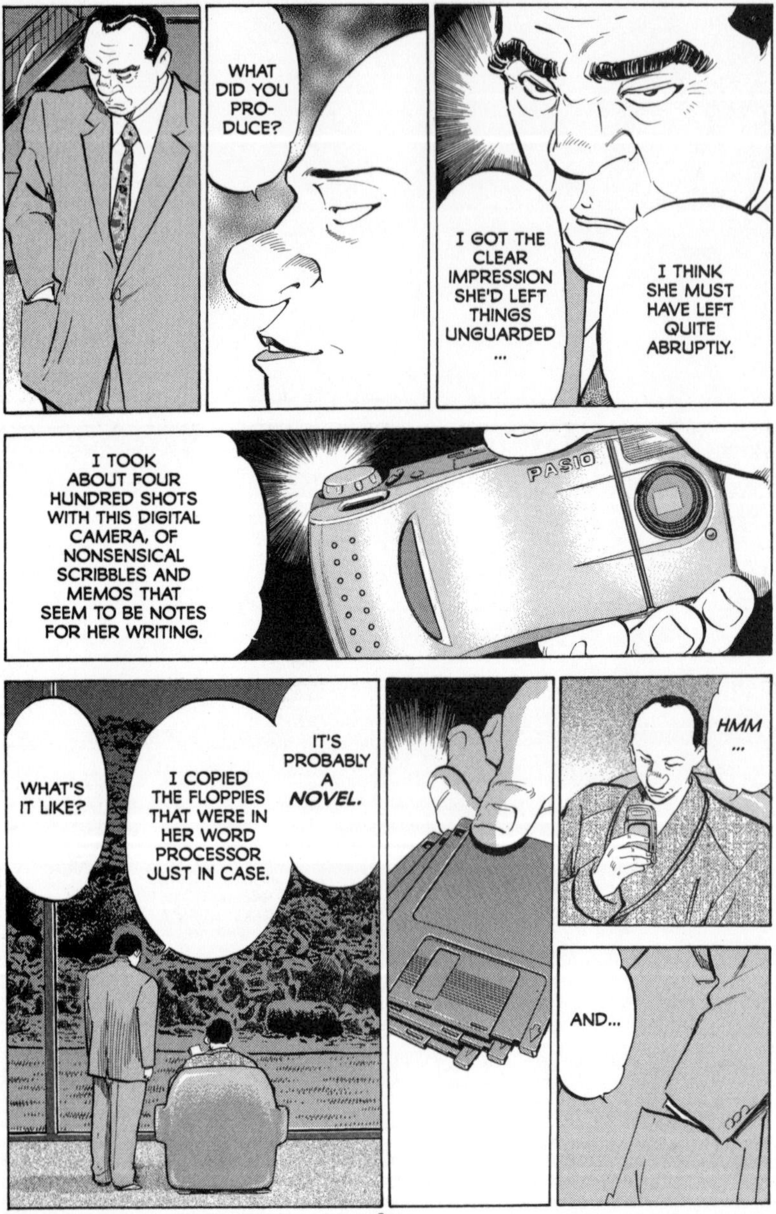

I THINK SHE MUST HAVE LEFT QUITE ABRUPTLY.
I GOT THE CLEAR IMPRESSION SHE'D LEFT THINGS UNGUARDED ...
WHAT DID YOU PRO-DUCE?
I TOOK ABOUT FOUR HUNDRED SHOTS WITH THIS DIGITAL CAMERA, OF NONSENSICAL SCRIBBLES AND MEMOS THAT SEEM TO BE NOTES FOR HER WRITING.
PASIO
HMM ...
AND...
I COPIED THE FLOPPIES THAT WERE IN HER WORD PROCESSOR JUST IN CASE.
WHAT'S IT LIKE?
IT'S PROBABLY A ***NOVEL.***

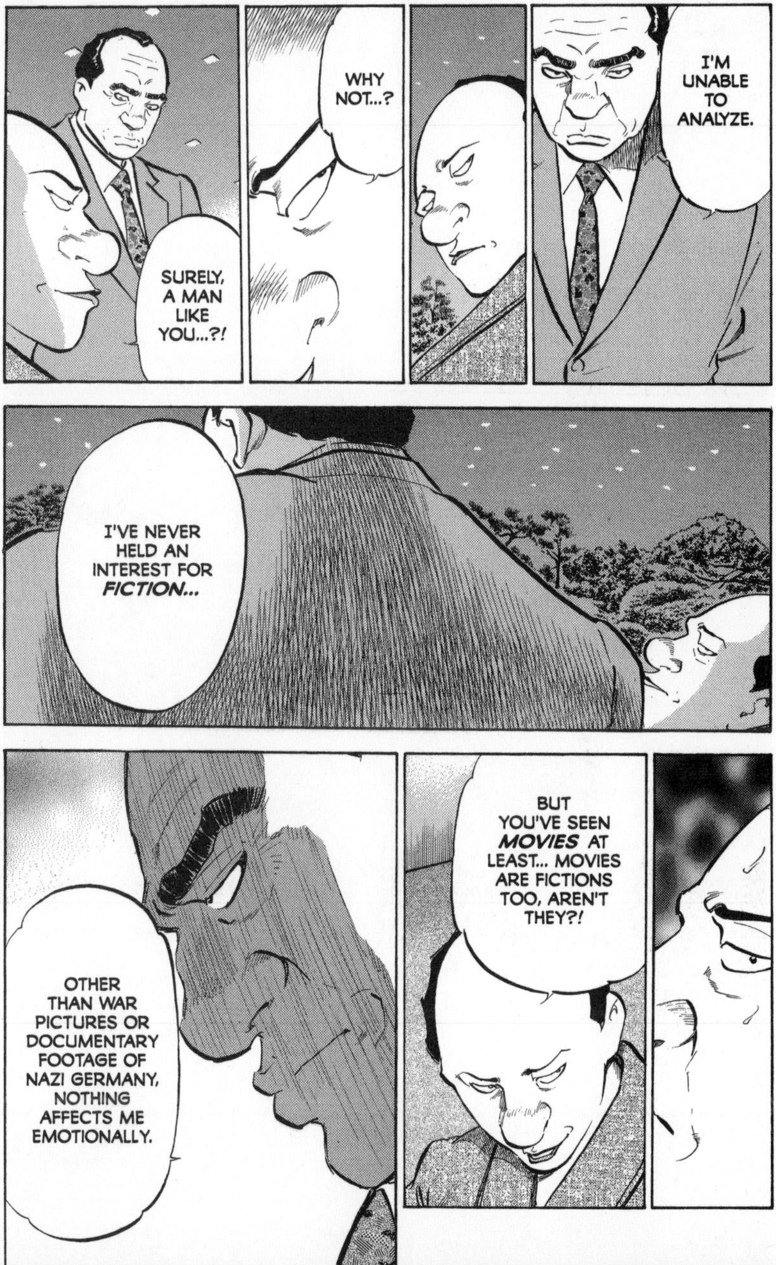
I'M UNABLE TO ANALYZE.
WHY NOT...?
SURELY, A MAN LIKE YOU...?!
I'VE NEVER HELD AN INTEREST FOR *FICTION...*
BUT YOU'VE SEEN *MOVIES* AT LEAST... MOVIES ARE FICTIONS TOO, AREN'T THEY?!
OTHER THAN WAR PICTURES OR DOCUMENTARY FOOTAGE OF NAZI GERMANY, NOTHING AFFECTS ME EMOTIONALLY.

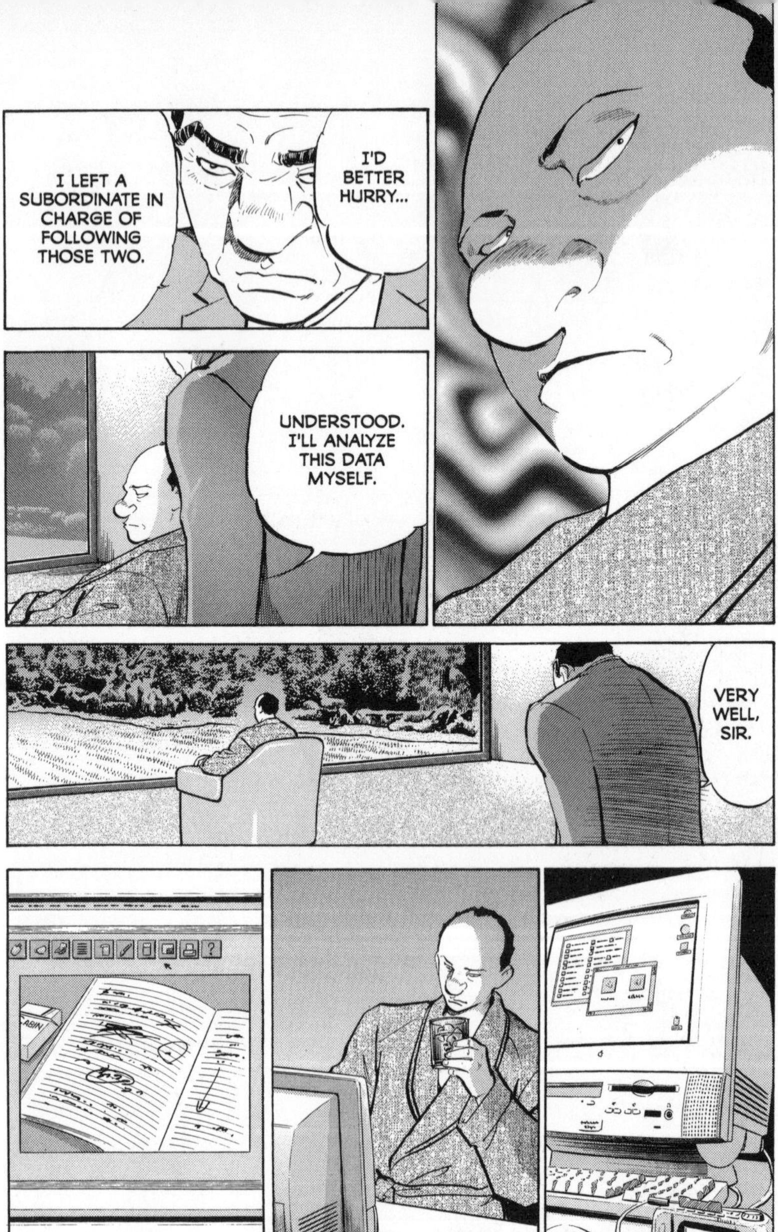
I'D BETTER HURRY...
I LEFT A SUBORDINATE IN CHARGE OF FOLLOWING THOSE TWO.
UNDERSTOOD. I'LL ANALYZE THIS DATA MYSELF.
VERY WELL, SIR.

WHEW... ALMOST HORRIFYING HAND-WRITING.

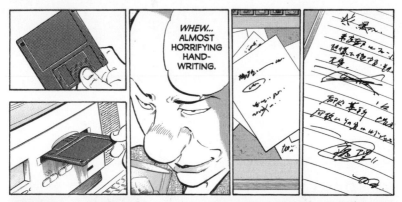

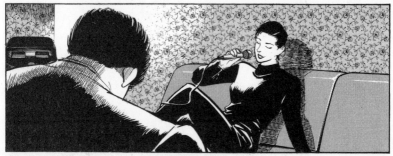

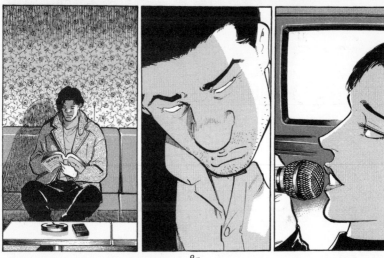

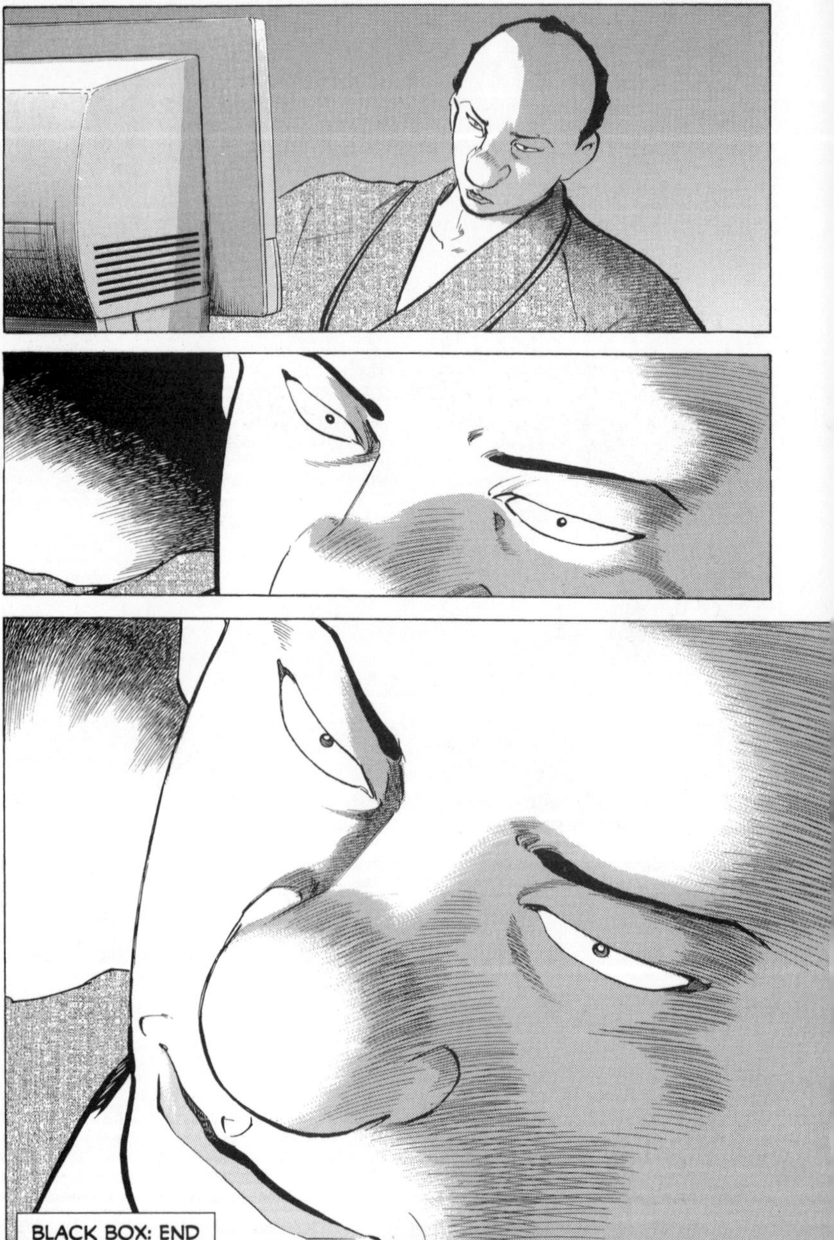
BLACK BOX: END

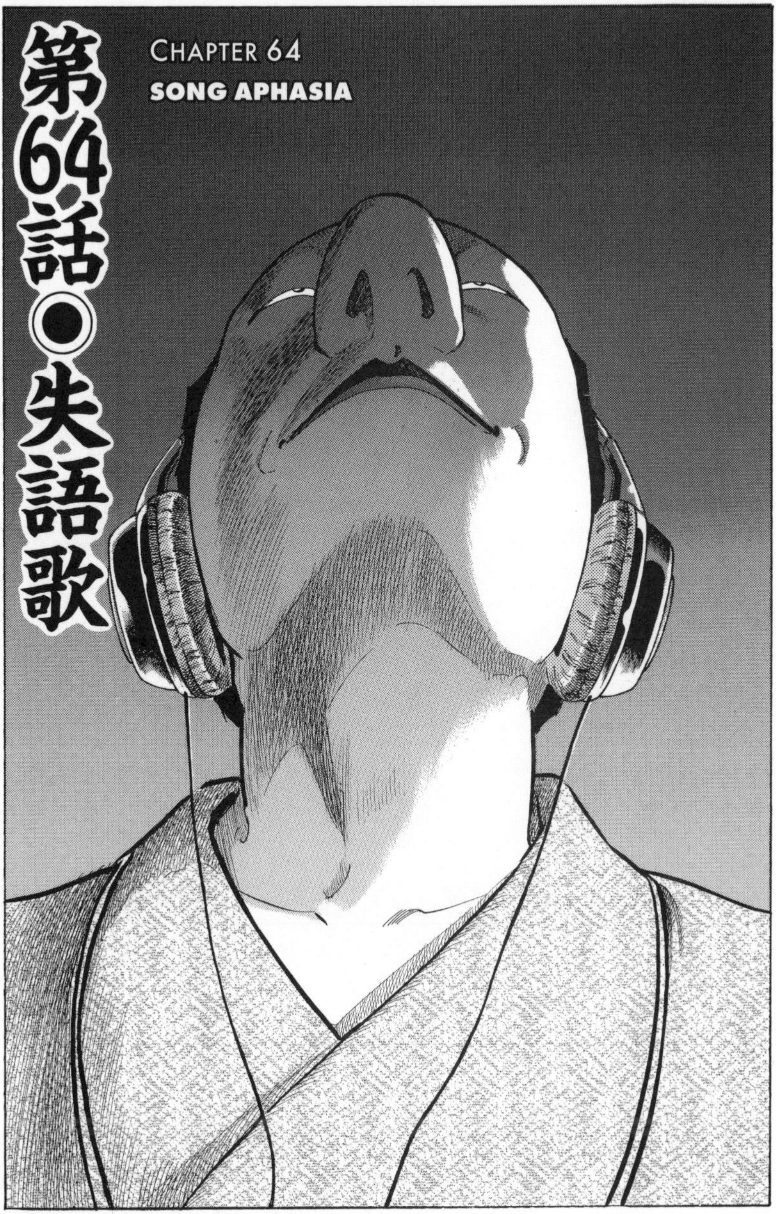
第64話●失語歌
CHAPTER 64
SONG APHASIA

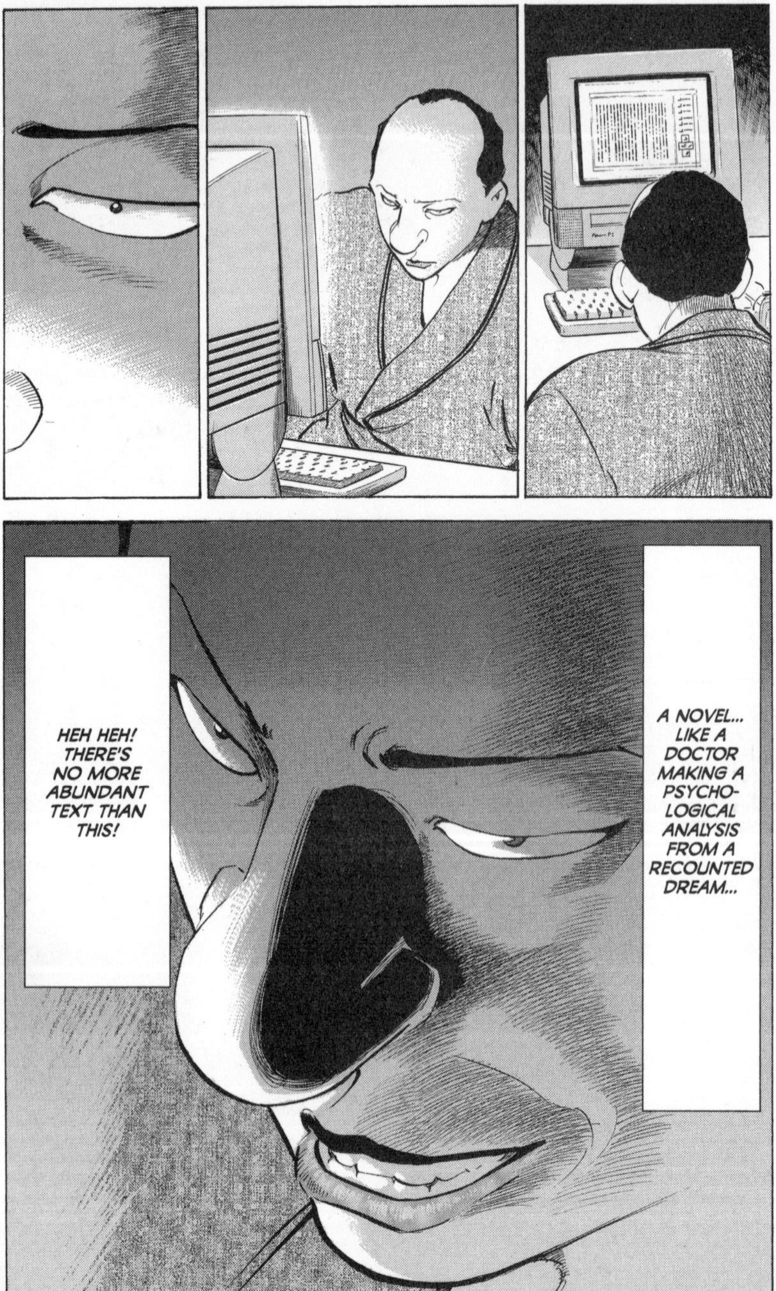
A NOVEL... LIKE A DOCTOR MAKING A PSYCHO-LOGICAL ANALYSIS FROM A RECOUNTED DREAM...
HEH HEH! THERE'S NO MORE ABUNDANT TEXT THAN THIS!

*SIGN: KARAOKE 2ND FLOOR

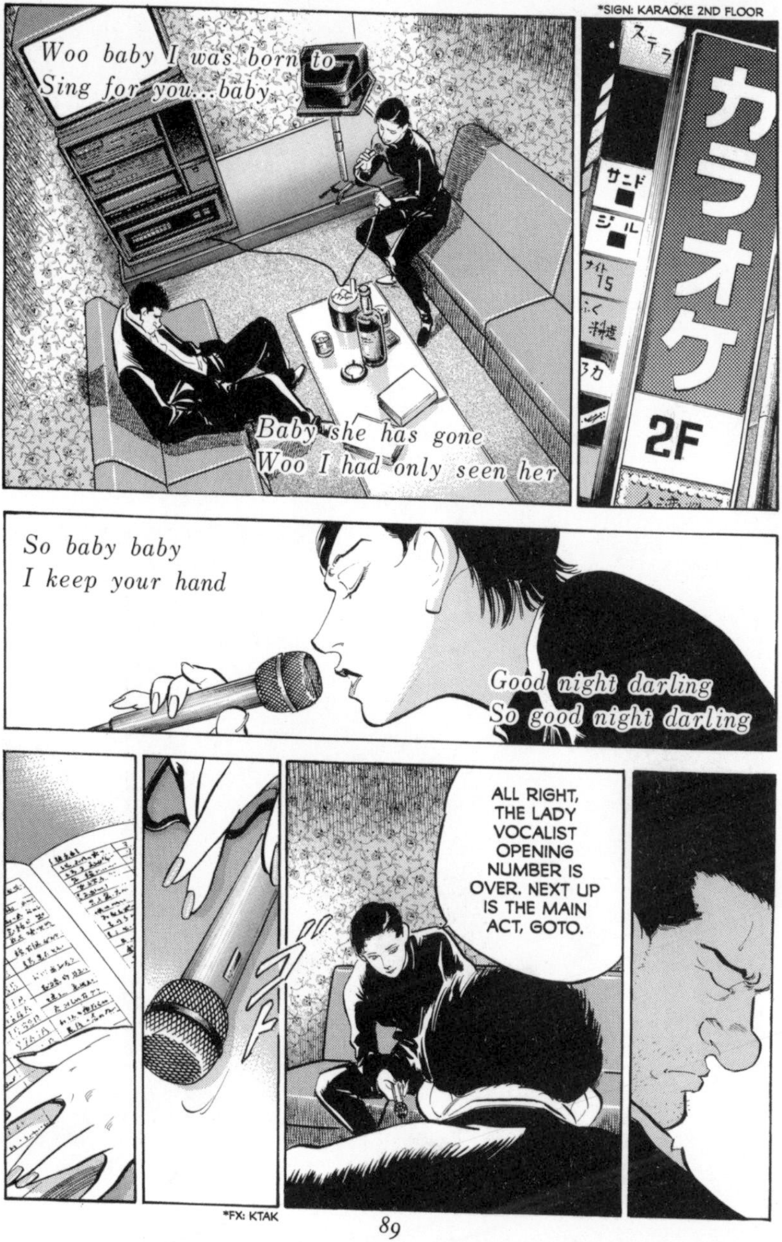
ステラ
カラオケ
2F
サンド
ジル
Woo baby I was born to
Sing for you...baby
Baby she has gone
Woo I had only seen her
So baby baby
I keep your hand
Good night darling
So good night darling
ALL RIGHT, THE LADY VOCALIST OPENING NUMBER IS OVER. NEXT UP IS THE MAIN ACT, GOTO.
ゴト

*FX: KTAK

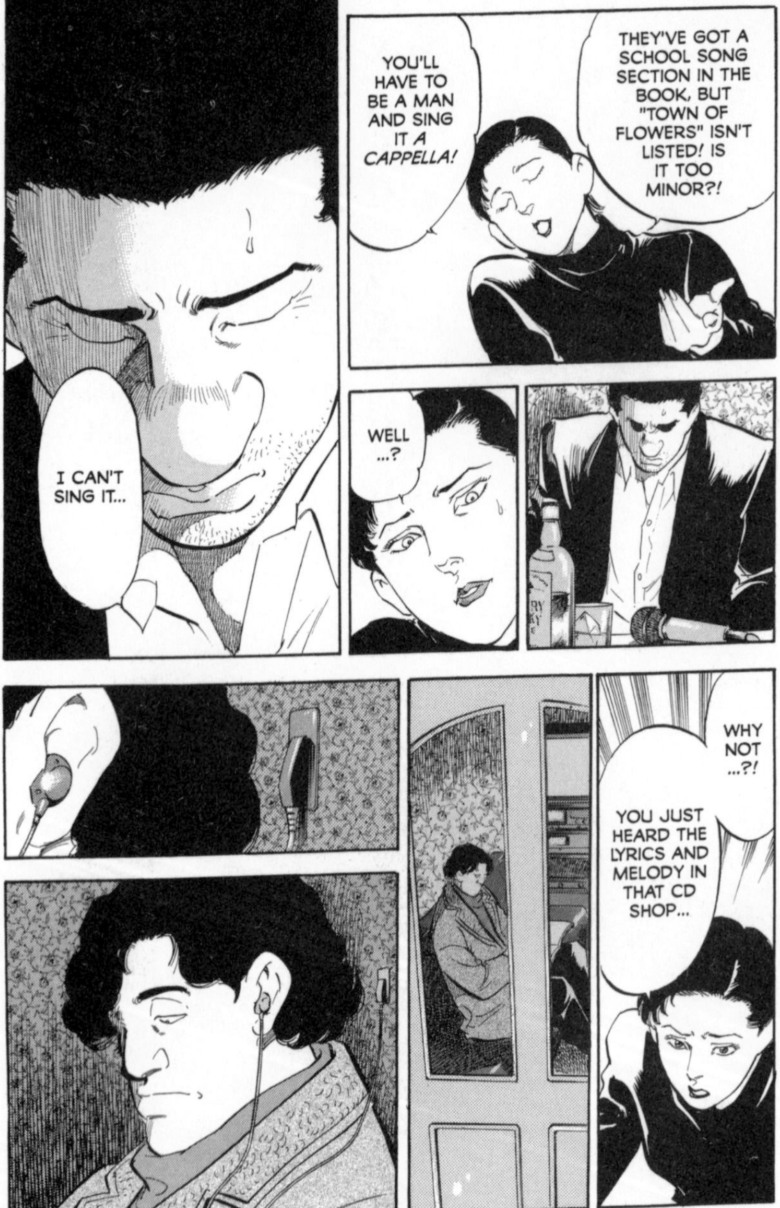
THEY'VE GOT A SCHOOL SONG SECTION IN THE BOOK, BUT "TOWN OF FLOWERS" ISN'T LISTED! IS IT TOO MINOR?!
YOU'LL HAVE TO BE A MAN AND SING IT *A CAPPELLA!*
WELL ...?
I CAN'T SING IT...
WHY NOT ...?!
YOU JUST HEARD THE LYRICS AND MELODY IN THAT CD SHOP...

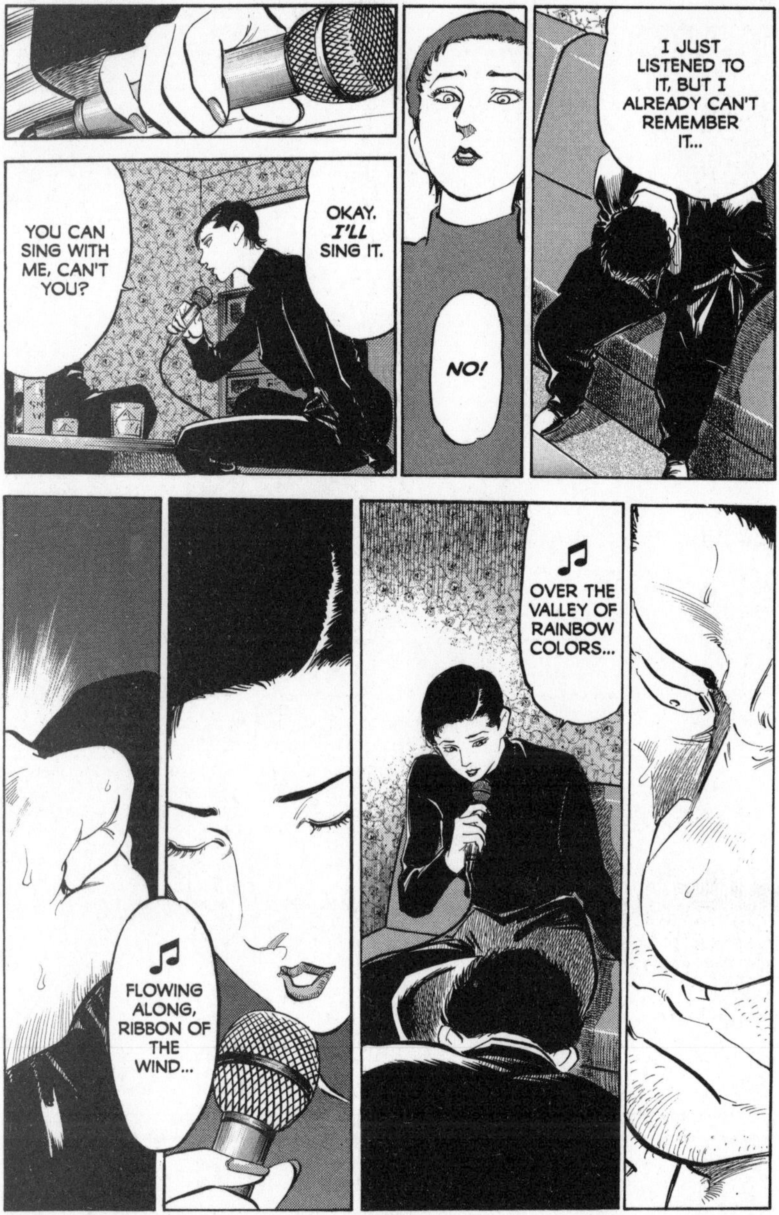
I JUST LISTENED TO IT, BUT I ALREADY CAN'T REMEMBER IT...
NO!
OKAY. *I'LL* SING IT.
YOU CAN SING WITH ME, CAN'T YOU?
♫ OVER THE VALLEY OF RAINBOW COLORS...
♫ FLOWING ALONG, RIBBON OF THE WIND...

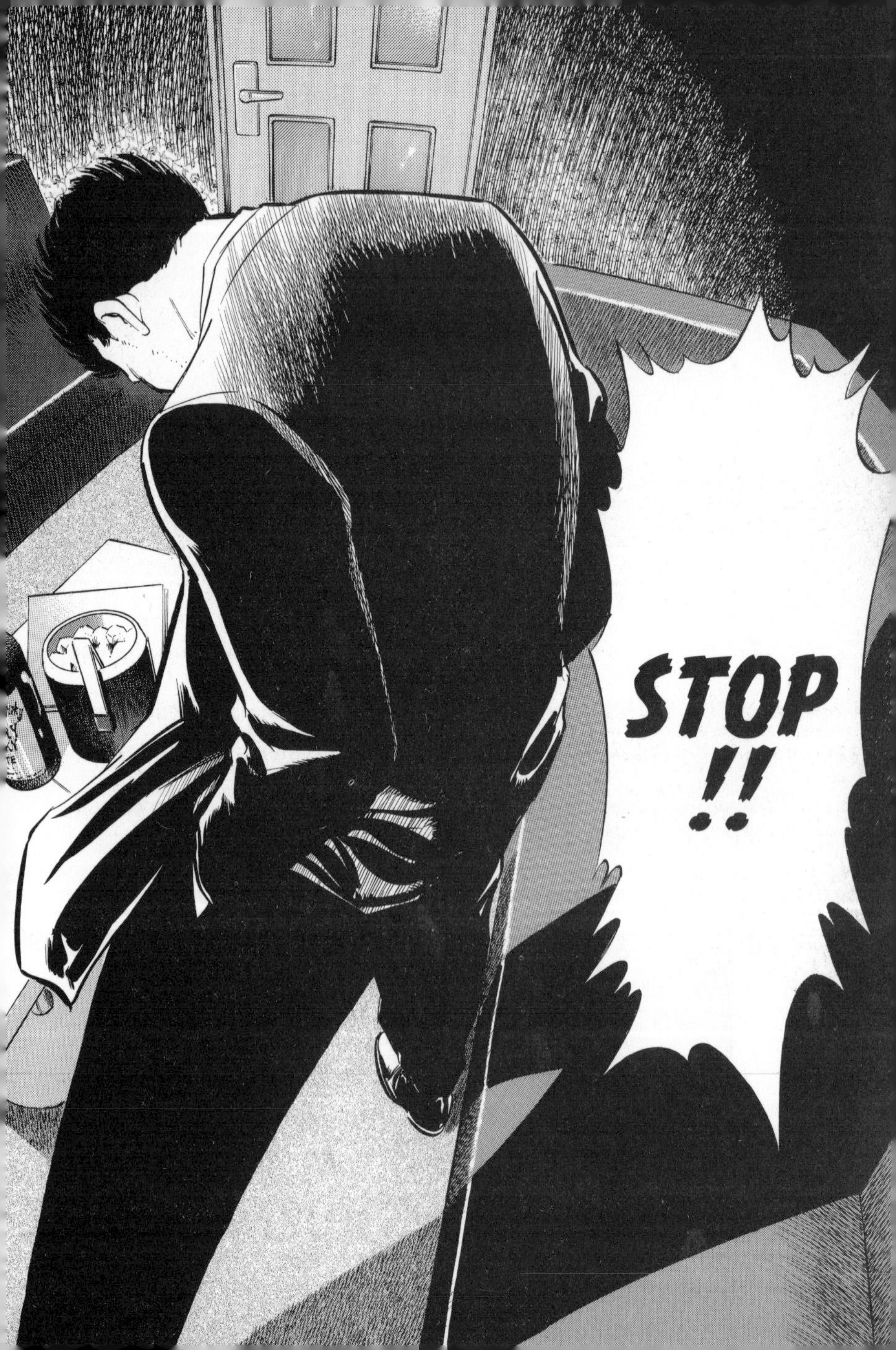
STOP!!

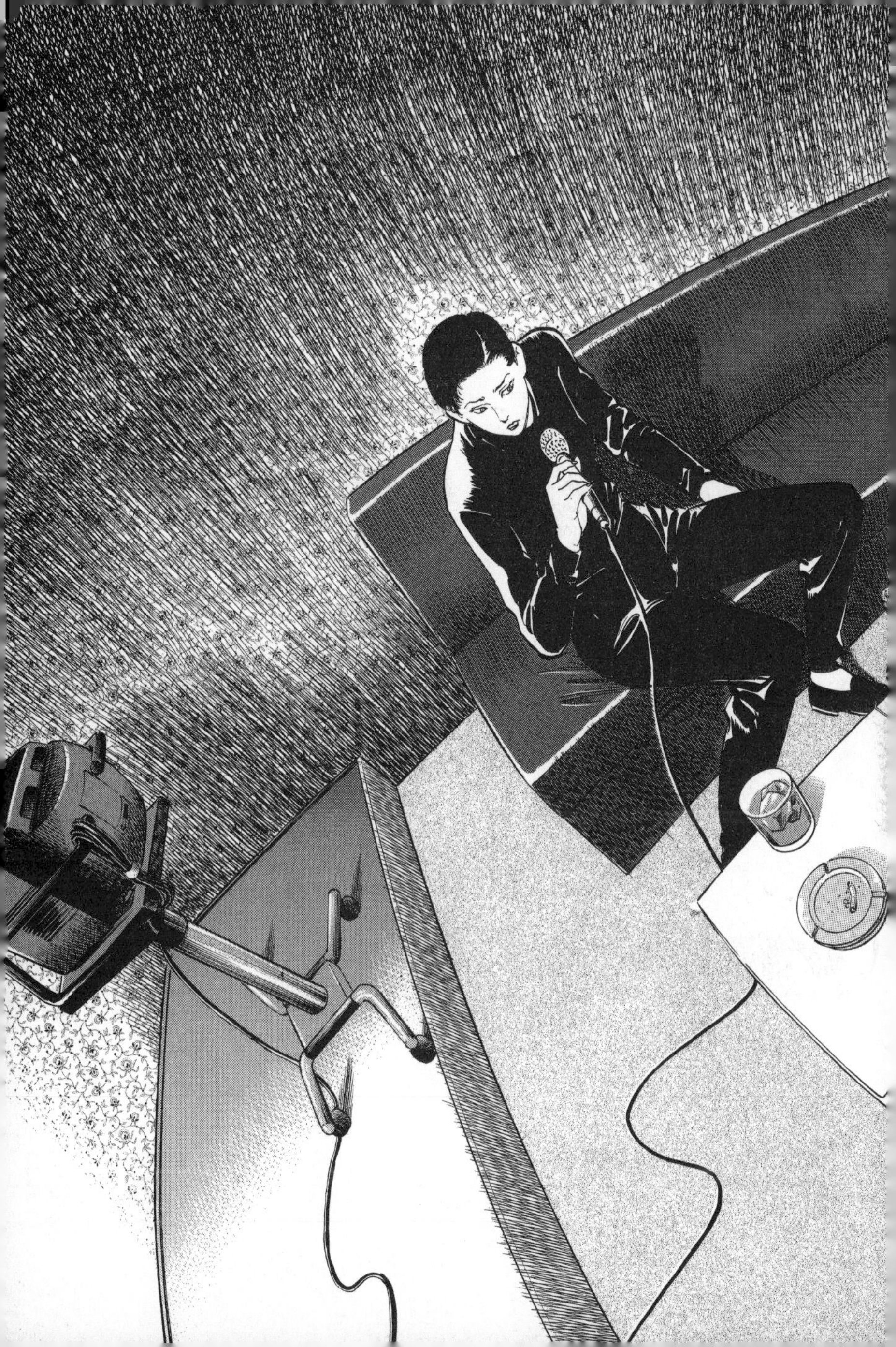

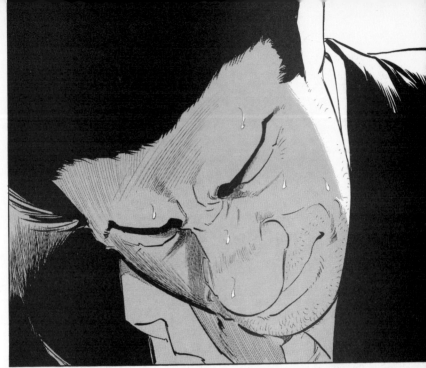

STOP,
PLEASE
...

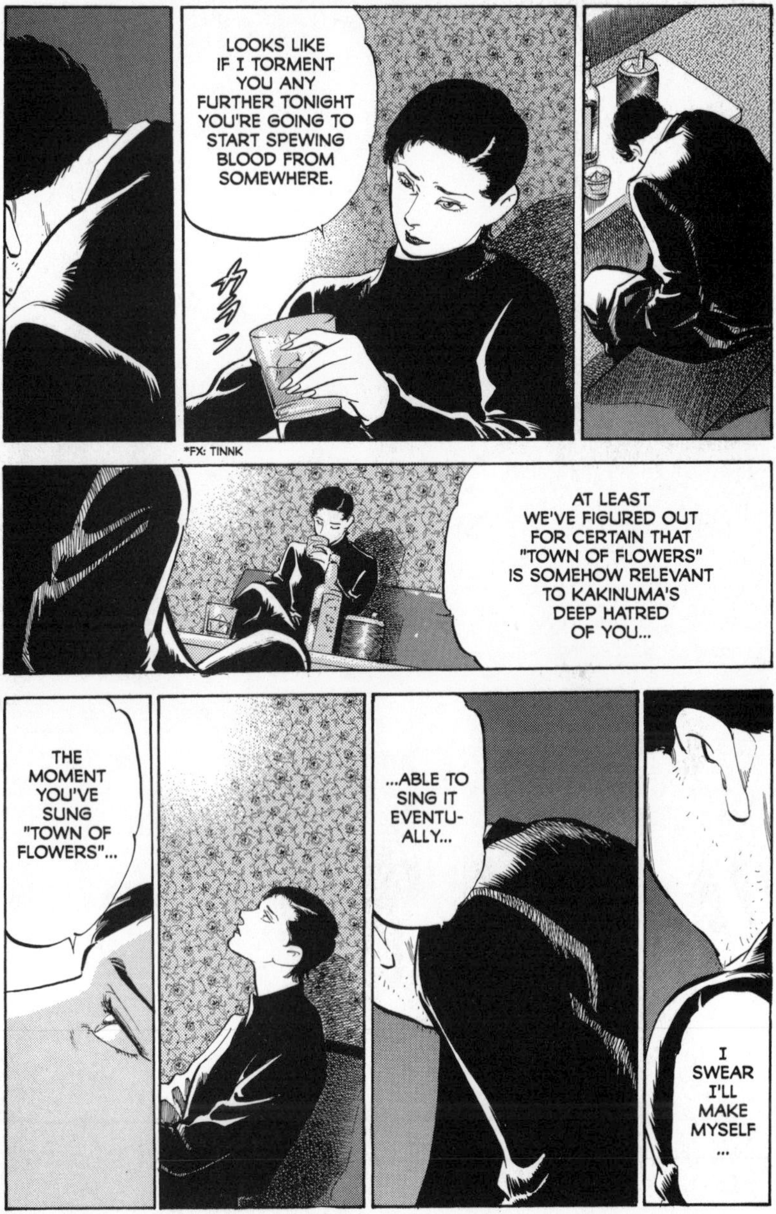
LOOKS LIKE IF I TORMENT YOU ANY FURTHER TONIGHT YOU'RE GOING TO START SPEWING BLOOD FROM SOMEWHERE.
*FX: TINNK
AT LEAST WE'VE FIGURED OUT FOR CERTAIN THAT "TOWN OF FLOWERS" IS SOMEHOW RELEVANT TO KAKINUMA'S DEEP HATRED OF YOU...
I SWEAR I'LL MAKE MYSELF ...
...ABLE TO SING IT EVENTU-ALLY...
THE MOMENT YOU'VE SUNG "TOWN OF FLOWERS"...

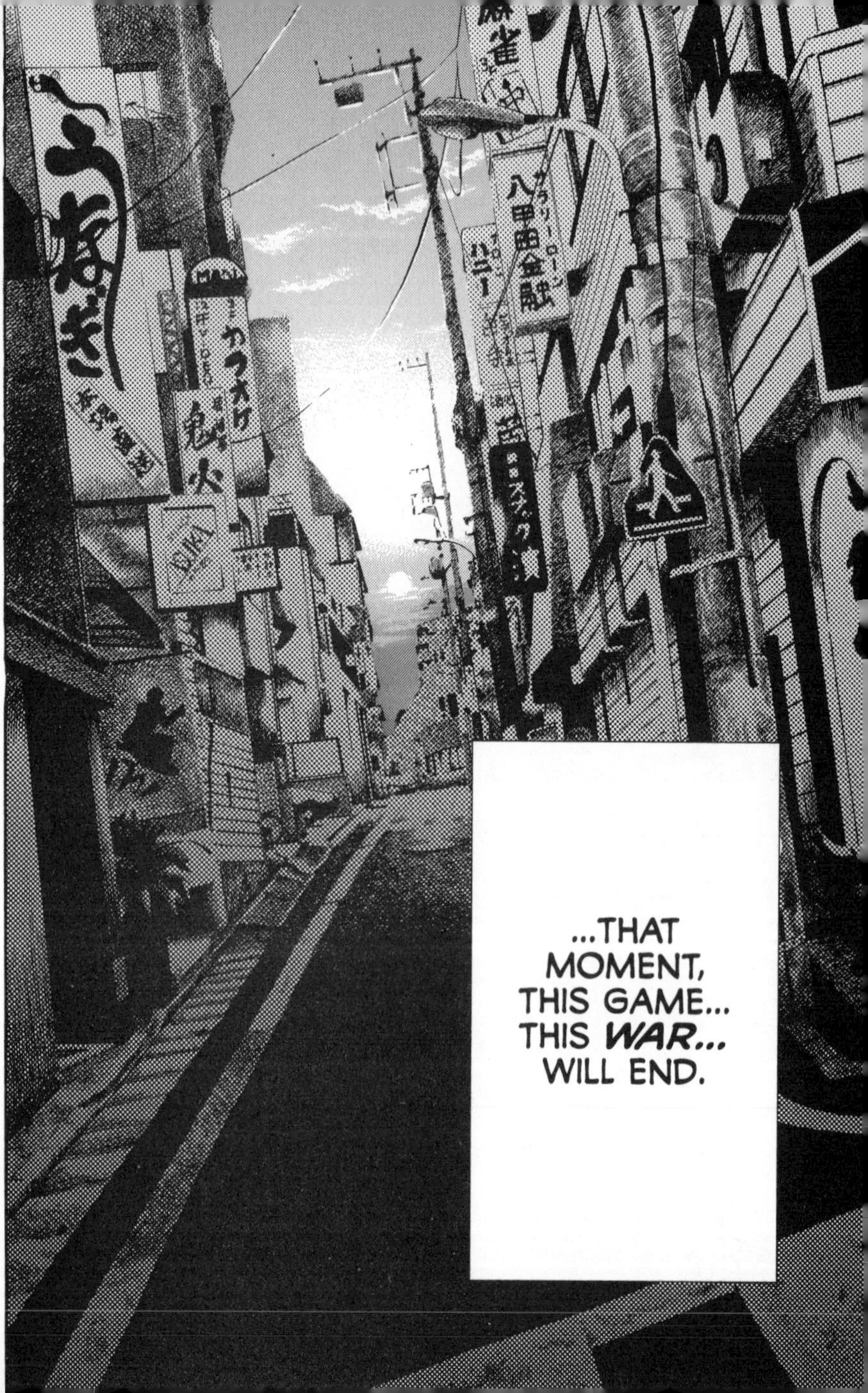
...THAT MOMENT, THIS GAME... THIS *WAR...* WILL END.
麻雀
サラリーローン
八甲田金融
カラオケ

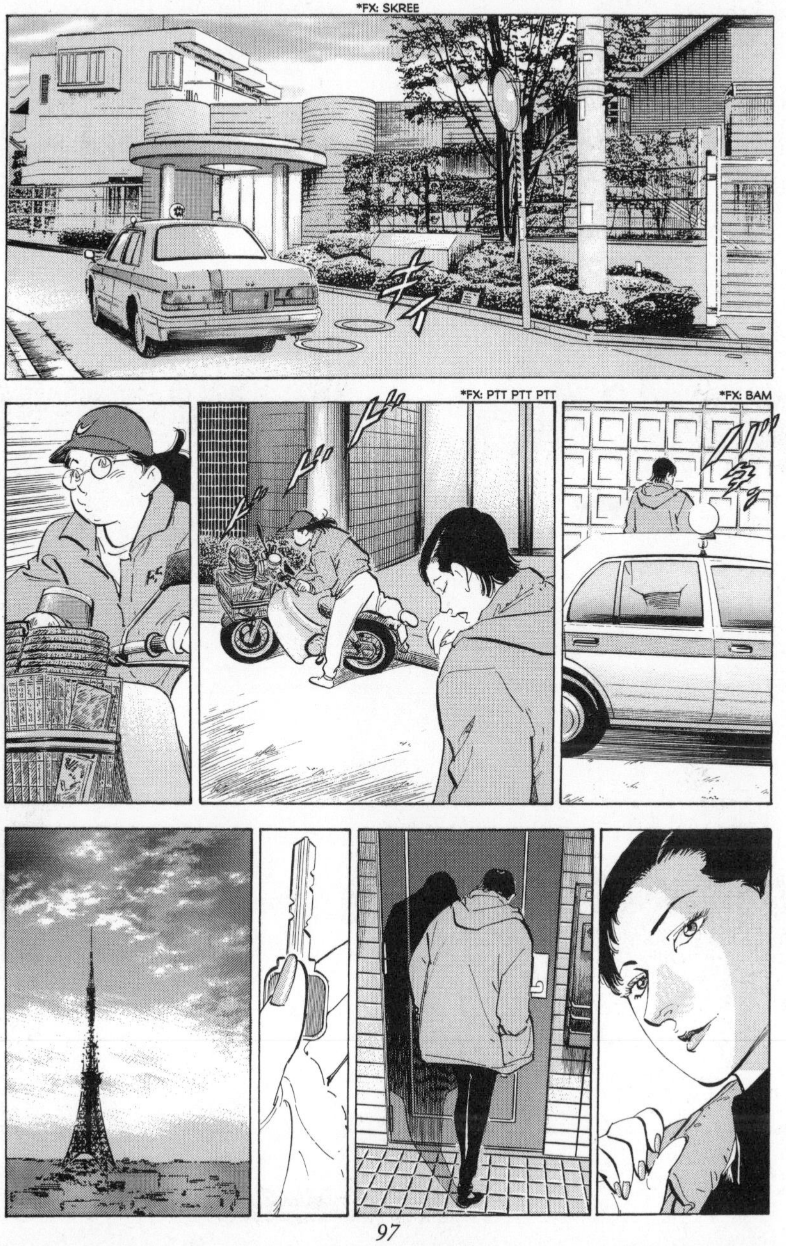
*FX: SKREE
*FX: BAM
*FX: PTT PTT PTT

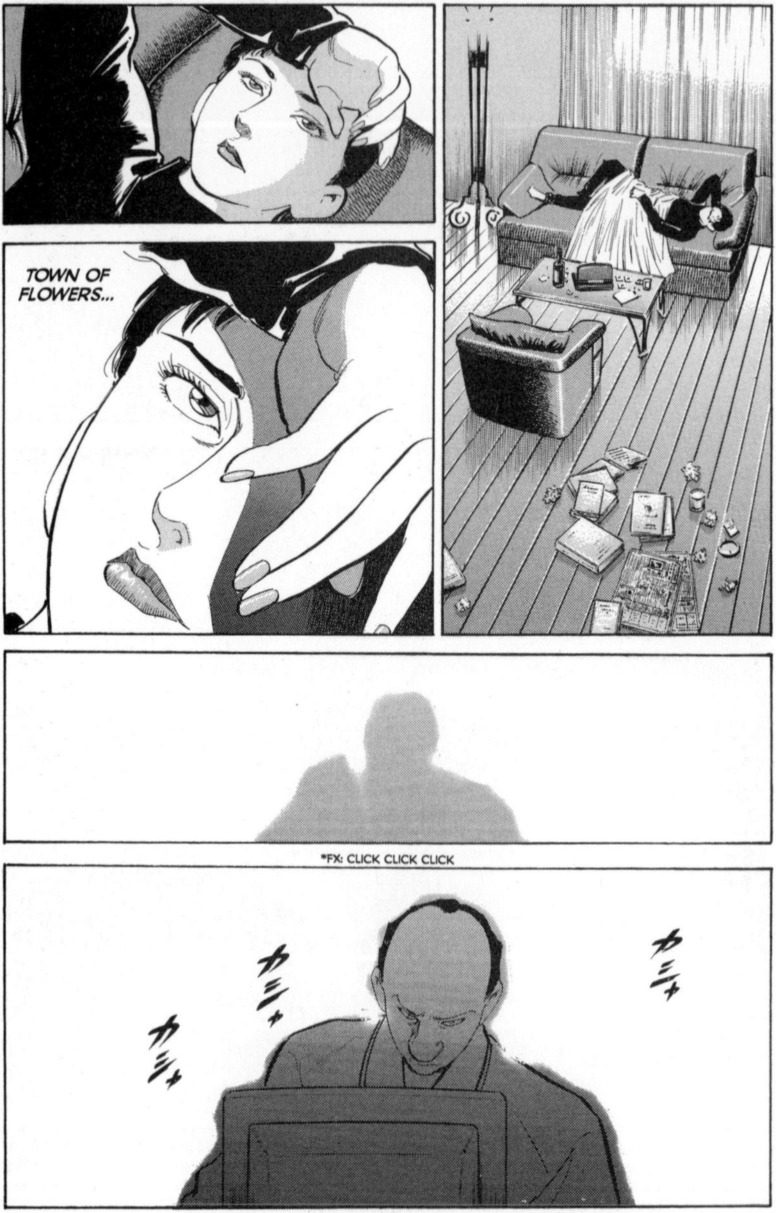
TOWN OF FLOWERS...
*FX: CLICK CLICK CLICK
カシャ
カシャ
カシャ

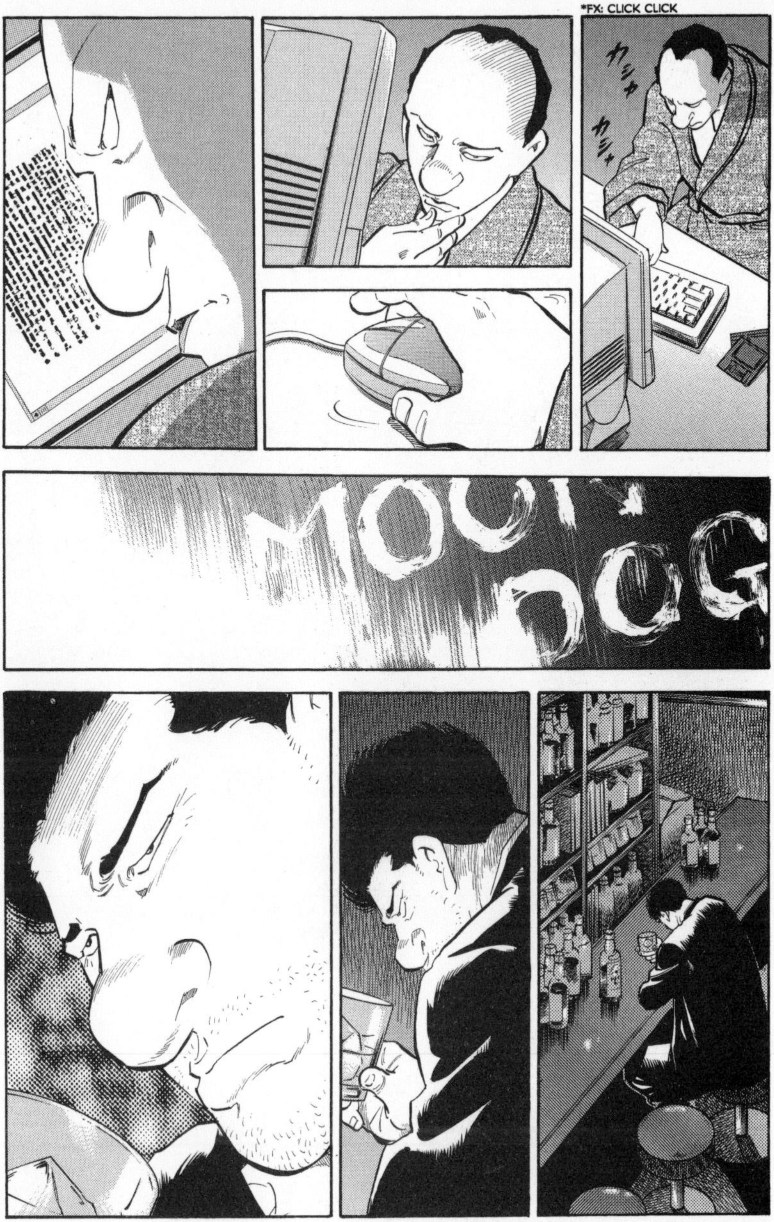
*FX: CLICK CLICK
カシャ
カシャ

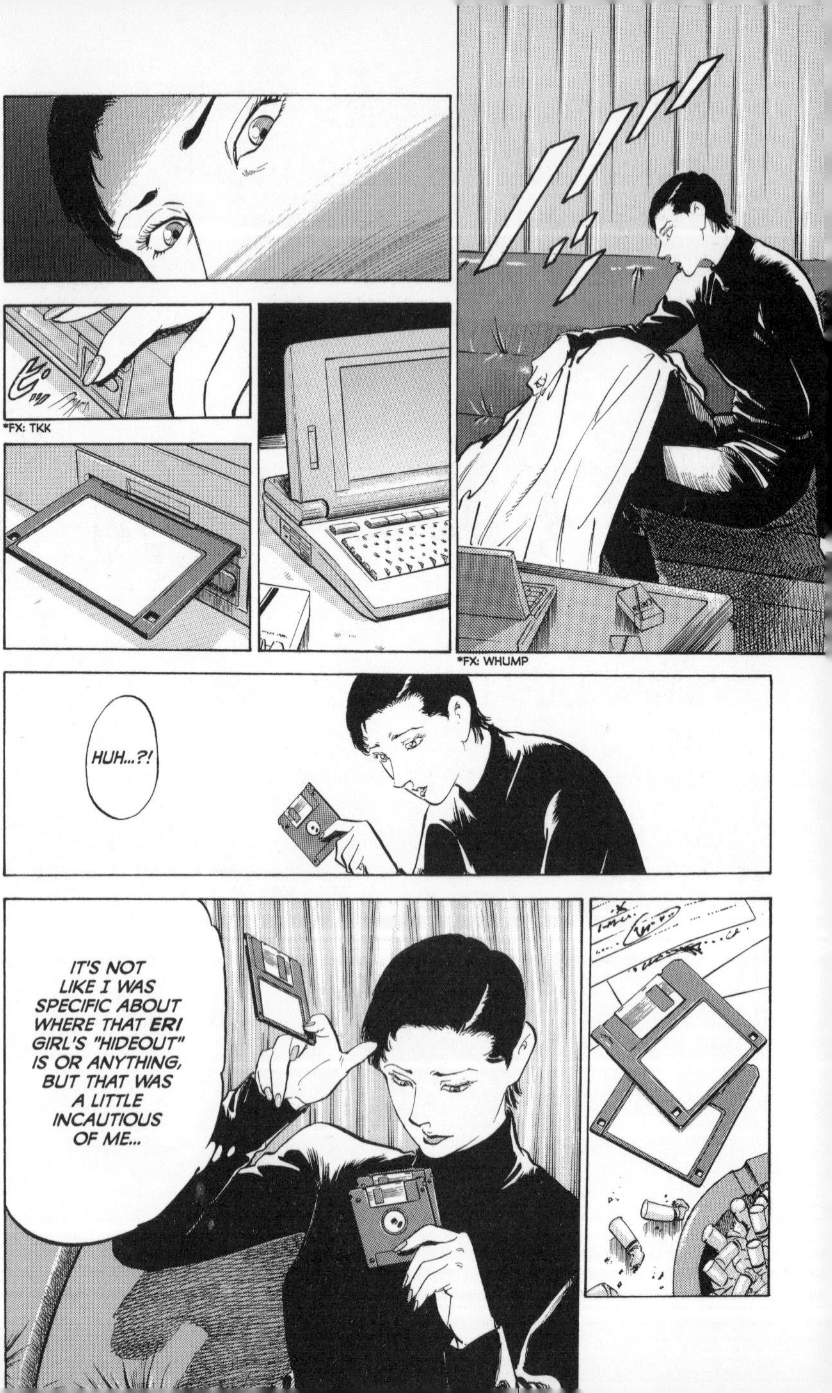
*FX: WHUMP
*FX: TKK
HUH...?!
IT'S NOT LIKE I WAS SPECIFIC ABOUT WHERE THAT ERI GIRL'S "HIDEOUT" IS OR ANYTHING, BUT THAT WAS A LITTLE INCAUTIOUS OF ME...

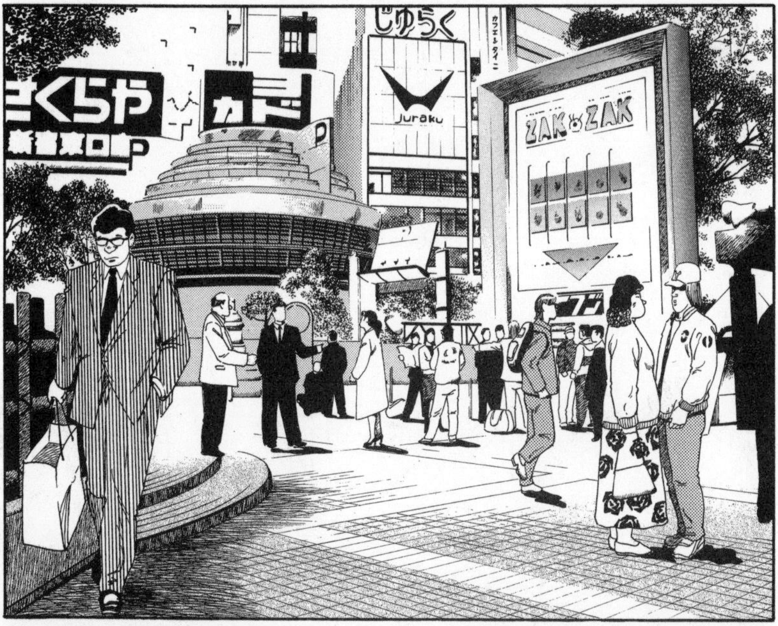
さくらや
じゅらく
Juraku
ZAK ZAK

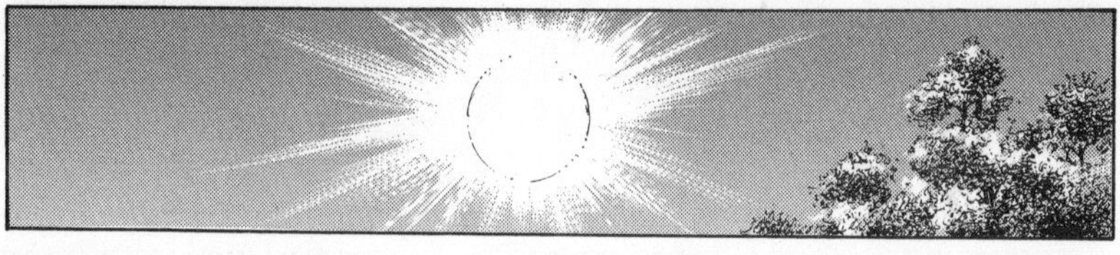

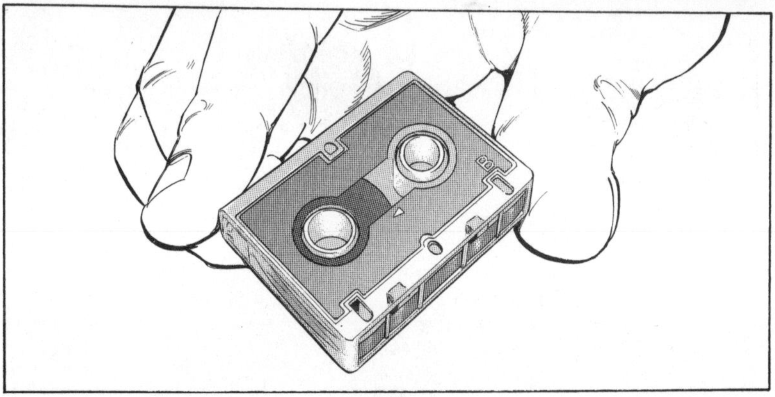

THE SURVEILLANCE TAPE FROM LAST NIGHT AT THE KARAOKE BOX.

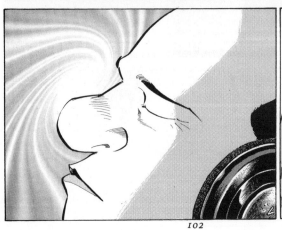

102

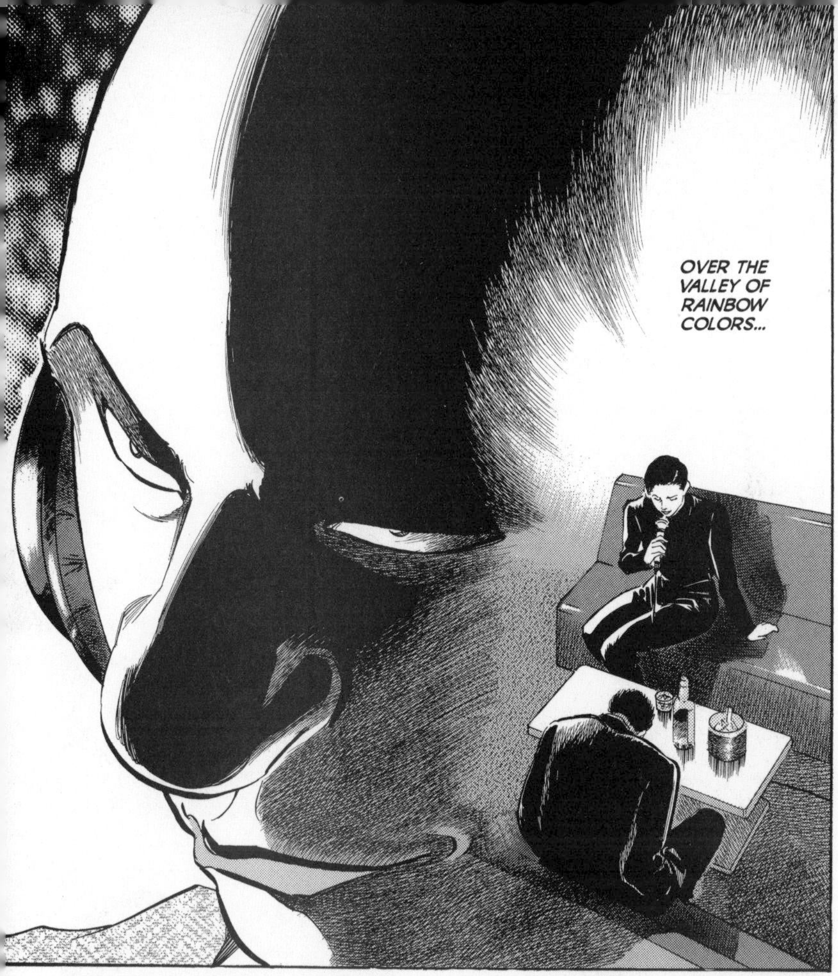
OVER THE
VALLEY OF
RAINBOW
COLORS...
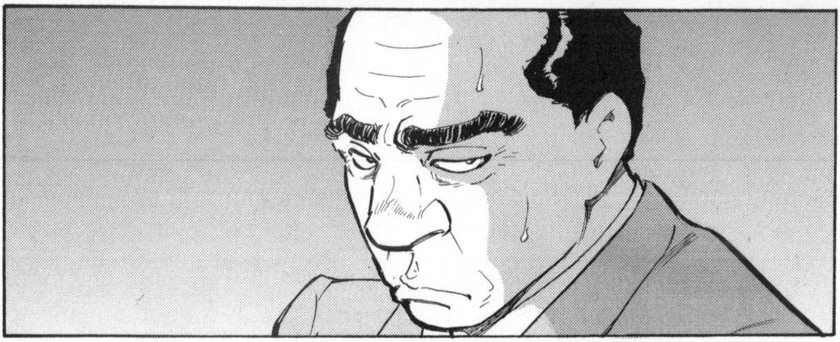

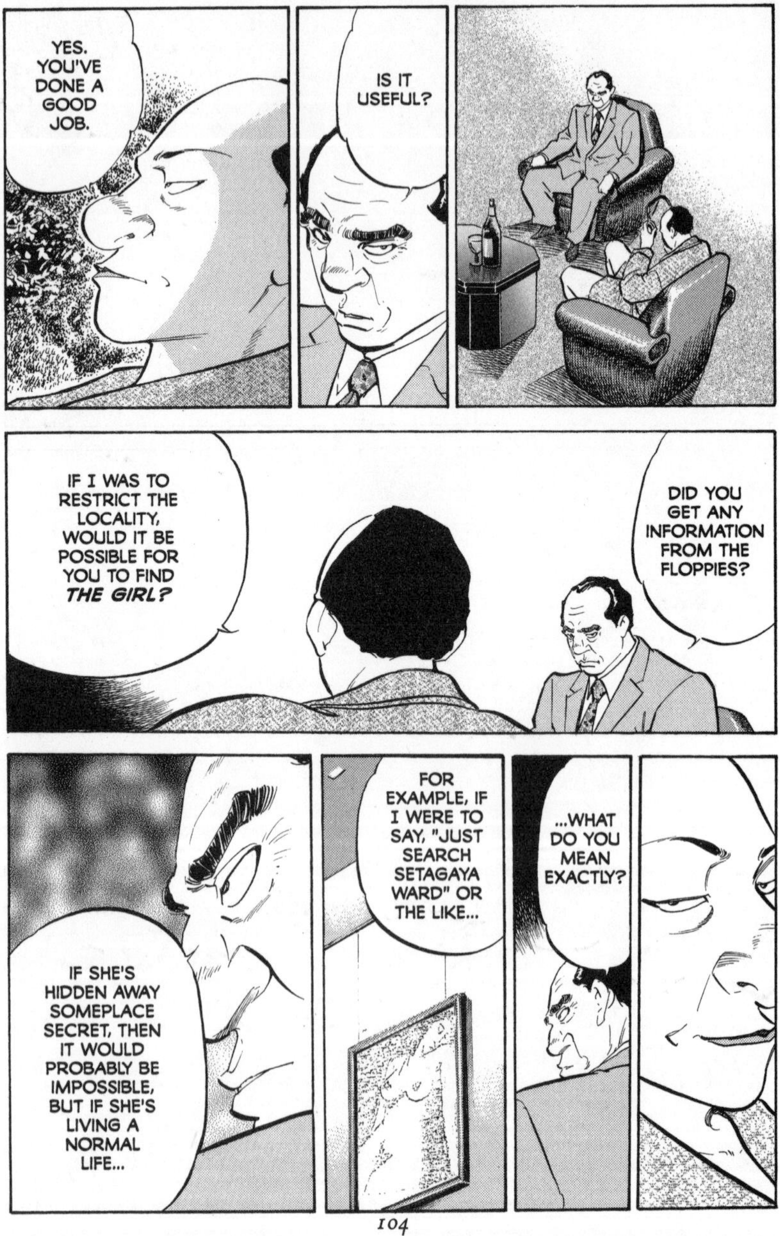
IS IT USEFUL?
YES. YOU'VE DONE A GOOD JOB.
DID YOU GET ANY INFORMATION FROM THE FLOPPIES?
IF I WAS TO RESTRICT THE LOCALITY, WOULD IT BE POSSIBLE FOR YOU TO FIND *THE GIRL?*
...WHAT DO YOU MEAN EXACTLY?
FOR EXAMPLE, IF I WERE TO SAY, "JUST SEARCH SETAGAYA WARD" OR THE LIKE...
IF SHE'S HIDDEN AWAY SOMEPLACE SECRET, THEN IT WOULD PROBABLY BE IMPOSSIBLE, BUT IF SHE'S LIVING A NORMAL LIFE...

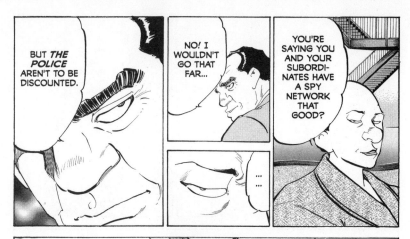

YOU'RE SAYING YOU AND YOUR SUBORDINATES HAVE A SPY NETWORK THAT GOOD?
NO! I WOULDN'T GO THAT FAR...
......
BUT *THE POLICE* AREN'T TO BE DISCOUNTED.
AS YOU KNOW, IN THE PAST I WAS ENGAGED IN A SECRET SERVICE CAPACITY FOR GOVERNMENT VIPs.
FOR SUCCESSIVE PRIME MINISTERS, CABINET MEMBERS, AND POLICE OFFICIALS, I SILENCED SCANDALS INVOLVING THEIR CHILDREN AND RELATIVES...AND PERFORMED OTHER PERSONAL "SERVICES."
I'M TALKING BASED ON THE ASSUMPTION THAT I CAN STILL USE THOSE CONNECTIONS...
TELL ME THE LOCALITY, PLEASE.

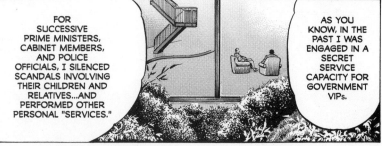

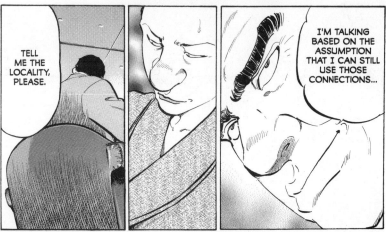

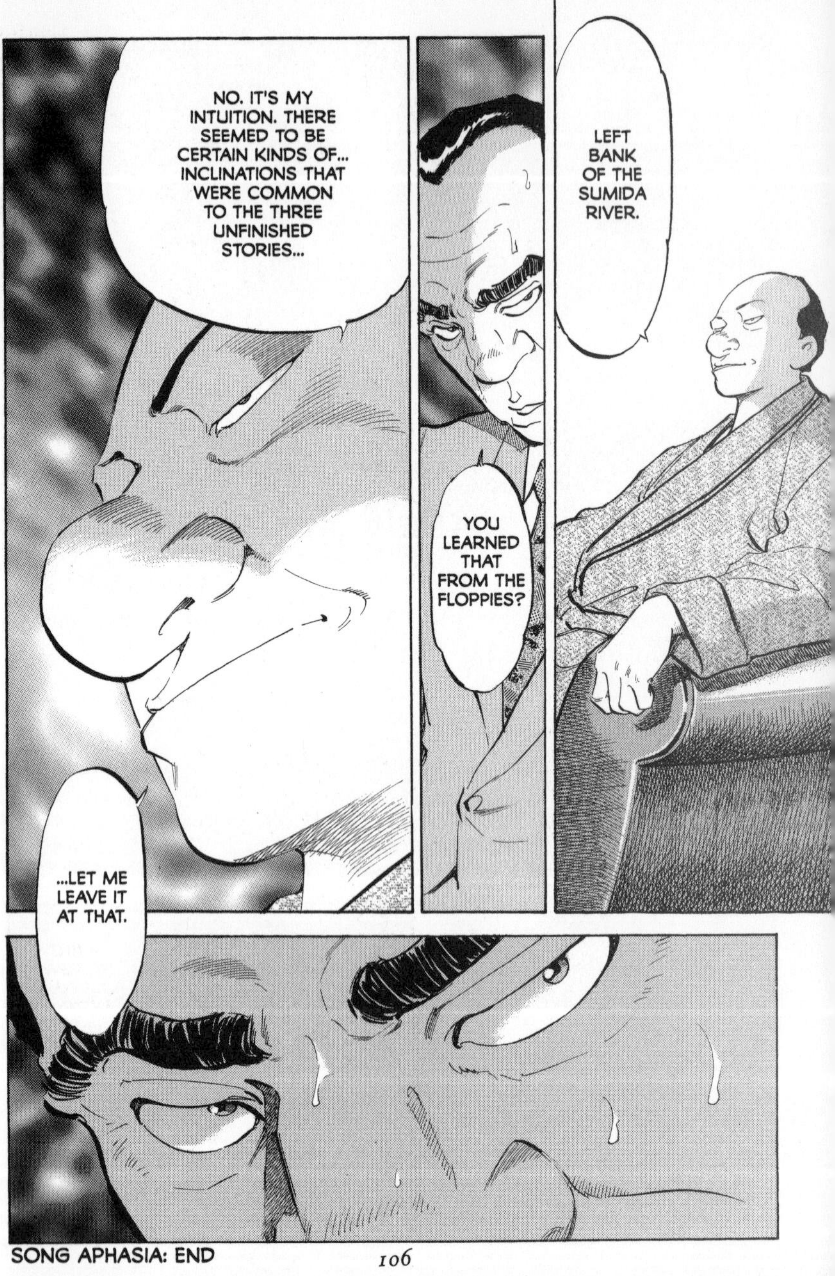
LEFT BANK OF THE SUMIDA RIVER.
YOU LEARNED THAT FROM THE FLOPPIES?
NO. IT'S MY INTUITION. THERE SEEMED TO BE CERTAIN KINDS OF... INCLINATIONS THAT WERE COMMON TO THE THREE UNFINISHED STORIES...
...LET ME LEAVE IT AT THAT.

SONG APHASIA: END

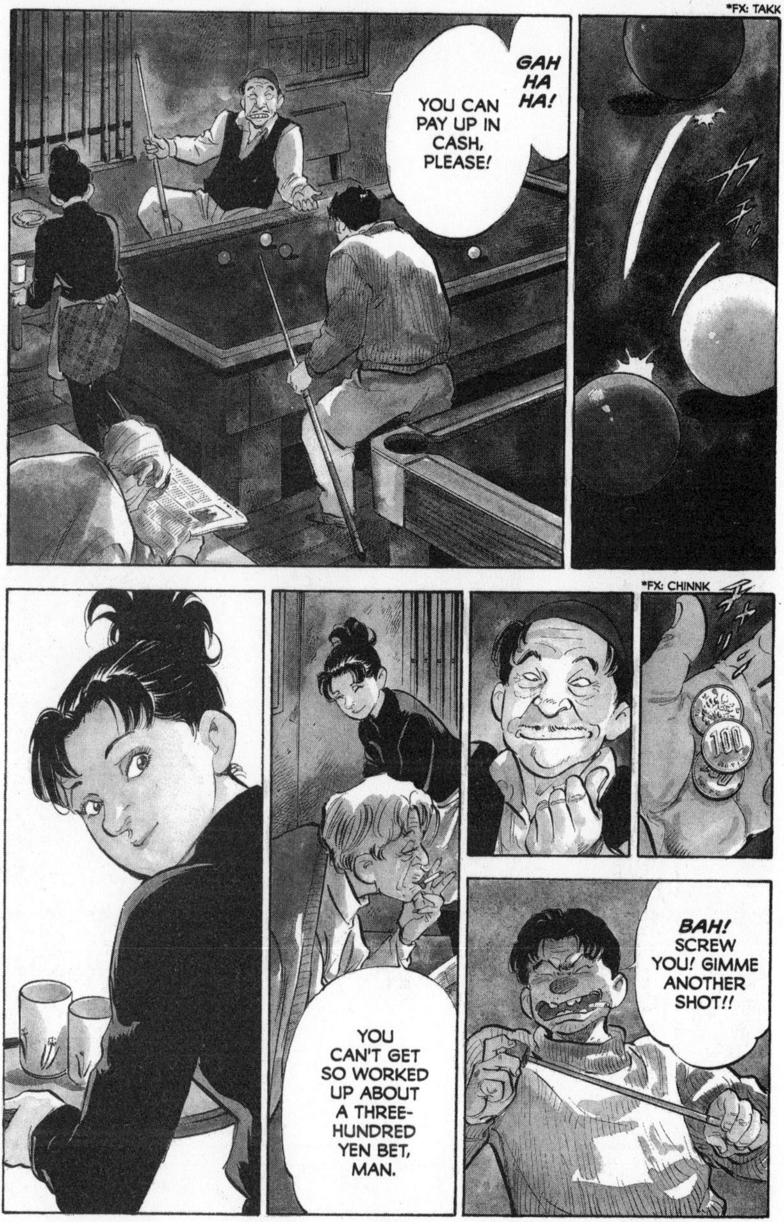
*FX: TAKK
GAH HA HA!
YOU CAN PAY UP IN CASH, PLEASE!
*FX: CHINNK
BAH! SCREW YOU! GIMME ANOTHER SHOT!!
YOU CAN'T GET SO WORKED UP ABOUT A THREE-HUNDRED YEN BET, MAN.

Chapter 65
Left Bank of the Sumida River
第65話◎隅田川左岸

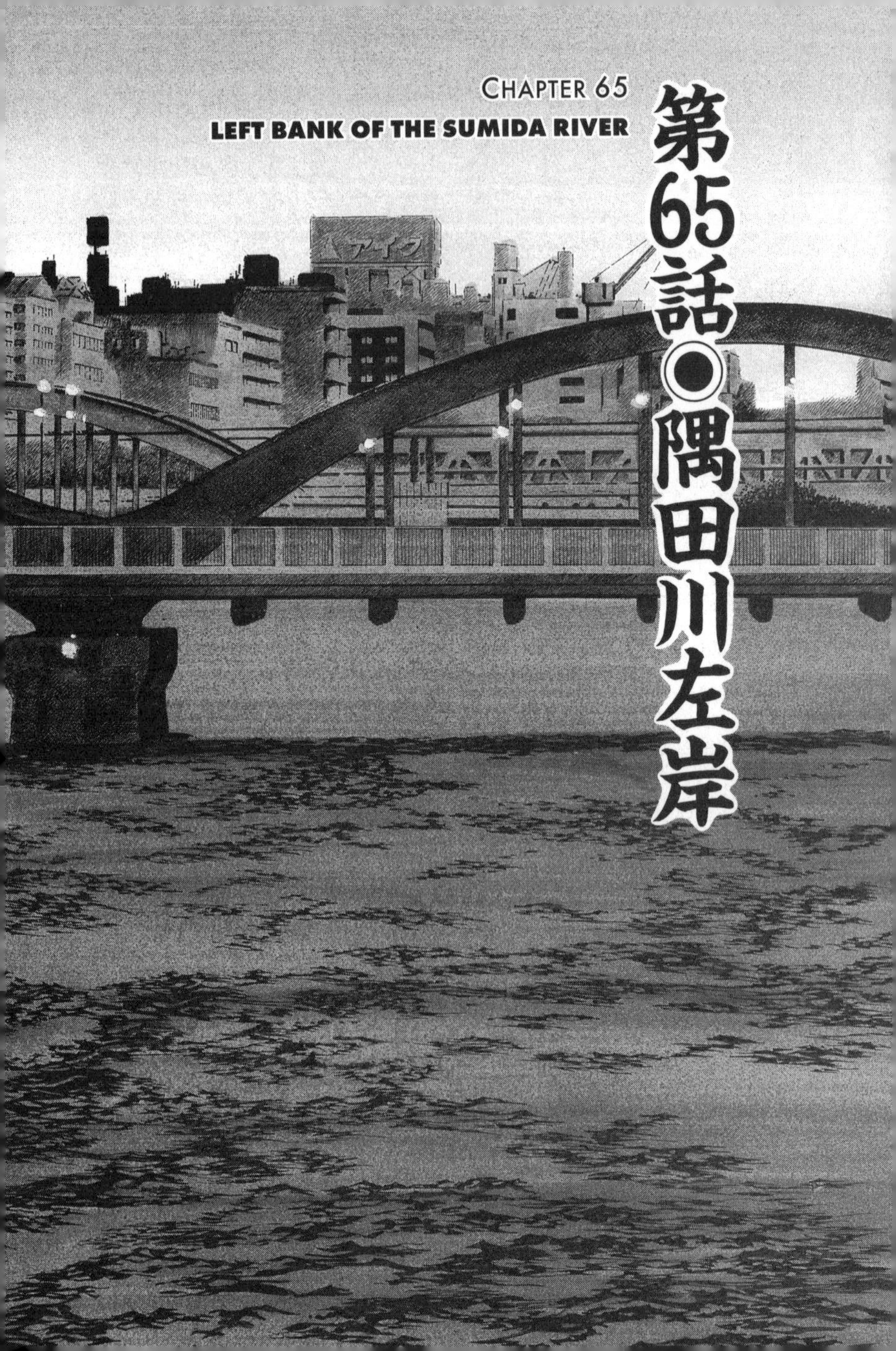
アイク

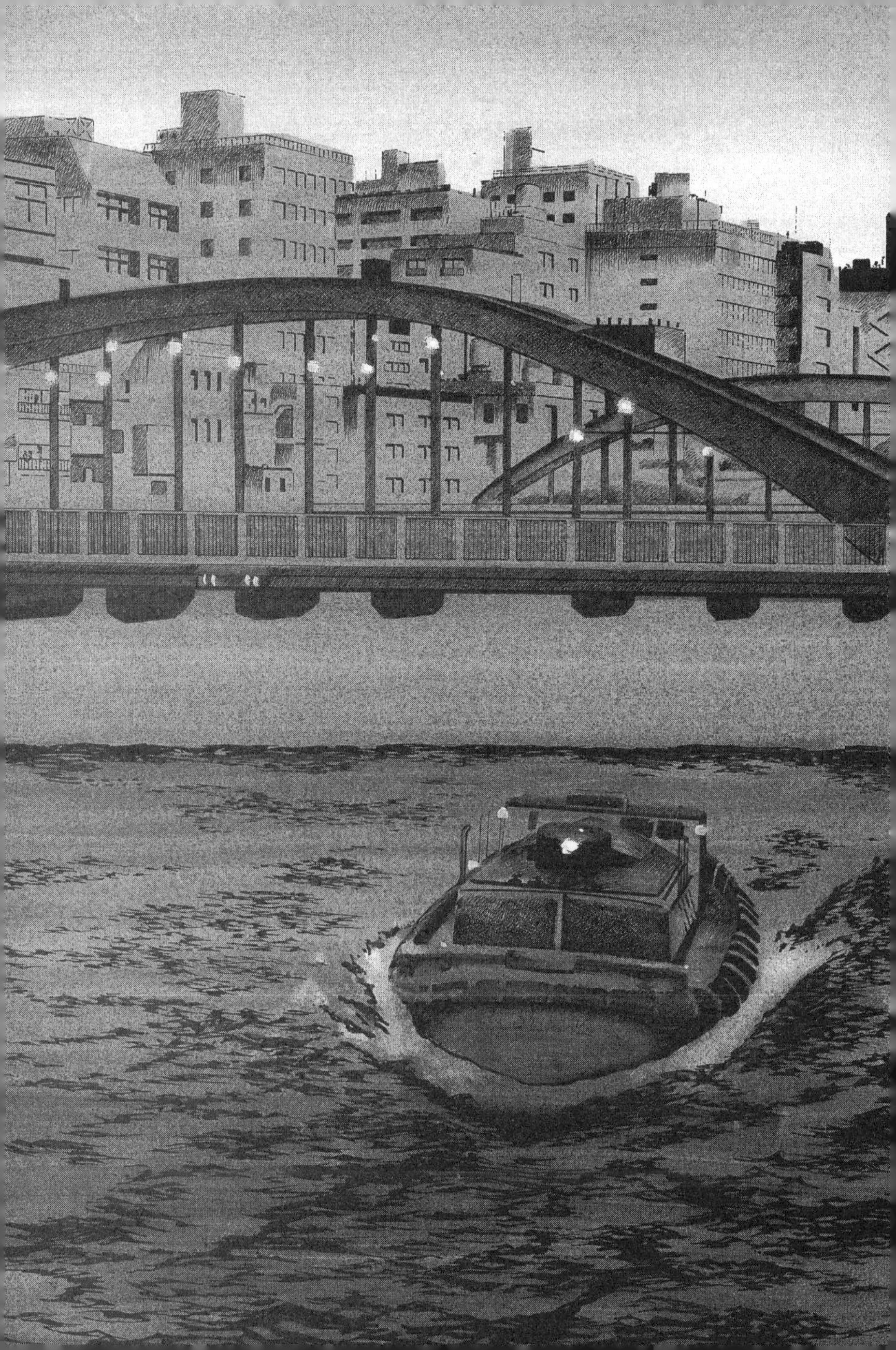

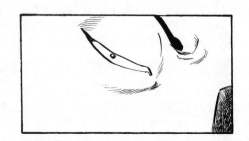

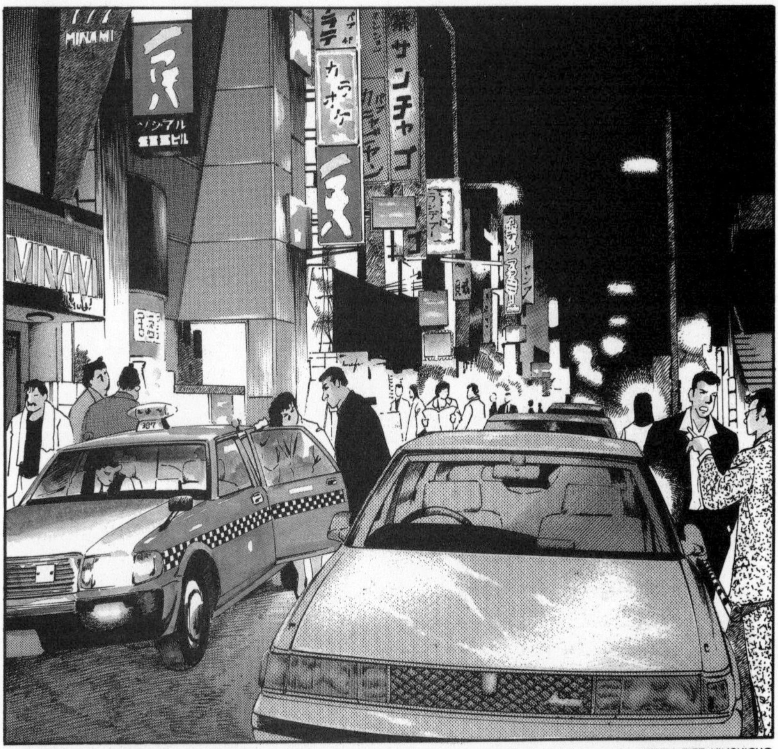
MINAMI
カラオケ
サンチャゴ
MINAMI

*SIGN: PIER KINSHICHO

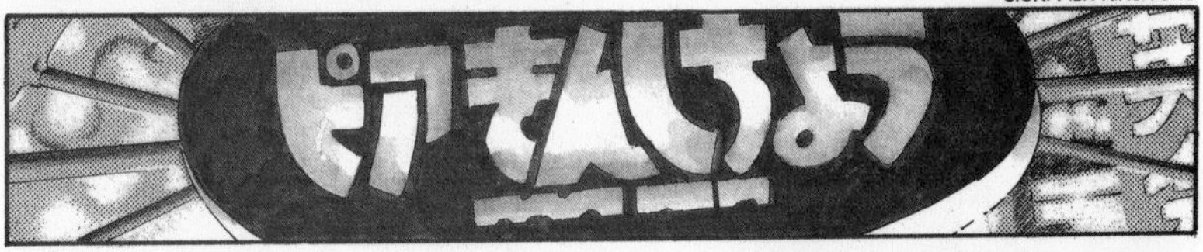
ピアきんしちょう

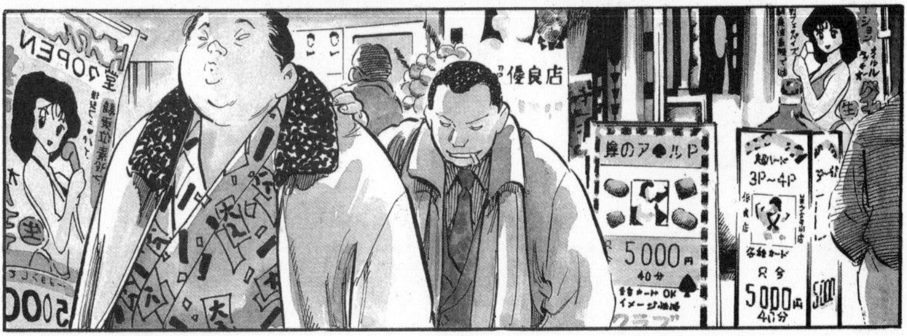
OPEN
優良店
5000円
40分
3P~4P
5000円
40分

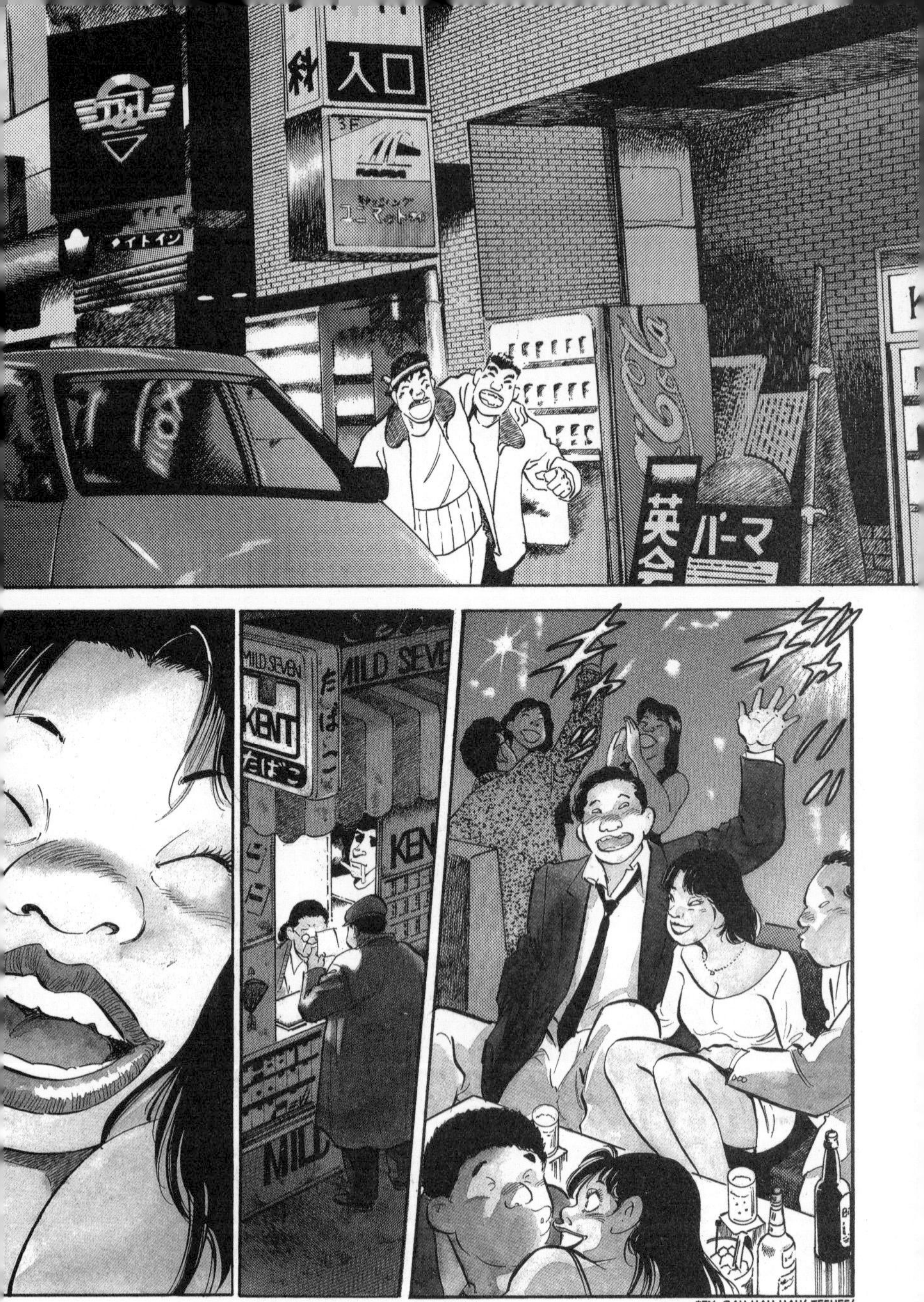
料
入口
英会
パーマ
MILD SEVEN
KENT
たばこ
MILD SEVEN
KENT
MILD

*FX: GAH HAH HAH! TEEHEE!

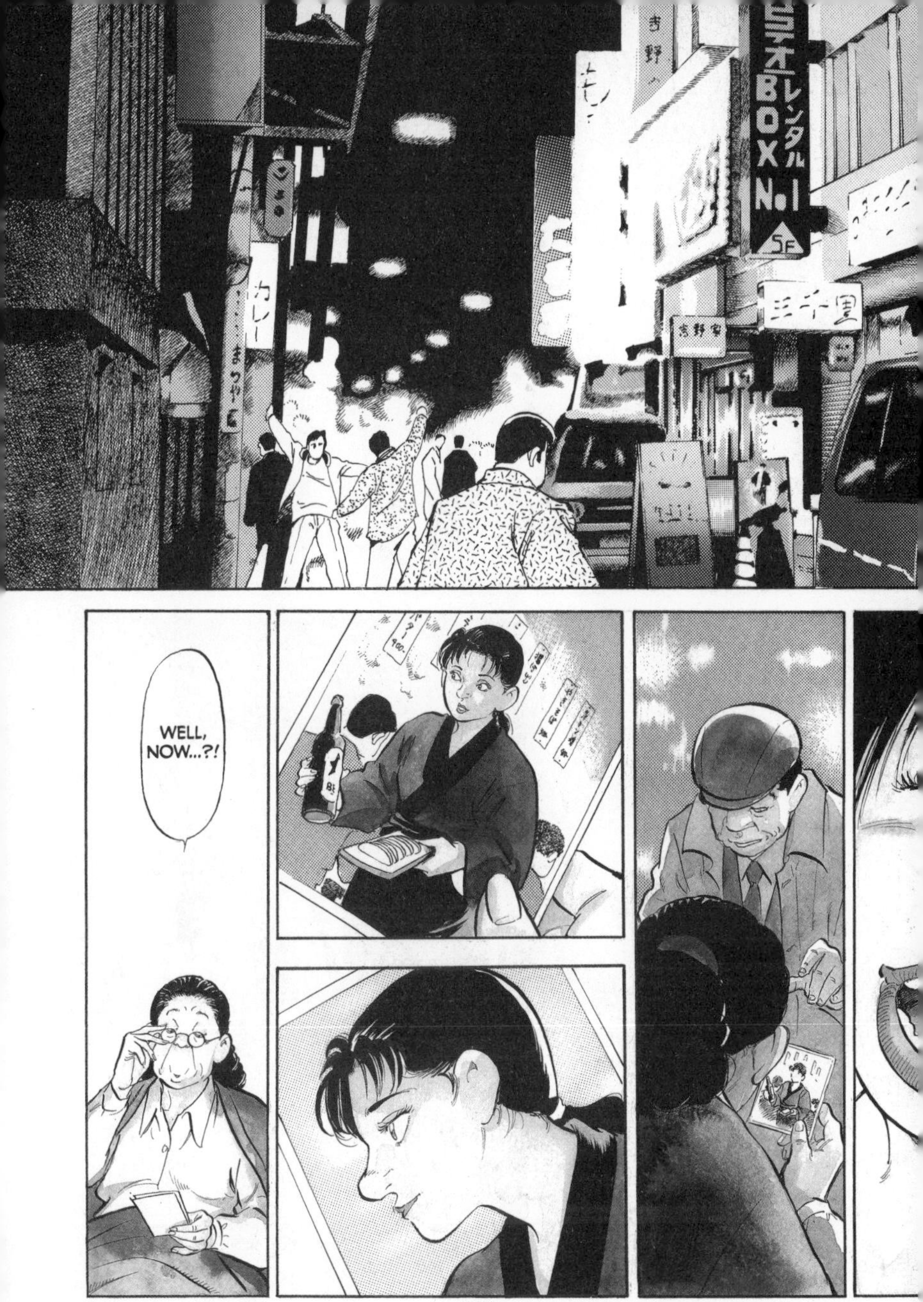

BOX
N.1
レンタル
5F
カレー
WELL, NOW...?!

*SIGN: IZUMI

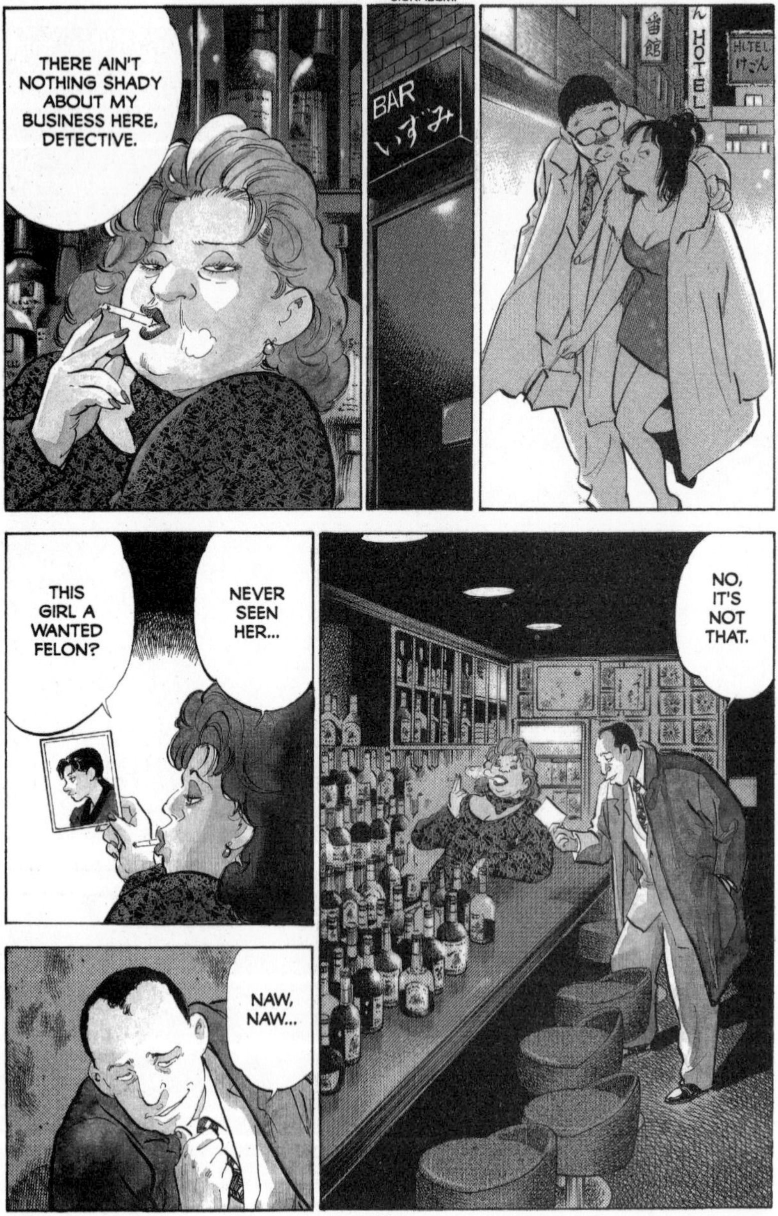
HOTEL
BAR
いずみ
THERE AIN'T NOTHING SHADY ABOUT MY BUSINESS HERE, DETECTIVE.
NO, IT'S NOT THAT.
NEVER SEEN HER...
THIS GIRL A WANTED FELON?
NAW, NAW...

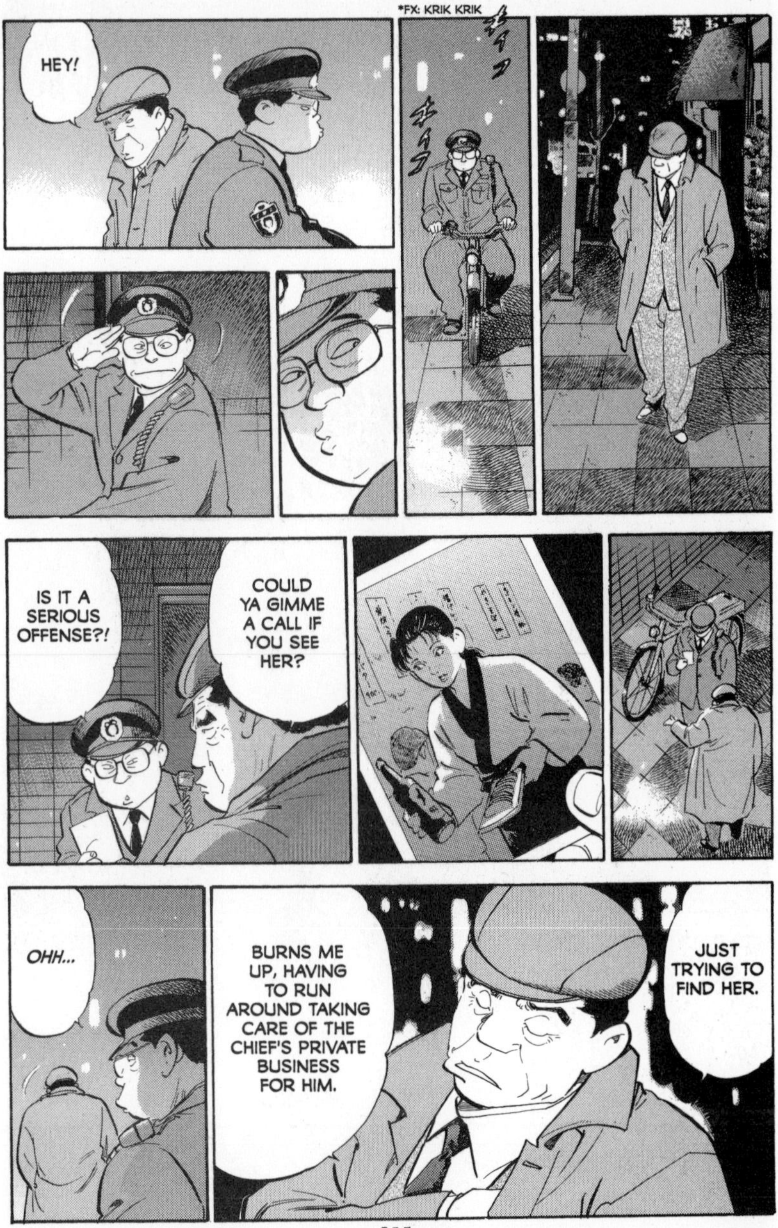
*FX: KRIK KRIK
HEY!
COULD YA GIMME A CALL IF YOU SEE HER?
IS IT A SERIOUS OFFENSE?!
JUST TRYING TO FIND HER.
BURNS ME UP, HAVING TO RUN AROUND TAKING CARE OF THE CHIEF'S PRIVATE BUSINESS FOR HIM.
OHH...

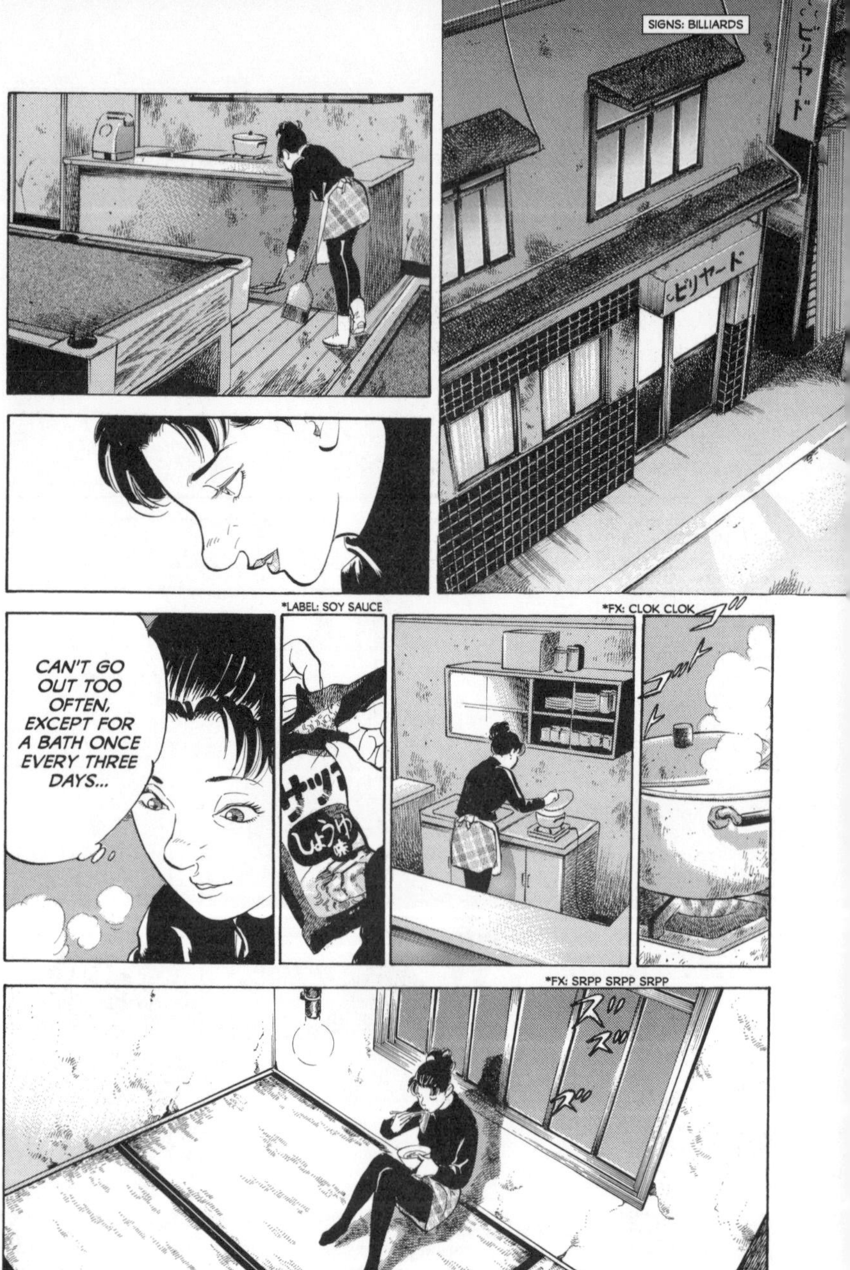
SIGNS: BILLIARDS
*FX: CLOK CLOK
*LABEL: SOY SAUCE
CAN'T GO OUT TOO OFTEN, EXCEPT FOR A BATH ONCE EVERY THREE DAYS...
*FX: SRPP SRPP SRPP

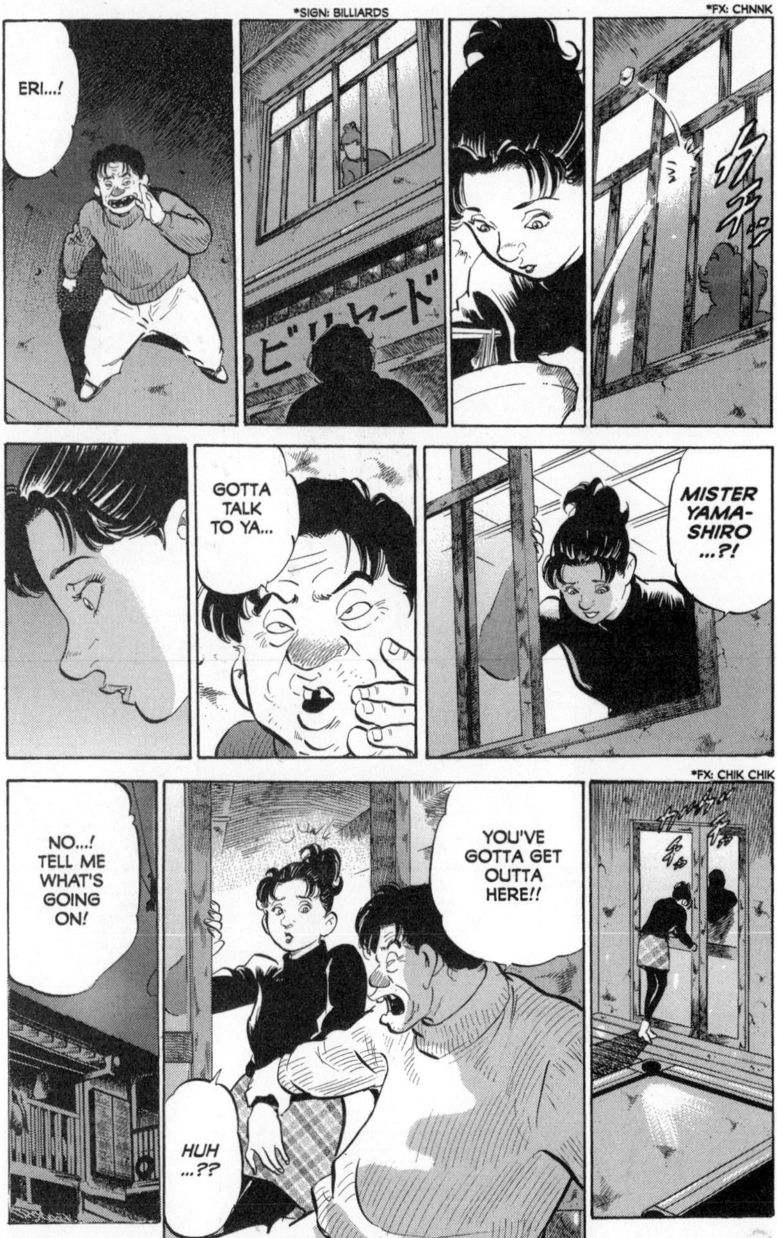
*FX: CHNNK
*SIGN: BILLIARDS
ERI...!
MISTER YAMA-SHIRO ...?!
GOTTA TALK TO YA...
*FX: CHIK CHIK
YOU'VE GOTTA GET OUTTA HERE!!
HUH ...??
NO...! TELL ME WHAT'S GOING ON!

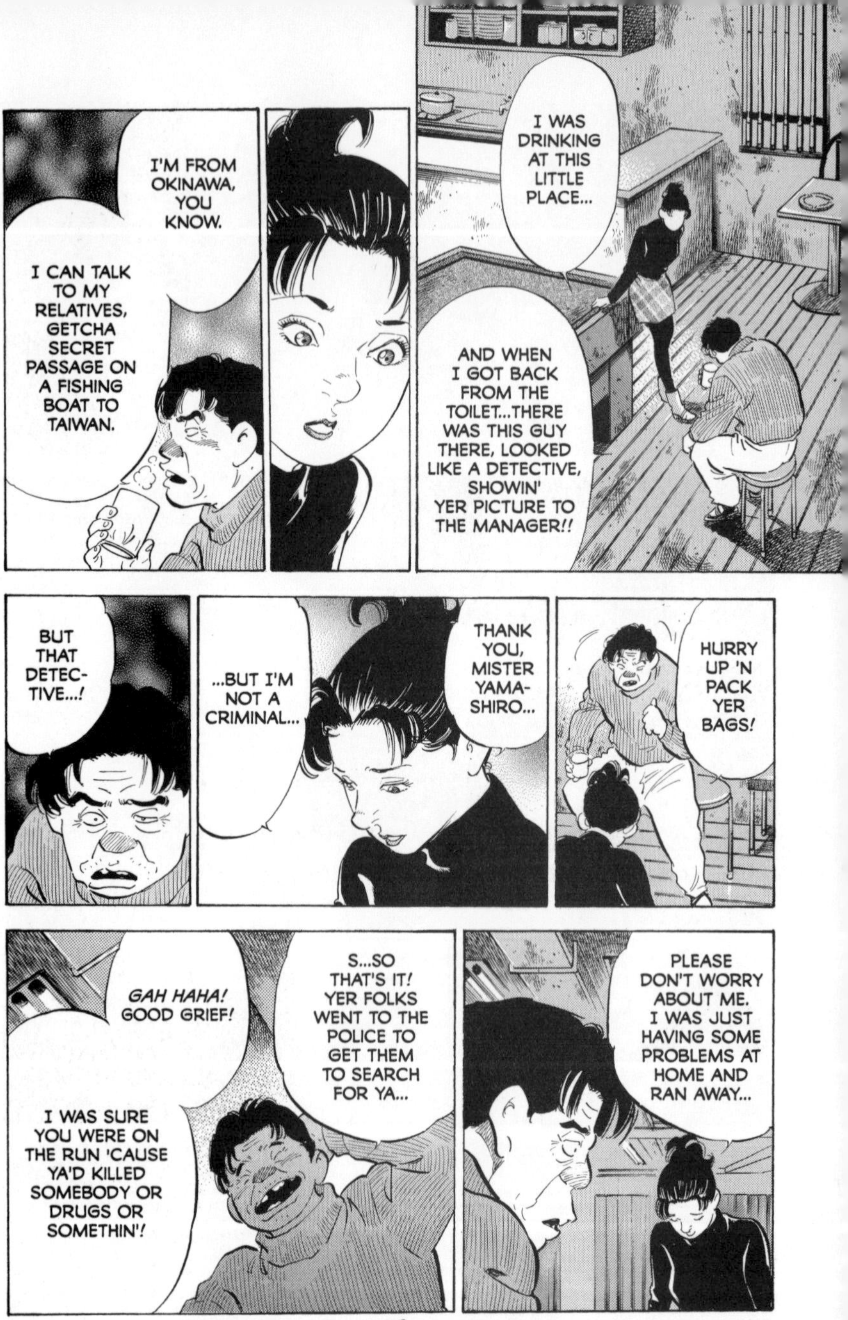
I WAS DRINKING AT THIS LITTLE PLACE...
AND WHEN I GOT BACK FROM THE TOILET...THERE WAS THIS GUY THERE, LOOKED LIKE A DETECTIVE, SHOWIN' YER PICTURE TO THE MANAGER!!
I'M FROM OKINAWA, YOU KNOW.
I CAN TALK TO MY RELATIVES, GETCHA SECRET PASSAGE ON A FISHING BOAT TO TAIWAN.
HURRY UP 'N PACK YER BAGS!
THANK YOU, MISTER YAMA-SHIRO...
...BUT I'M NOT A CRIMINAL...
BUT THAT DETEC-TIVE...!
PLEASE DON'T WORRY ABOUT ME. I WAS JUST HAVING SOME PROBLEMS AT HOME AND RAN AWAY...
S...SO THAT'S IT! YER FOLKS WENT TO THE POLICE TO GET THEM TO SEARCH FOR YA...
GAH HAHA! GOOD GRIEF!
I WAS SURE YOU WERE ON THE RUN 'CAUSE YA'D KILLED SOMEBODY OR DRUGS OR SOMETHIN'!

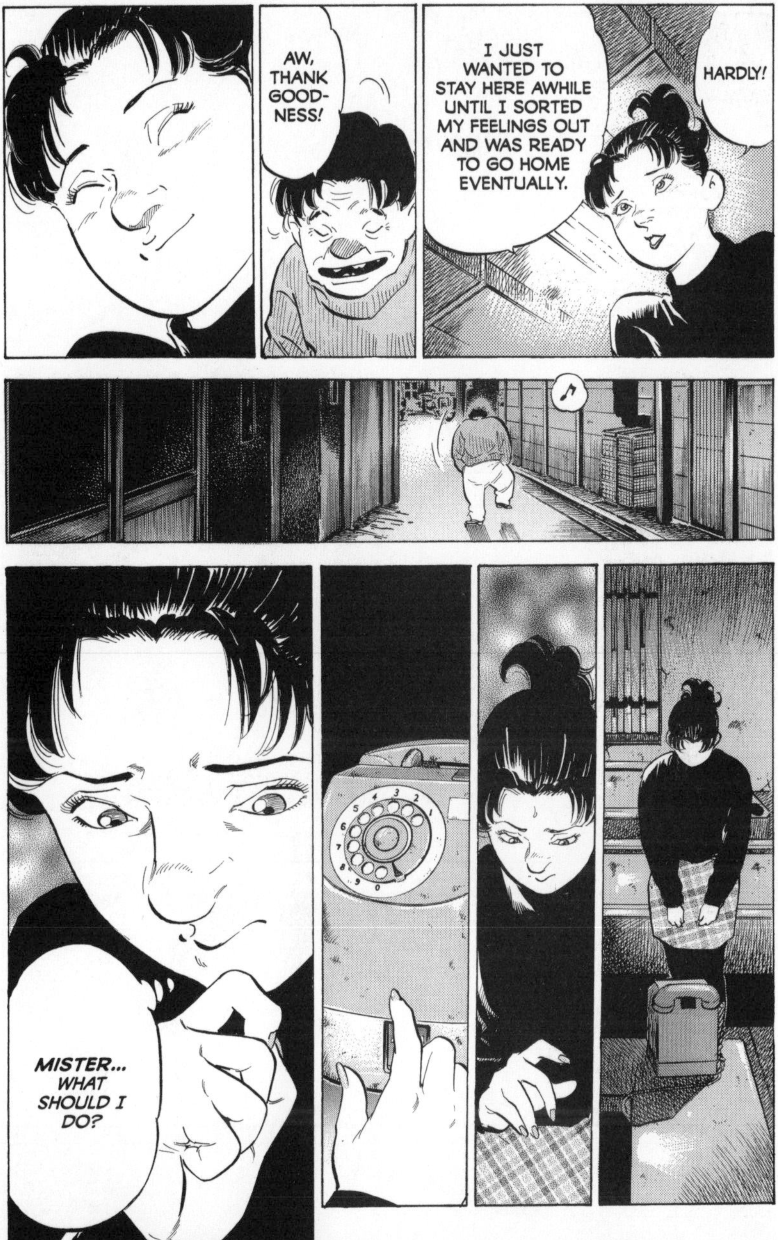
HARDLY!
I JUST WANTED TO STAY HERE AWHILE UNTIL I SORTED MY FEELINGS OUT AND WAS READY TO GO HOME EVENTUALLY.
AW, THANK GOOD-NESS!
MISTER... WHAT SHOULD I DO?

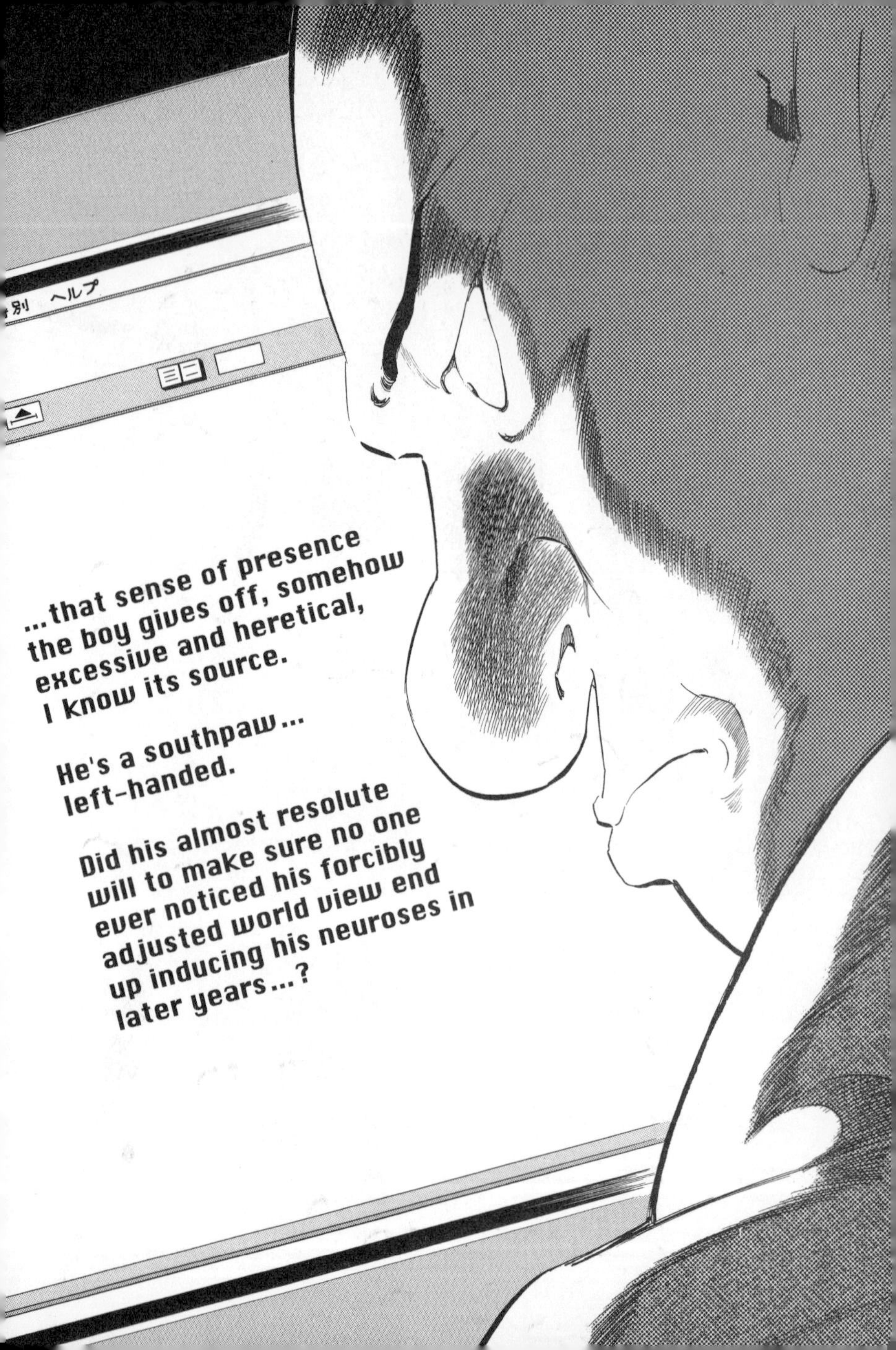
ヘルプ
...that sense of presence the boy gives off, somehow excessive and heretical, I know its source.
He's a southpaw... left-handed.
Did his almost resolute will to make sure no one ever noticed his forcibly adjusted world view end up inducing his neuroses in later years...?

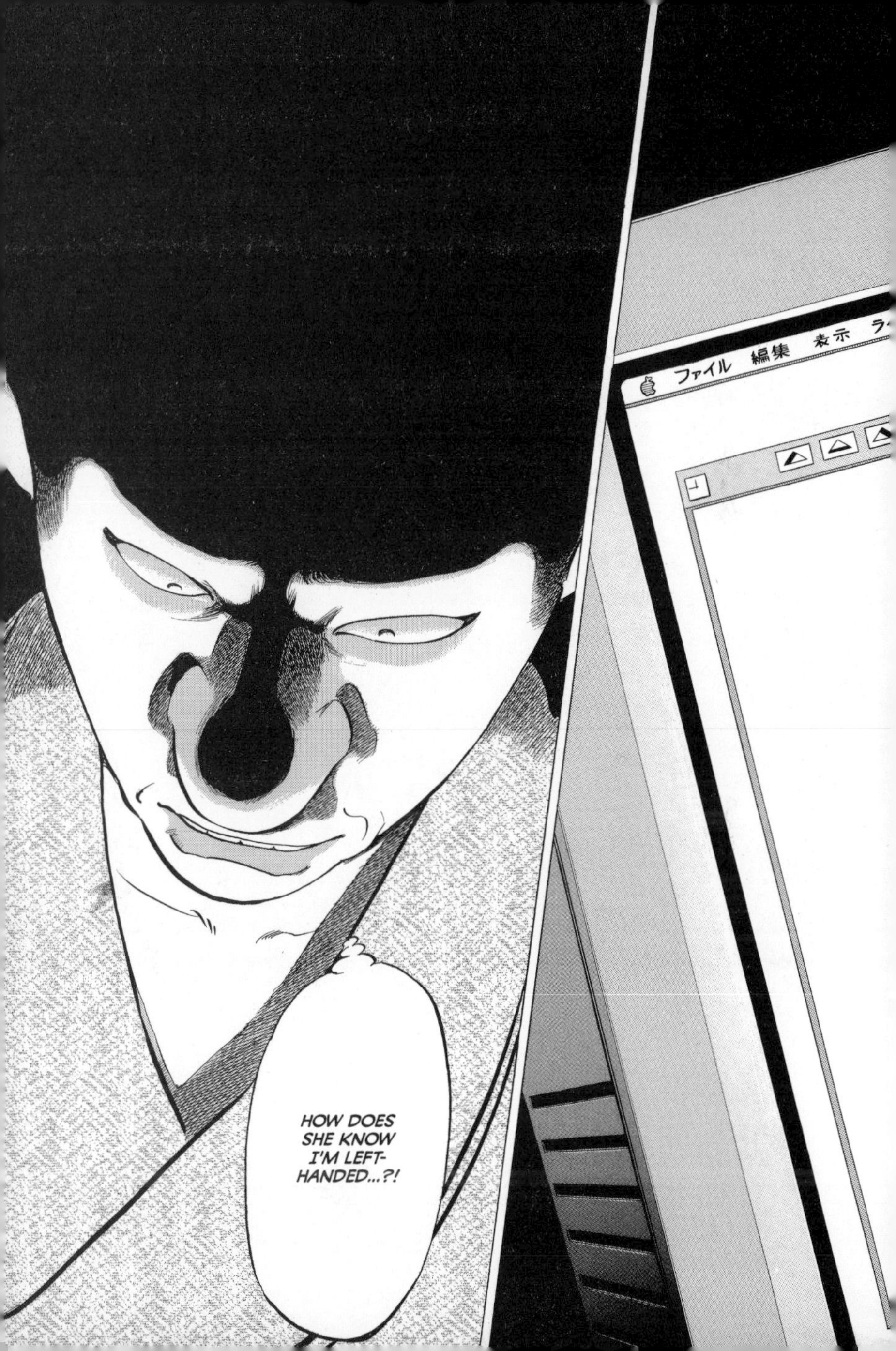
ファイル　編集　表示
HOW DOES SHE KNOW I'M LEFT-HANDED...?!

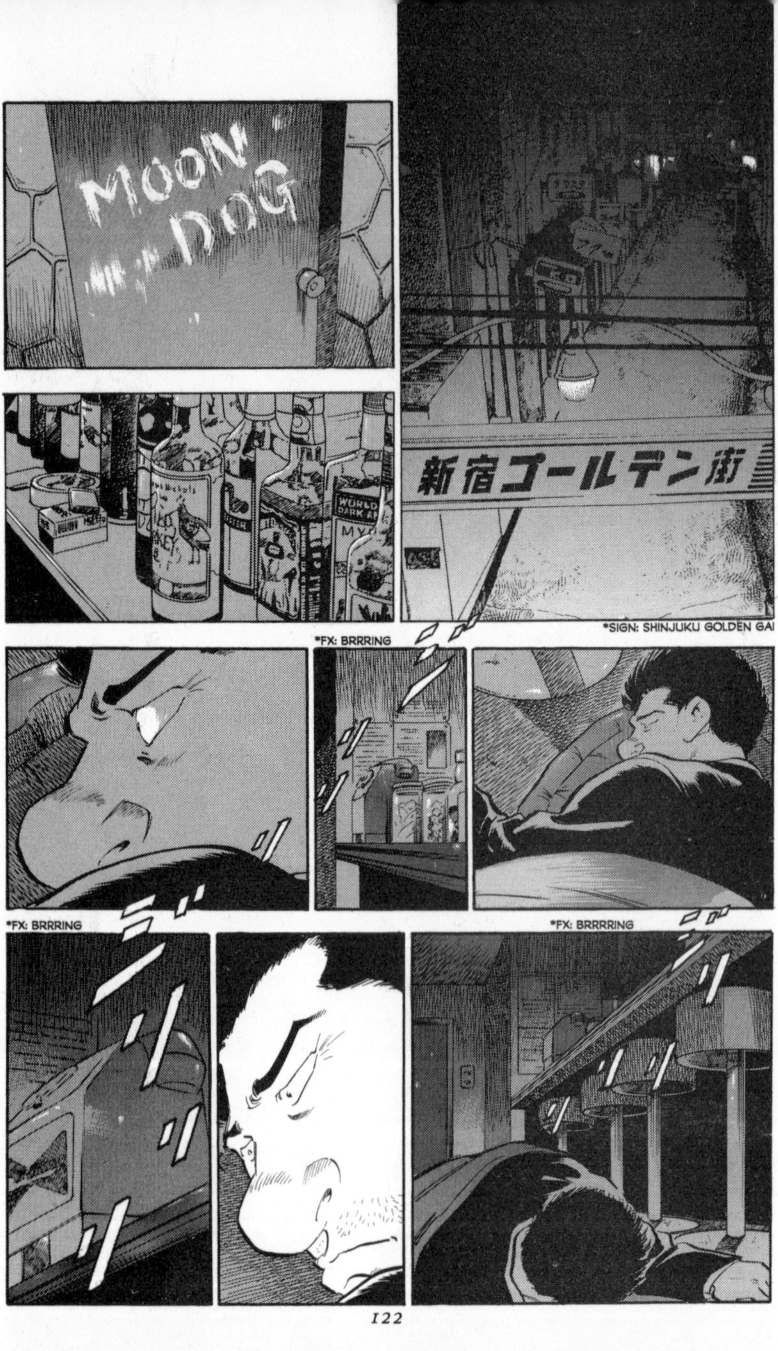
新宿ゴールデン街
*SIGN: SHINJUKU GOLDEN GA
MOON DOG
*FX: BRRRING
*FX: BRRRRING
*FX: BRRING

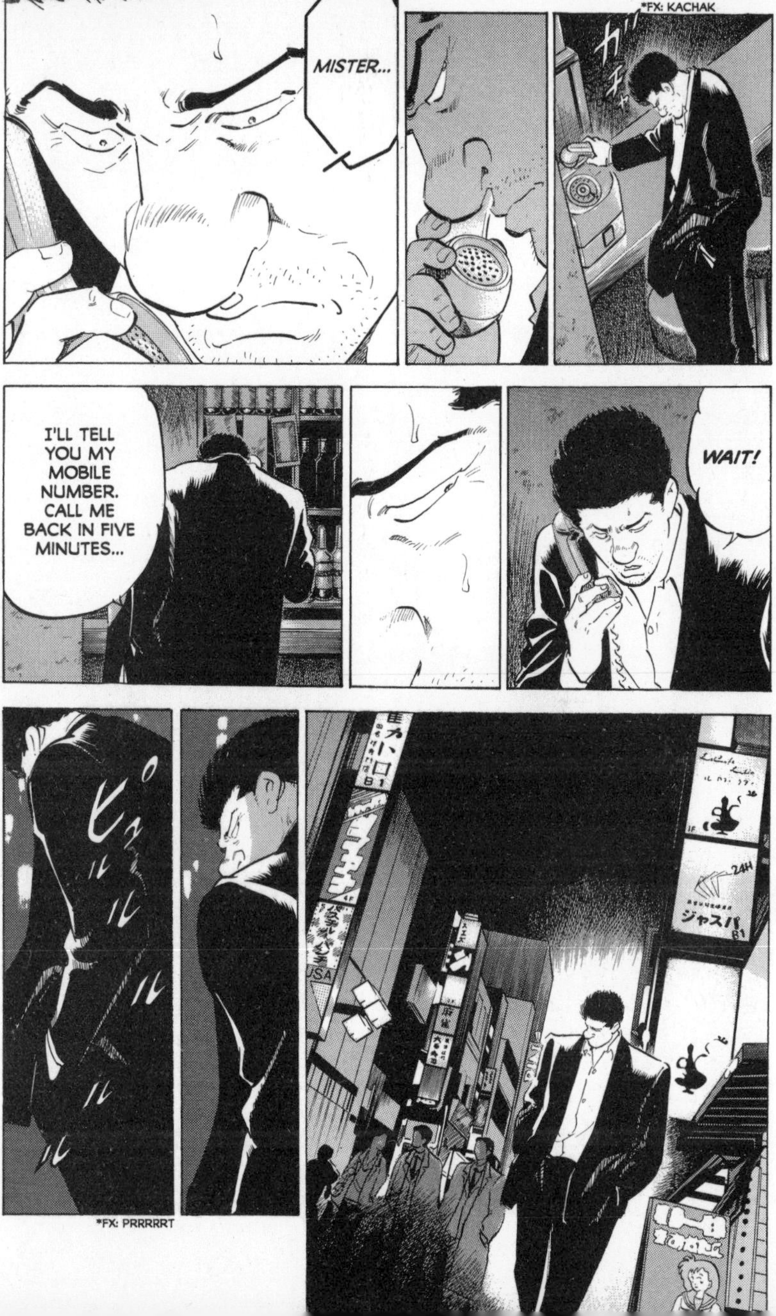
*FX: KACHAK
MISTER...
WAIT!
I'LL TELL YOU MY MOBILE NUMBER. CALL ME BACK IN FIVE MINUTES...
24H
ジャスパ
*FX: PRRRRRT

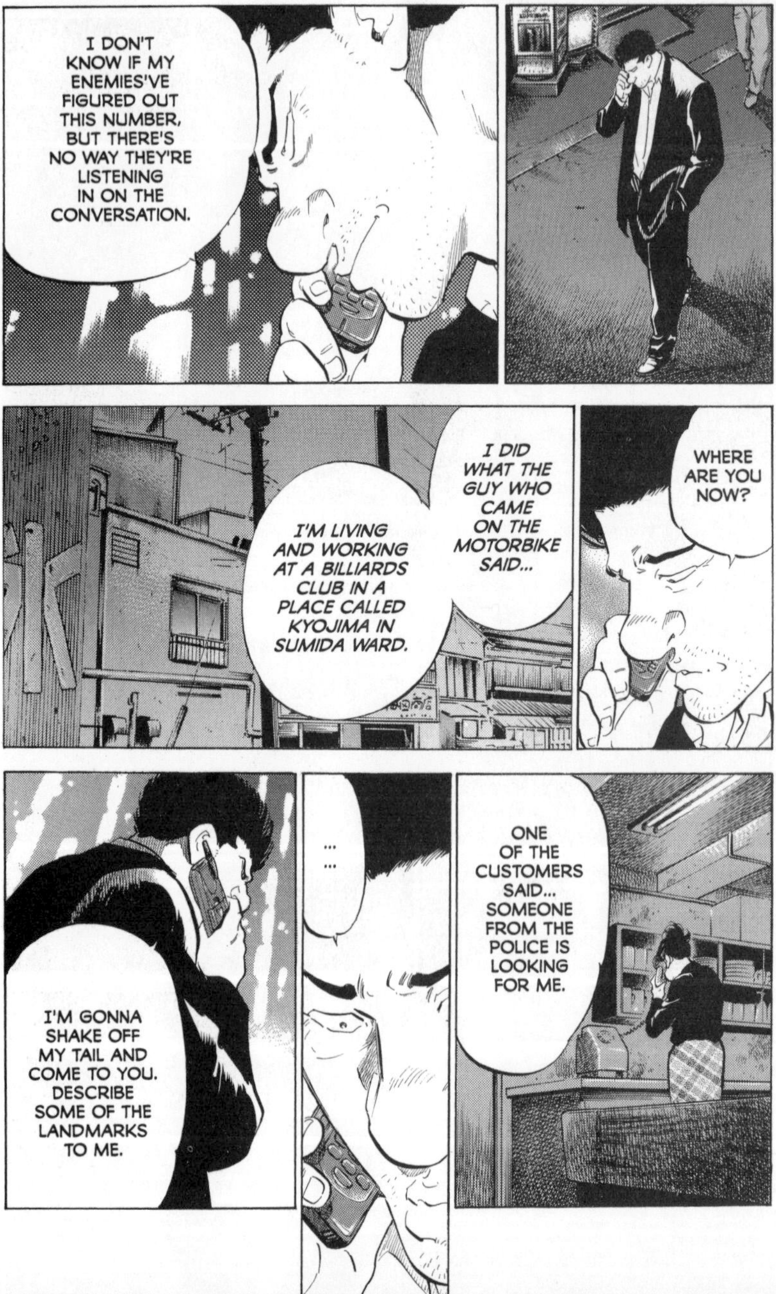
I DON'T KNOW IF MY ENEMIES'VE FIGURED OUT THIS NUMBER, BUT THERE'S NO WAY THEY'RE LISTENING IN ON THE CONVERSATION.
WHERE ARE YOU NOW?
I DID WHAT THE GUY WHO CAME ON THE MOTORBIKE SAID...
I'M LIVING AND WORKING AT A BILLIARDS CLUB IN A PLACE CALLED KYOJIMA IN SUMIDA WARD.
ONE OF THE CUSTOMERS SAID... SOMEONE FROM THE POLICE IS LOOKING FOR ME.
... ...
I'M GONNA SHAKE OFF MY TAIL AND COME TO YOU. DESCRIBE SOME OF THE LANDMARKS TO ME.

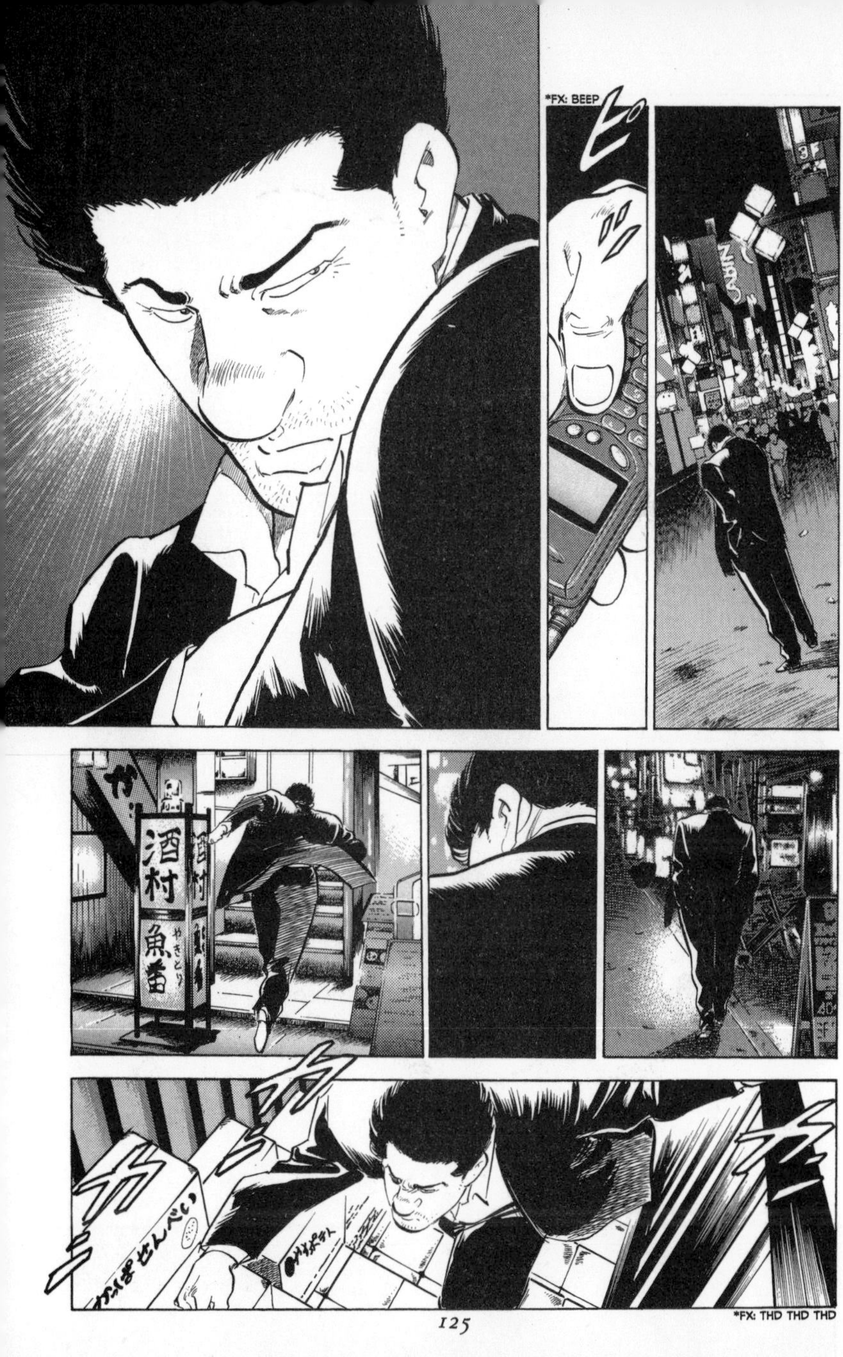
*FX: BEEP
酒村
かっぱせんべい
*FX: THD THD THD

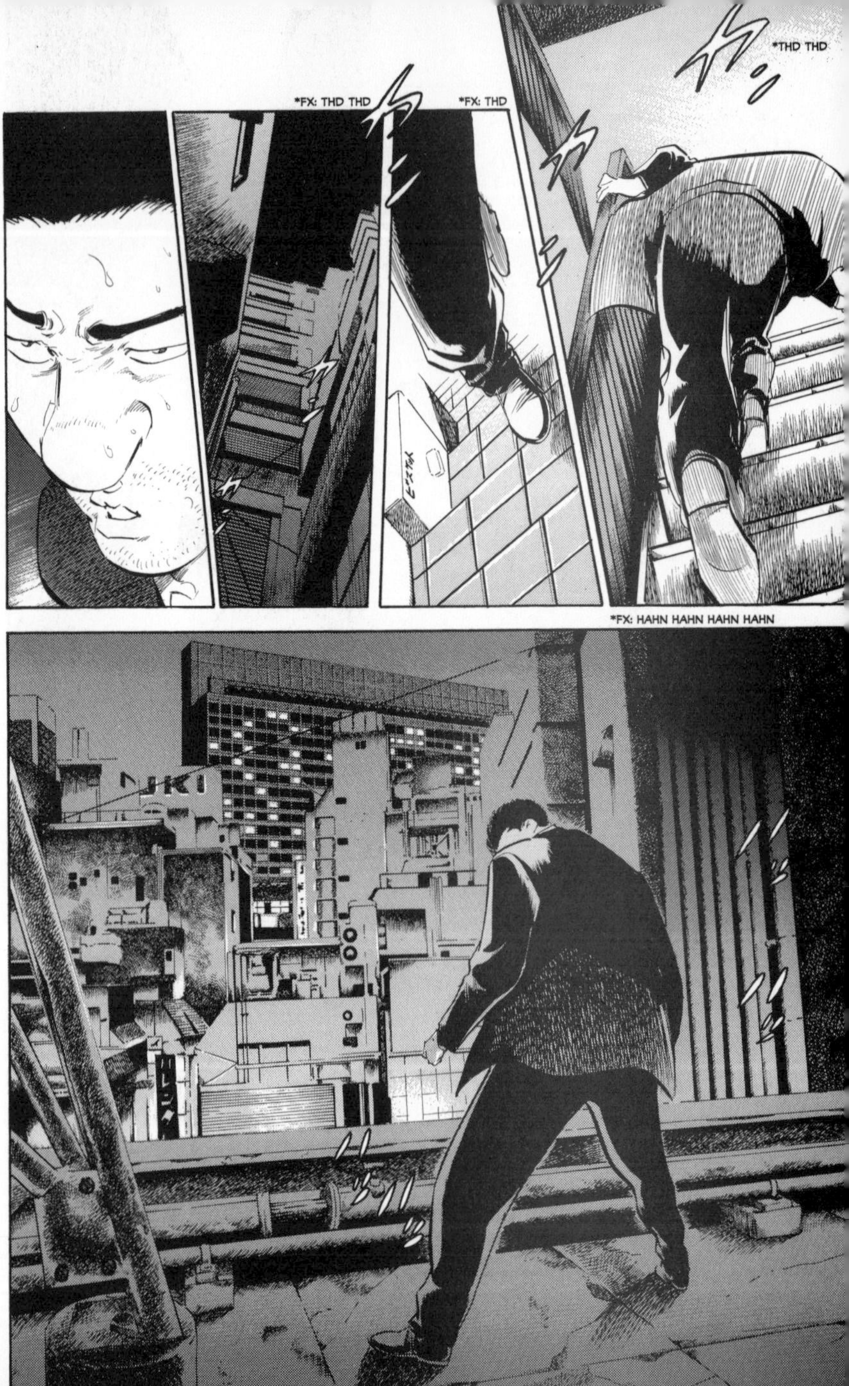
*THD THD
*FX: THD
*FX: THD THD
*FX: HAHN HAHN HAHN HAHN

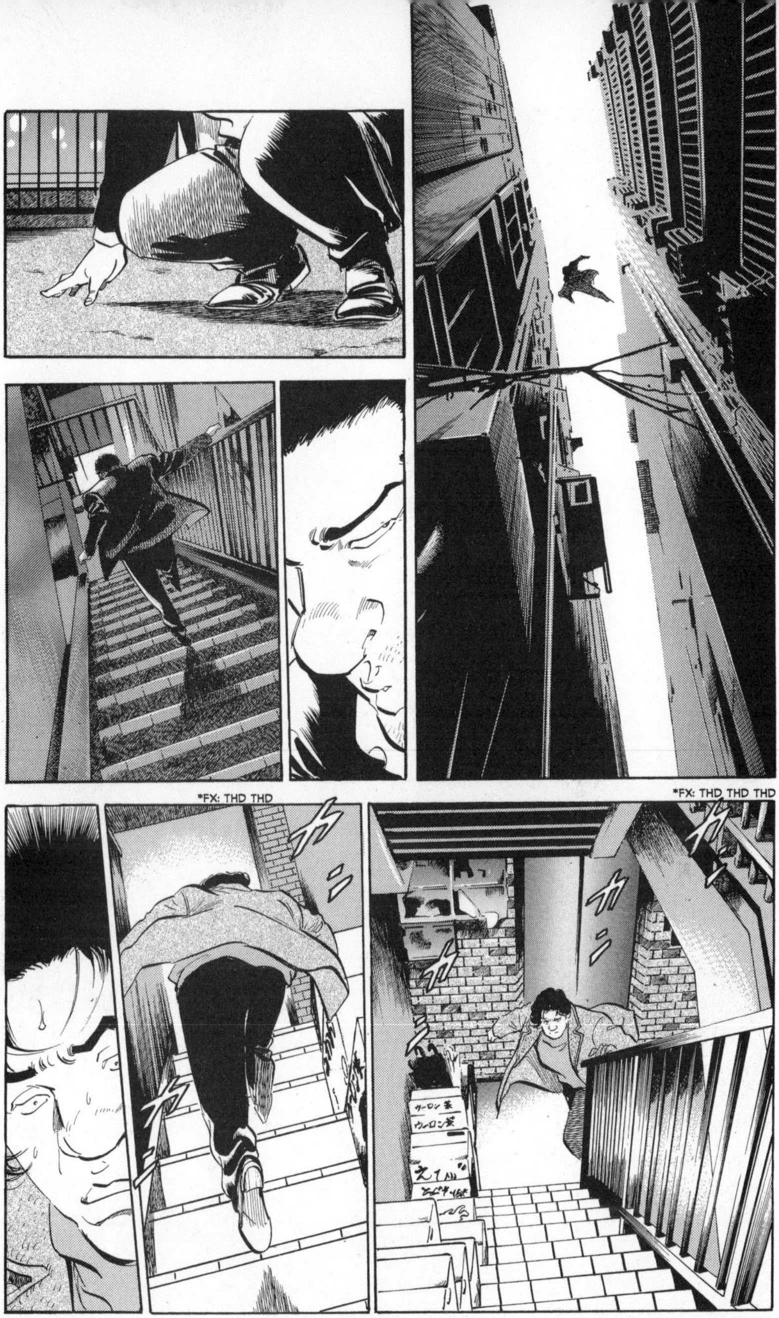
*FX: THD THD THD
*FX: THD THD

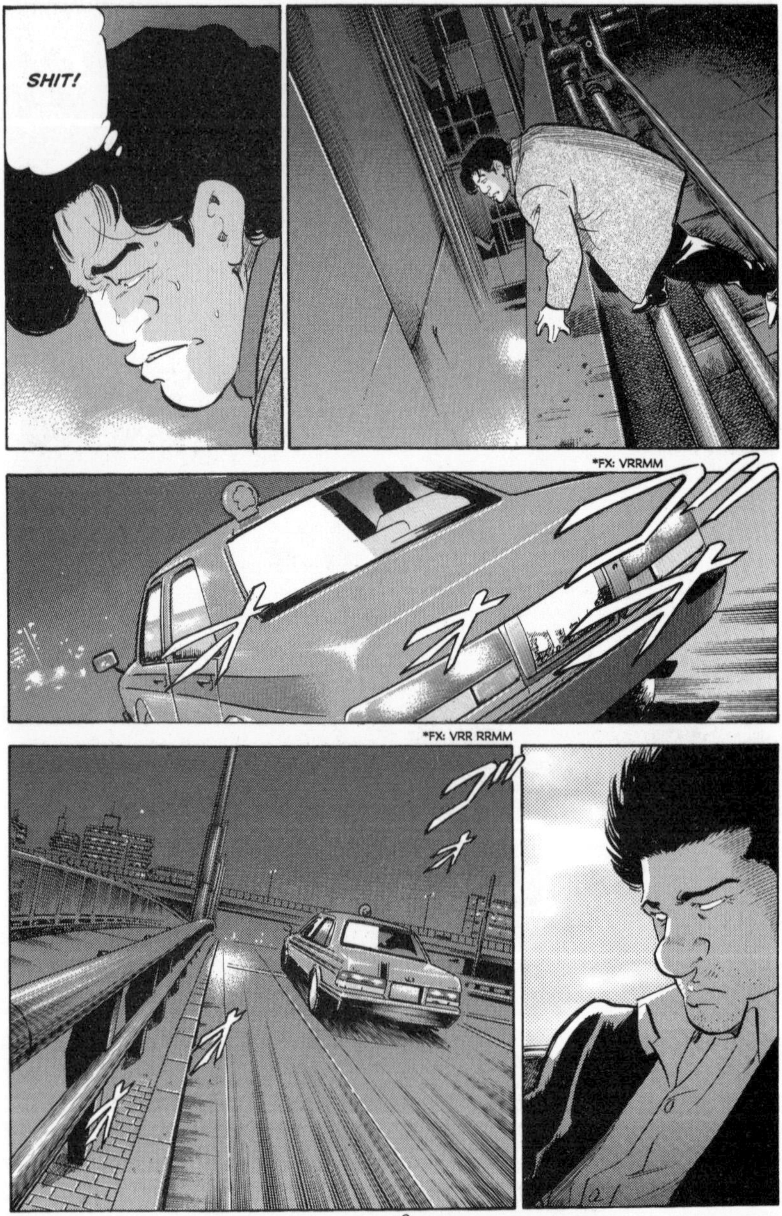
SHIT!
*FX: VRRMM
*FX: VRR RRMM

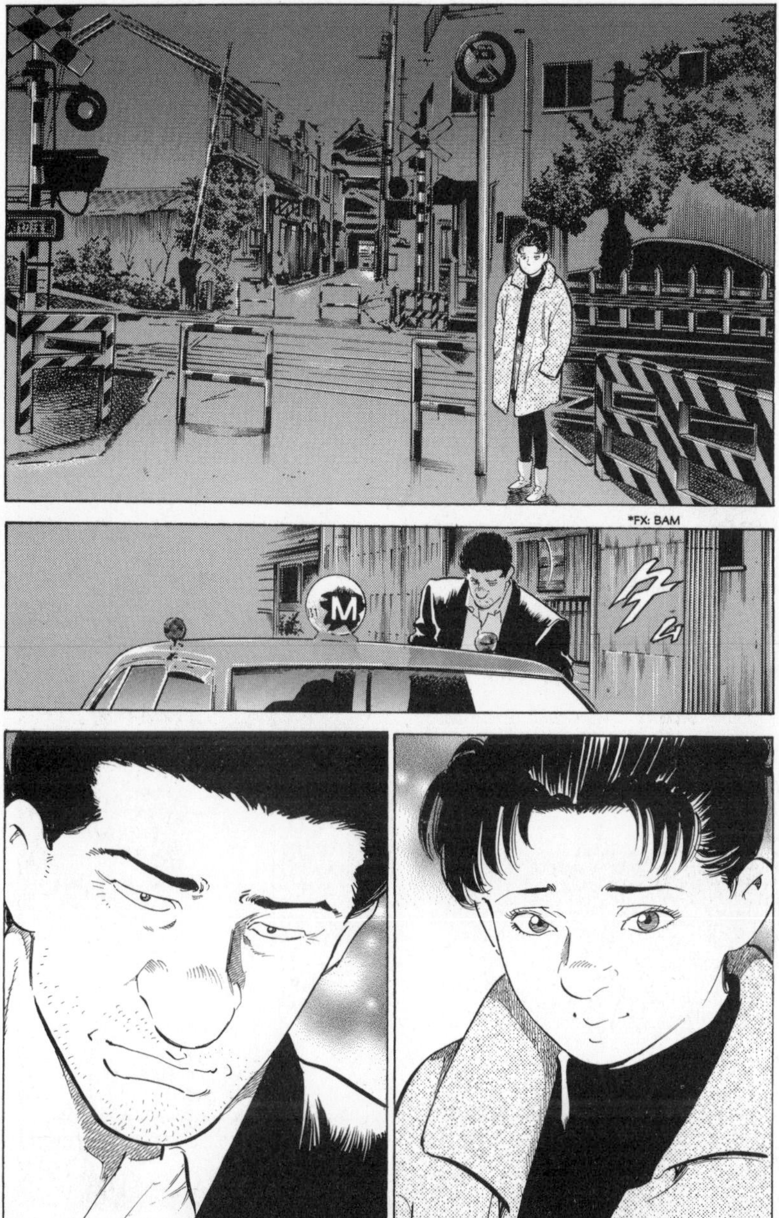
*FX: BAM

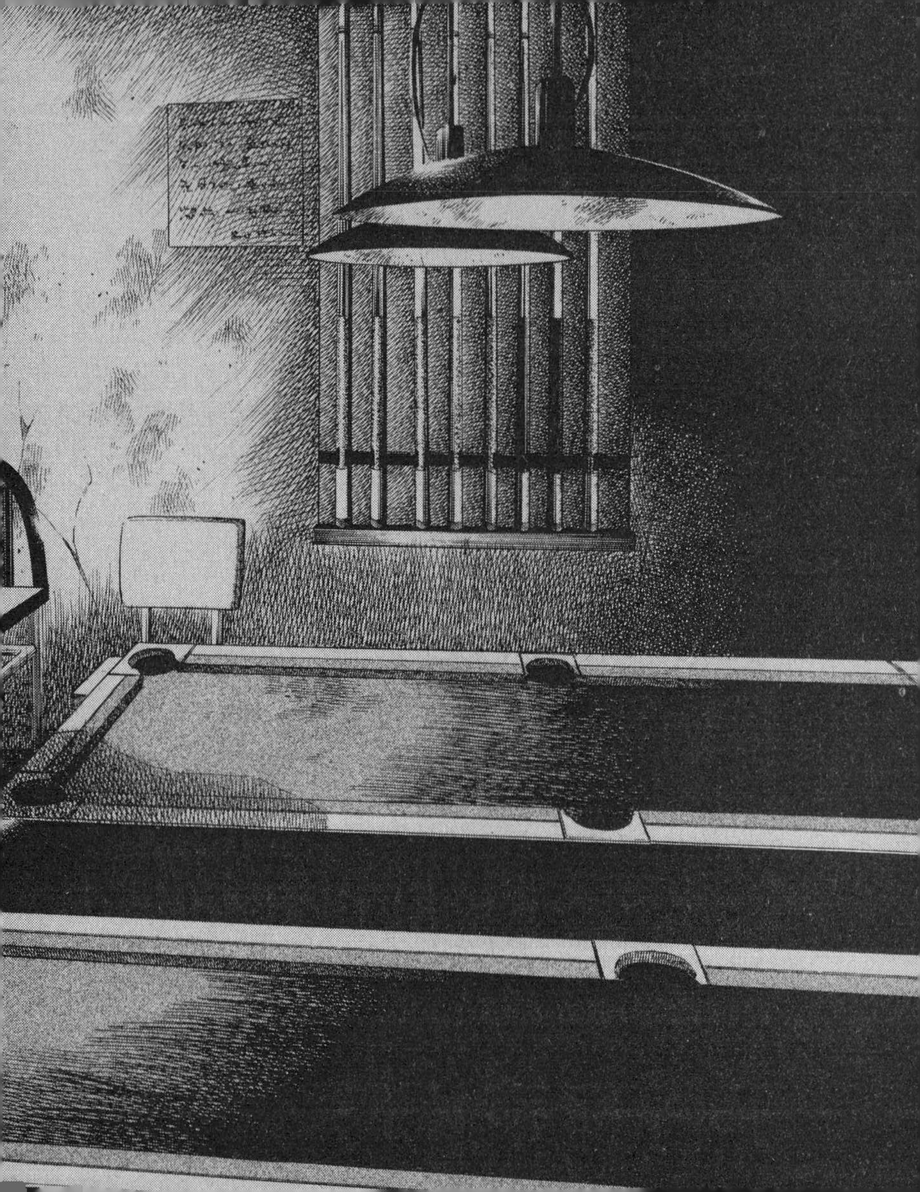

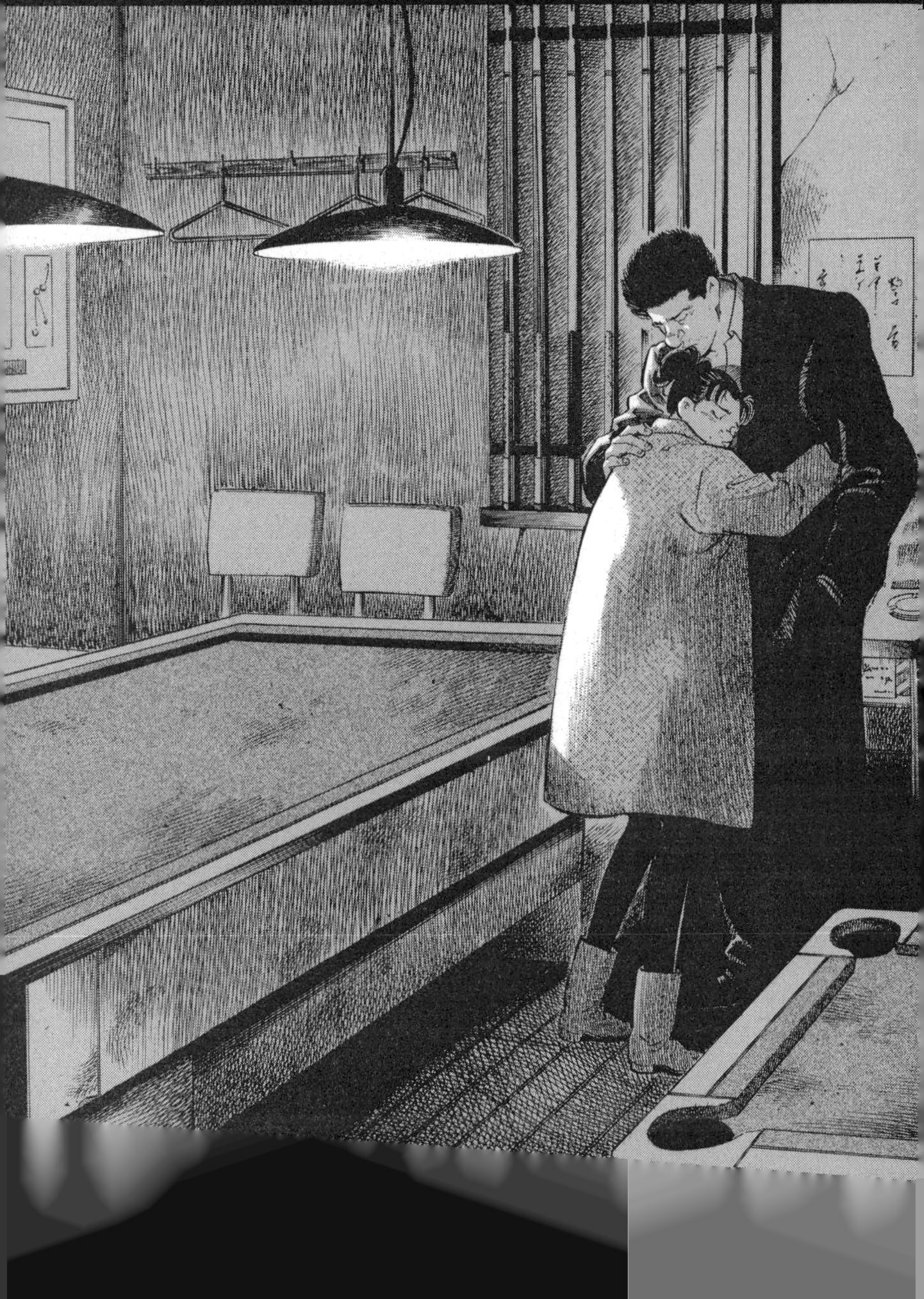

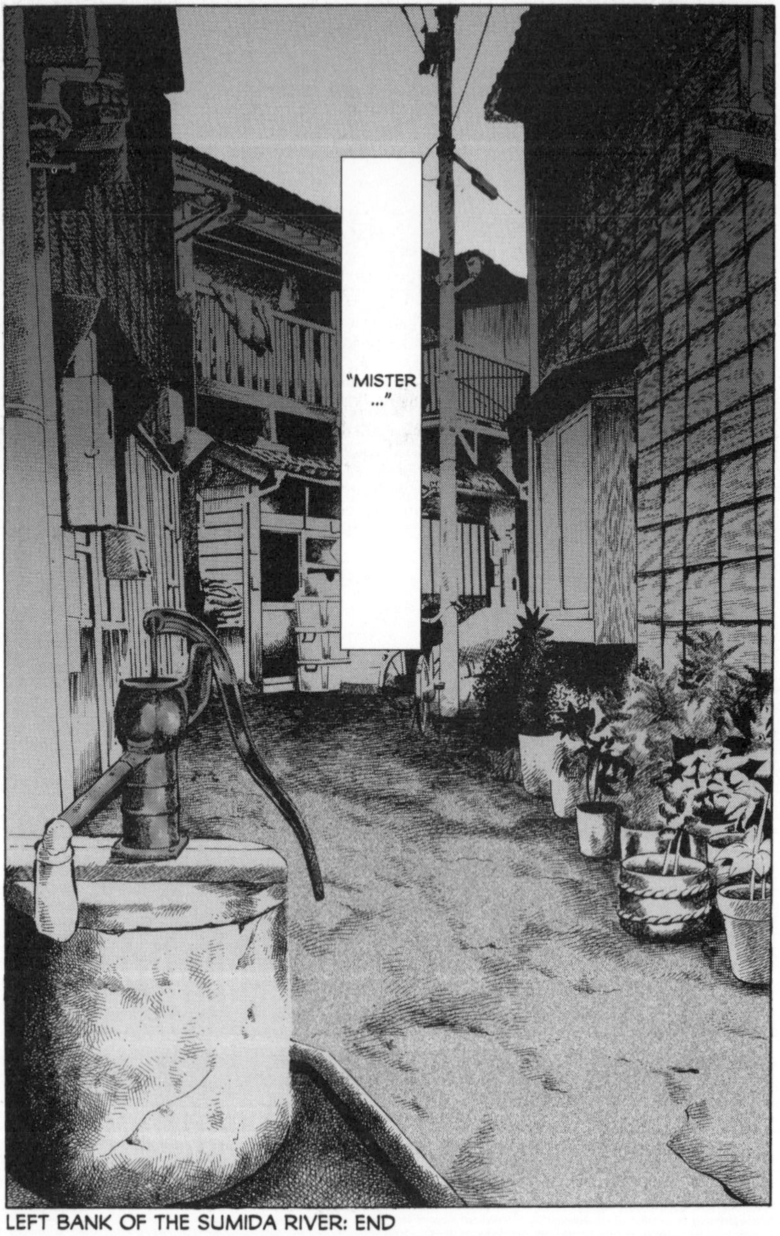
"MISTER ..."
LEFT BANK OF THE SUMIDA RIVER: END

CHAPTER 66
ESCAPE FROM KYOJIMA

第66話●京島脱出

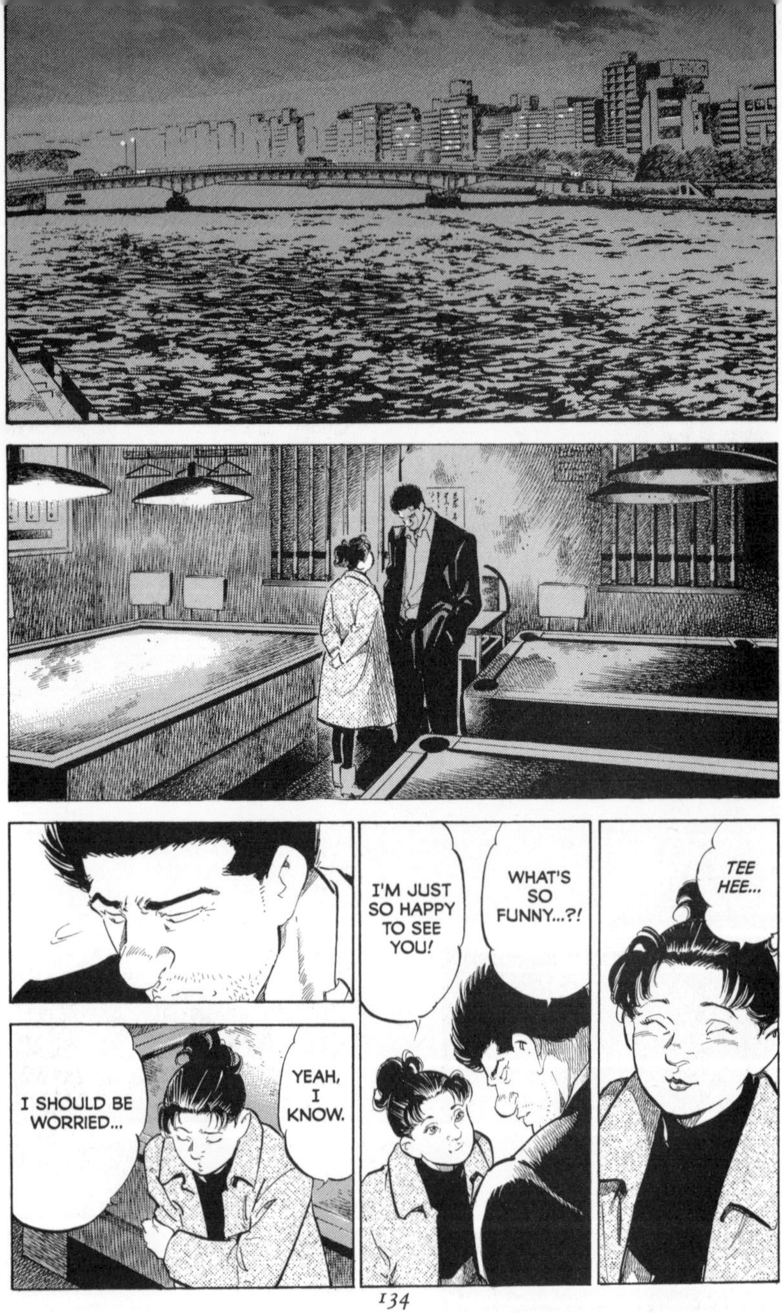
TEE HEE...
WHAT'S SO FUNNY...?!
I'M JUST SO HAPPY TO SEE YOU!
YEAH, I KNOW.
I SHOULD BE WORRIED...

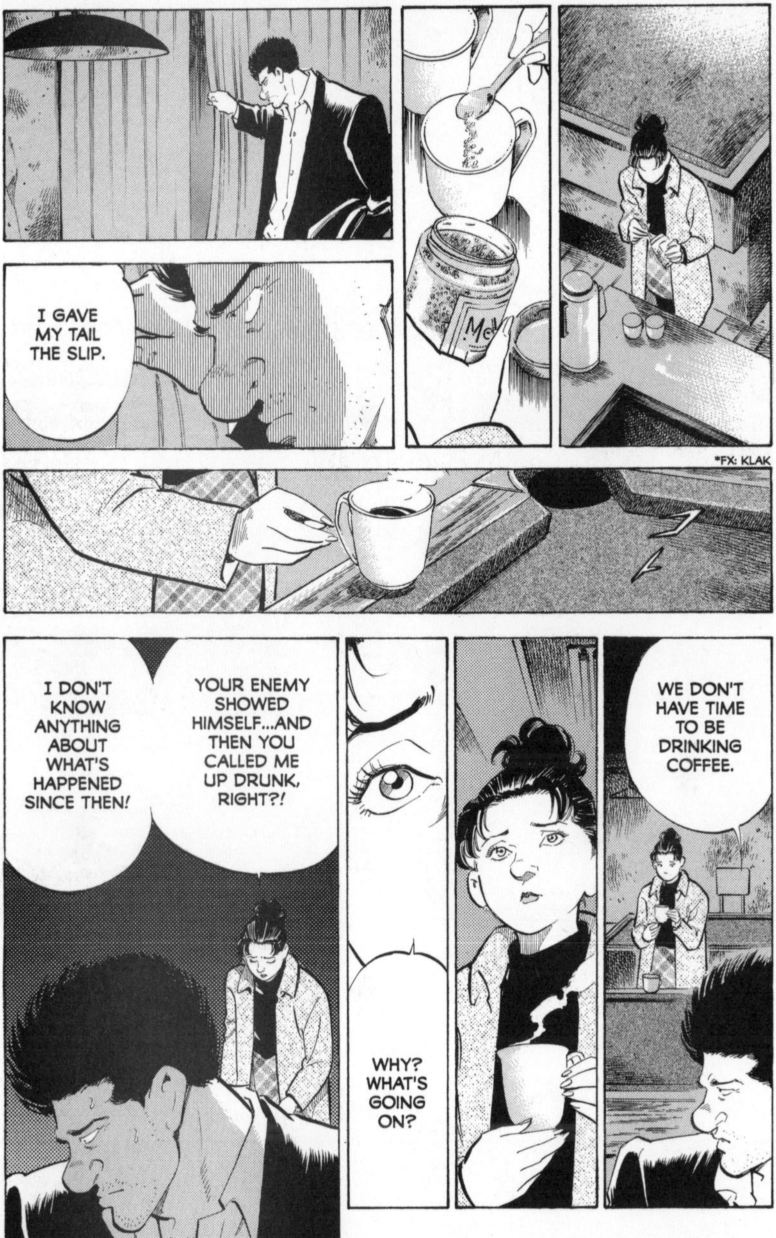
I GAVE MY TAIL THE SLIP.
*FX: KLAK
WE DON'T HAVE TIME TO BE DRINKING COFFEE.
WHY? WHAT'S GOING ON?
YOUR ENEMY SHOWED HIMSELF...AND THEN YOU CALLED ME UP DRUNK, RIGHT?!
I DON'T KNOW ANYTHING ABOUT WHAT'S HAPPENED SINCE THEN!

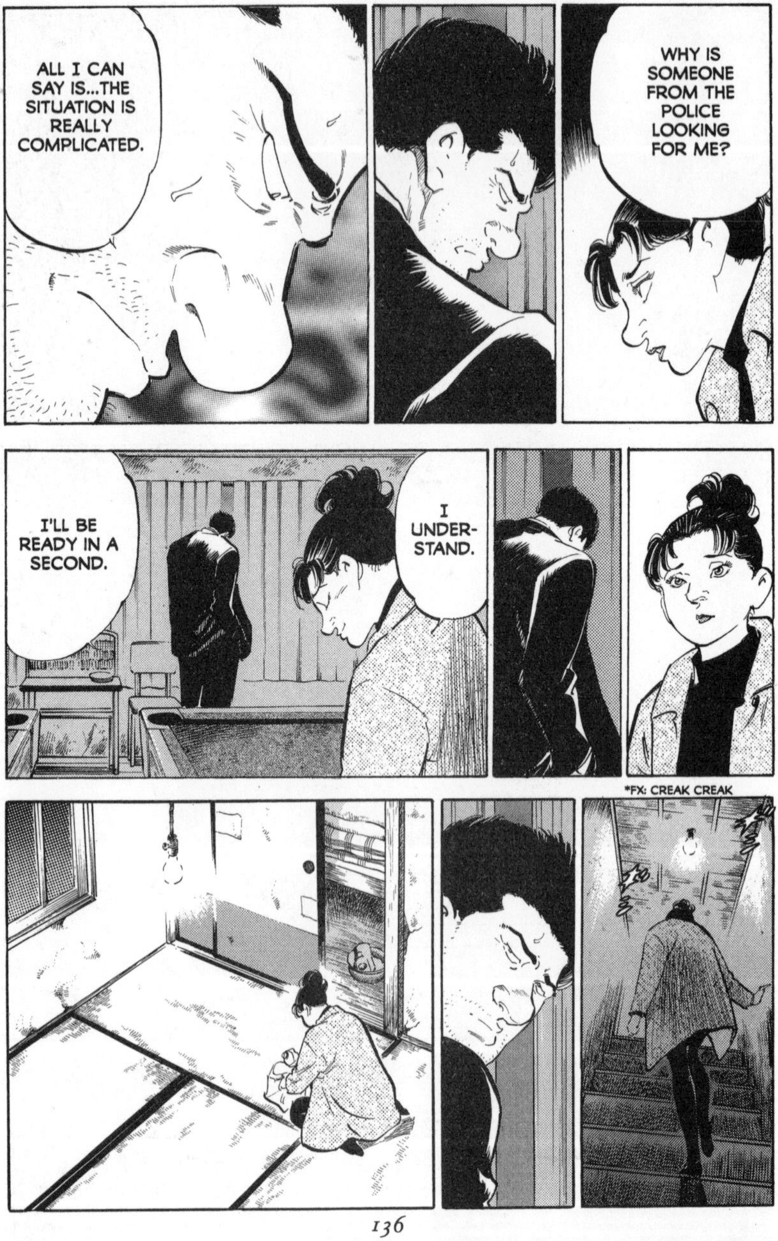
WHY IS SOMEONE FROM THE POLICE LOOKING FOR ME?
ALL I CAN SAY IS...THE SITUATION IS REALLY COMPLICATED.
I UNDER-STAND.
I'LL BE READY IN A SECOND.
*FX: CREAK CREAK

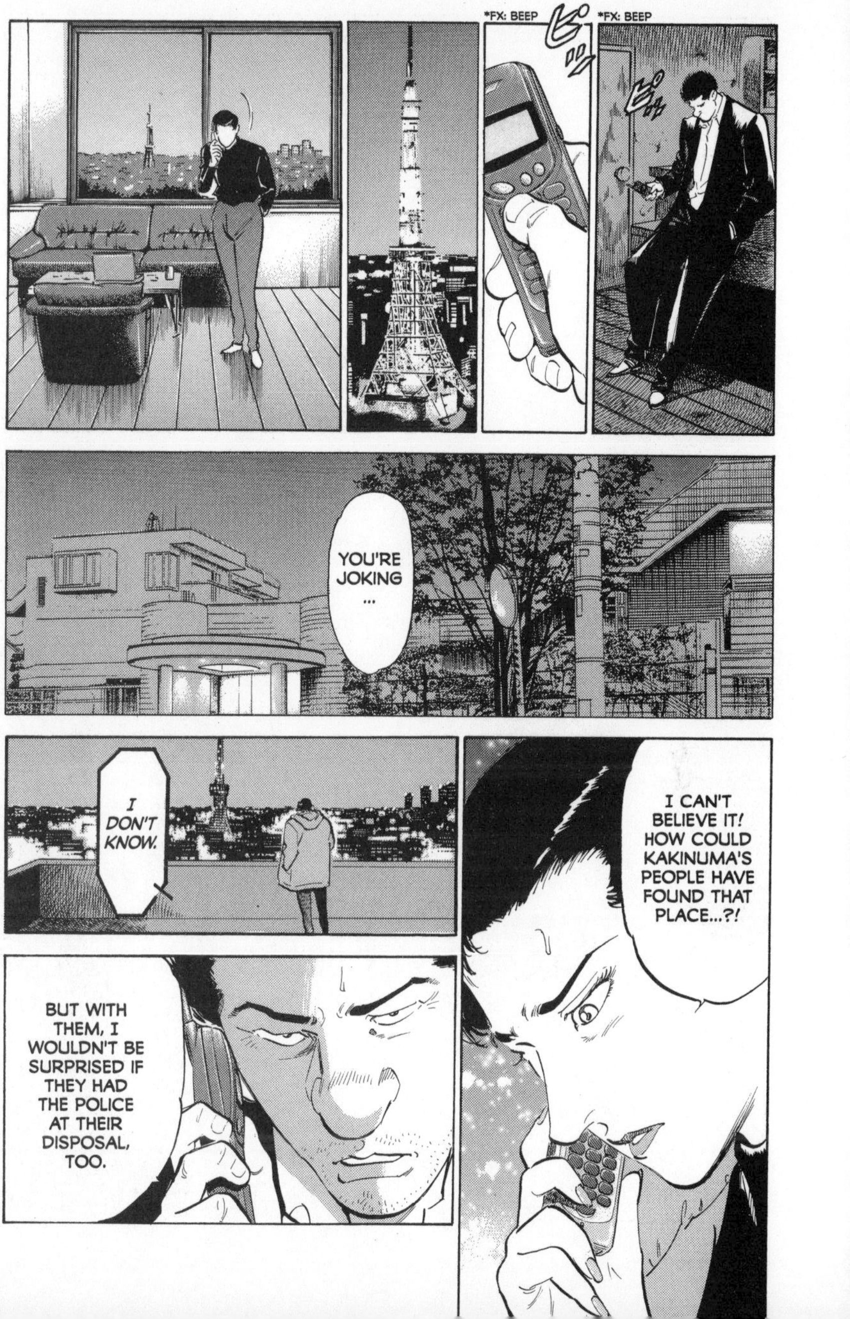
*FX: BEEP
*FX: BEEP
YOU'RE JOKING ...
I CAN'T BELIEVE IT! HOW COULD KAKINUMA'S PEOPLE HAVE FOUND THAT PLACE...?!
I DON'T KNOW.
BUT WITH THEM, I WOULDN'T BE SURPRISED IF THEY HAD THE POLICE AT THEIR DISPOSAL, TOO.

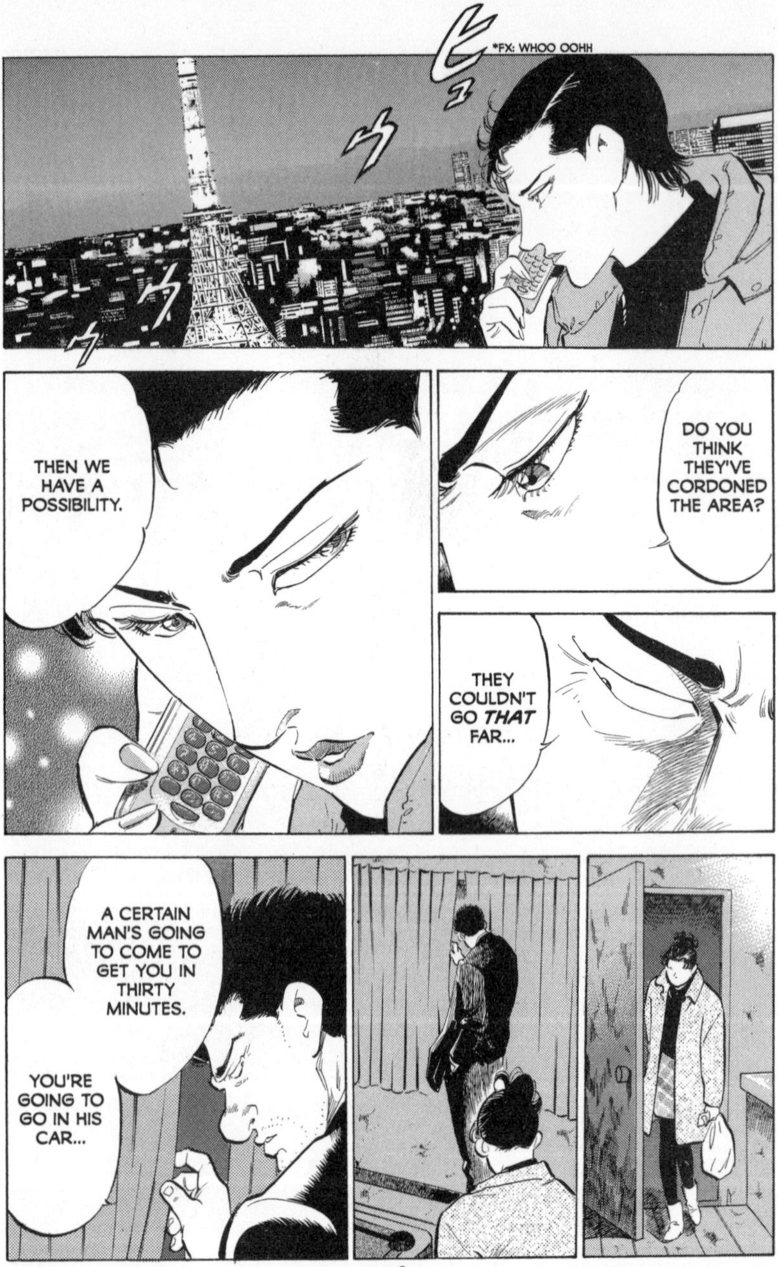
*FX: WHOO OOHH
DO YOU THINK THEY'VE CORDONED THE AREA?
THEY COULDN'T GO *THAT* FAR...
THEN WE HAVE A POSSIBILITY.
A CERTAIN MAN'S GOING TO COME TO GET YOU IN THIRTY MINUTES.
YOU'RE GOING TO GO IN HIS CAR...

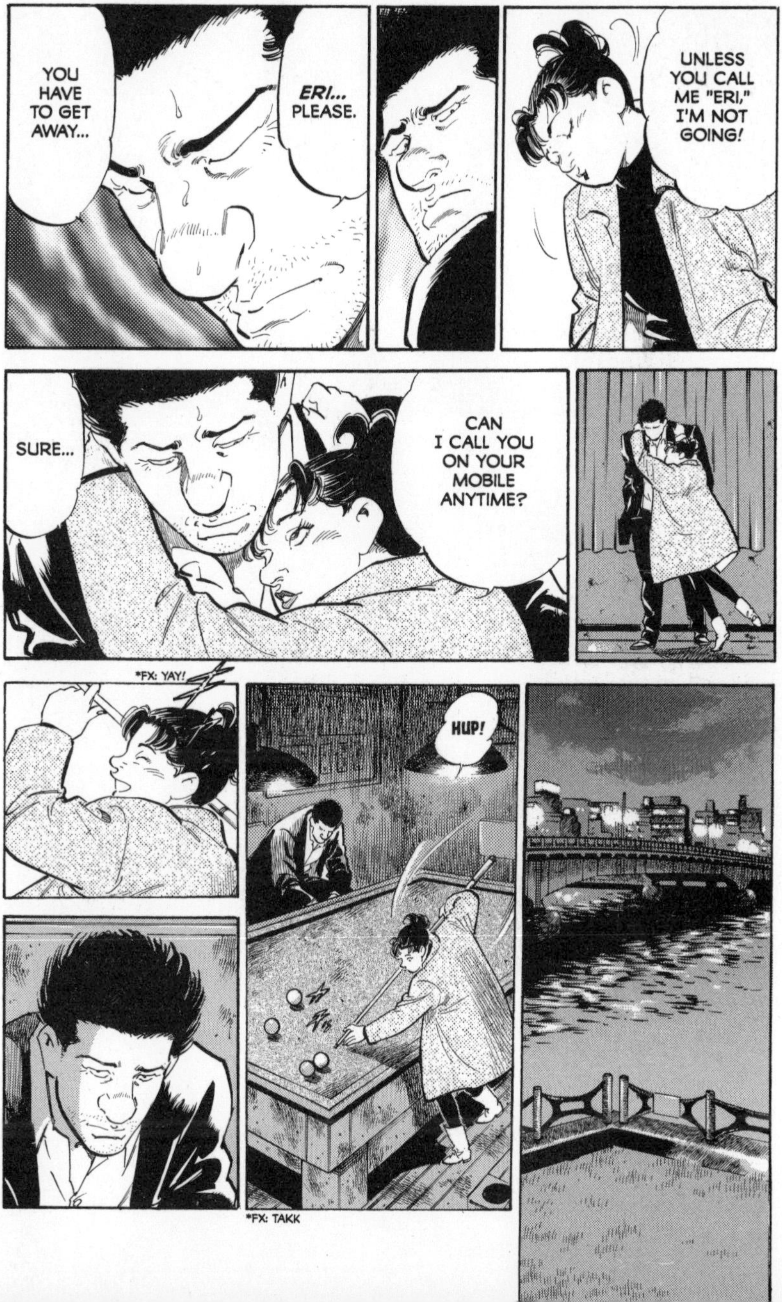
UNLESS YOU CALL ME "ERI," I'M NOT GOING!
ERI... PLEASE.
YOU HAVE TO GET AWAY...
CAN I CALL YOU ON YOUR MOBILE ANYTIME?
SURE...
HUP!
*FX: TAKK
*FX: YAY!

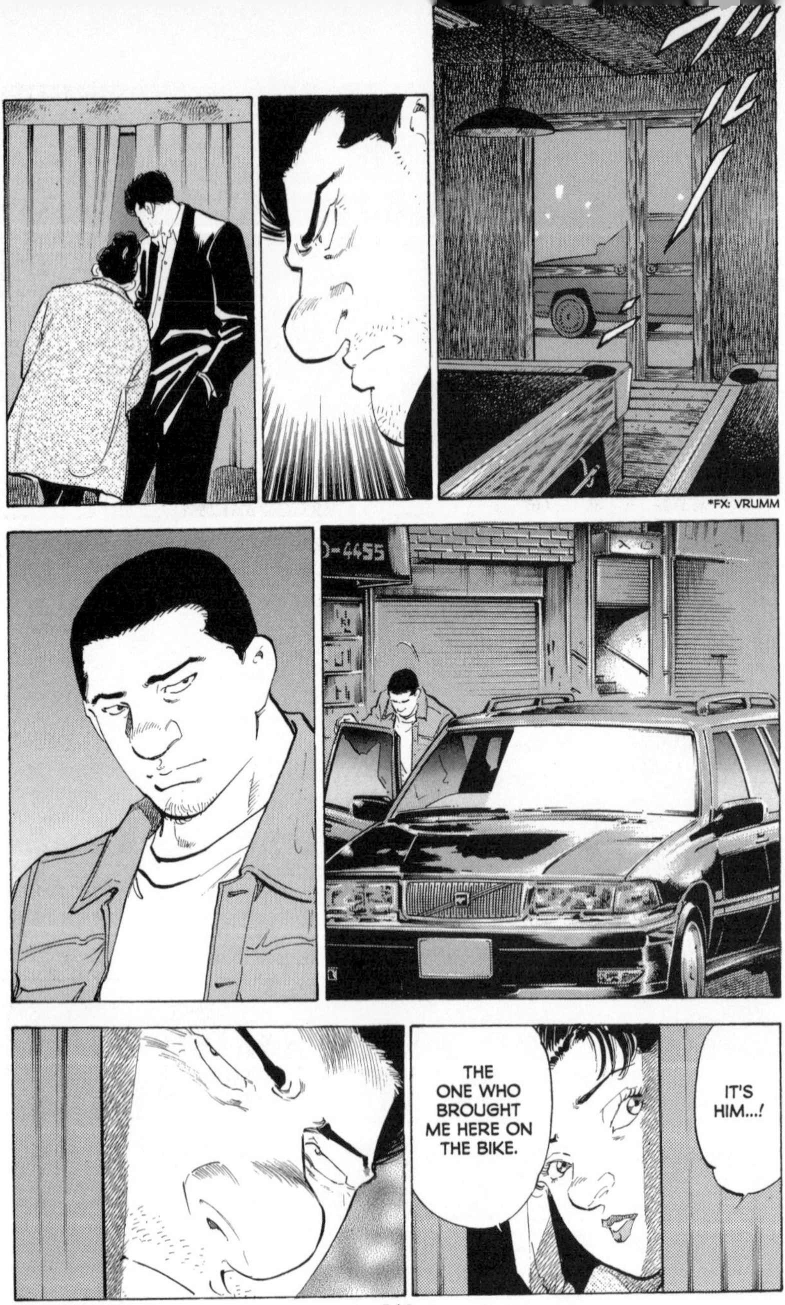
*FX: VRUMM
IT'S HIM...!
THE ONE WHO BROUGHT ME HERE ON THE BIKE.

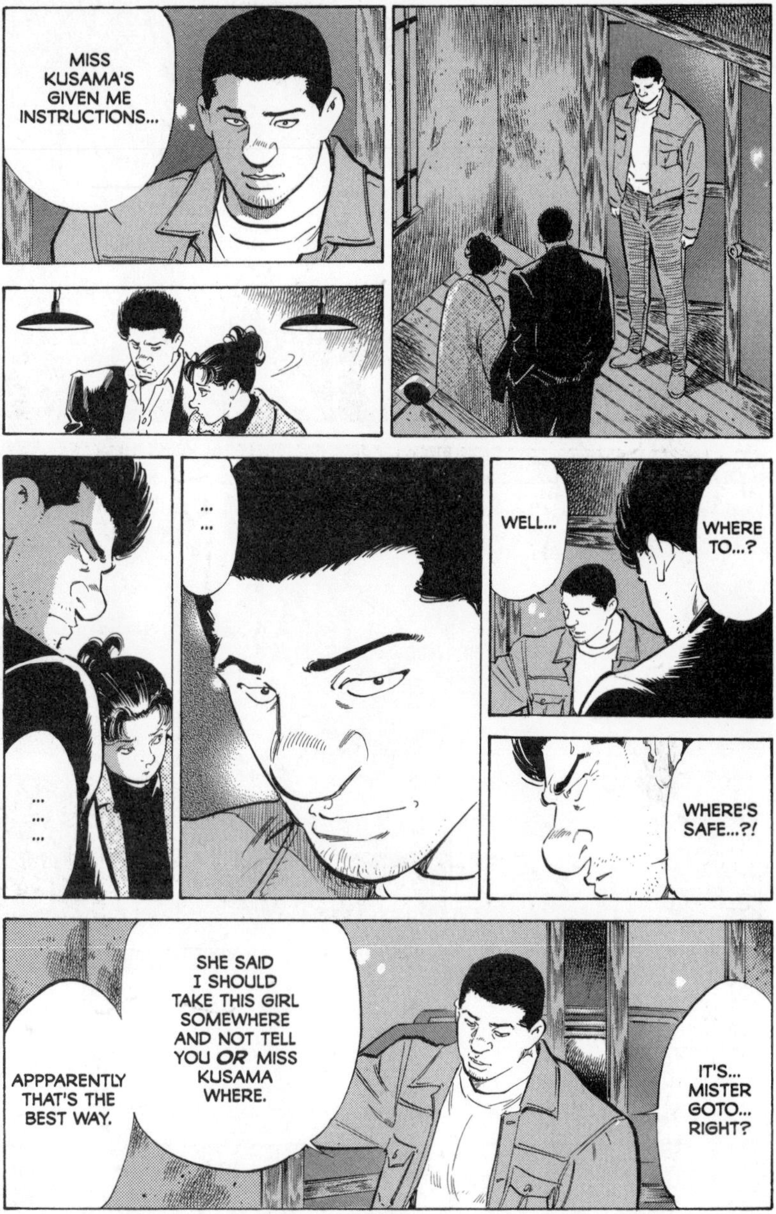
MISS KUSAMA'S GIVEN ME INSTRUCTIONS...
WHERE TO...?
WELL...
WHERE'S SAFE...?!
... ...
... ...
IT'S... MISTER GOTO... RIGHT?
SHE SAID I SHOULD TAKE THIS GIRL SOMEWHERE AND NOT TELL YOU *OR* MISS KUSAMA WHERE.
APPPARENTLY THAT'S THE BEST WAY.

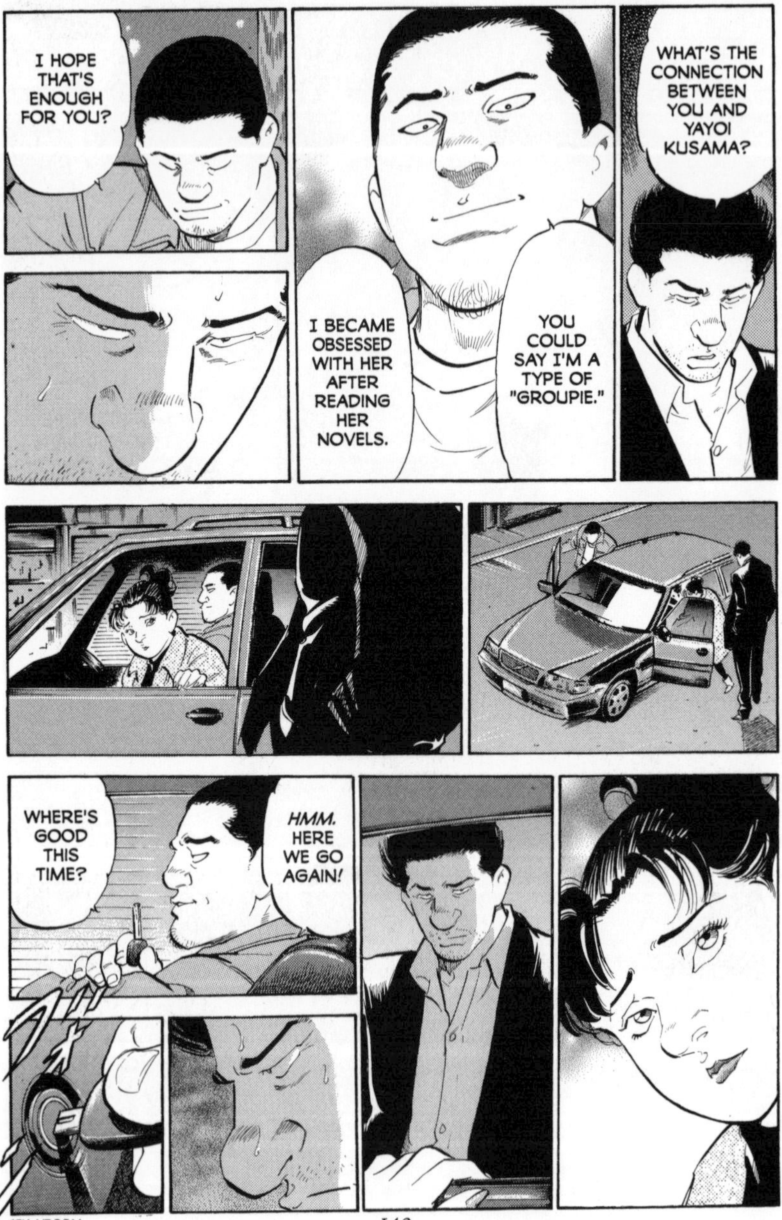
WHAT'S THE CONNECTION BETWEEN YOU AND YAYOI KUSAMA?
YOU COULD SAY I'M A TYPE OF "GROUPIE."
I BECAME OBSESSED WITH HER AFTER READING HER NOVELS.
I HOPE THAT'S ENOUGH FOR YOU?
HMM. HERE WE GO AGAIN!
WHERE'S GOOD THIS TIME?

*FX: VROOM

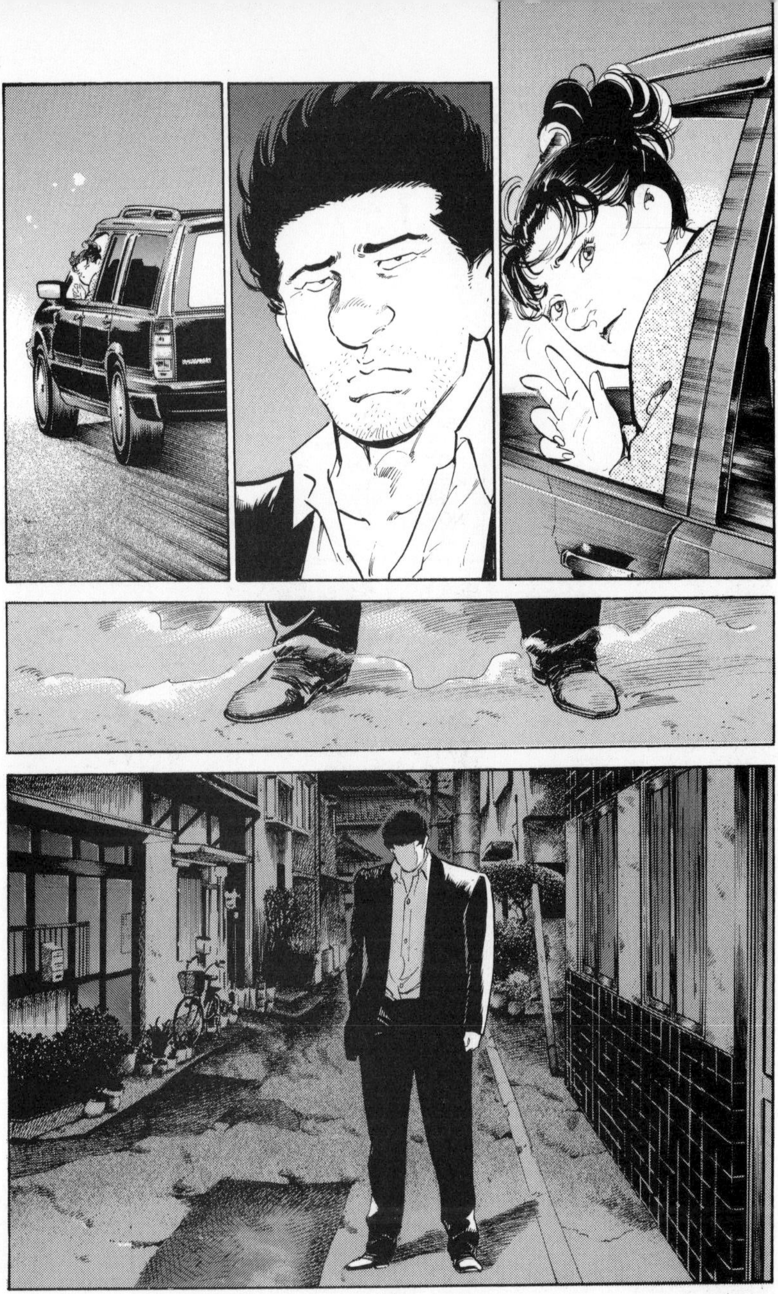

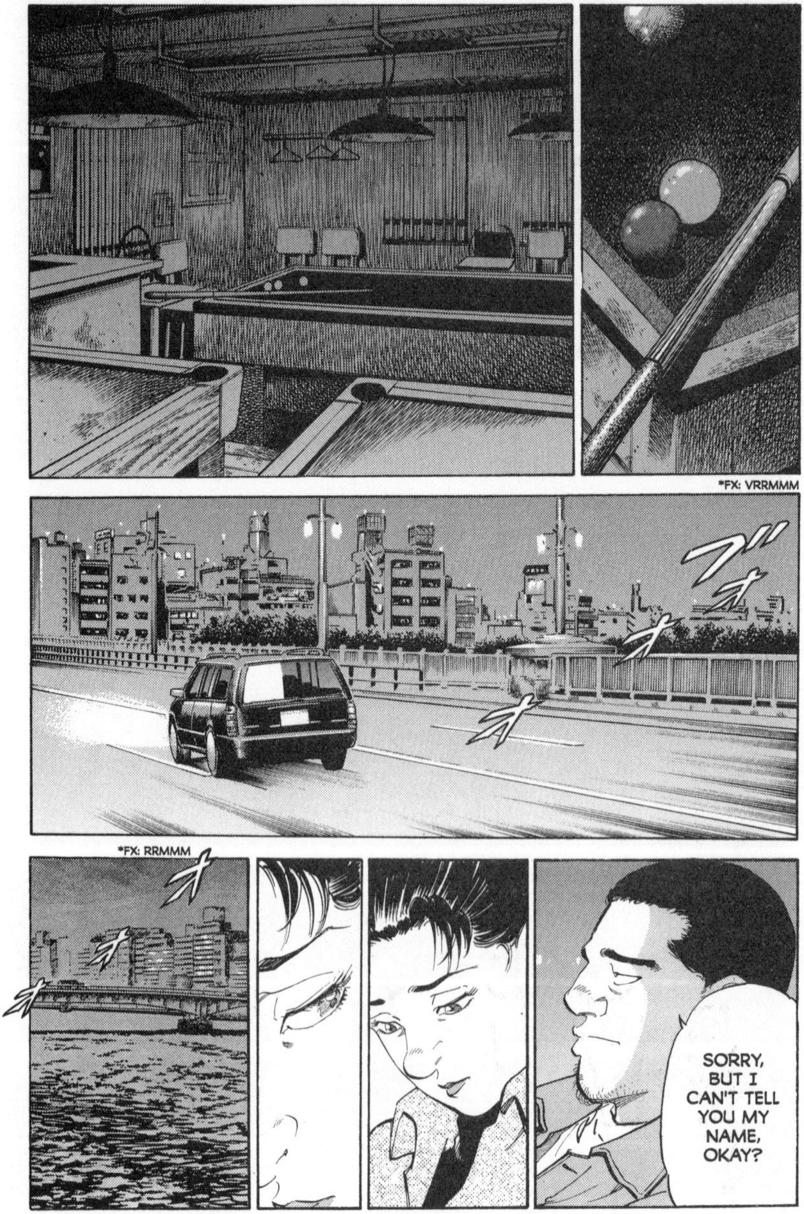
*FX: VRRMMM
ブォォォ
SORRY, BUT I CAN'T TELL YOU MY NAME, OKAY?
*FX: RRMMM
ォォォ

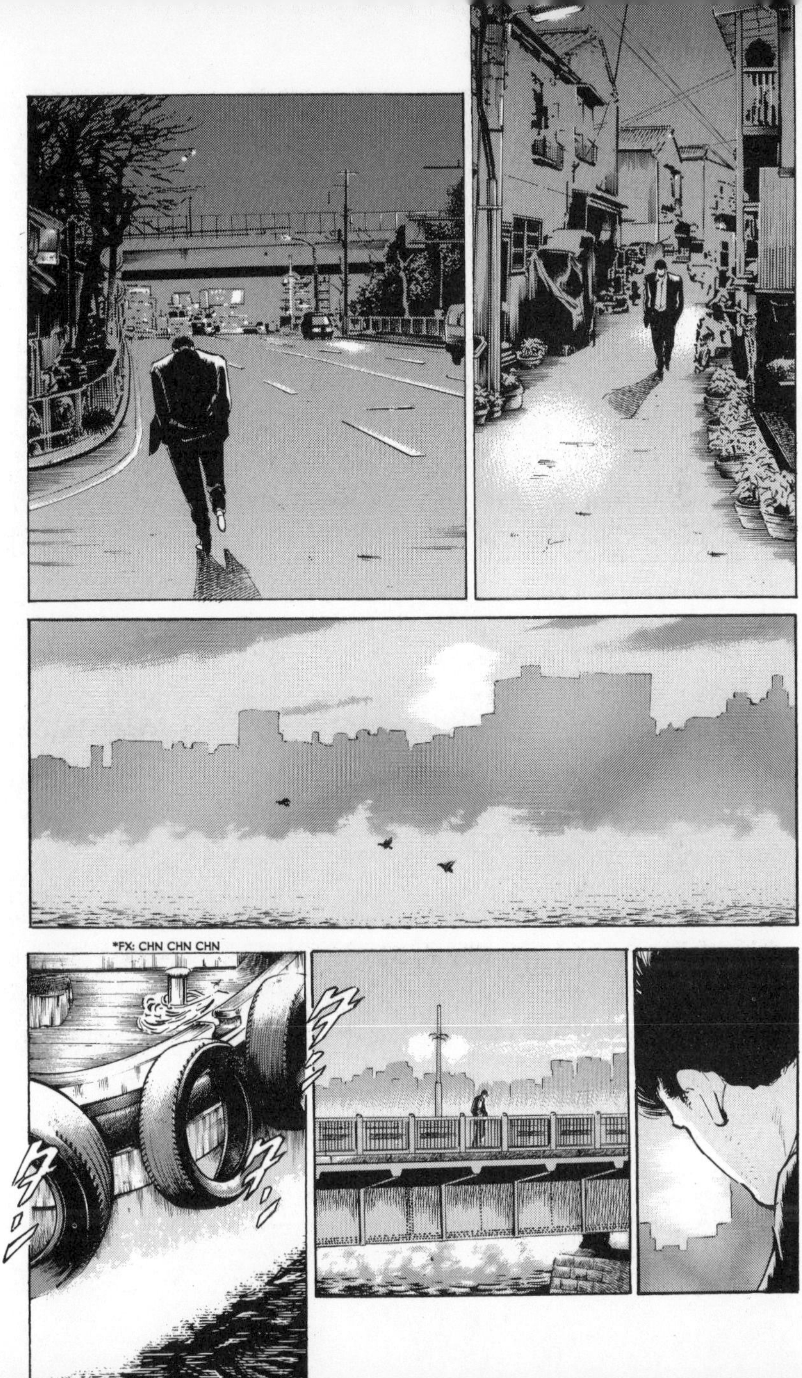
*FX: CHN CHN CHN

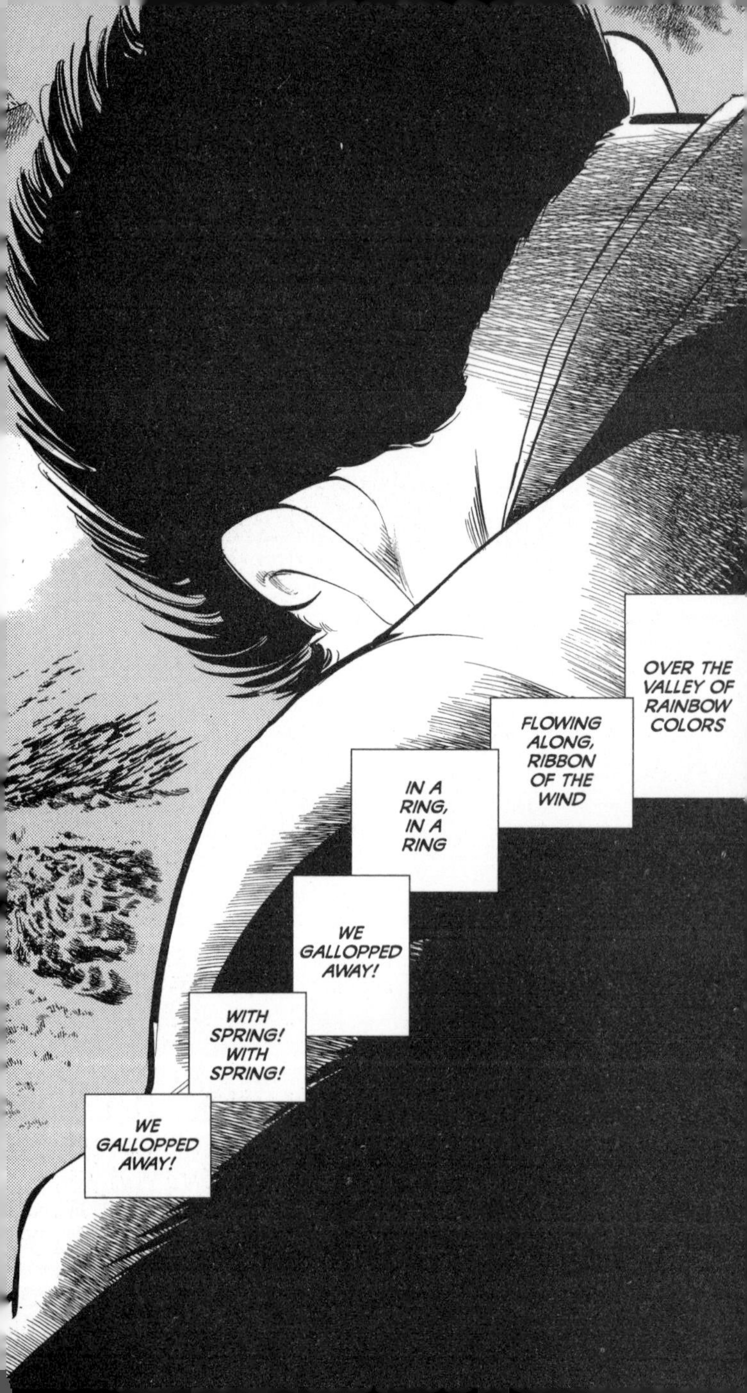

OVER THE VALLEY OF RAINBOW COLORS
FLOWING ALONG, RIBBON OF THE WIND
IN A RING, IN A RING
WE GALLOPPED AWAY!
WITH SPRING! WITH SPRING!
WE GALLOPPED AWAY!

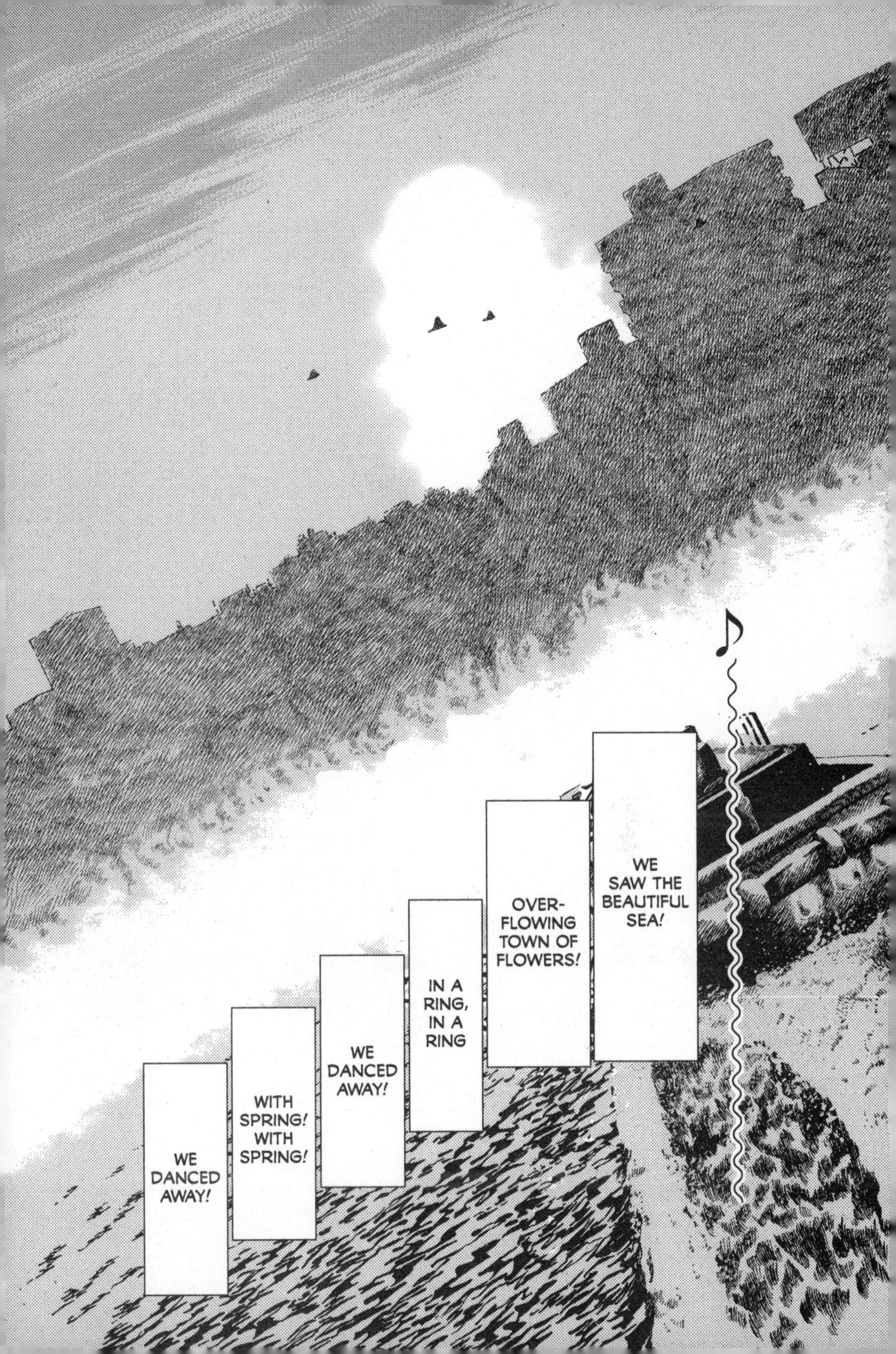
WE SAW THE BEAUTIFUL SEA!
OVER-FLOWING TOWN OF FLOWERS!
IN A RING, IN A RING
WE DANCED AWAY!
WITH SPRING! WITH SPRING!
WE DANCED AWAY!

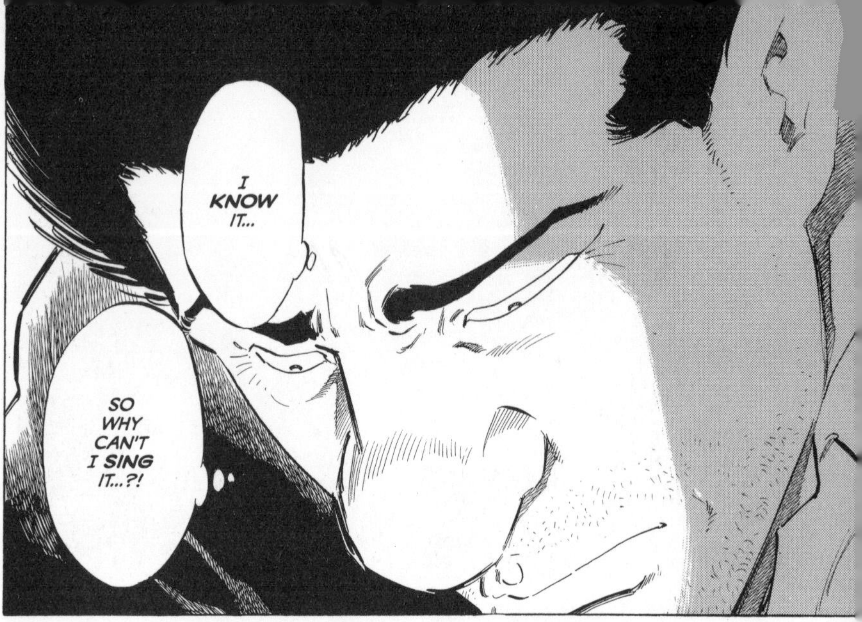
I KNOW IT...
SO WHY CAN'T I SING IT...?!
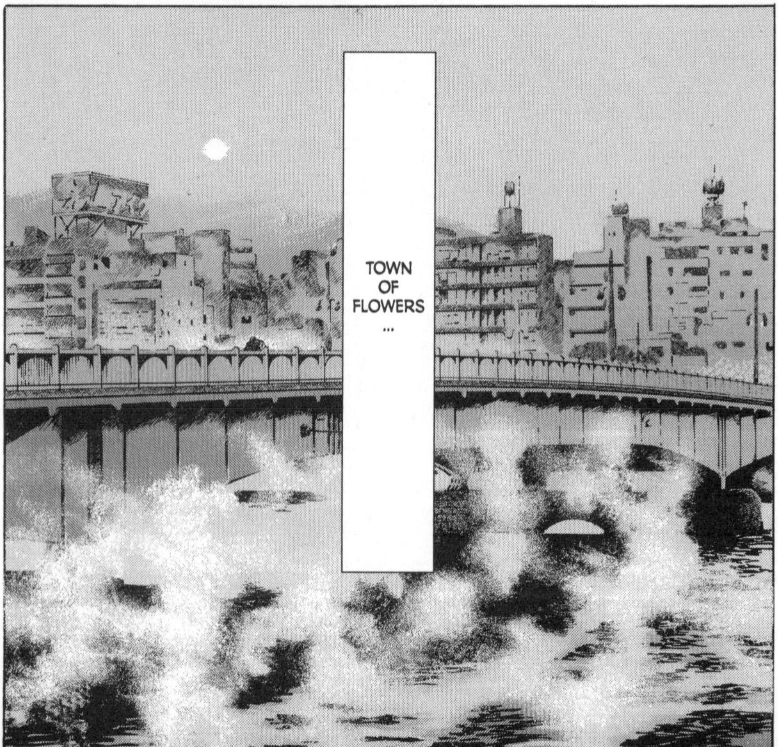
TOWN OF FLOWERS ...

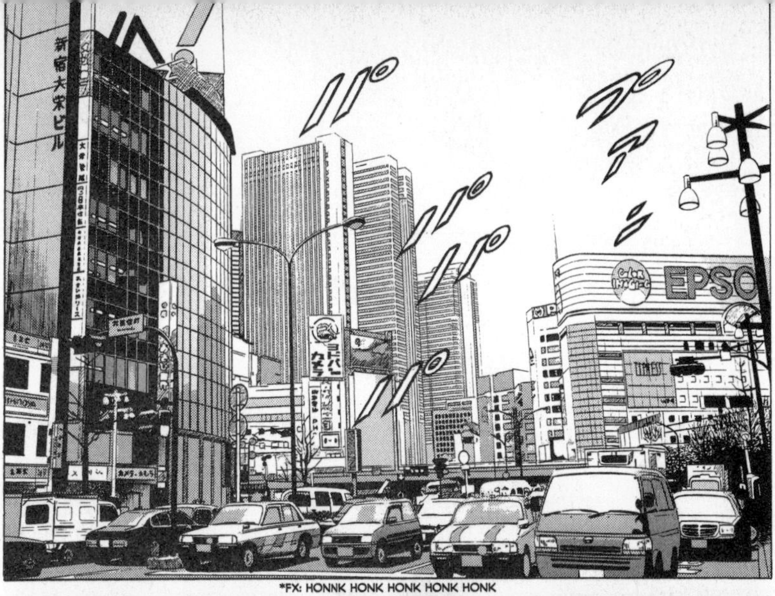
新宿大宋ビル
EPSO

*FX: HONNK HONK HONK HONK HONK

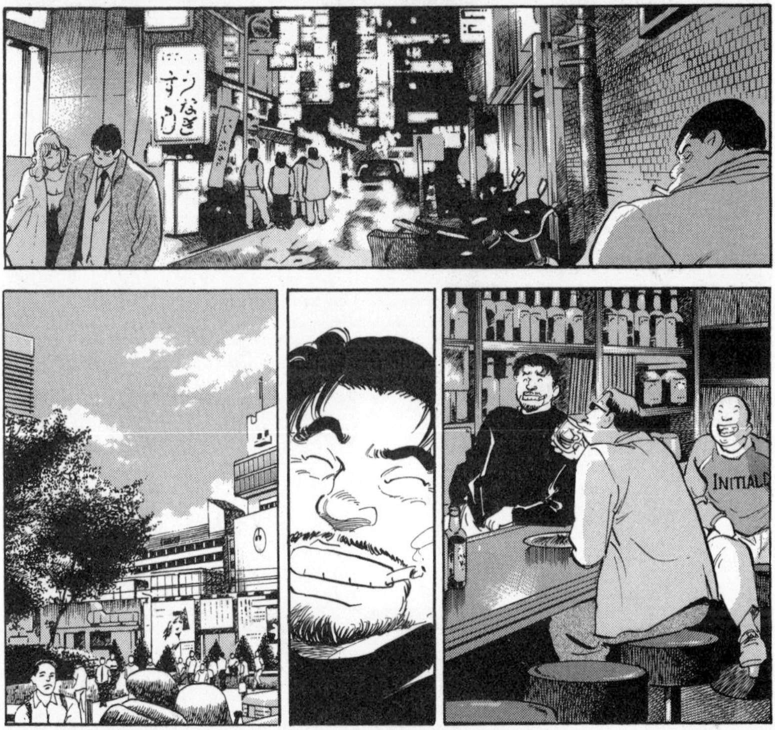
INITIAL D

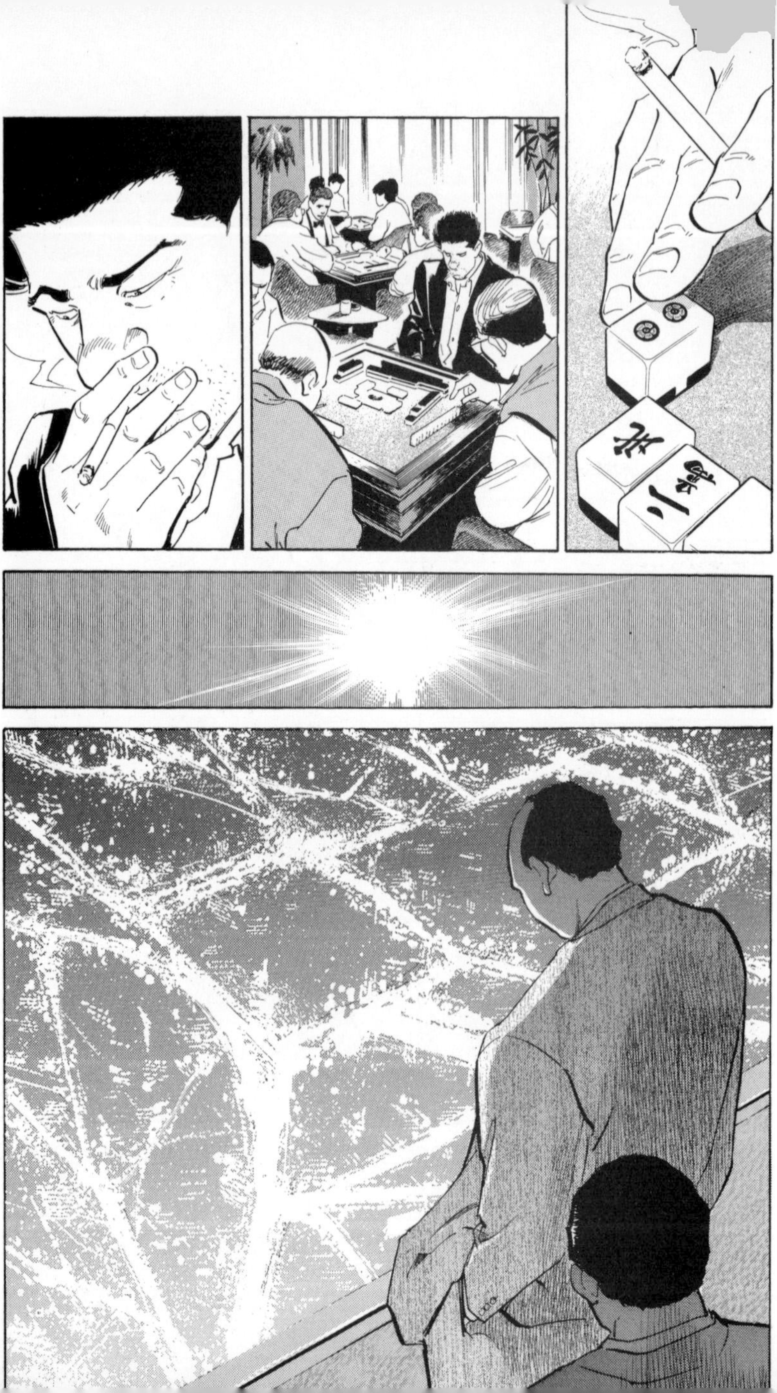

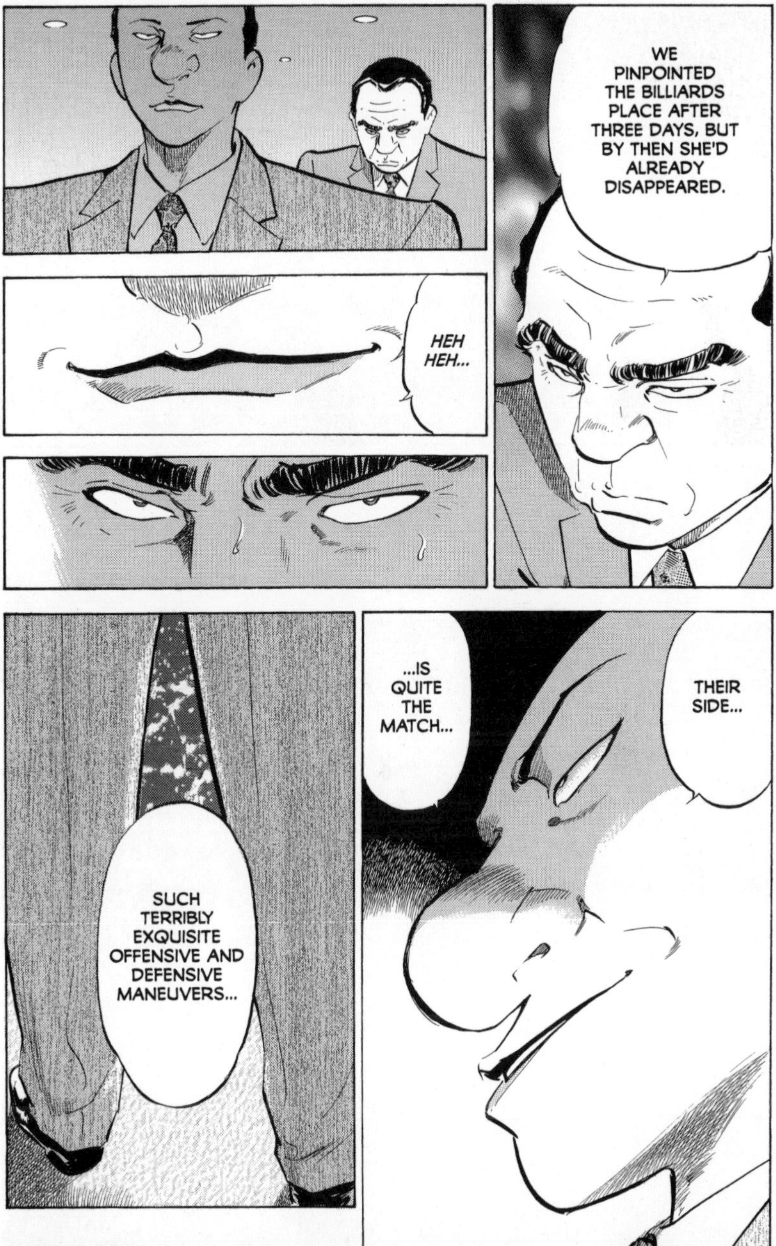
WE PINPOINTED THE BILLIARDS PLACE AFTER THREE DAYS, BUT BY THEN SHE'D ALREADY DISAPPEARED.
HEH HEH...
THEIR SIDE...
...IS QUITE THE MATCH...
SUCH TERRIBLY EXQUISITE OFFENSIVE AND DEFENSIVE MANEUVERS...

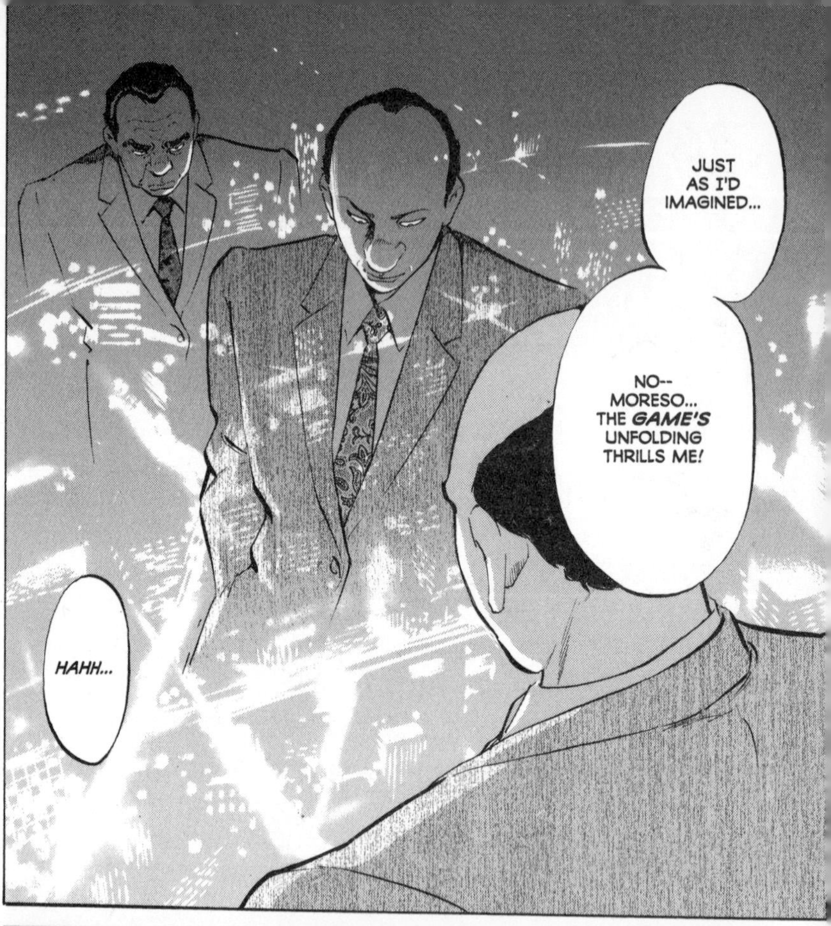
JUST AS I'D IMAGINED...
NO-- MORESO... THE *GAME'S* UNFOLDING THRILLS ME!
HAHH...

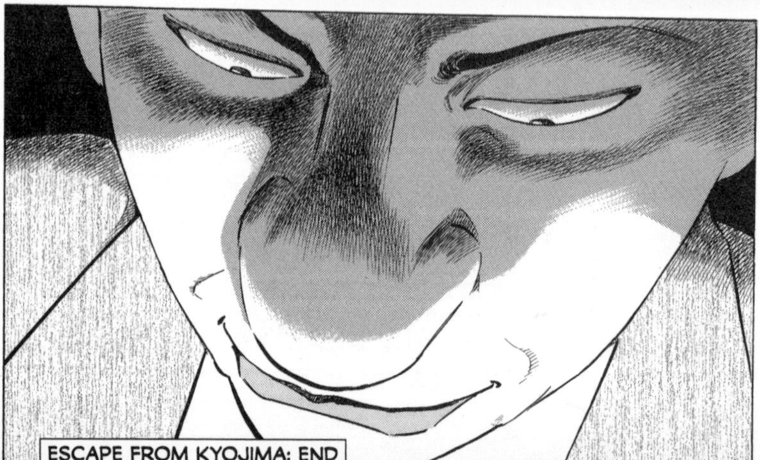
ESCAPE FROM KYOJIMA: END

第67話◉コンタクト

CHAPTER 67
CONTACT

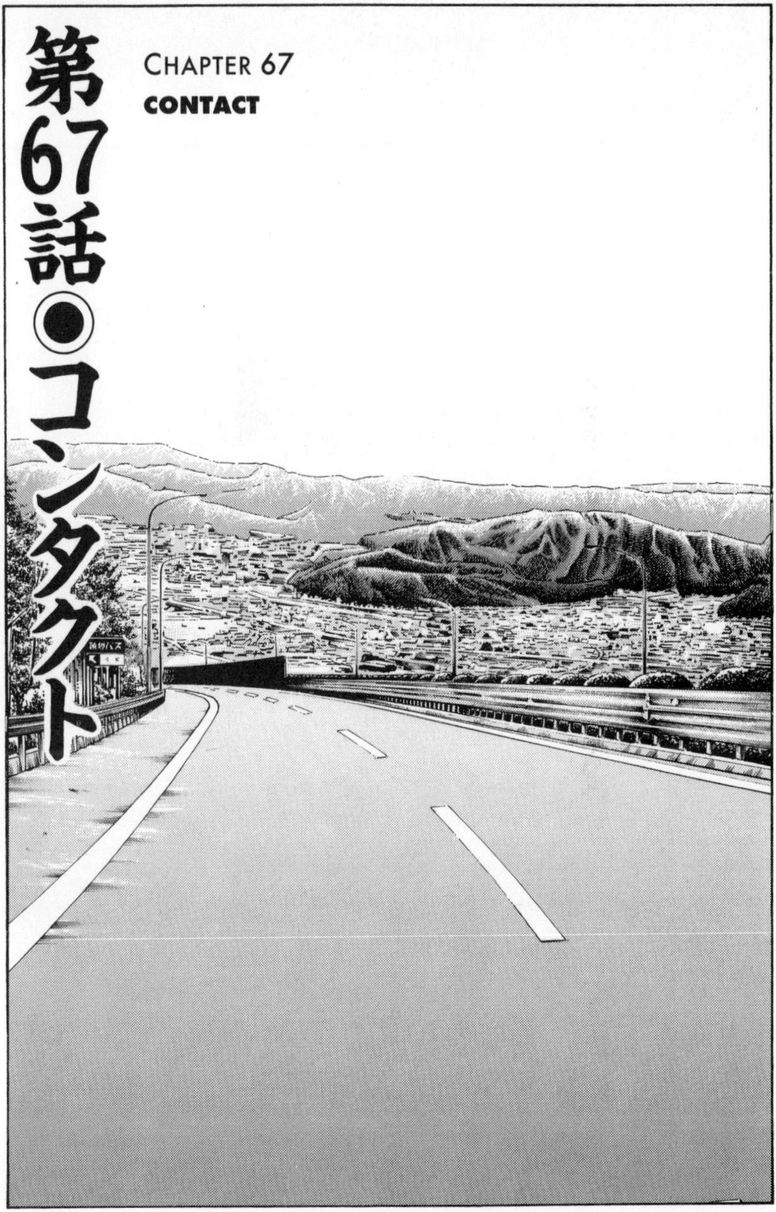

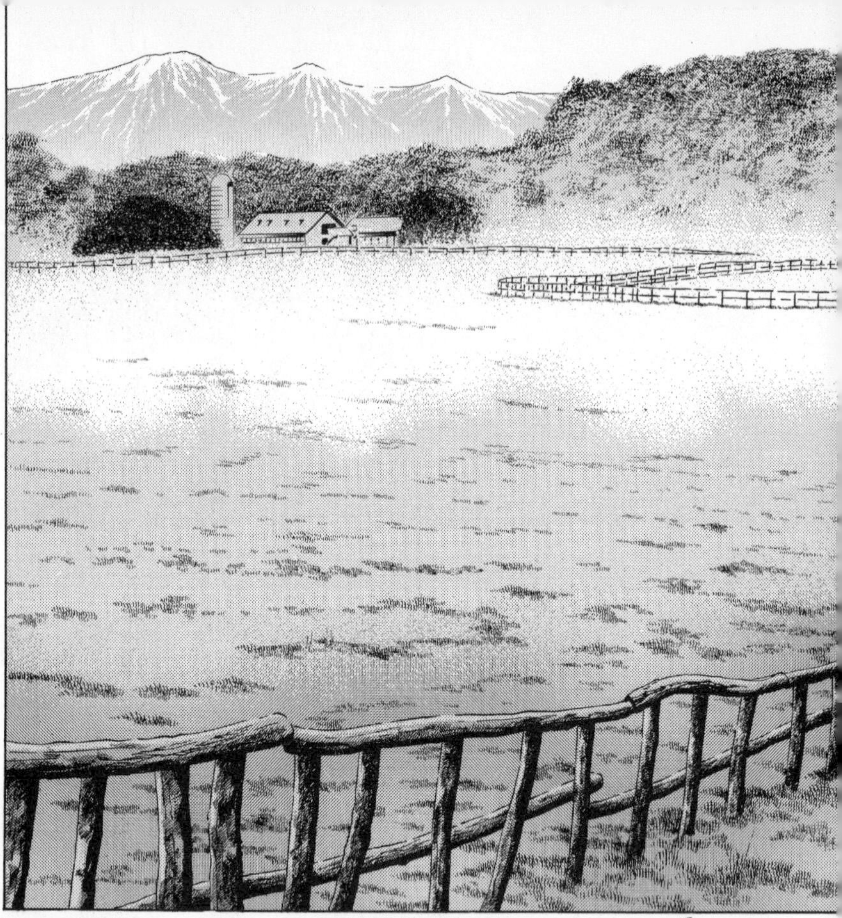

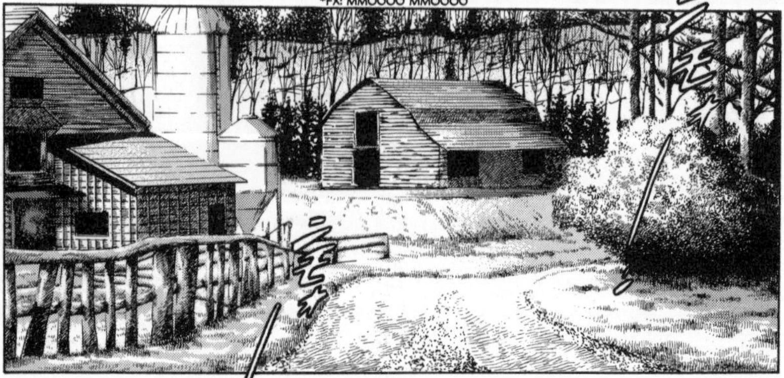
*FX: MMOOOO MMOOOO

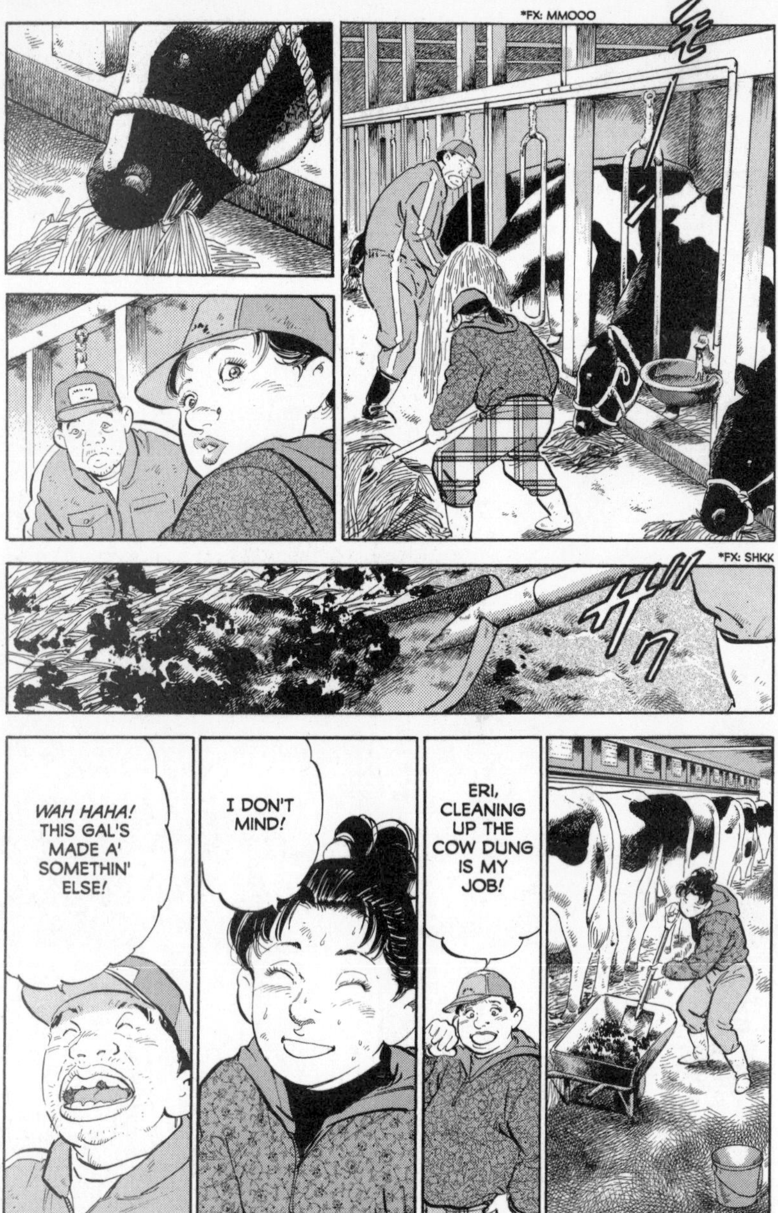
*FX: MMOOO
*FX: SHKK
ERI, CLEANING UP THE COW DUNG IS MY JOB!
I DON'T MIND!
WAH HAHA! THIS GAL'S MADE A' SOMETHIN' ELSE!

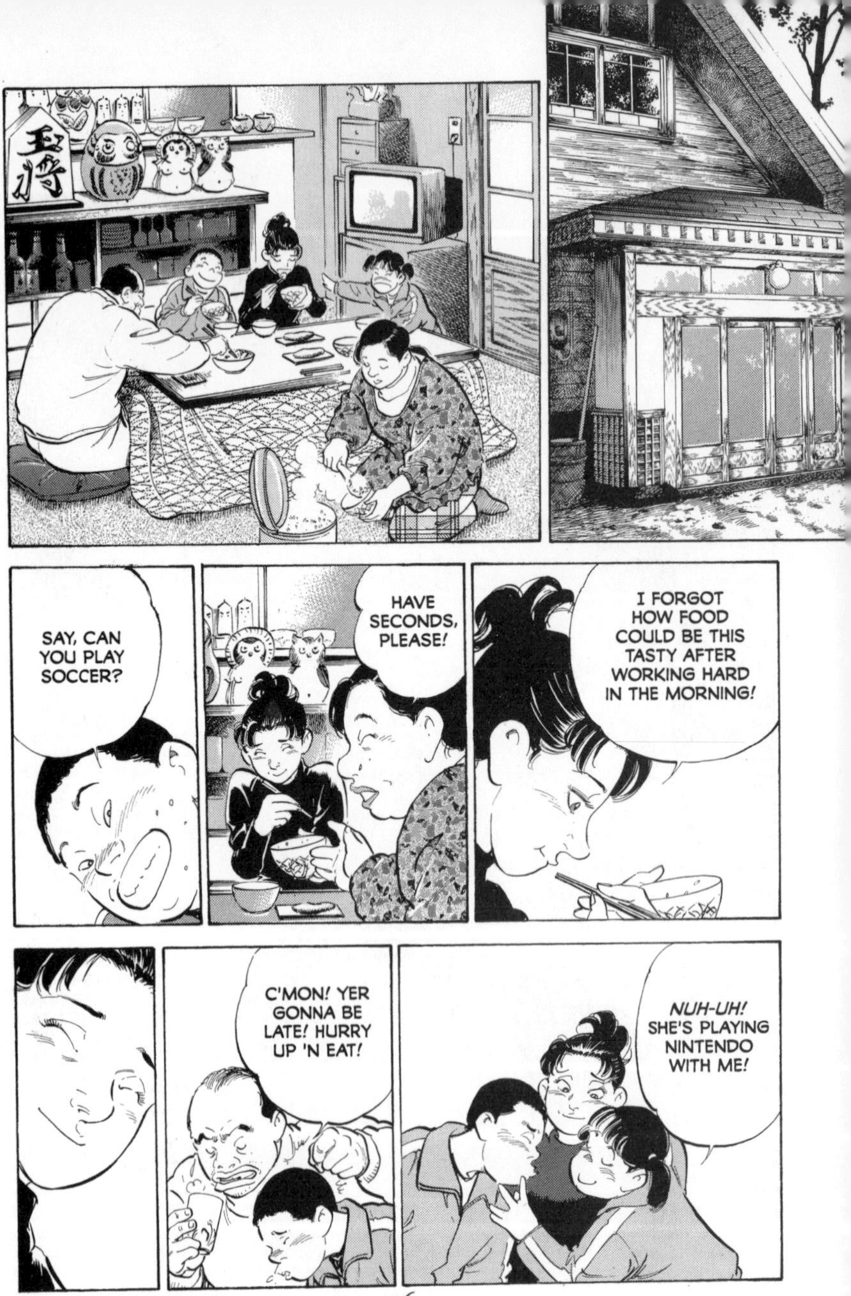
I FORGOT HOW FOOD COULD BE THIS TASTY AFTER WORKING HARD IN THE MORNING!
HAVE SECONDS, PLEASE!
SAY, CAN YOU PLAY SOCCER?
NUH-UH! SHE'S PLAYING NINTENDO WITH ME!
C'MON! YER GONNA BE LATE! HURRY UP 'N EAT!

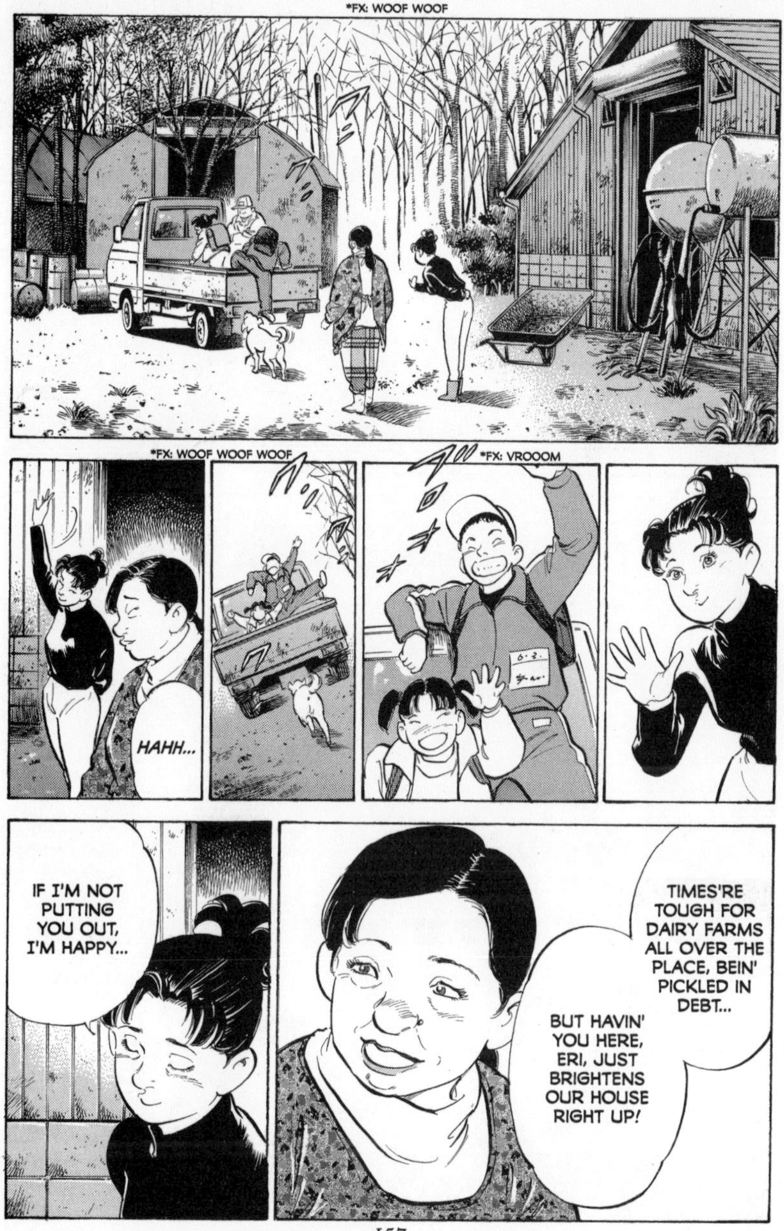
*FX: WOOF WOOF
*FX: VROOOM
*FX: WOOF WOOF WOOF
HAHH...
TIMES'RE TOUGH FOR DAIRY FARMS ALL OVER THE PLACE, BEIN' PICKLED IN DEBT...
BUT HAVIN' YOU HERE, ERI, JUST BRIGHTENS OUR HOUSE RIGHT UP!
IF I'M NOT PUTTING YOU OUT, I'M HAPPY...

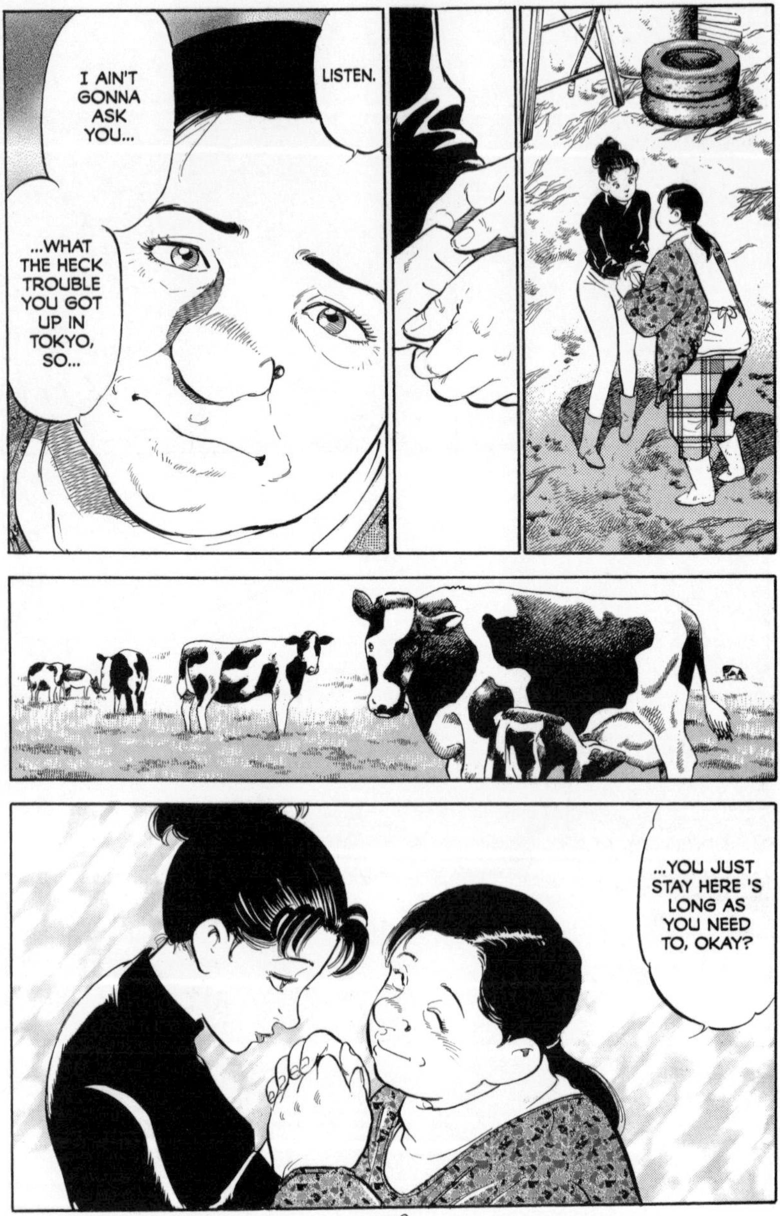
LISTEN.
I AIN'T GONNA ASK YOU...
...WHAT THE HECK TROUBLE YOU GOT UP IN TOKYO, SO...
...YOU JUST STAY HERE 'S LONG AS YOU NEED TO, OKAY?

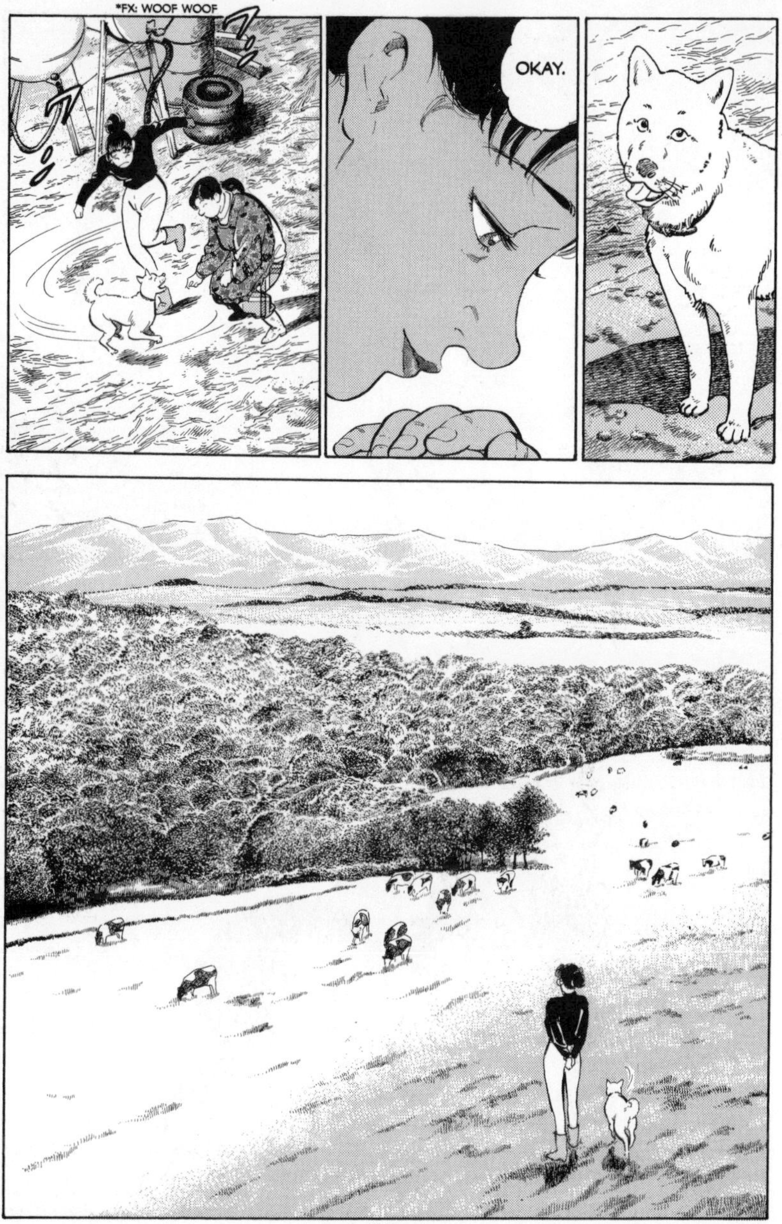
OKAY.
*FX: WOOF WOOF

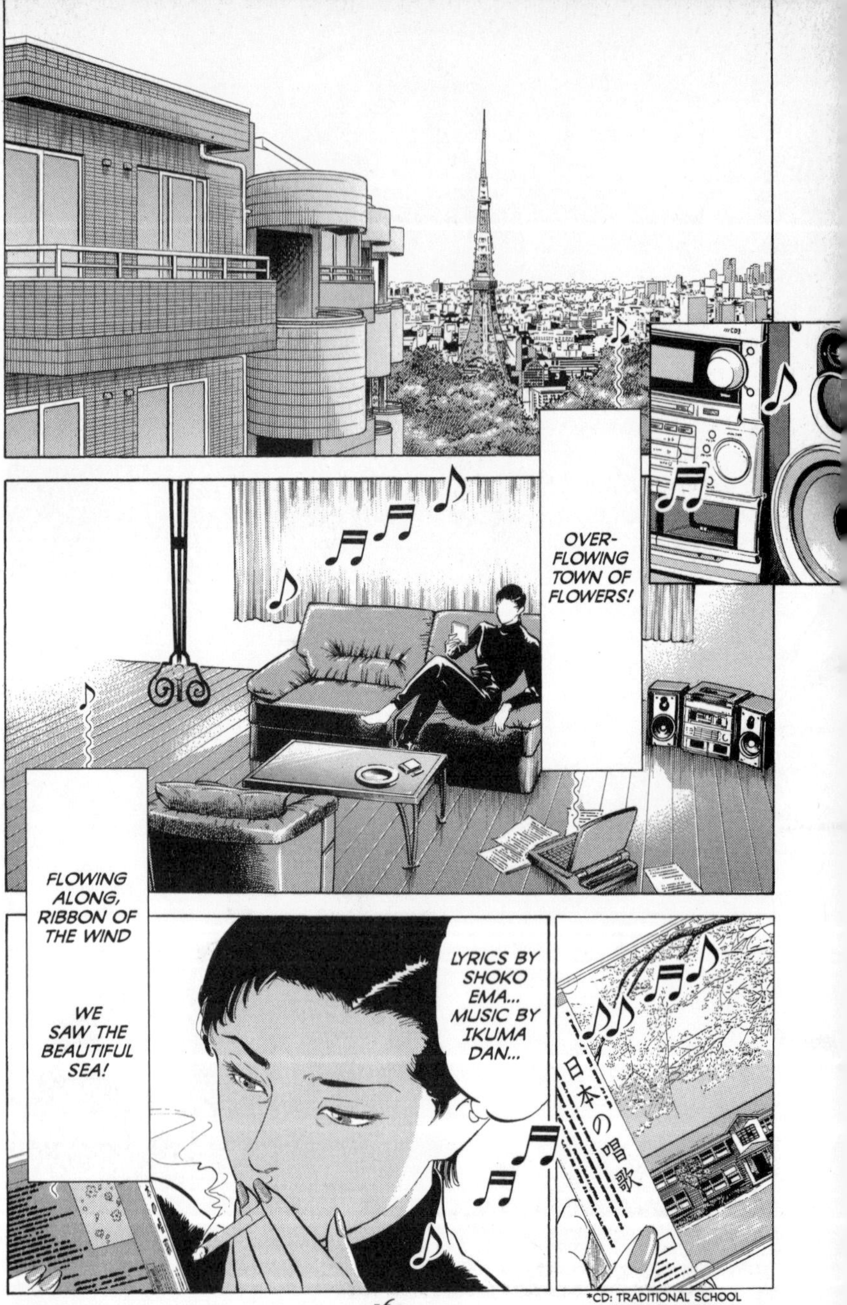
OVER-FLOWING TOWN OF FLOWERS!
FLOWING ALONG, RIBBON OF THE WIND
WE SAW THE BEAUTIFUL SEA!
日本の唱歌
LYRICS BY SHOKO EMA... MUSIC BY IKUMA DAN...

*CD: TRADITIONAL SCHOOL SONGS OF JAPAN

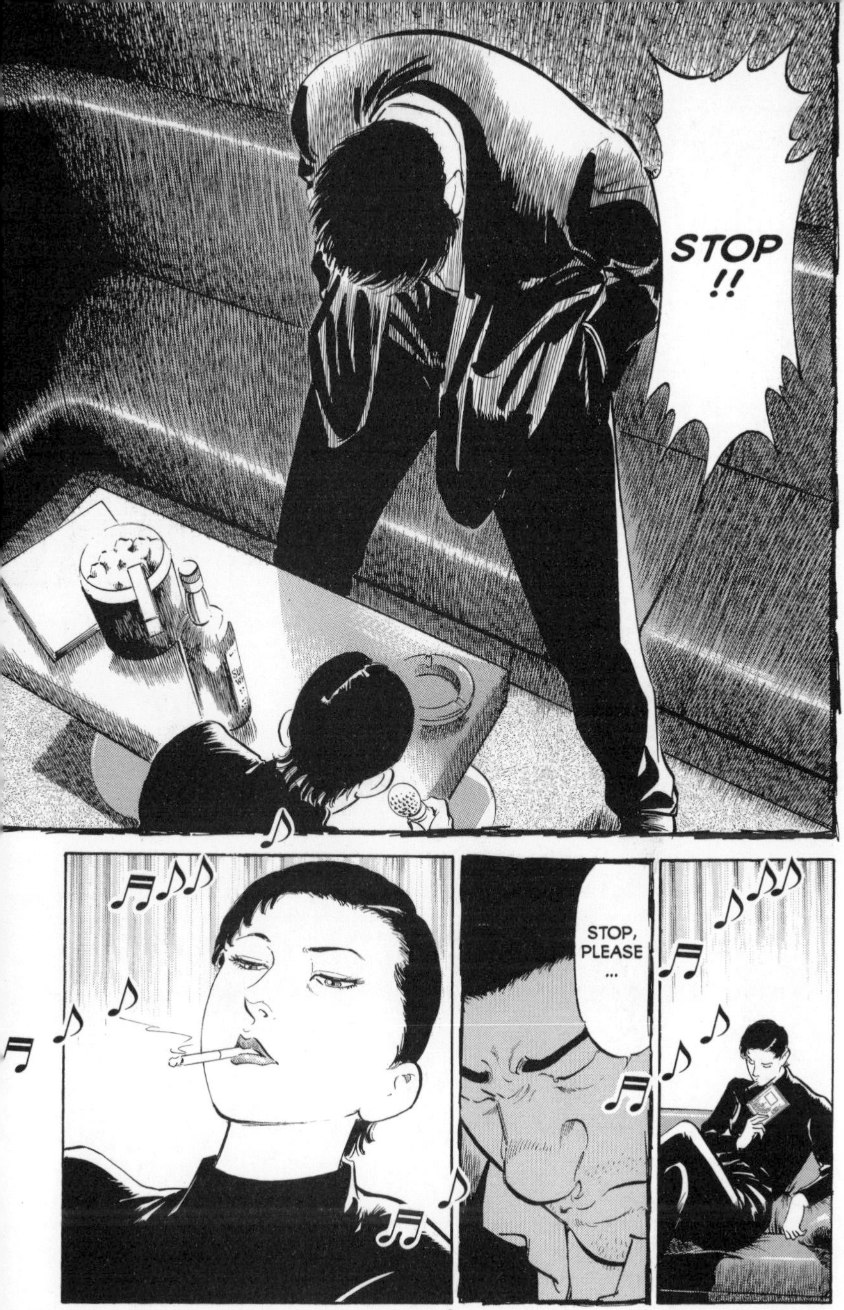
STOP !!
STOP, PLEASE ...

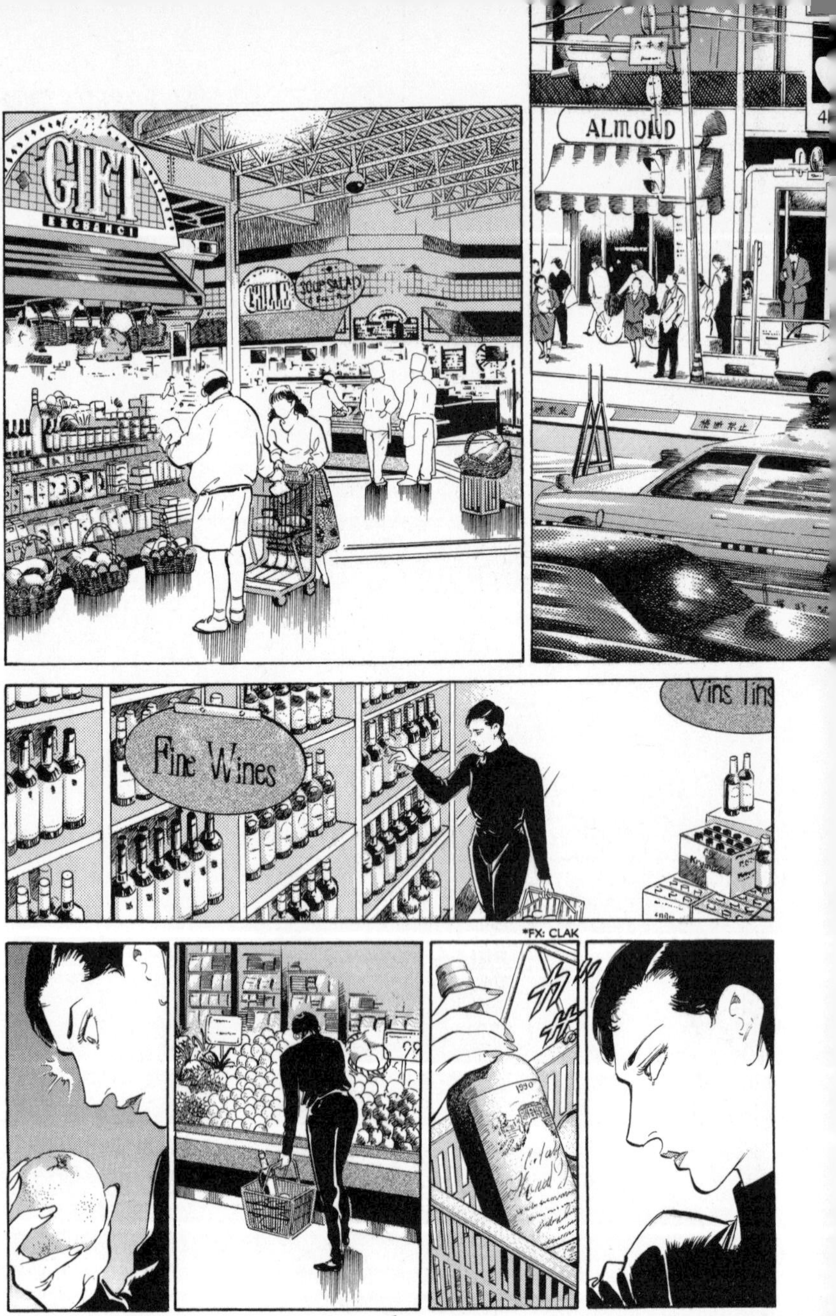
ALMOND
GIFT
GRILLE
SOUP SALAD
Fine Wines
*FX: CLAK

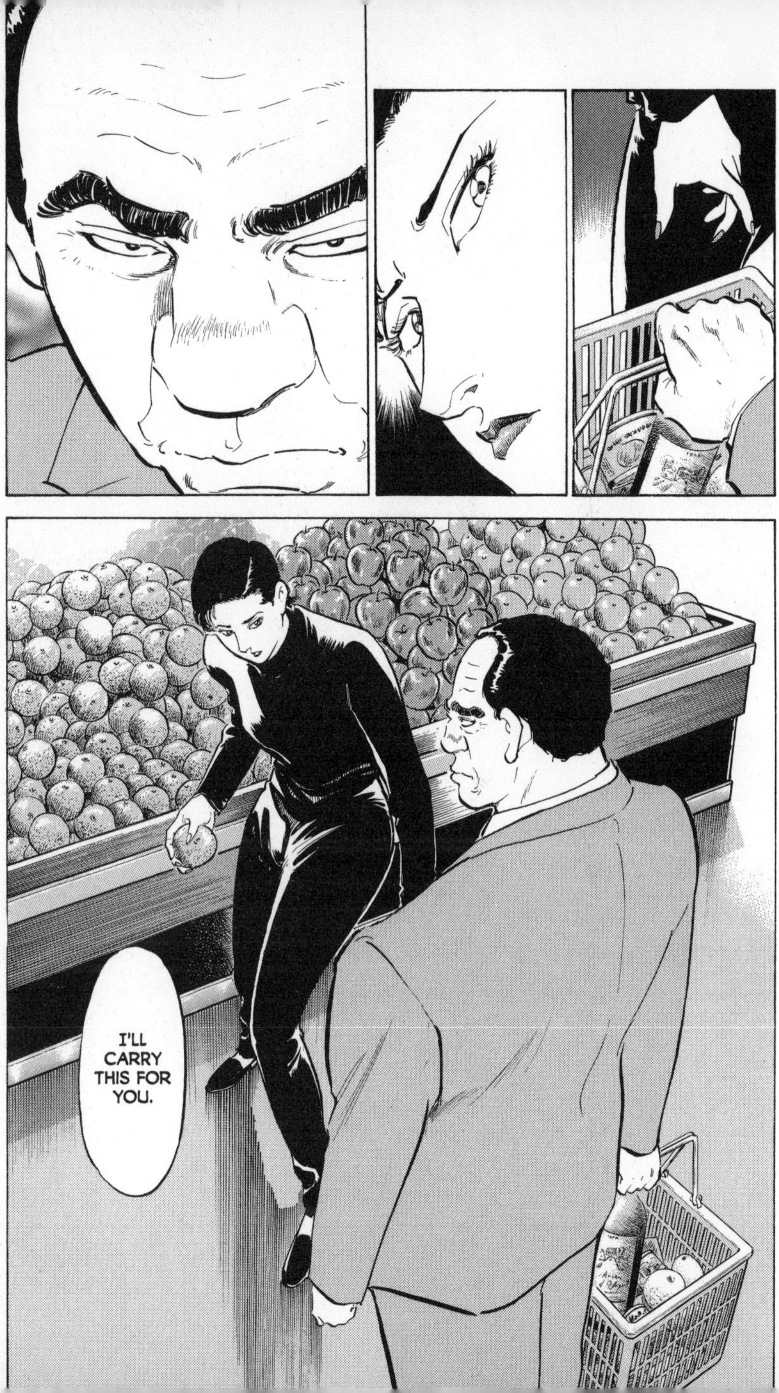
I'LL CARRY THIS FOR YOU.

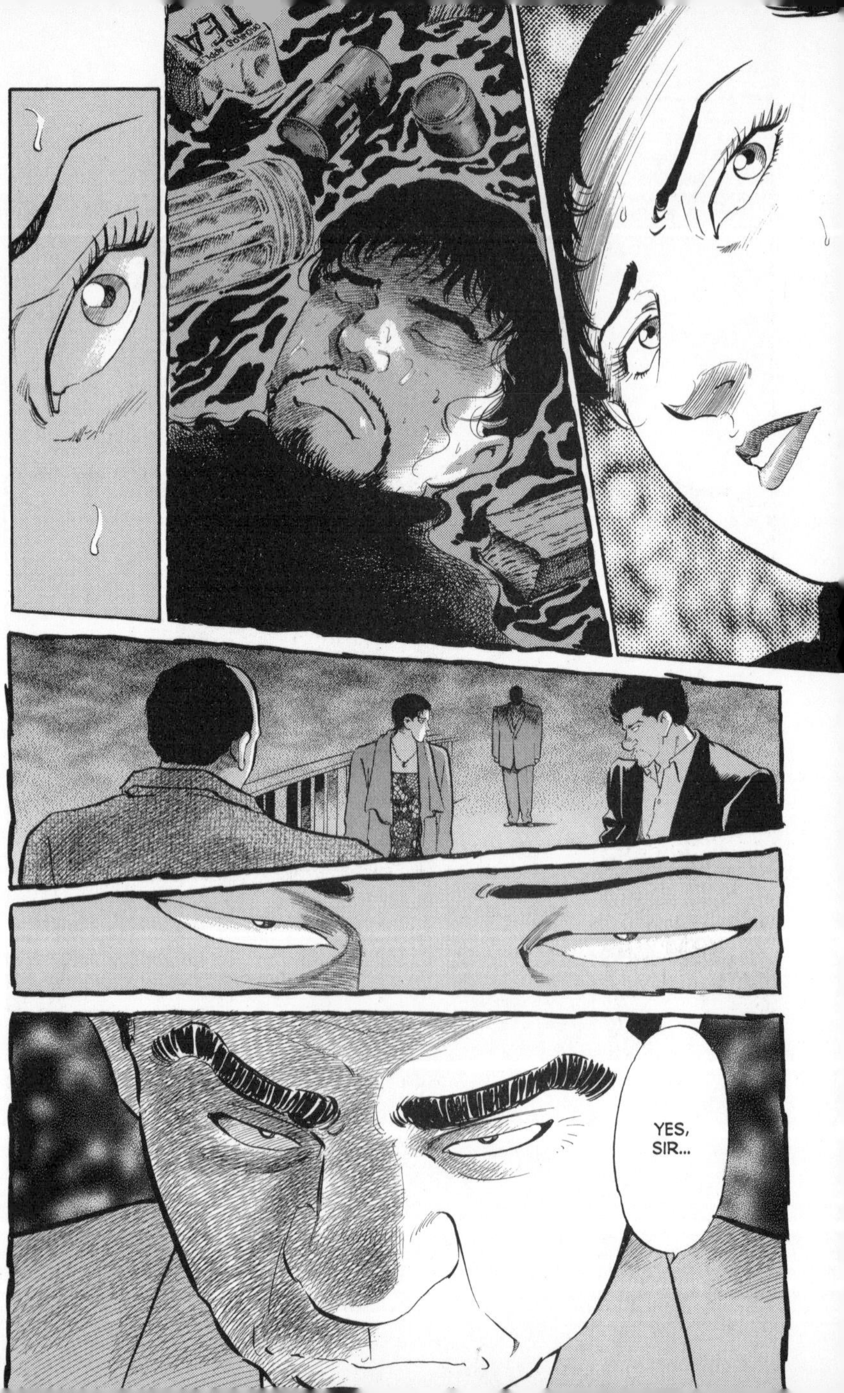
YES, SIR...

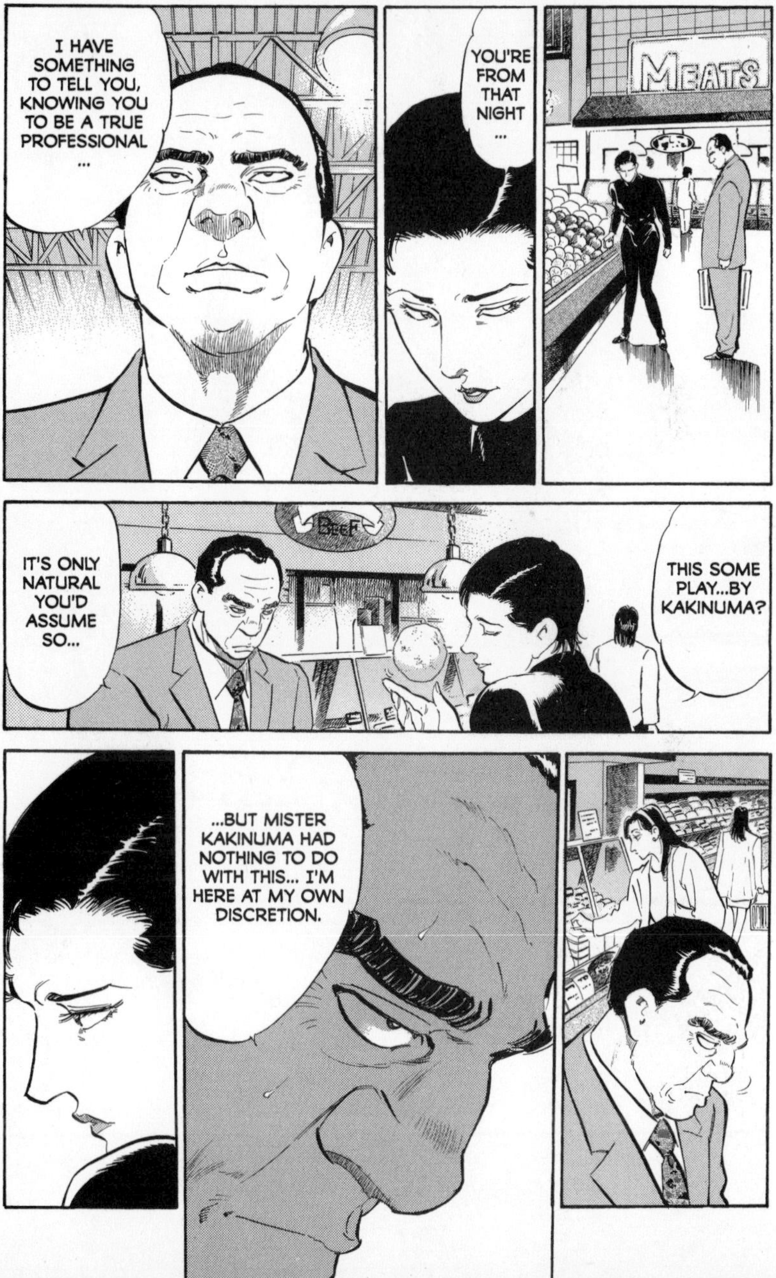
MEATS
YOU'RE FROM THAT NIGHT ...
I HAVE SOMETHING TO TELL YOU, KNOWING YOU TO BE A TRUE PROFESSIONAL ...
THIS SOME PLAY...BY KAKINUMA?
BEEF
IT'S ONLY NATURAL YOU'D ASSUME SO...
...BUT MISTER KAKINUMA HAD NOTHING TO DO WITH THIS... I'M HERE AT MY OWN DISCRETION.

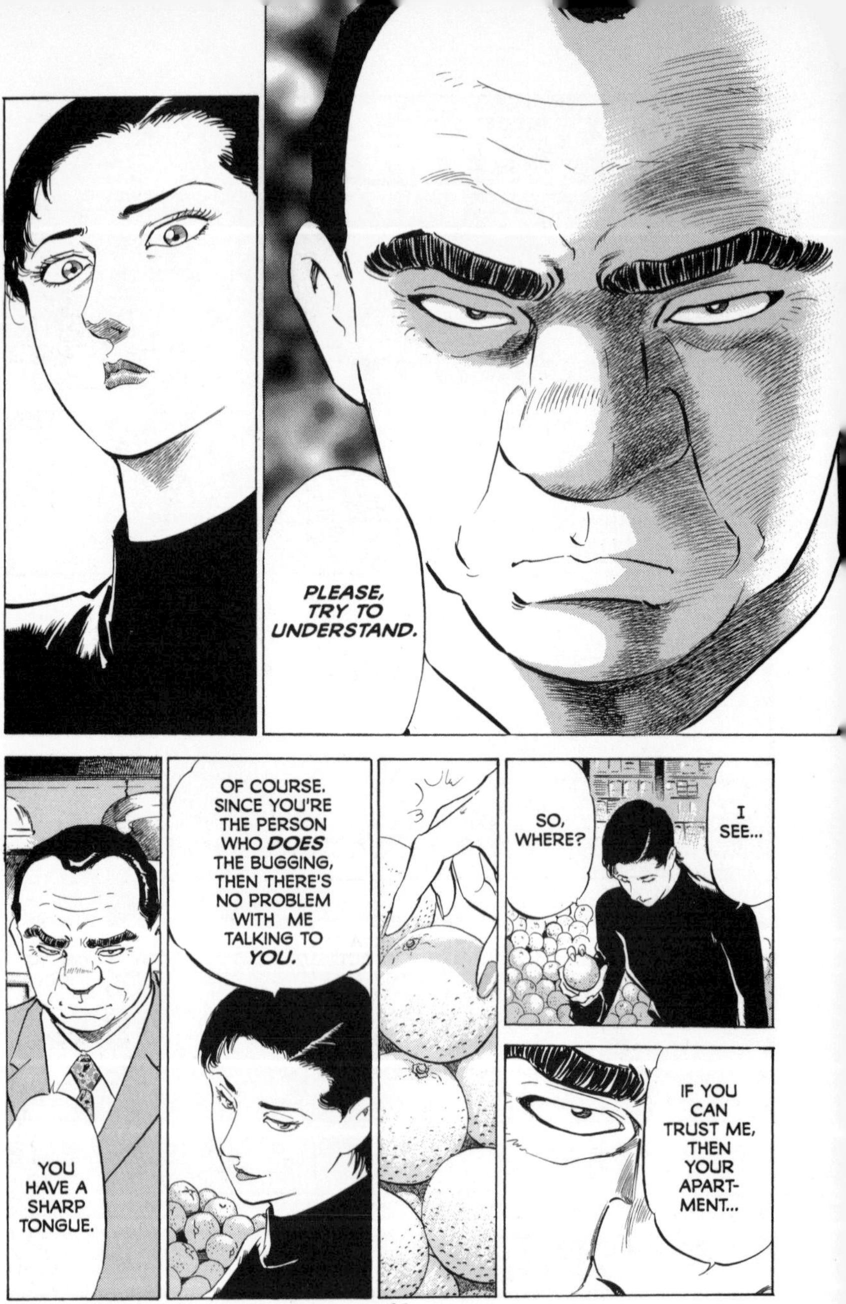
PLEASE, TRY TO UNDERSTAND.
I SEE...
SO, WHERE?
IF YOU CAN TRUST ME, THEN YOUR APARTMENT...
OF COURSE. SINCE YOU'RE THE PERSON WHO *DOES* THE BUGGING, THEN THERE'S NO PROBLEM WITH ME TALKING TO *YOU*.
YOU HAVE A SHARP TONGUE.

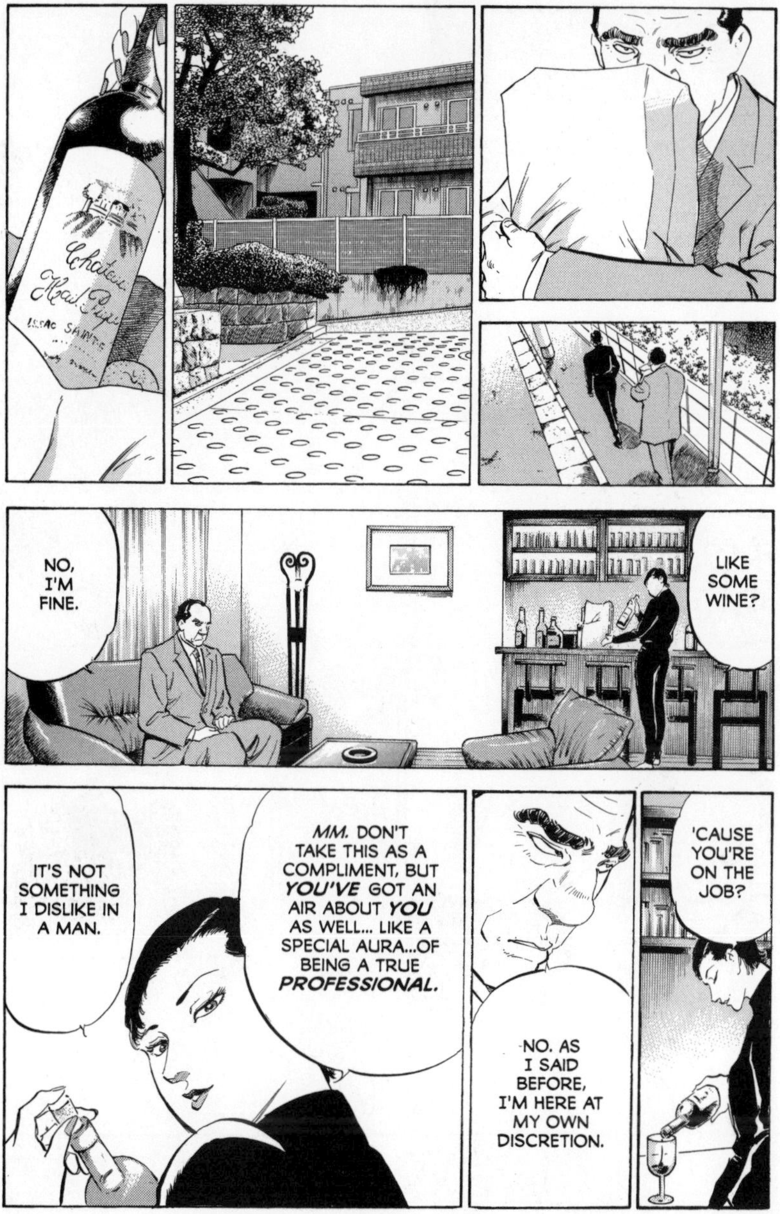
LIKE SOME WINE?
NO, I'M FINE.
'CAUSE YOU'RE ON THE JOB?
NO. AS I SAID BEFORE, I'M HERE AT MY OWN DISCRETION.
MM. DON'T TAKE THIS AS A COMPLIMENT, BUT ***YOU'VE*** GOT AN AIR ABOUT ***YOU*** AS WELL... LIKE A SPECIAL AURA...OF BEING A TRUE ***PROFESSIONAL.***
IT'S NOT SOMETHING I DISLIKE IN A MAN.

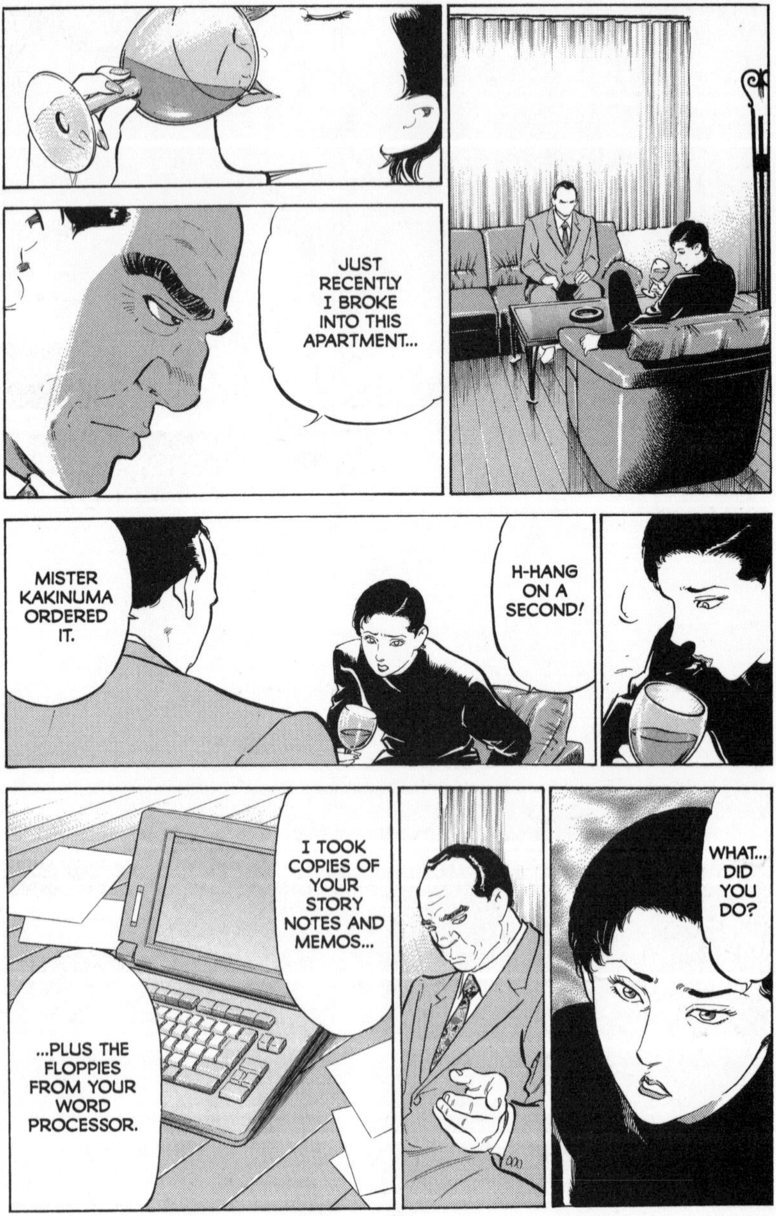
JUST RECENTLY I BROKE INTO THIS APARTMENT...
H-HANG ON A SECOND!
MISTER KAKINUMA ORDERED IT.
WHAT... DID YOU DO?
I TOOK COPIES OF YOUR STORY NOTES AND MEMOS...
...PLUS THE FLOPPIES FROM YOUR WORD PROCESSOR.

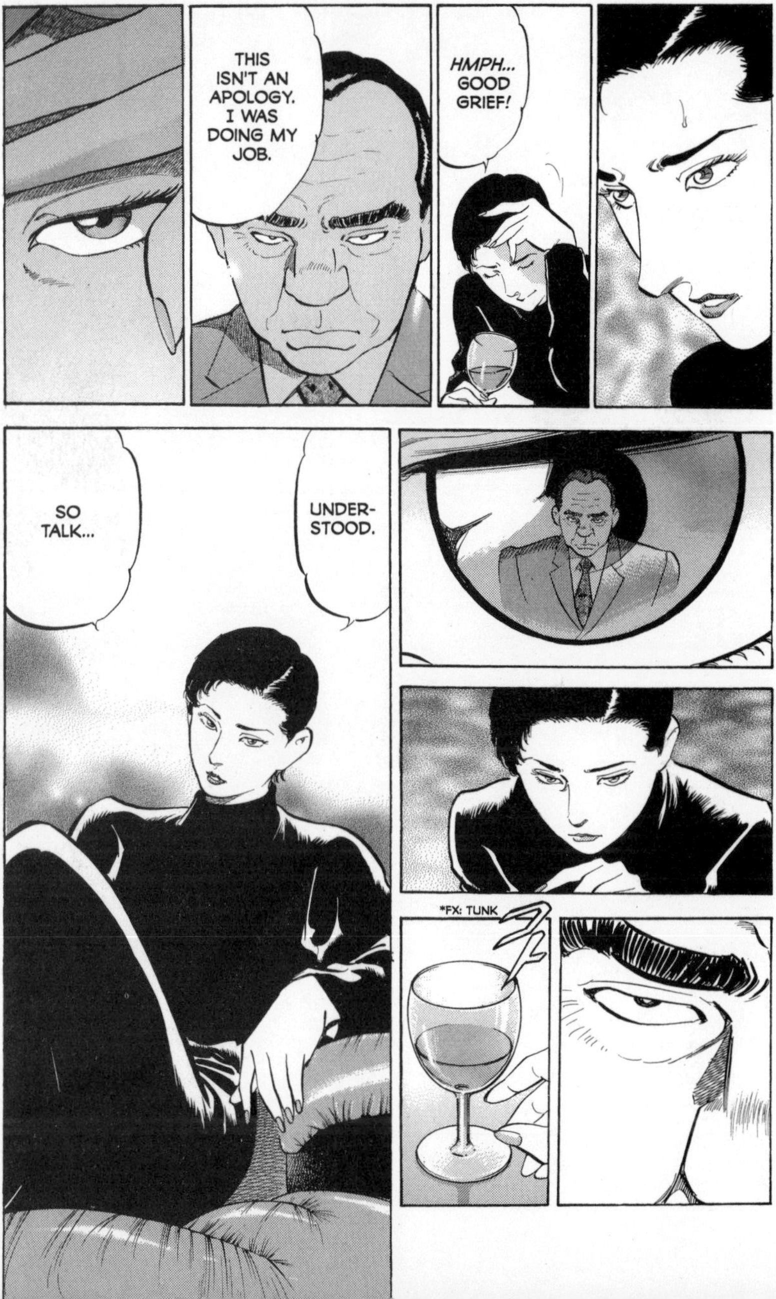
HMPH... GOOD GRIEF!
THIS ISN'T AN APOLOGY. I WAS DOING MY JOB.
*FX: TUNK
UNDER-STOOD.
SO TALK...

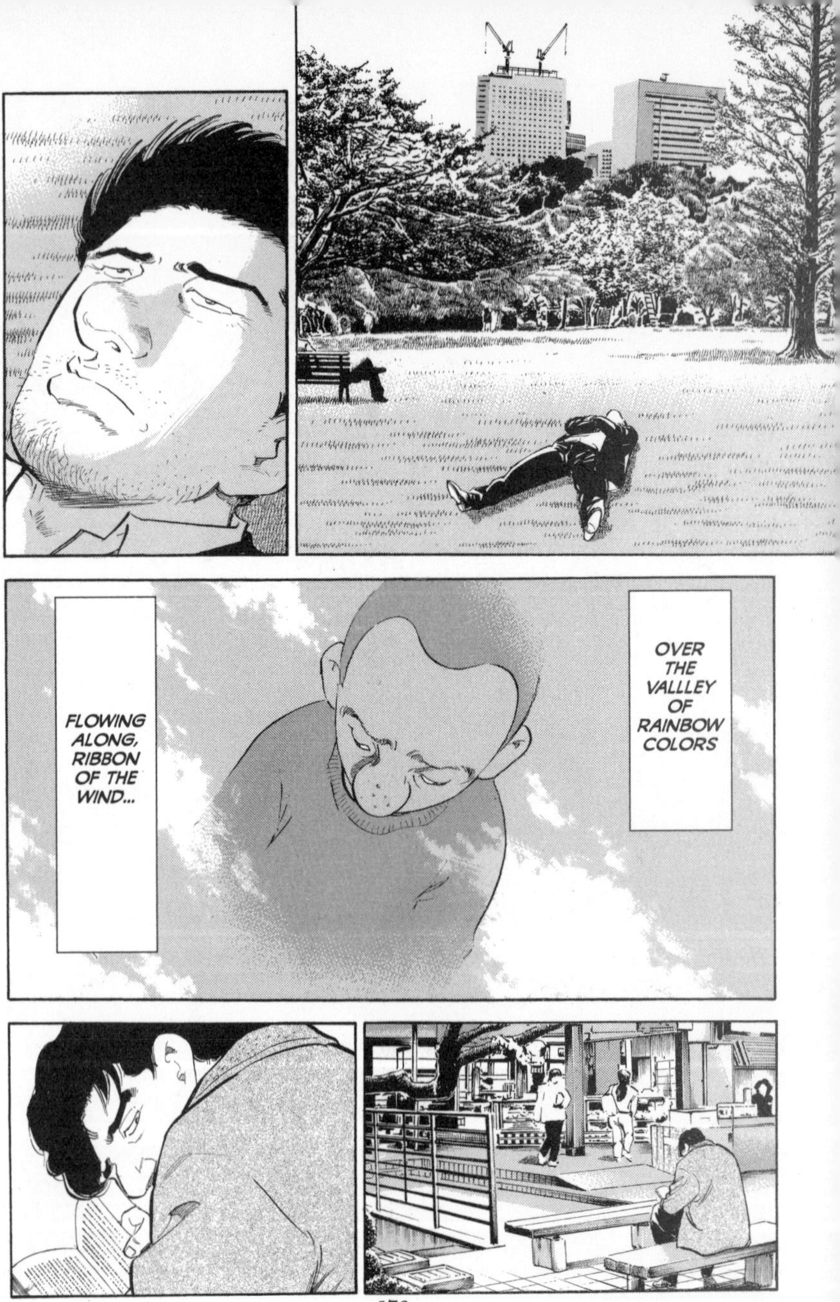
OVER THE VALLLEY OF RAINBOW COLORS
FLOWING ALONG, RIBBON OF THE WIND...

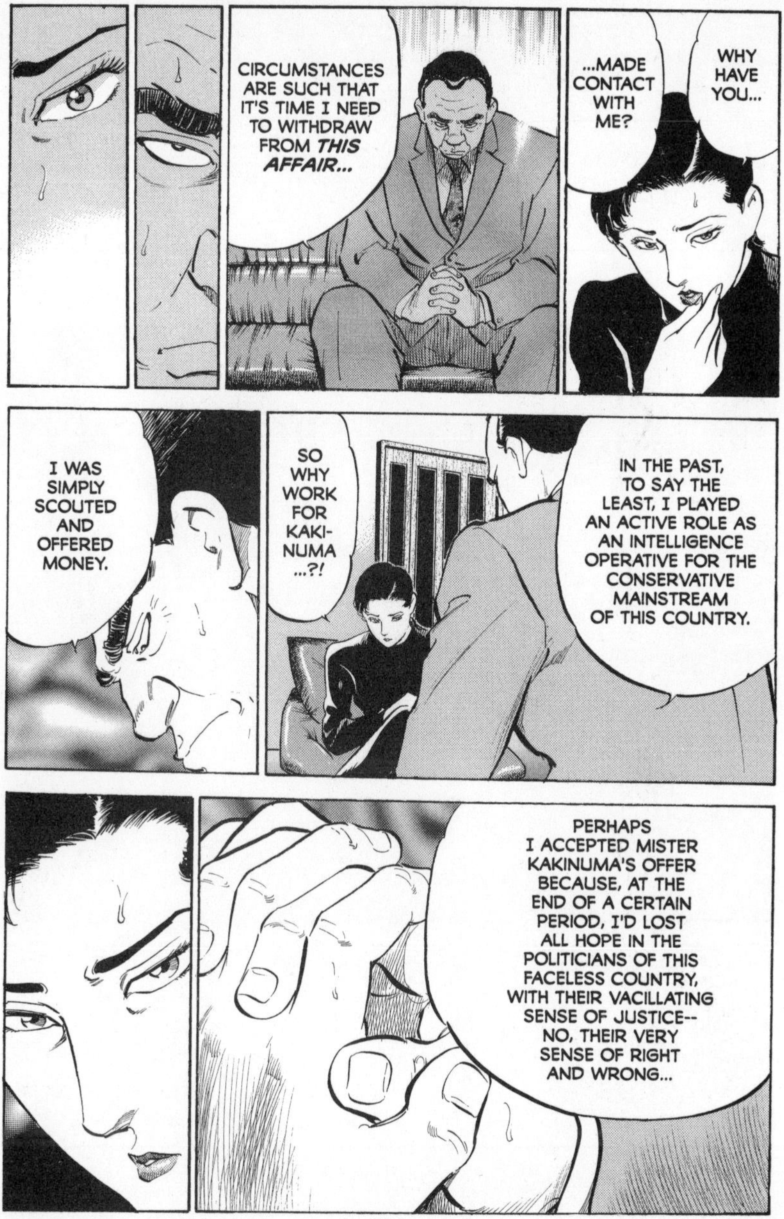
WHY HAVE YOU...
...MADE CONTACT WITH ME?
CIRCUMSTANCES ARE SUCH THAT IT'S TIME I NEED TO WITHDRAW FROM *THIS AFFAIR...*
IN THE PAST, TO SAY THE LEAST, I PLAYED AN ACTIVE ROLE AS AN INTELLIGENCE OPERATIVE FOR THE CONSERVATIVE MAINSTREAM OF THIS COUNTRY.
SO WHY WORK FOR KAKI-NUMA ...?!
I WAS SIMPLY SCOUTED AND OFFERED MONEY.
PERHAPS I ACCEPTED MISTER KAKINUMA'S OFFER BECAUSE, AT THE END OF A CERTAIN PERIOD, I'D LOST ALL HOPE IN THE POLITICIANS OF THIS FACELESS COUNTRY, WITH THEIR VACILLATING SENSE OF JUSTICE-- NO, THEIR VERY SENSE OF RIGHT AND WRONG...

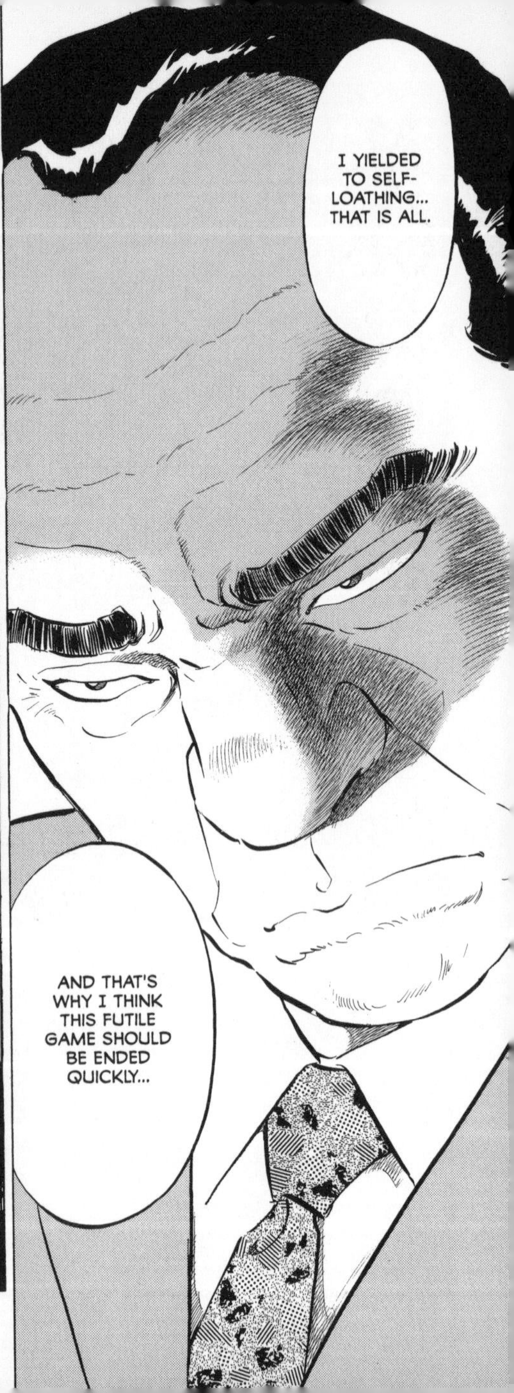
I YIELDED TO SELF-LOATHING... THAT IS ALL.
AND THAT'S WHY I THINK THIS FUTILE GAME SHOULD BE ENDED QUICKLY...

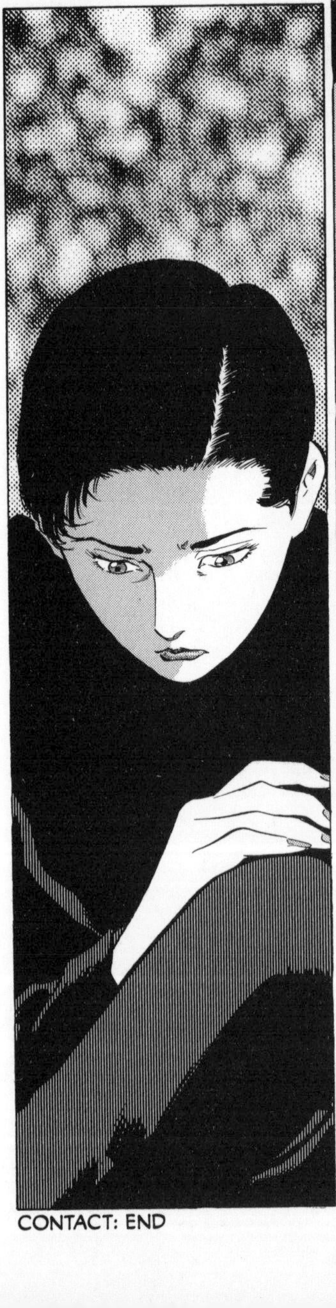

CONTACT: END

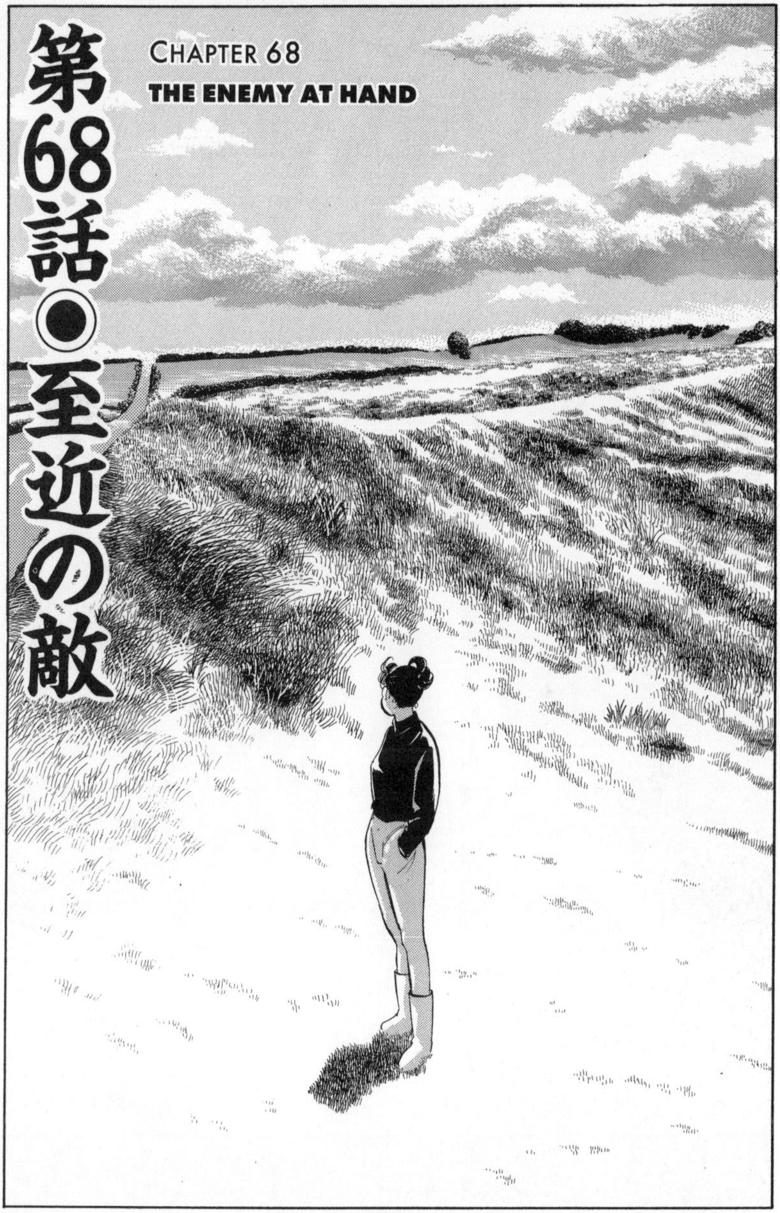
第68話●至近の敵
CHAPTER 68
THE ENEMY AT HAND

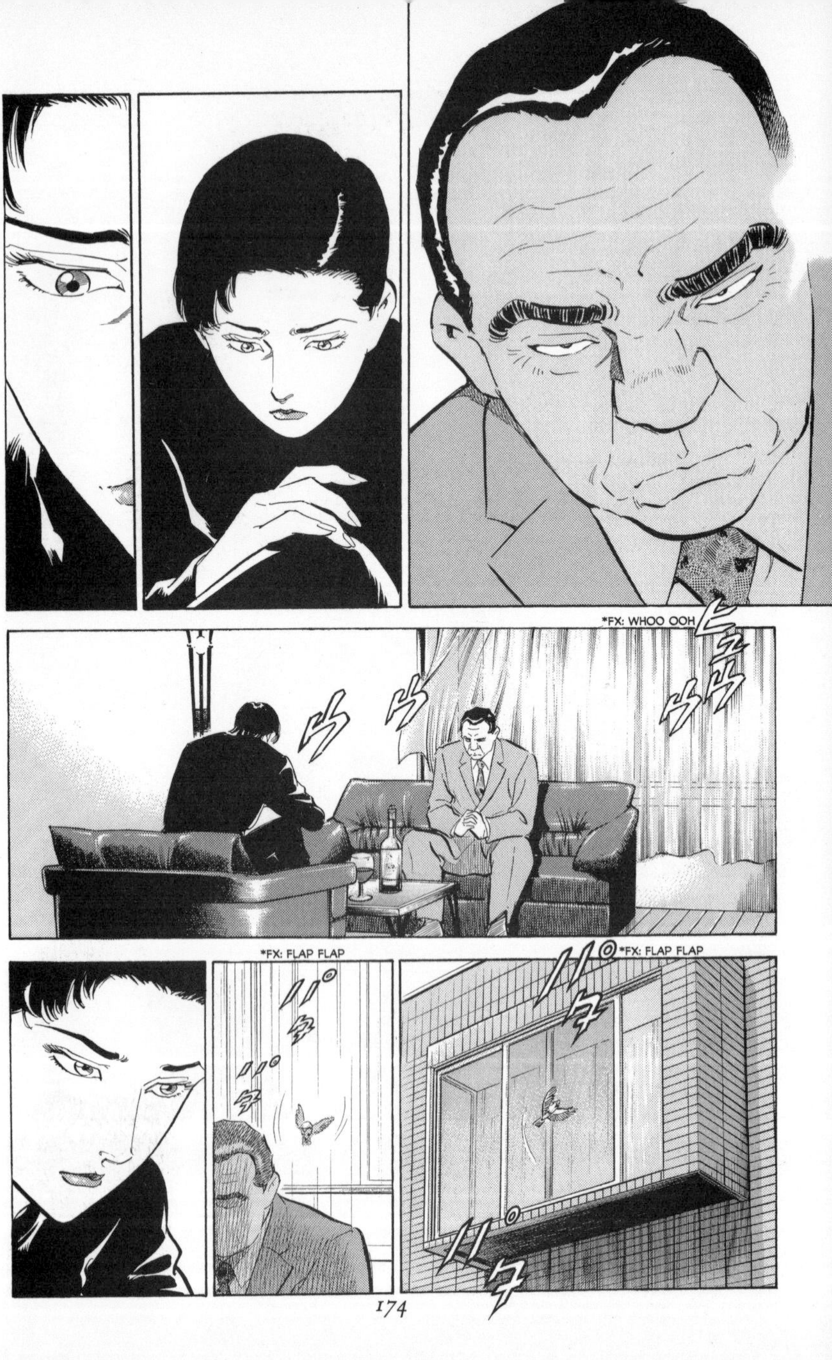
*FX: WHOO OOH
*FX: FLAP FLAP
*FX: FLAP FLAP

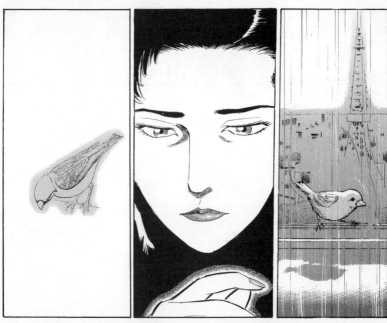

PHEW...
YOU
ALMOST
HAD ME
THERE.

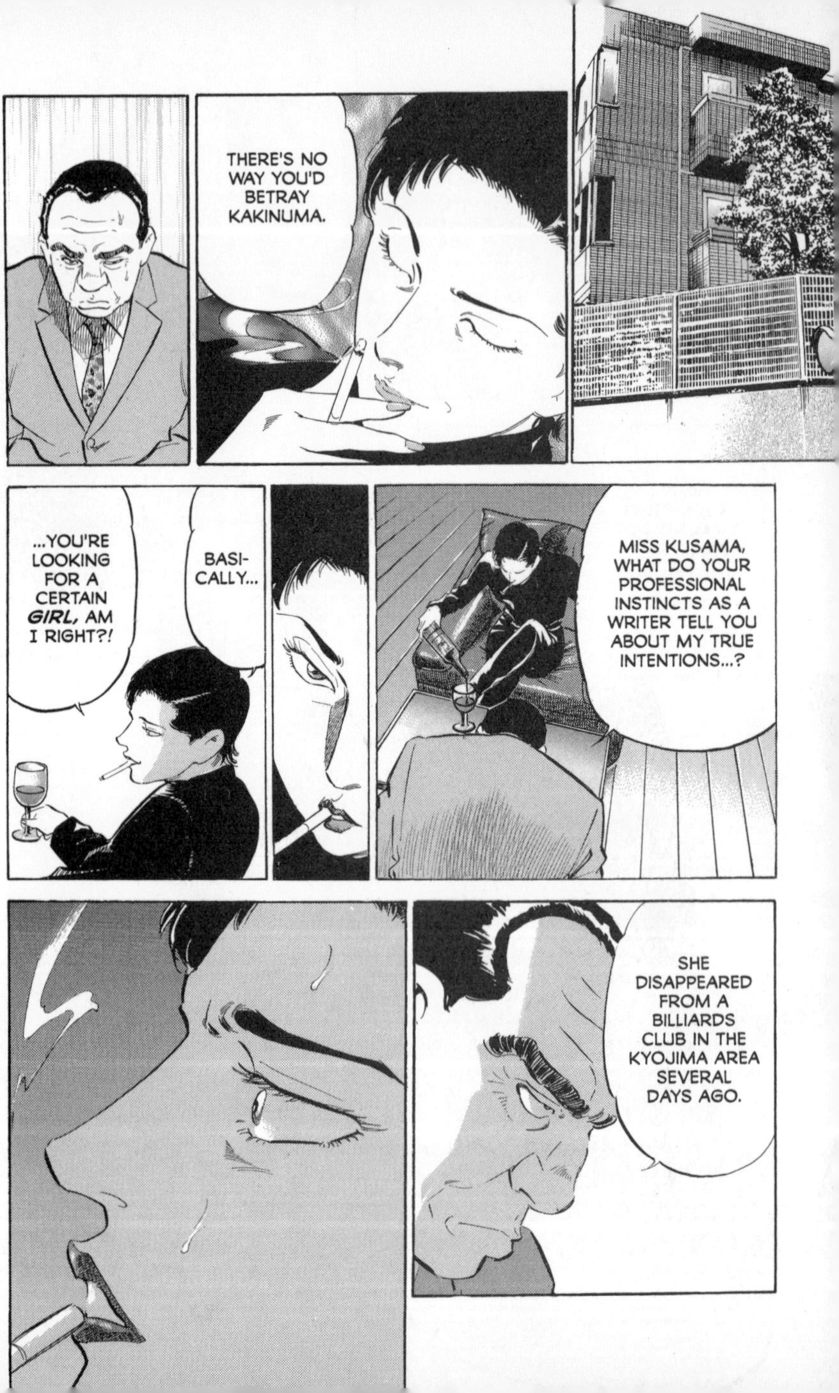
THERE'S NO WAY YOU'D BETRAY KAKINUMA.
MISS KUSAMA, WHAT DO YOUR PROFESSIONAL INSTINCTS AS A WRITER TELL YOU ABOUT MY TRUE INTENTIONS...?
BASI-CALLY...
...YOU'RE LOOKING FOR A CERTAIN *GIRL*, AM I RIGHT?!
SHE DISAPPEARED FROM A BILLIARDS CLUB IN THE KYOJIMA AREA SEVERAL DAYS AGO.

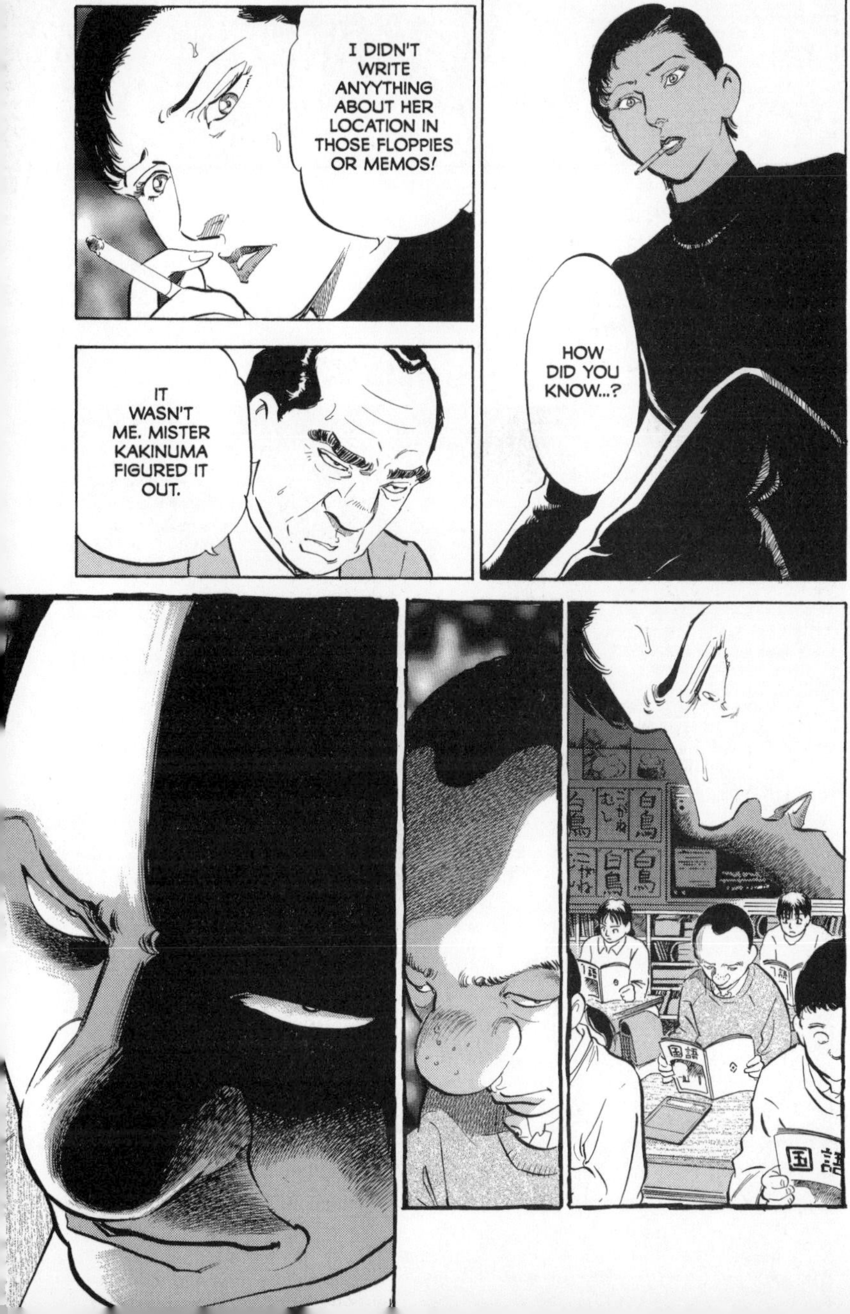
HOW DID YOU KNOW...?
I DIDN'T WRITE ANYYTHING ABOUT HER LOCATION IN THOSE FLOPPIES OR MEMOS!
IT WASN'T ME. MISTER KAKINUMA FIGURED IT OUT.
国語

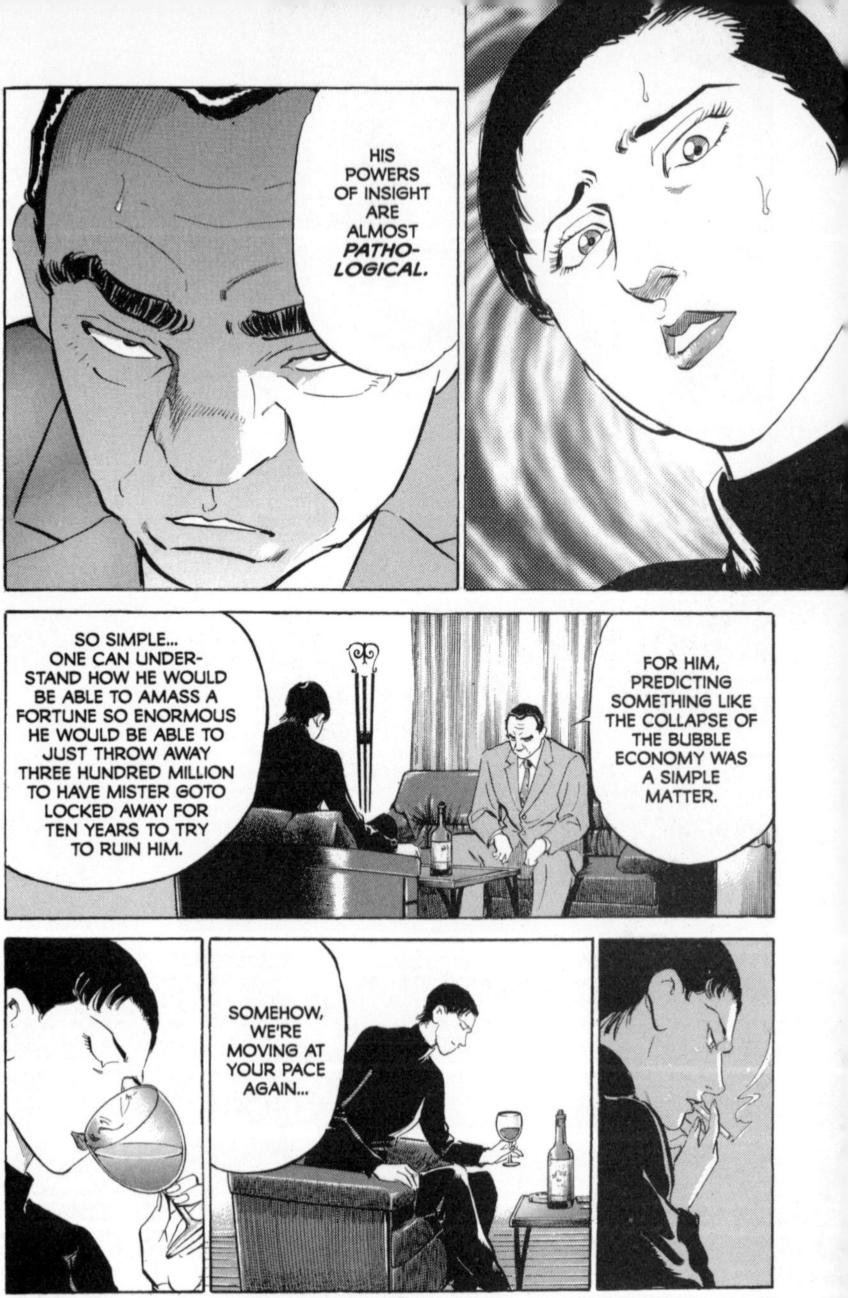
HIS POWERS OF INSIGHT ARE ALMOST *PATHO-LOGICAL.*
FOR HIM, PREDICTING SOMETHING LIKE THE COLLAPSE OF THE BUBBLE ECONOMY WAS A SIMPLE MATTER.
SO SIMPLE... ONE CAN UNDER-STAND HOW HE WOULD BE ABLE TO AMASS A FORTUNE SO ENORMOUS HE WOULD BE ABLE TO JUST THROW AWAY THREE HUNDRED MILLION TO HAVE MISTER GOTO LOCKED AWAY FOR TEN YEARS TO TRY TO RUIN HIM.
SOMEHOW, WE'RE MOVING AT YOUR PACE AGAIN...

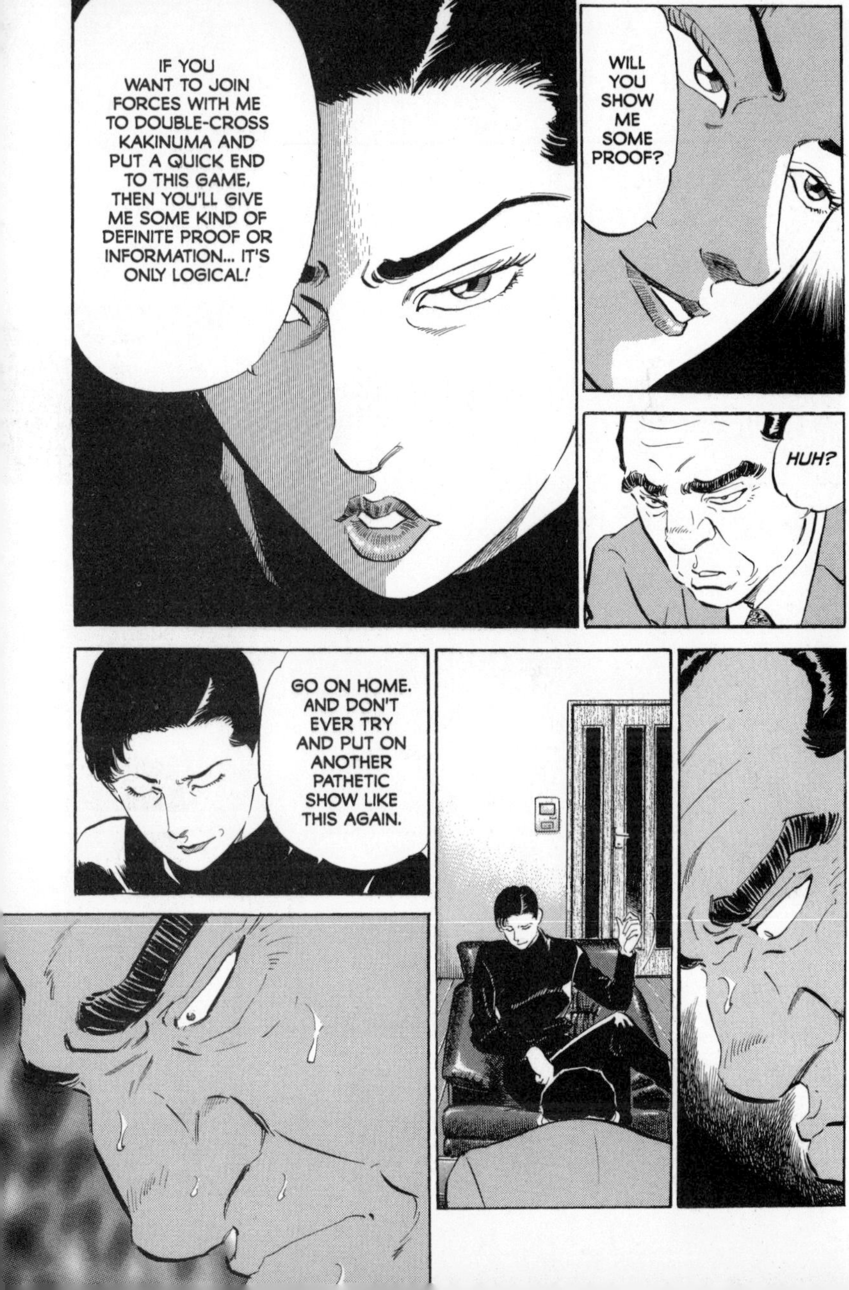
WILL YOU SHOW ME SOME PROOF?
HUH?
IF YOU WANT TO JOIN FORCES WITH ME TO DOUBLE-CROSS KAKINUMA AND PUT A QUICK END TO THIS GAME, THEN YOU'LL GIVE ME SOME KIND OF DEFINITE PROOF OR INFORMATION... IT'S ONLY LOGICAL!
GO ON HOME. AND DON'T EVER TRY AND PUT ON ANOTHER PATHETIC SHOW LIKE THIS AGAIN.

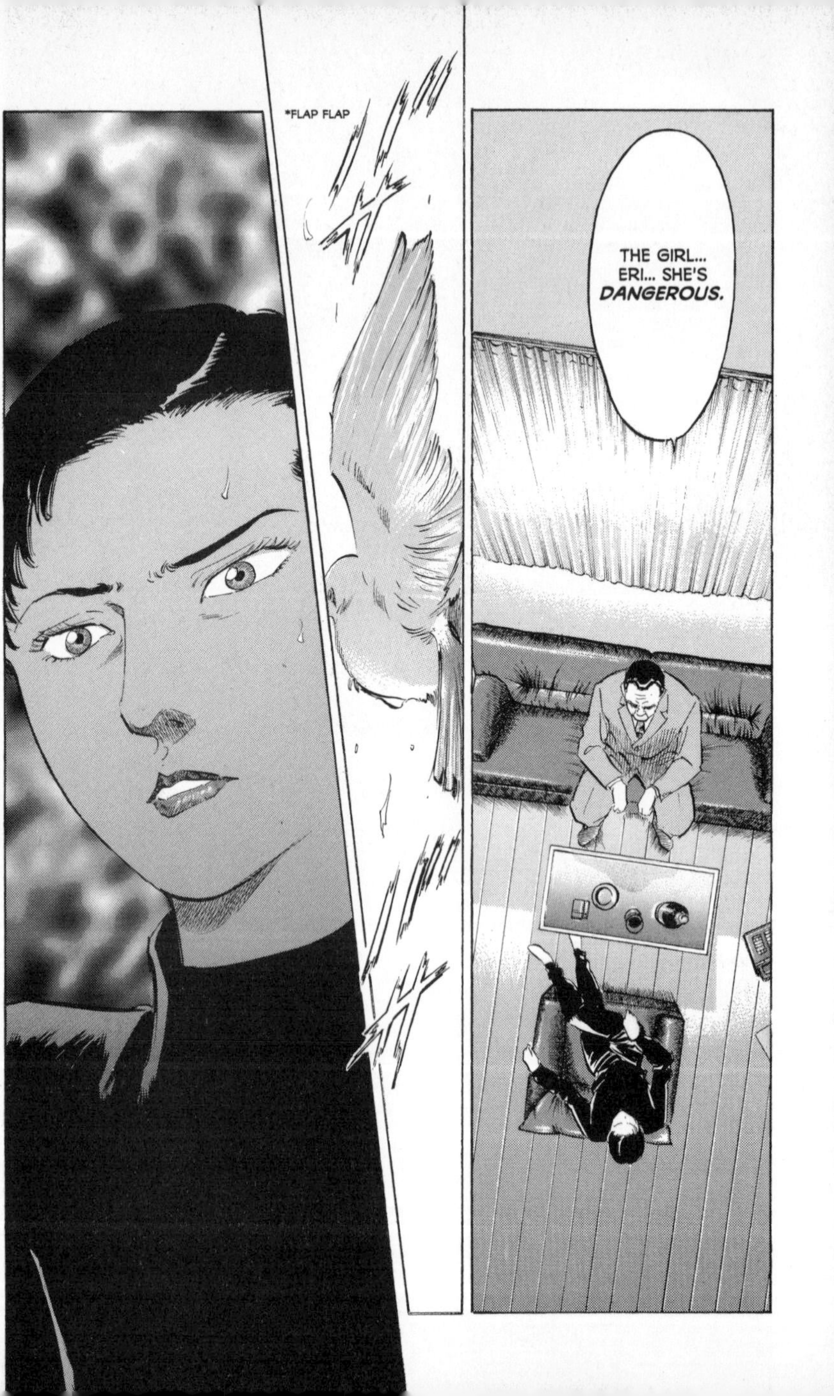
THE GIRL... ERI... SHE'S DANGEROUS.
*FLAP FLAP

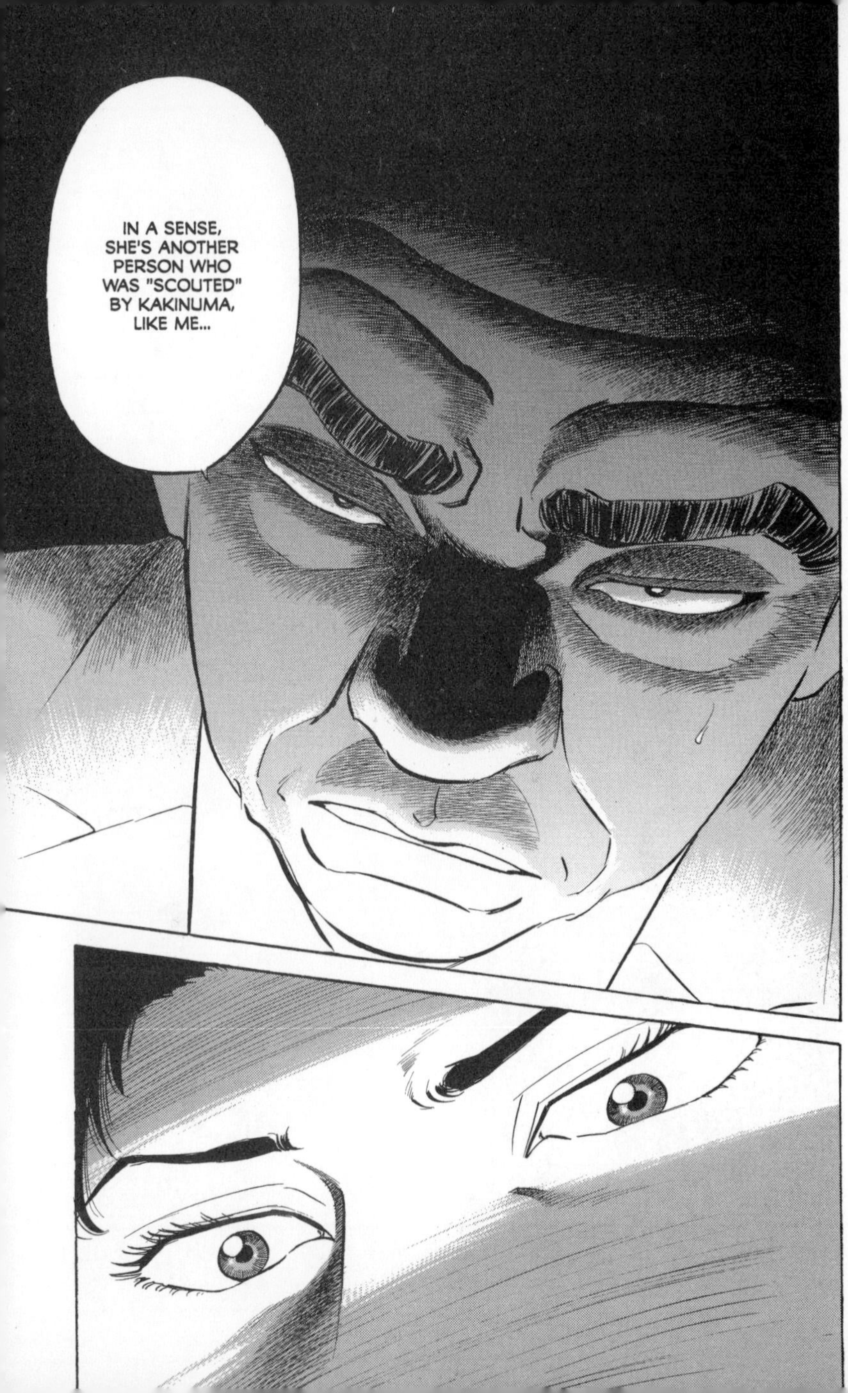
IN A SENSE, SHE'S ANOTHER PERSON WHO WAS "SCOUTED" BY KAKINUMA, LIKE ME...

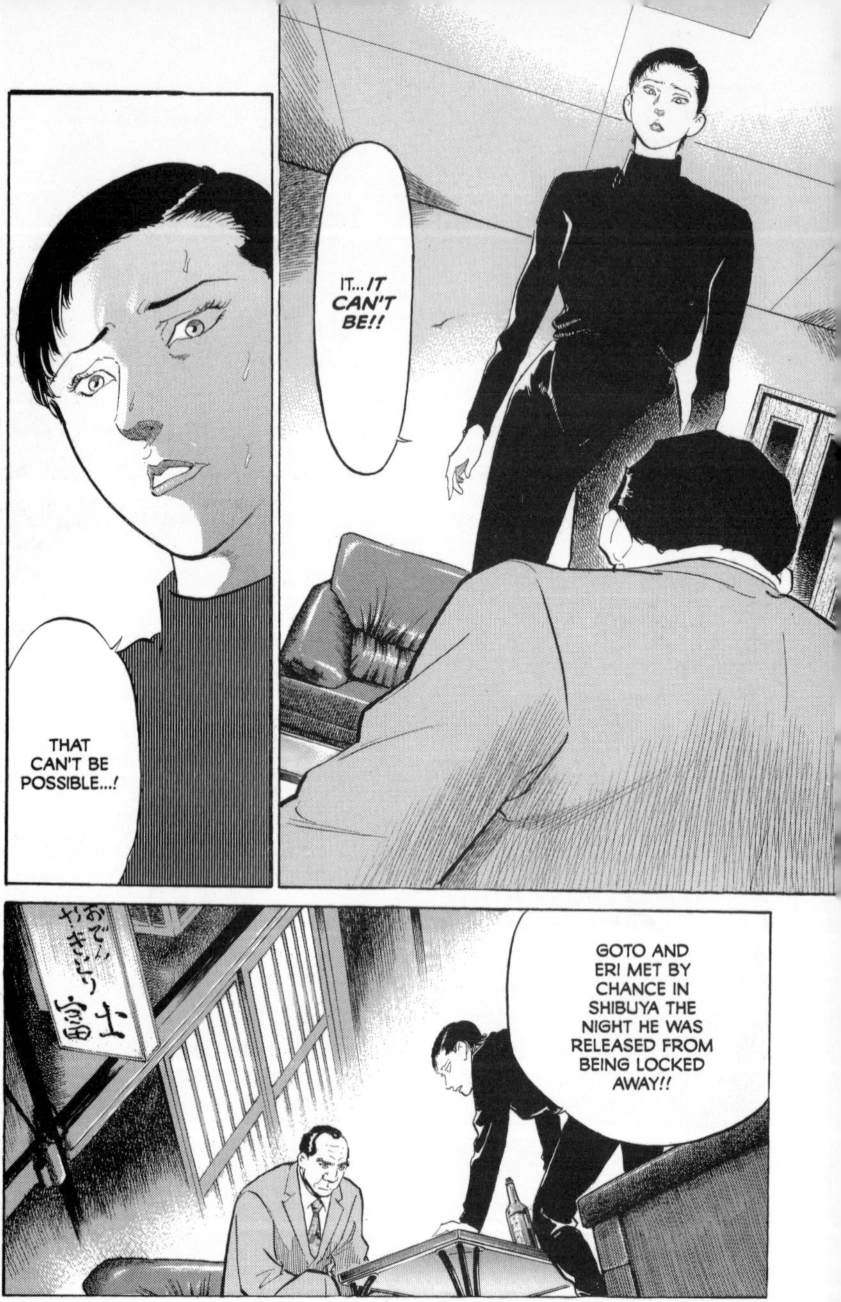
IT... IT CAN'T BE!!
THAT CAN'T BE POSSIBLE...!
おでん
やきとり
富士
GOTO AND ERI MET BY CHANCE IN SHIBUYA THE NIGHT HE WAS RELEASED FROM BEING LOCKED AWAY!!

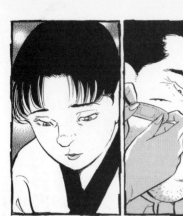

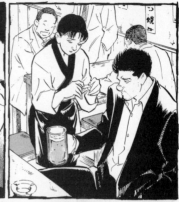

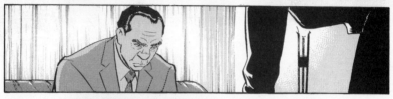

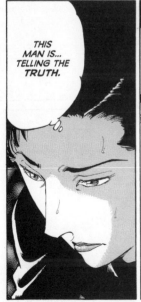

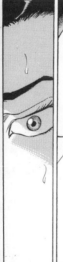

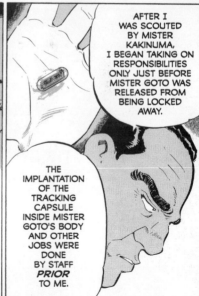

AFTER I WAS SCOUTED BY MISTER KAKINUMA, I BEGAN TAKING ON RESPONSIBILITIES ONLY JUST BEFORE MISTER GOTO WAS RELEASED FROM BEING LOCKED AWAY.
THE IMPLANTATION OF THE TRACKING CAPSULE INSIDE MISTER GOTO'S BODY AND OTHER JOBS WERE DONE BY STAFF *PRIOR* TO ME.
THIS MAN IS... TELLING THE ***TRUTH.***

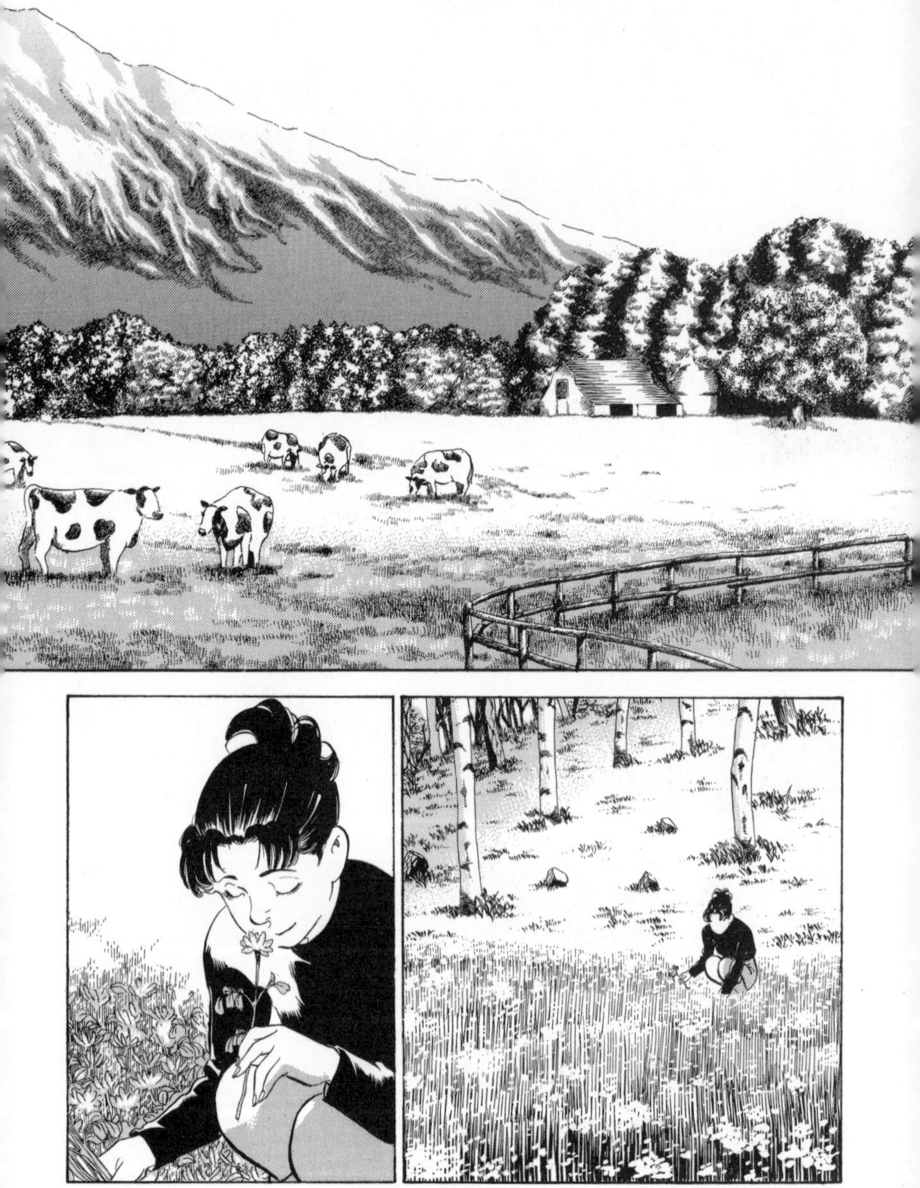

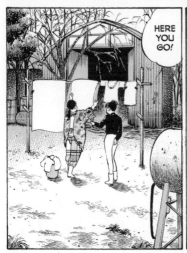

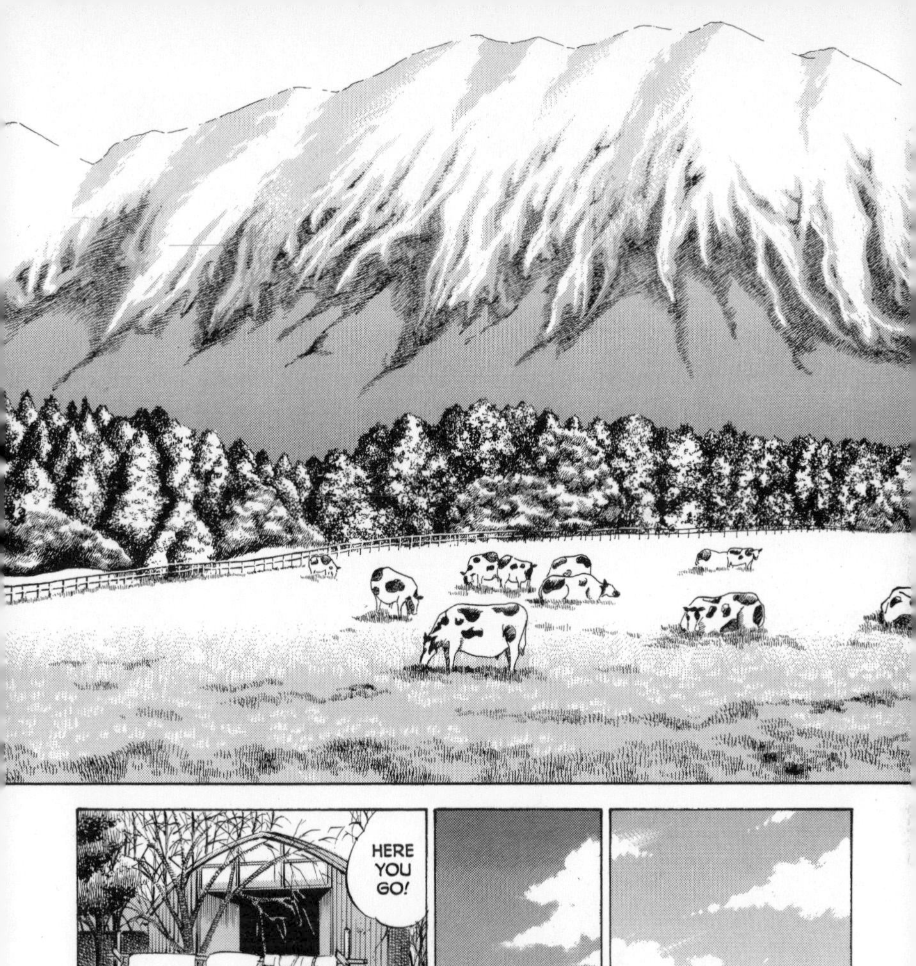
HERE YOU GO!

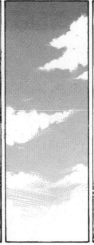

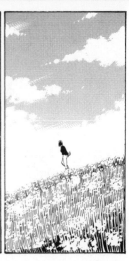

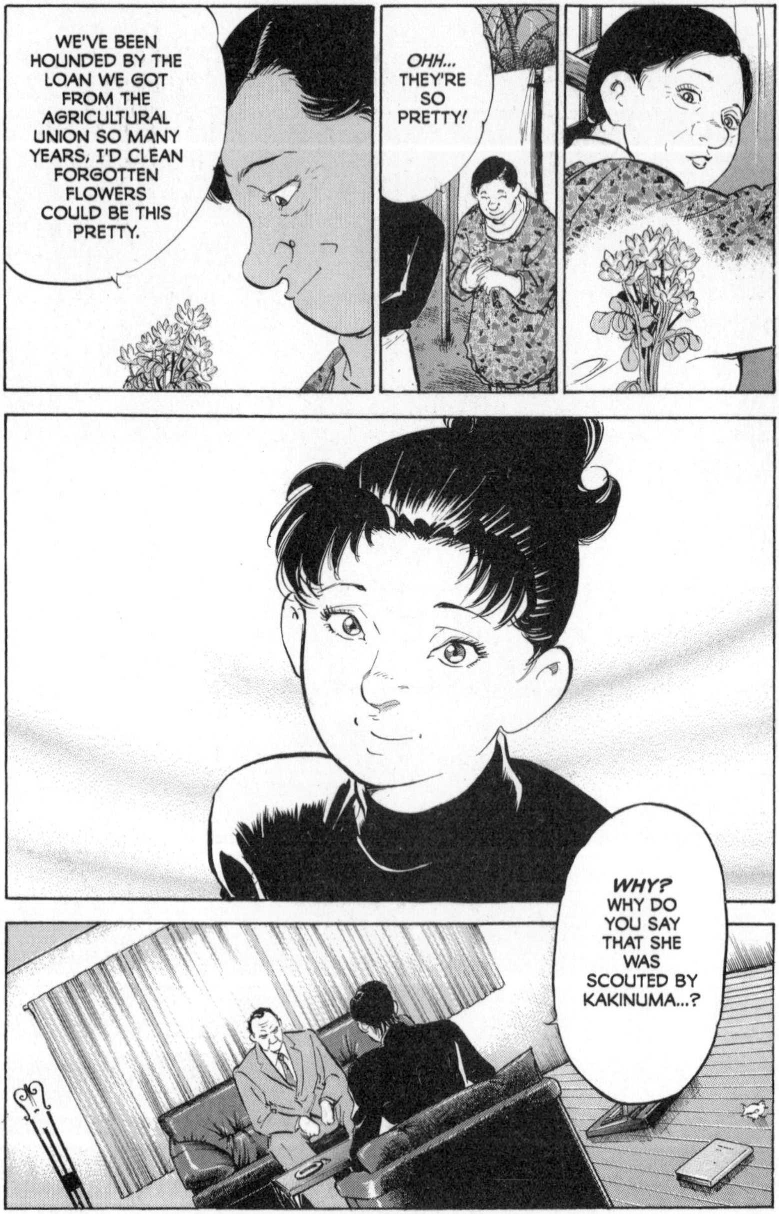
OHH... THEY'RE SO PRETTY!
WE'VE BEEN HOUNDED BY THE LOAN WE GOT FROM THE AGRICULTURAL UNION SO MANY YEARS, I'D CLEAN FORGOTTEN FLOWERS COULD BE THIS PRETTY.
WHY? WHY DO YOU SAY THAT SHE WAS SCOUTED BY KAKINUMA...?

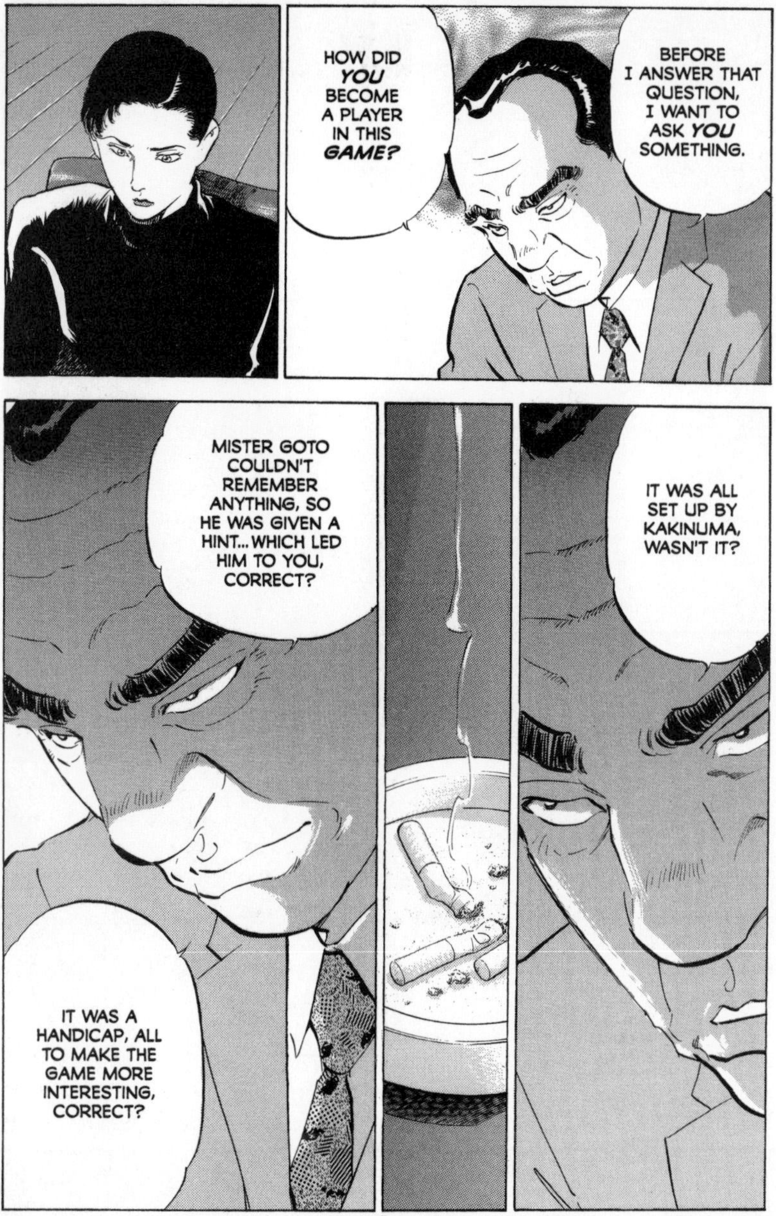
HOW DID *YOU* BECOME A PLAYER IN THIS *GAME?*
BEFORE I ANSWER THAT QUESTION, I WANT TO ASK *YOU* SOMETHING.
IT WAS ALL SET UP BY KAKINUMA, WASN'T IT?
MISTER GOTO COULDN'T REMEMBER ANYTHING, SO HE WAS GIVEN A HINT...WHICH LED HIM TO YOU, CORRECT?
IT WAS A HANDICAP, ALL TO MAKE THE GAME MORE INTERESTING, CORRECT?

MOST LIKELY...

ERI... TOO.

SO WHAT SHOULD I DO...?!

SHIT!!

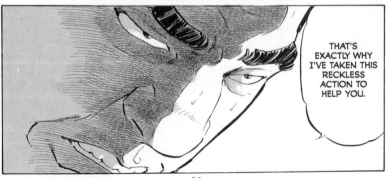

THAT'S EXACTLY WHY I'VE TAKEN THIS RECKLESS ACTION TO HELP YOU.

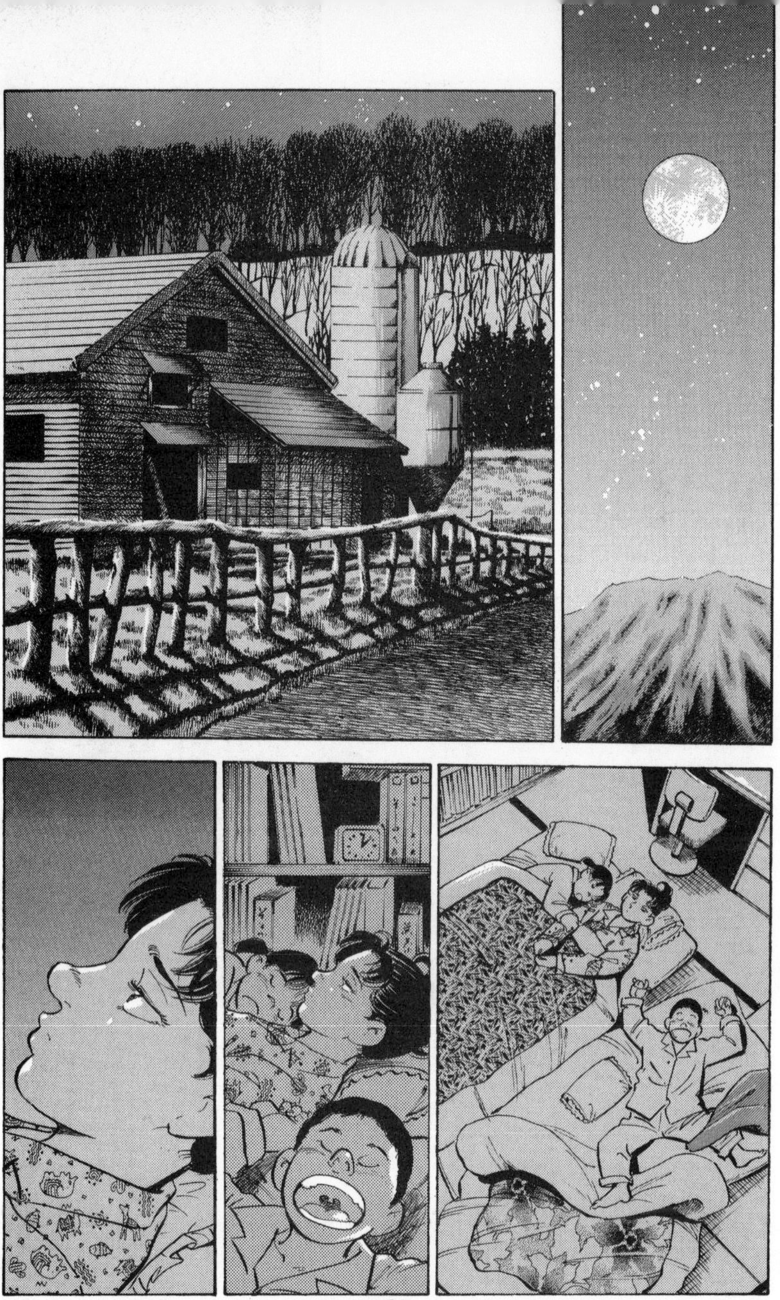

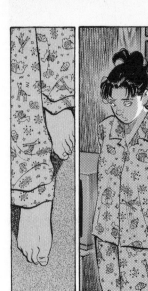

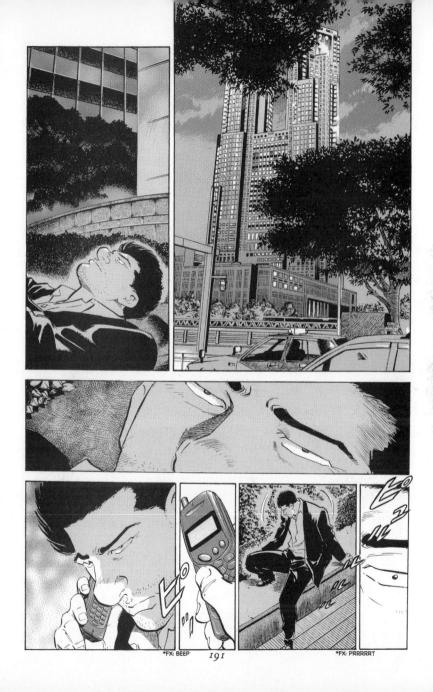

*FX: BEEP
191
*FX: PRRRRRT

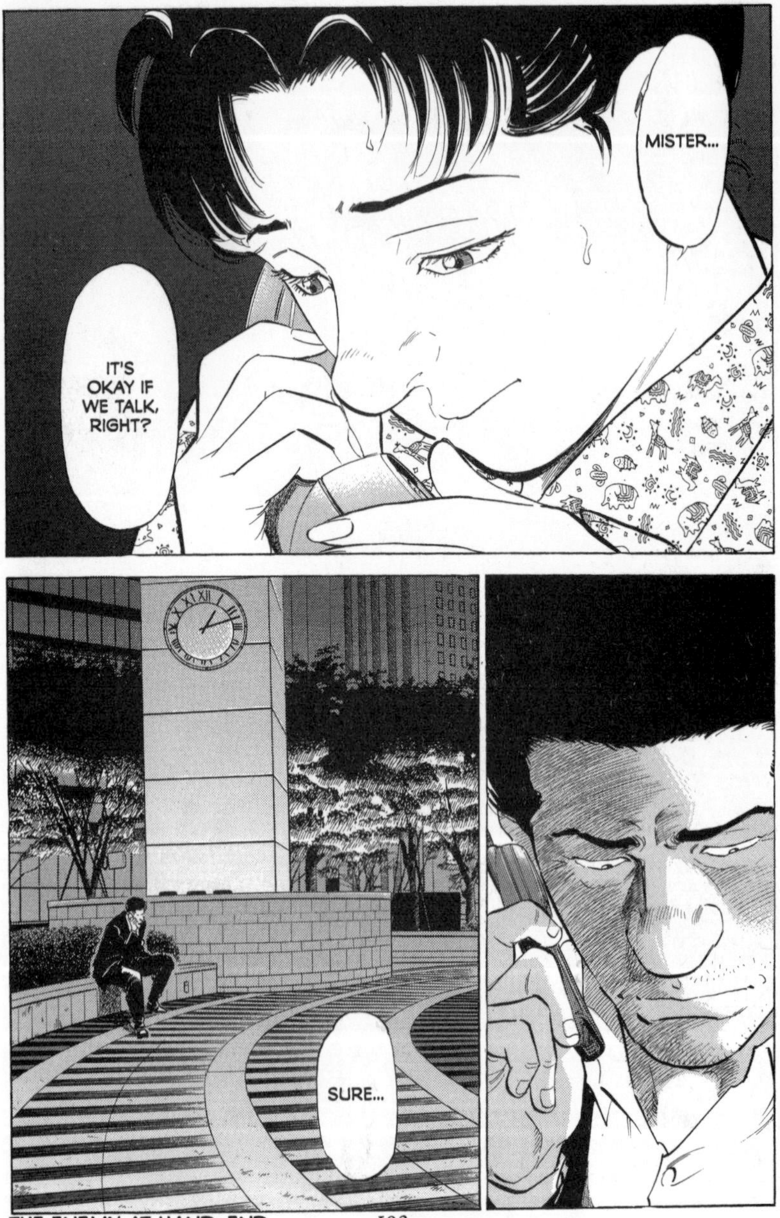
MISTER...
IT'S OKAY IF WE TALK, RIGHT?
SURE...

THE ENEMY AT HAND: END

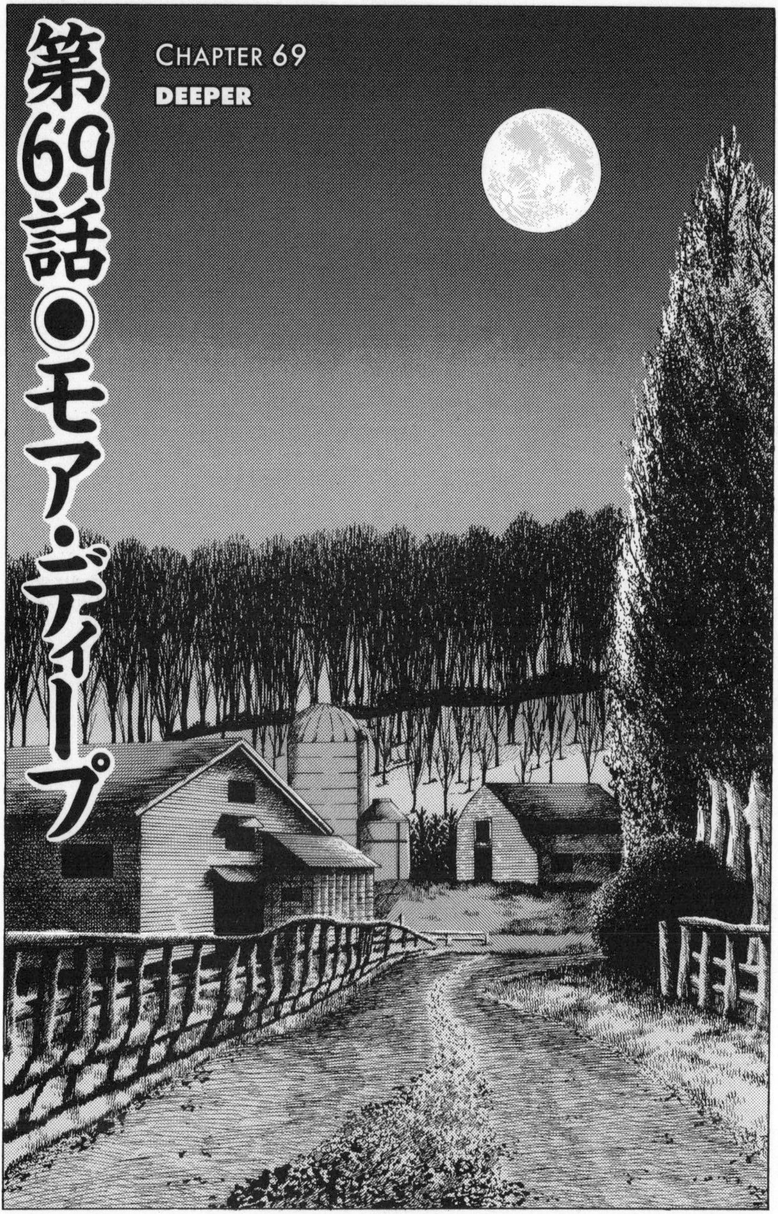
第69話●モア・ディープ
CHAPTER 69
DEEPER

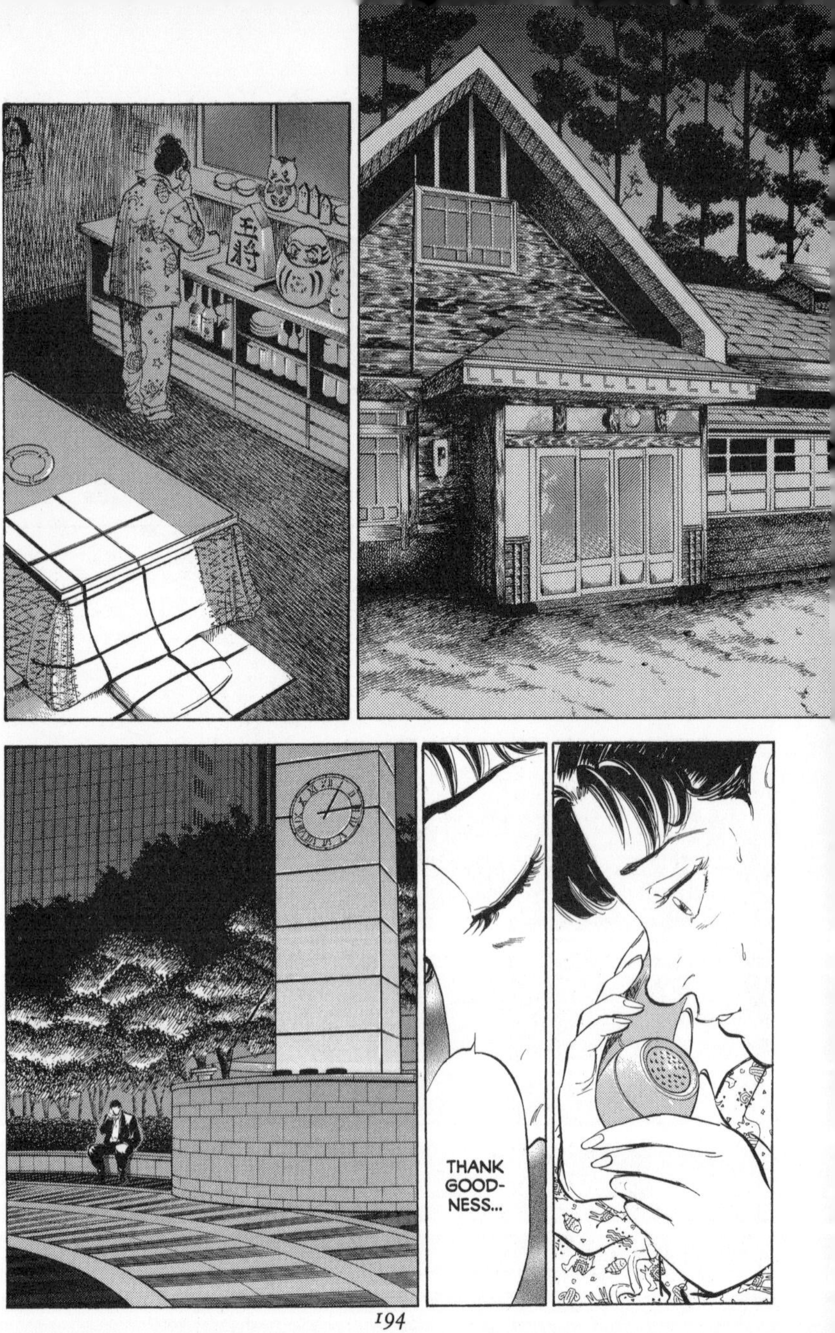
THANK GOOD-NESS...

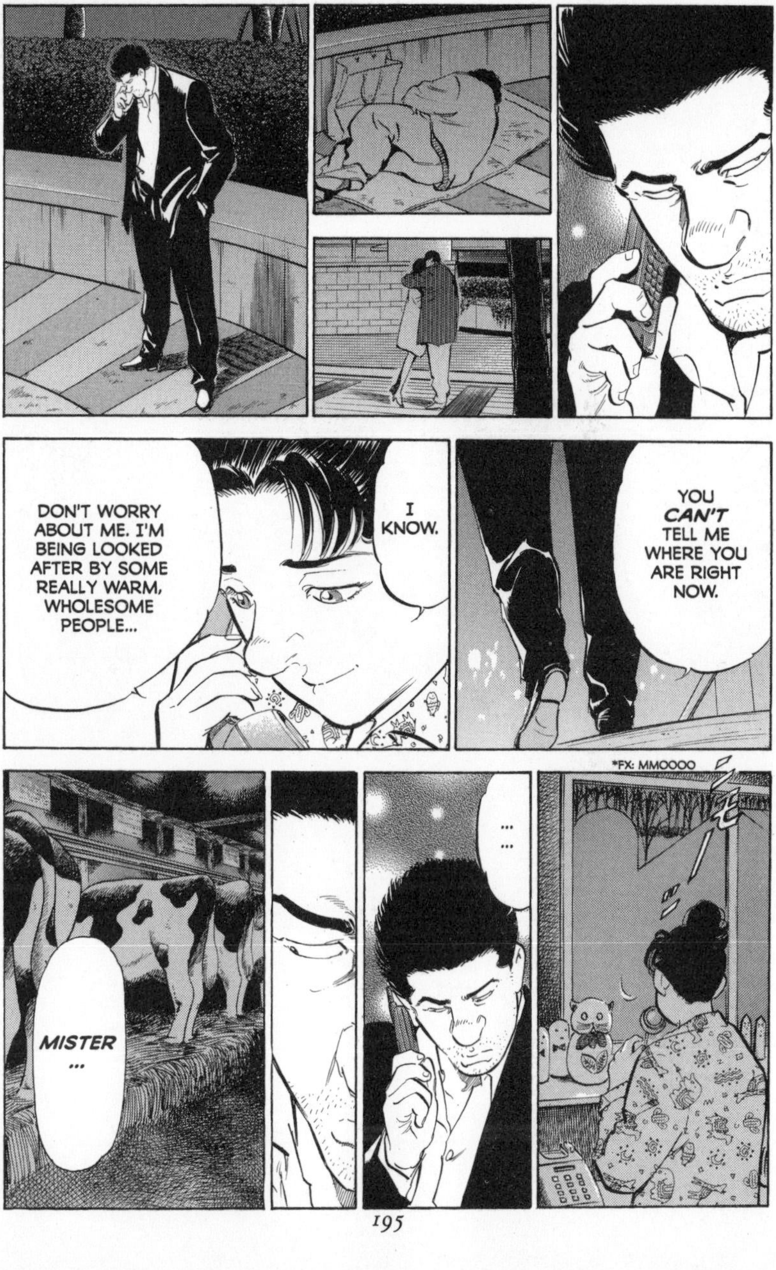
YOU *CAN'T* TELL ME WHERE YOU ARE RIGHT NOW.
I KNOW.
DON'T WORRY ABOUT ME. I'M BEING LOOKED AFTER BY SOME REALLY WARM, WHOLESOME PEOPLE...
*FX: MMOOOO
... ...
MISTER ...

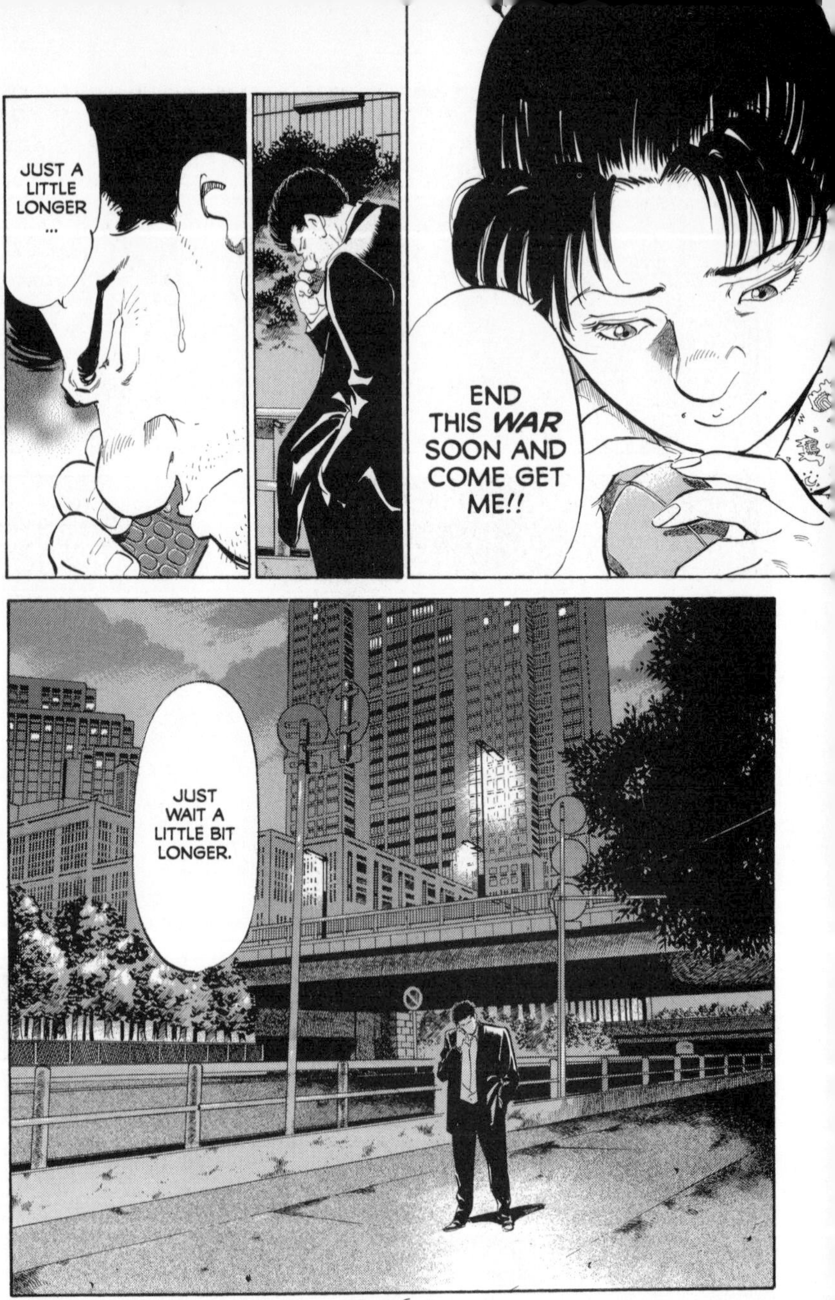
END THIS WAR SOON AND COME GET ME!!
JUST A LITTLE LONGER ...
JUST WAIT A LITTLE BIT LONGER.

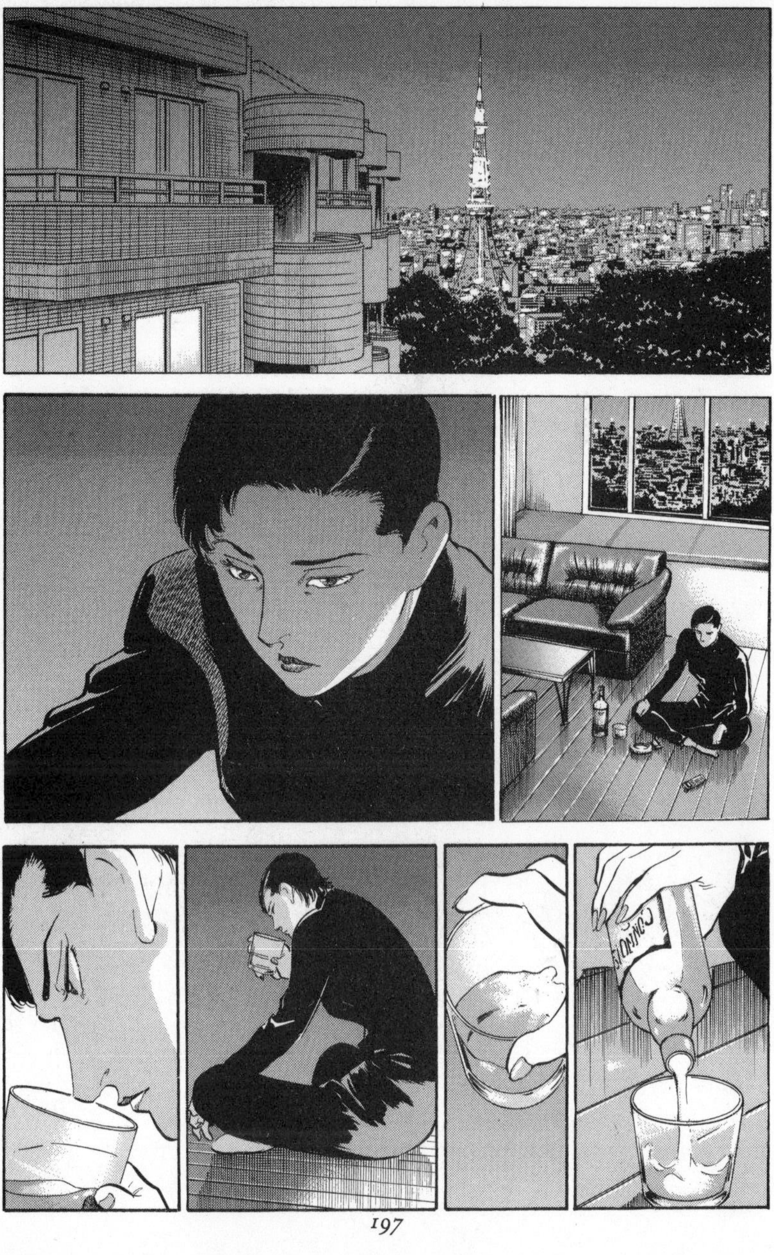

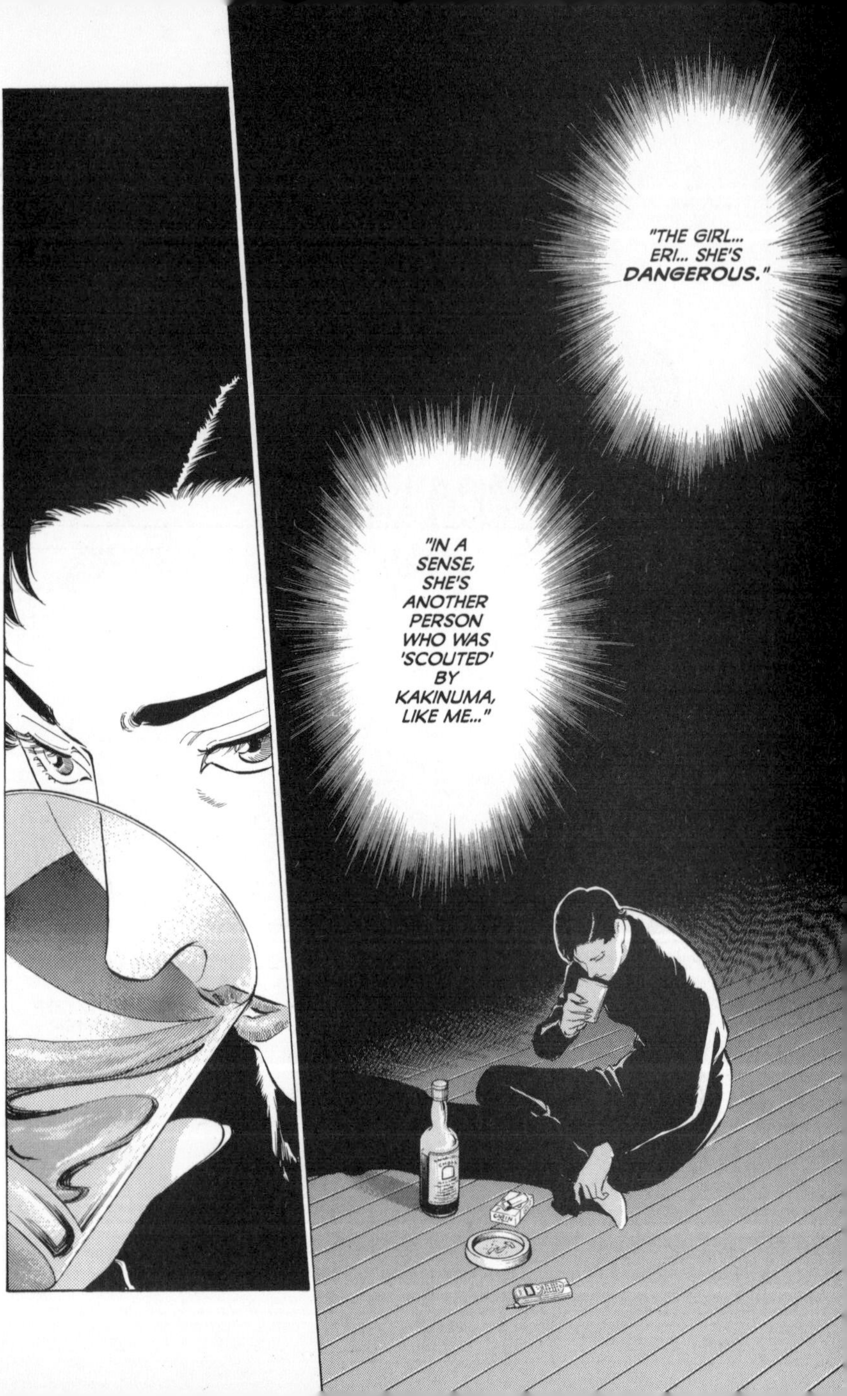
"THE GIRL... ERI... SHE'S DANGEROUS."
"IN A SENSE, SHE'S ANOTHER PERSON WHO WAS 'SCOUTED' BY KAKINUMA, LIKE ME..."

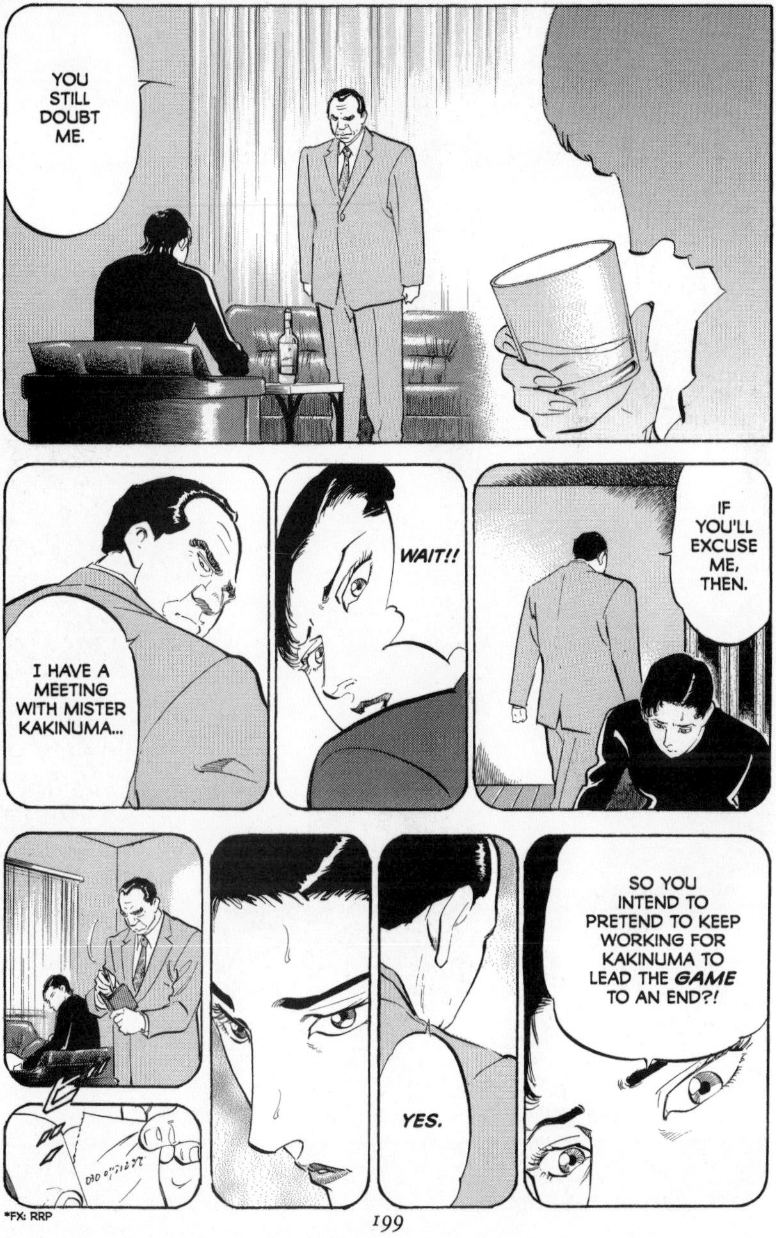
YOU STILL DOUBT ME.
IF YOU'LL EXCUSE ME, THEN.
WAIT!!
I HAVE A MEETING WITH MISTER KAKINUMA...
SO YOU INTEND TO PRETEND TO KEEP WORKING FOR KAKINUMA TO LEAD THE *GAME* TO AN END?!
YES.

*FX: RRP

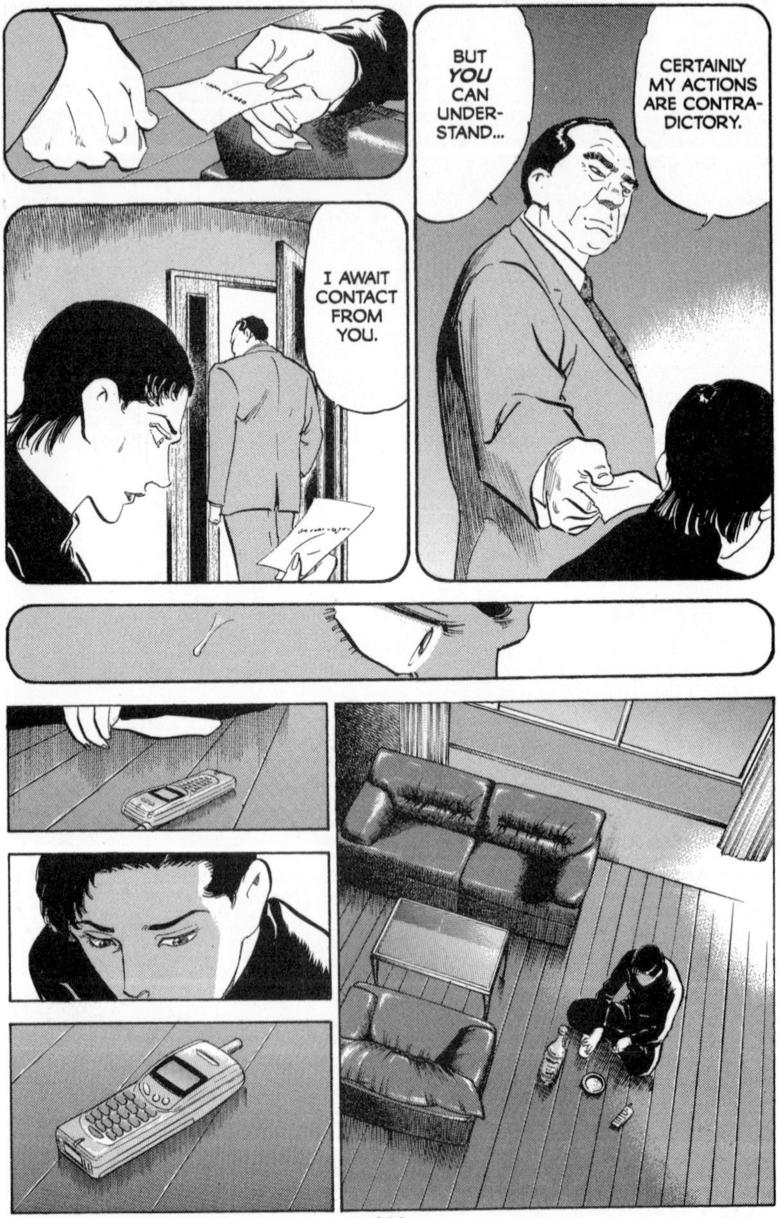
CERTAINLY MY ACTIONS ARE CONTRA-DICTORY.
BUT *YOU* CAN UNDER-STAND...
I AWAIT CONTACT FROM YOU.

MAKING THIS DECISION WILL BRING THE **STORY** TO ITS CLIMAX IN A BREATH...

IT'S A GAMBLE...

PRR-RT...

PRR-RT...

*FX: BEEP BEEP

030 048

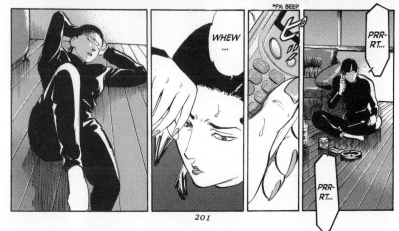

WHEW...

*FX: BEEP

PRR-RT...

PRR-RT...

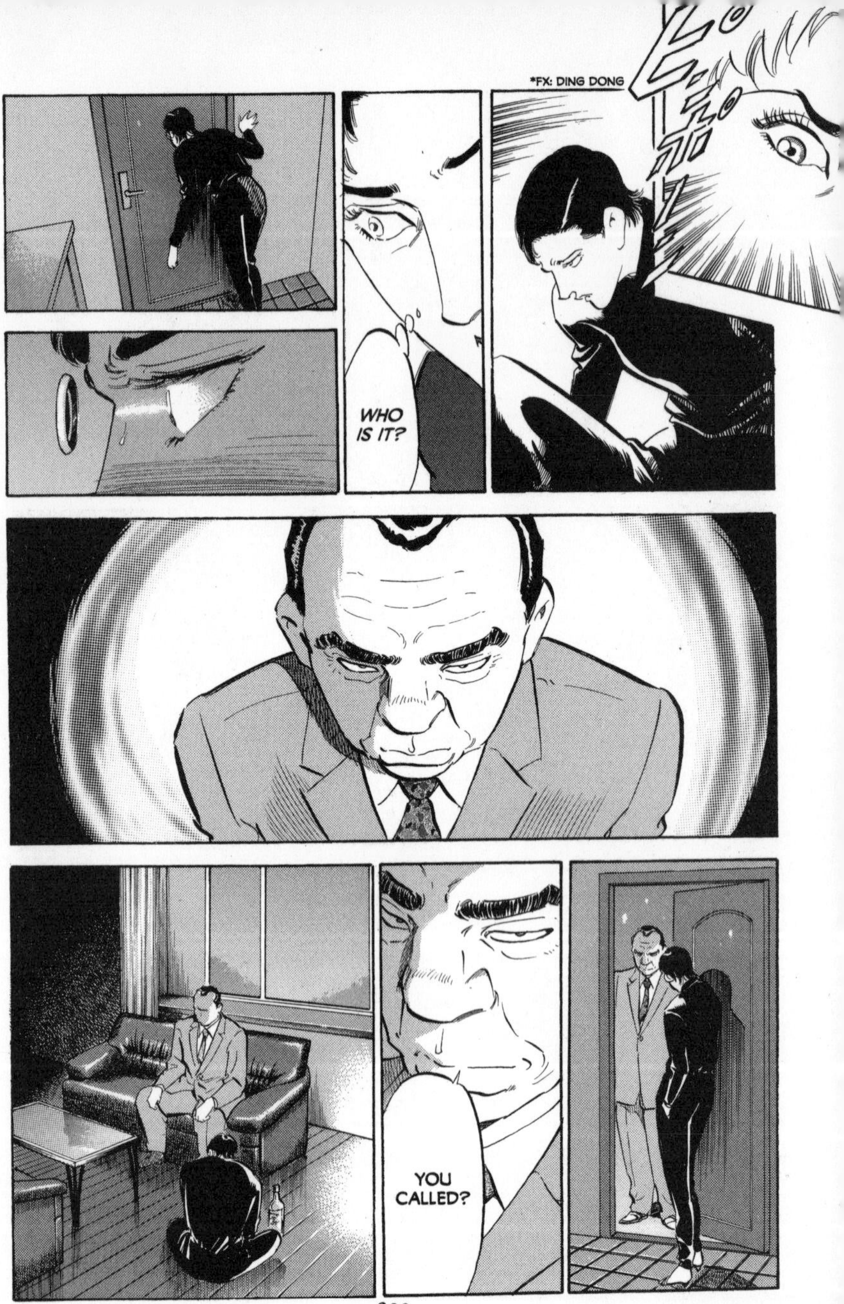
*FX: DING DONG
WHO IS IT?
YOU CALLED?

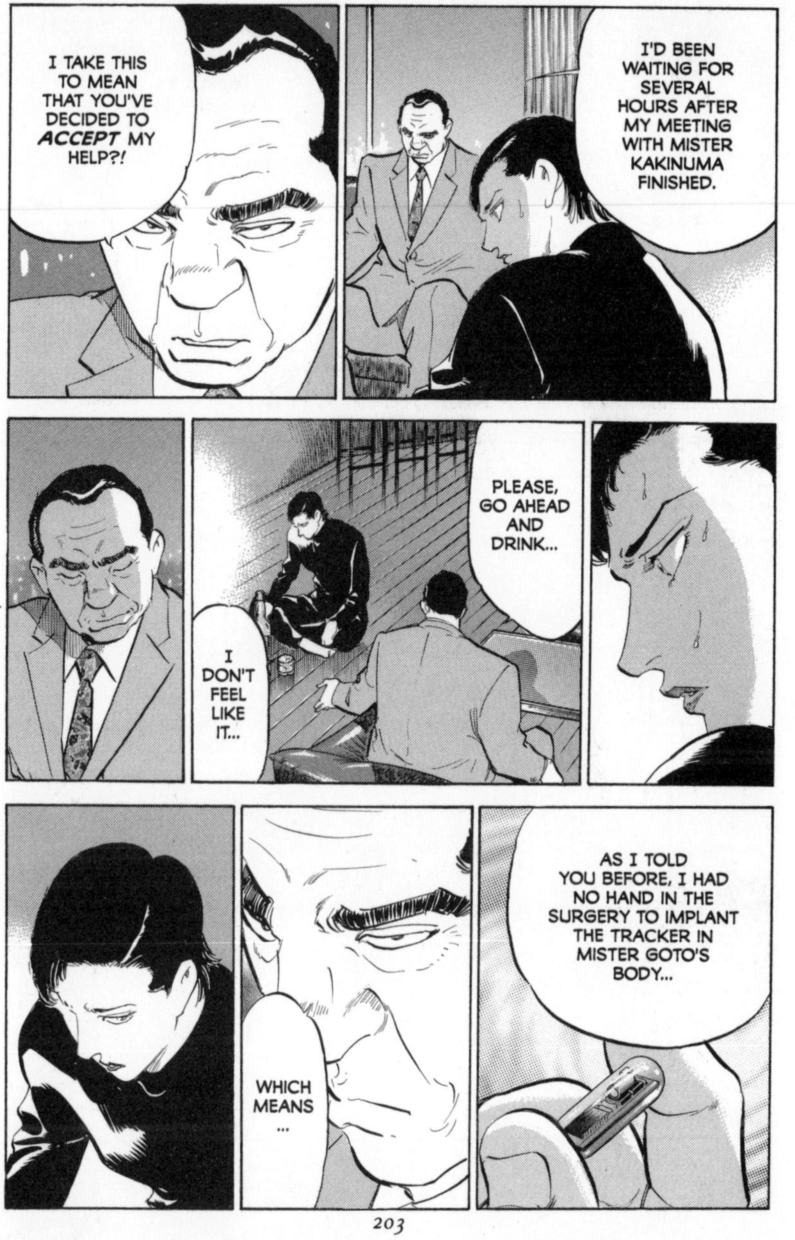
I'D BEEN WAITING FOR SEVERAL HOURS AFTER MY MEETING WITH MISTER KAKINUMA FINISHED.
I TAKE THIS TO MEAN THAT YOU'VE DECIDED TO *ACCEPT* MY HELP?!
PLEASE, GO AHEAD AND DRINK...
I DON'T FEEL LIKE IT...
AS I TOLD YOU BEFORE, I HAD NO HAND IN THE SURGERY TO IMPLANT THE TRACKER IN MISTER GOTO'S BODY...
WHICH MEANS ...

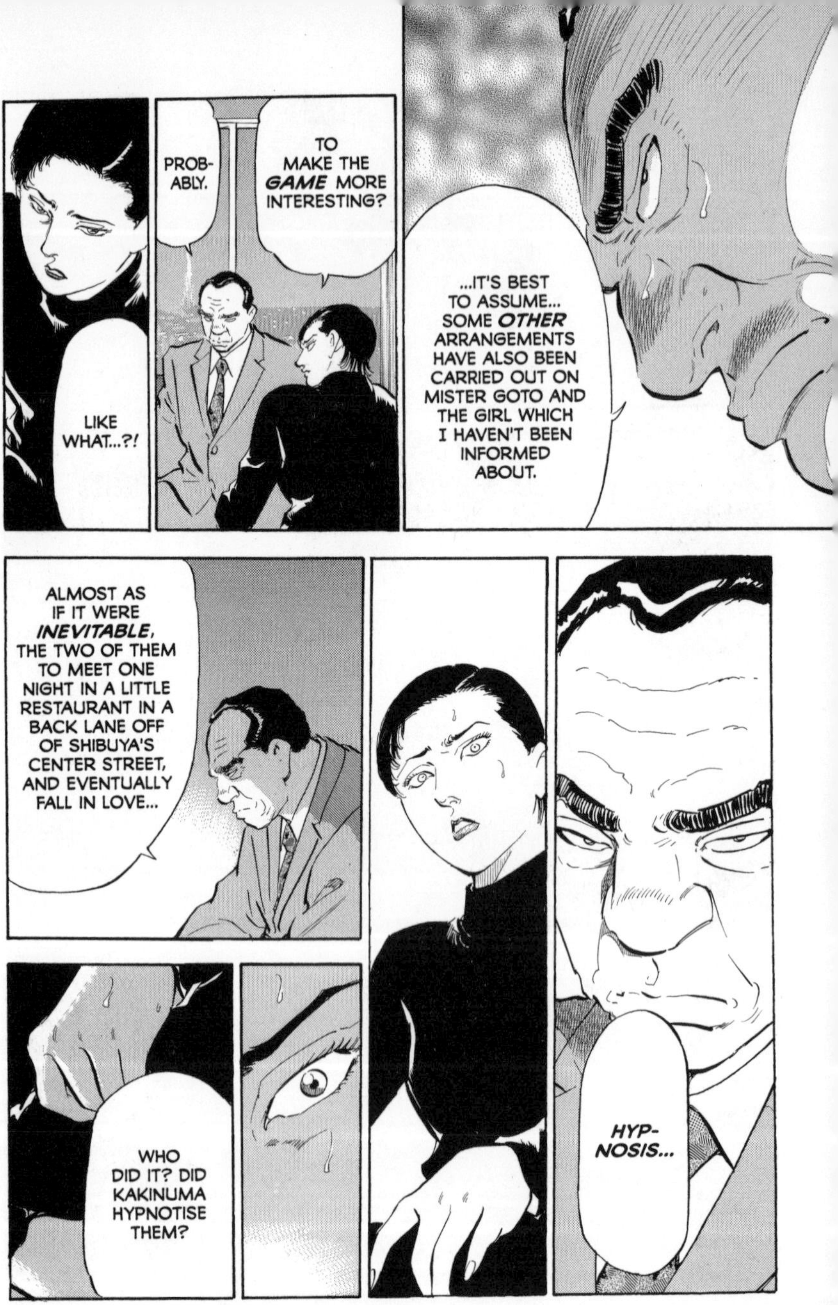
...IT'S BEST TO ASSUME... SOME *OTHER* ARRANGEMENTS HAVE ALSO BEEN CARRIED OUT ON MISTER GOTO AND THE GIRL WHICH I HAVEN'T BEEN INFORMED ABOUT.
TO MAKE THE *GAME* MORE INTERESTING?
PROB-ABLY.
LIKE WHAT...?!
HYP-NOSIS...
ALMOST AS IF IT WERE *INEVITABLE*, THE TWO OF THEM TO MEET ONE NIGHT IN A LITTLE RESTAURANT IN A BACK LANE OFF OF SHIBUYA'S CENTER STREET, AND EVENTUALLY FALL IN LOVE...
WHO DID IT? DID KAKINUMA HYPNOTISE THEM?

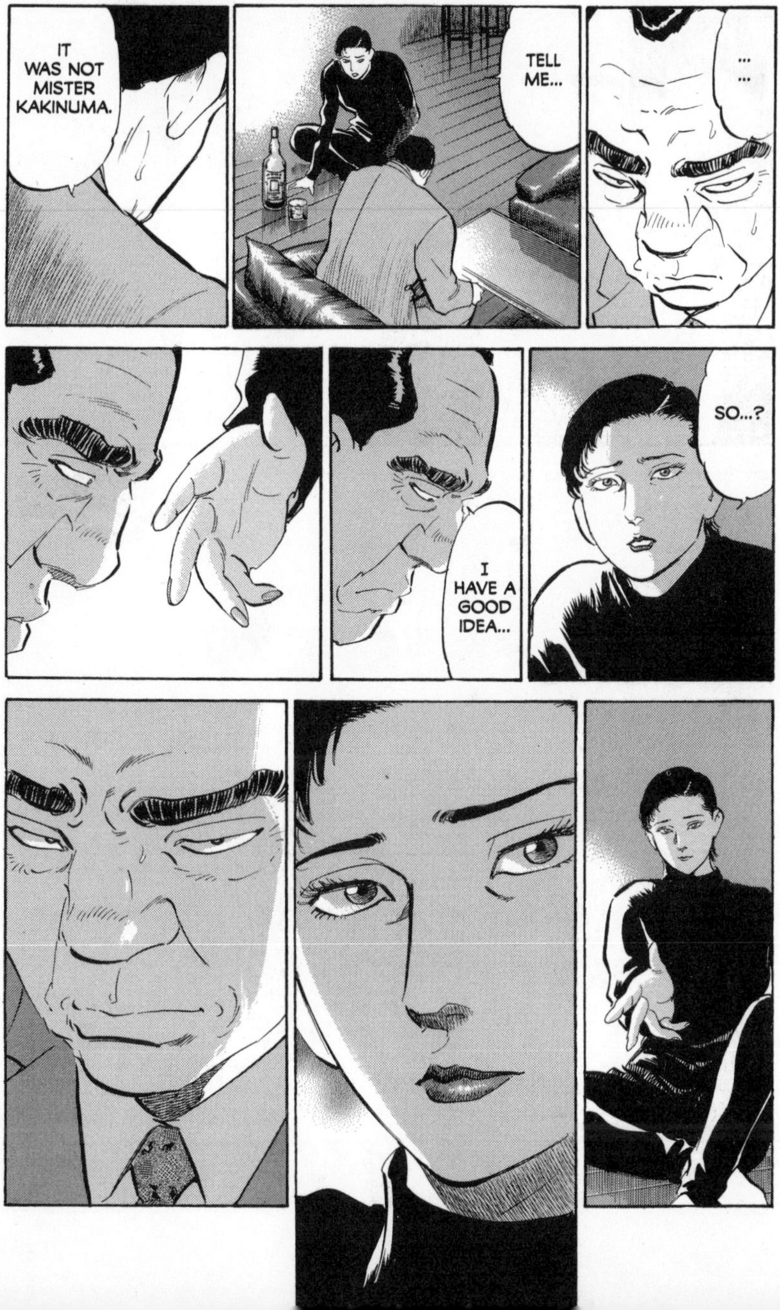
......
TELL ME...
IT WAS NOT MISTER KAKINUMA.
SO...?
I HAVE A GOOD IDEA...

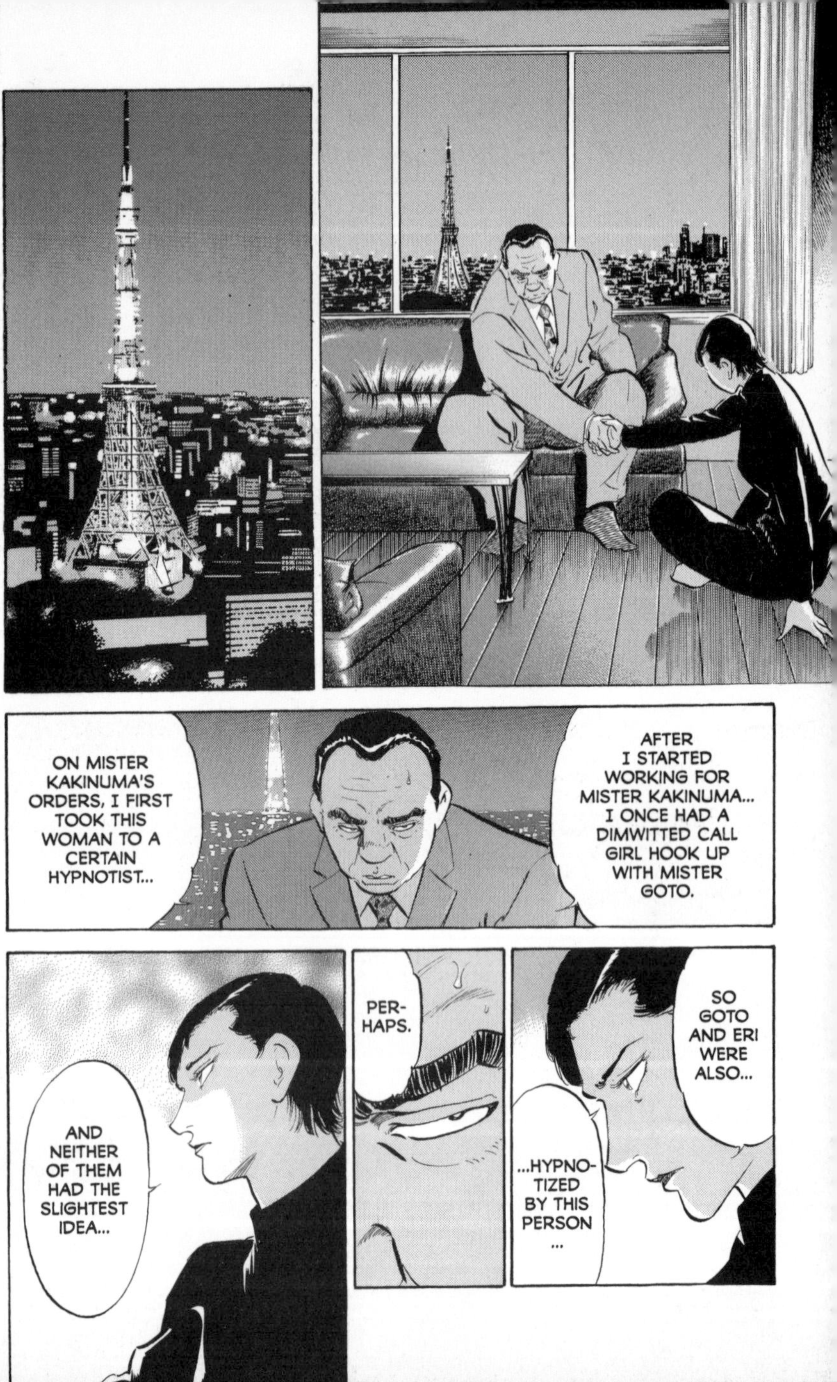
AFTER I STARTED WORKING FOR MISTER KAKINUMA... I ONCE HAD A DIMWITTED CALL GIRL HOOK UP WITH MISTER GOTO.
ON MISTER KAKINUMA'S ORDERS, I FIRST TOOK THIS WOMAN TO A CERTAIN HYPNOTIST...
SO GOTO AND ERI WERE ALSO...
...HYPNOTIZED BY THIS PERSON ...
PERHAPS.
AND NEITHER OF THEM HAD THE SLIGHTEST IDEA...

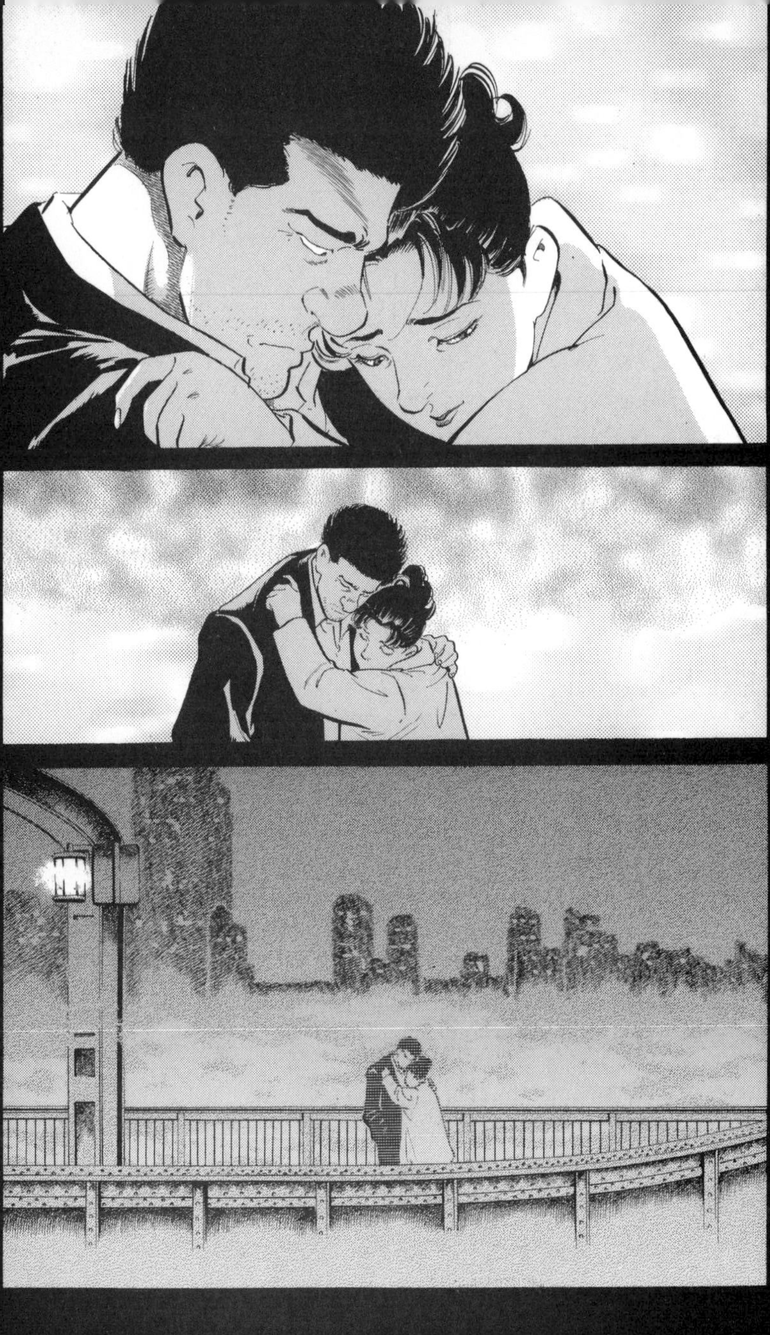

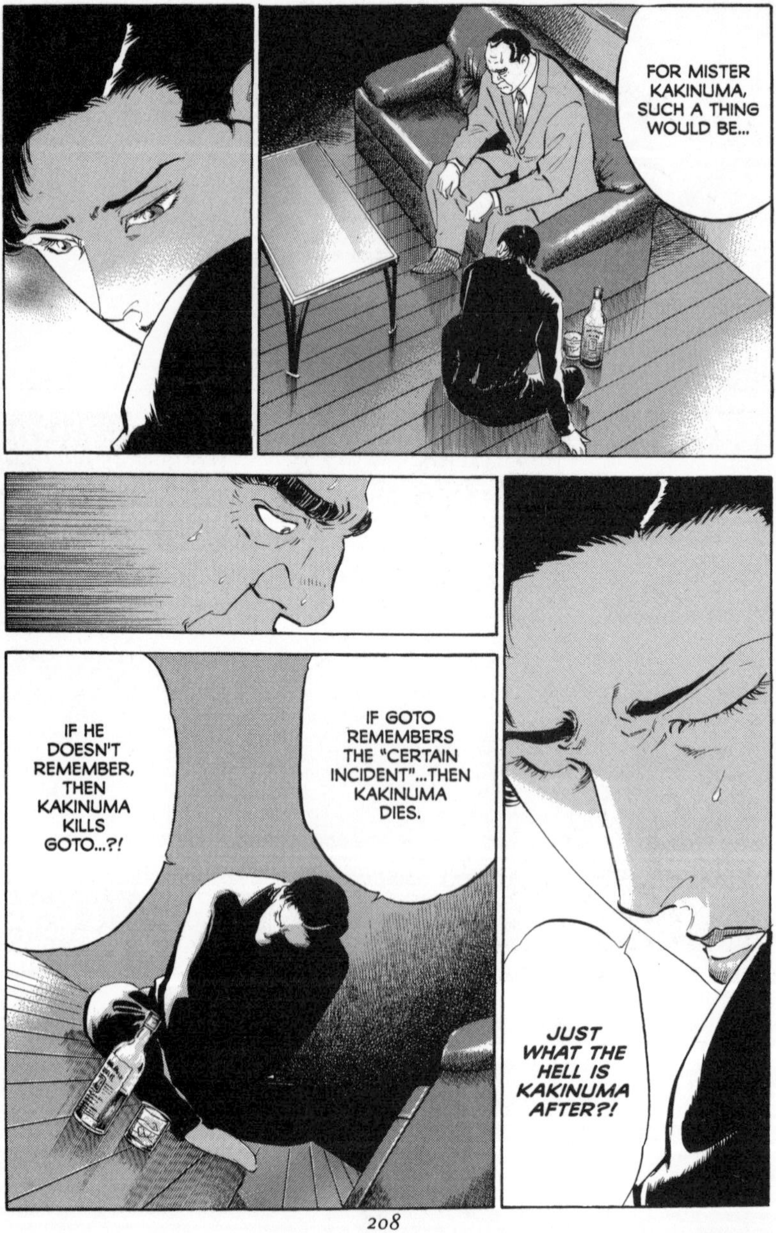
FOR MISTER KAKINUMA, SUCH A THING WOULD BE...
JUST WHAT THE HELL IS KAKINUMA AFTER?!
IF GOTO REMEMBERS THE "CERTAIN INCIDENT"...THEN KAKINUMA DIES.
IF HE DOESN'T REMEMBER, THEN KAKINUMA KILLS GOTO...?!

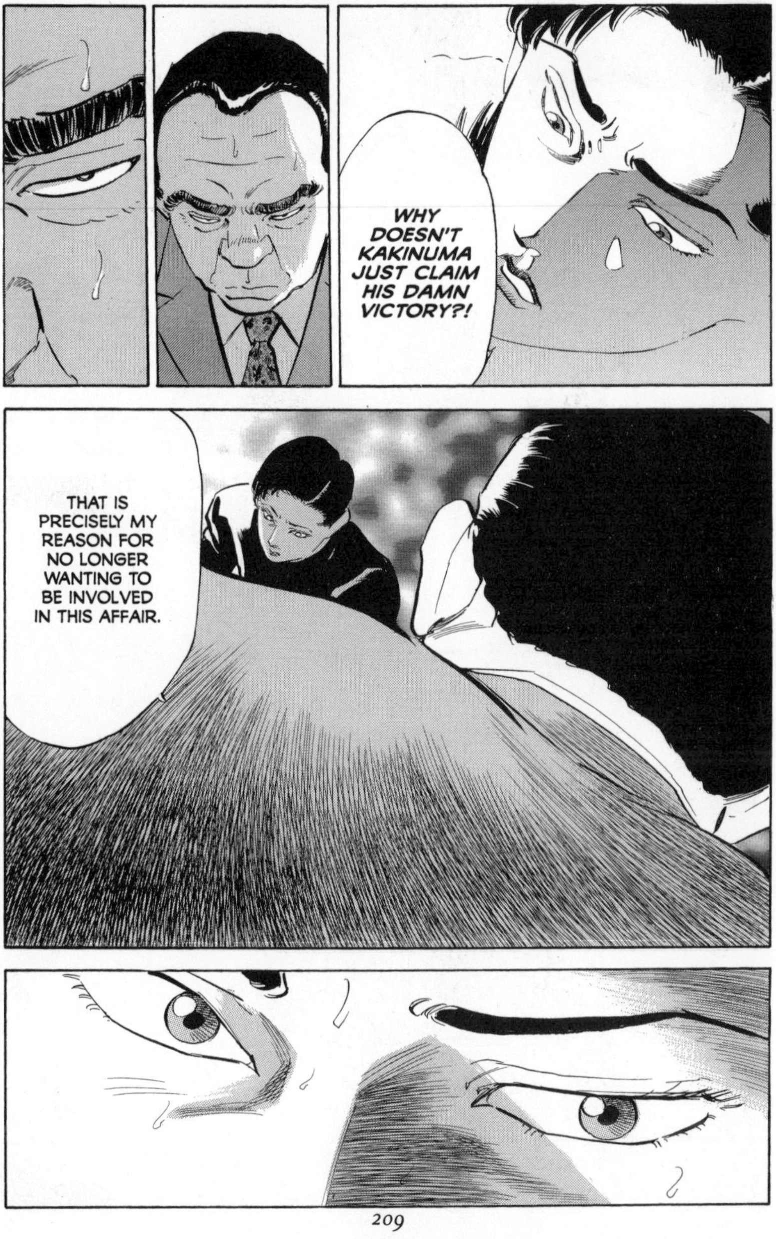
WHY DOESN'T KAKINUMA JUST CLAIM HIS DAMN VICTORY?!
THAT IS PRECISELY MY REASON FOR NO LONGER WANTING TO BE INVOLVED IN THIS AFFAIR.

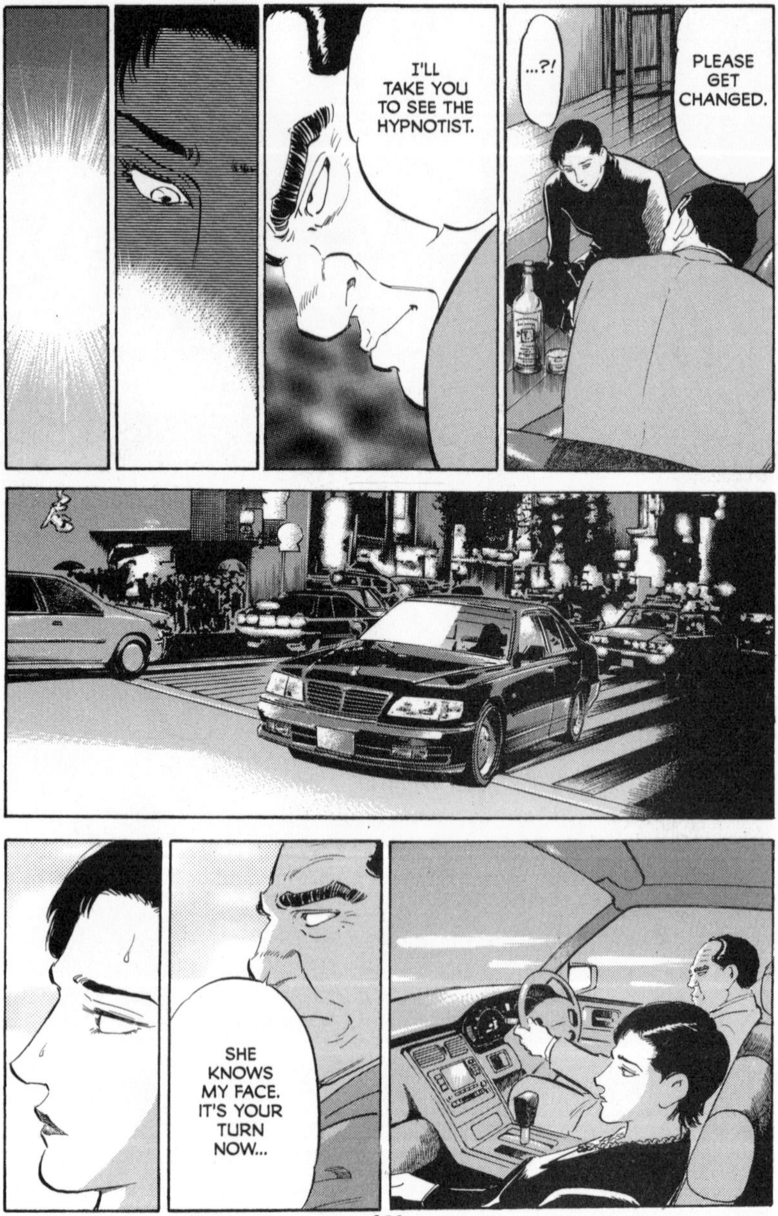
PLEASE GET CHANGED.
...?!
I'LL TAKE YOU TO SEE THE HYPNOTIST.
SHE KNOWS MY FACE. IT'S YOUR TURN NOW...

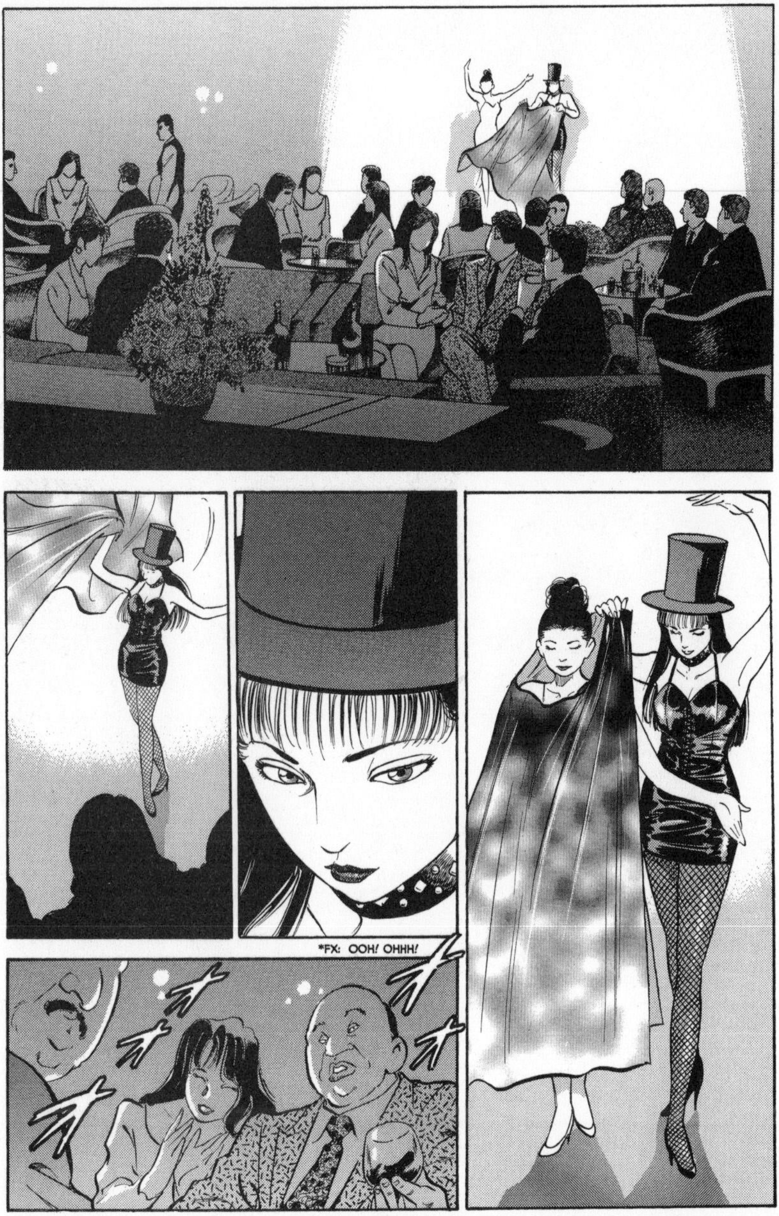
*FX: OOH! OHHH!

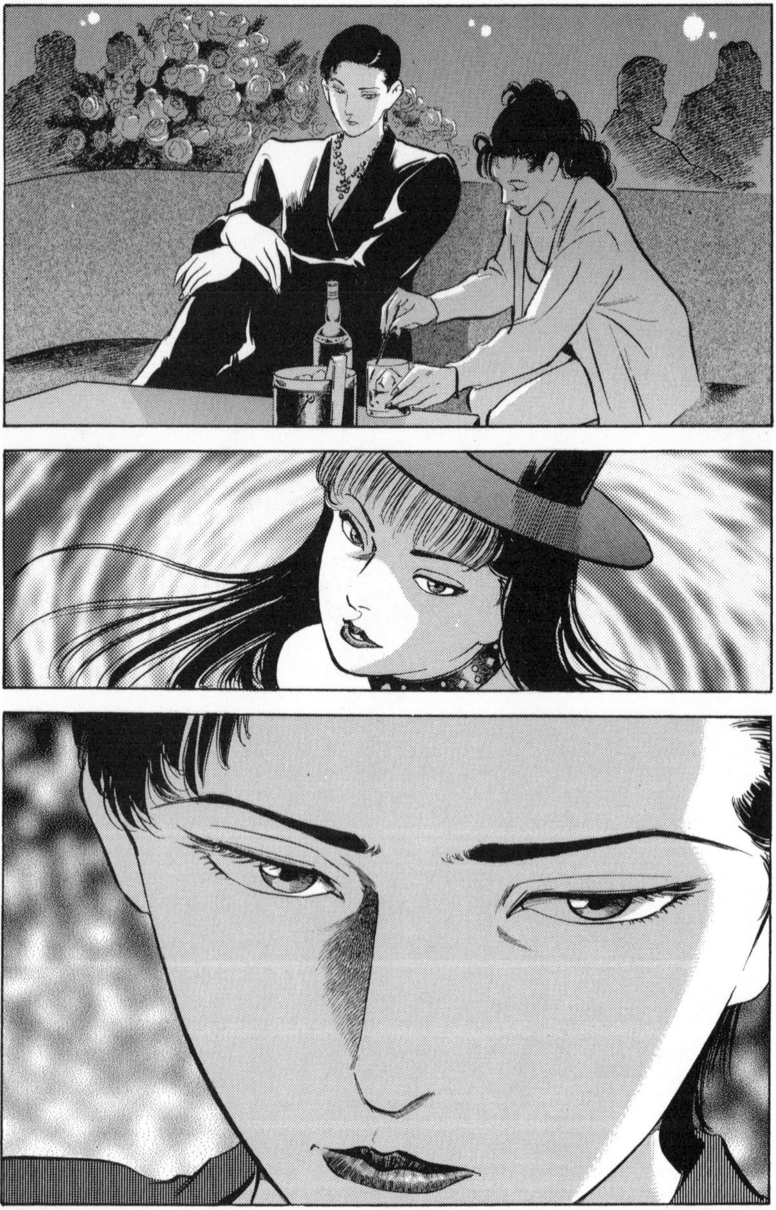

DEEPER: END

OLDBOY

Ten years ago, he was abducted and confined to a private prison. He was never told why he was there, or who put him there. Suddenly his incarceration has ended, again without explanation. He is sedated, stuffed inside a trunk, and dumped in a park. When he awakes, he is free to reclaim what's left of his life . . . and what's left is revenge.

This series is the inspiration of the *Oldboy* film directed by Chan-wook Park, which was awarded the Grand Jury Prize at the 2004 Cannes Film Festival!

VOLUME 1:
ISBN-10: 1-59307-568-5
ISBN-13: 978-1-59307-568-2

VOLUME 2:
ISBN-10: 1-59307-569-3
ISBN-13: 978-1-59307-569-9

VOLUME 3:
ISBN-10: 1-59307-570-7
ISBN-13: 978-1-59307-570-5

VOLUME 4:
ISBN-10: 1-59307-703-3
ISBN-13: 978-1-59307-703-7

VOLUME 5:
ISBN-10: 1-59307-714-9
ISBN-13: 978-1-59307-714-3

VOLUME 6:
ISBN-10: 1-59307-720-3
ISBN-13: 978-1-59307-720-4

VOLUME 7:
ISBN-10: 1-59307-721-1
ISBN-13: 978-1-59307-721-1

VOLUME 8:
ISBN-10: 1-59307-722-X
ISBN-13: 978-1-59307-722-8

$12.95 EACH!

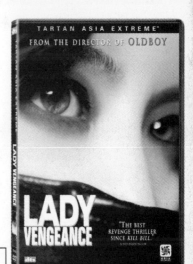

darkhorse.com | DARK HORSE TWENTY YEARS

COMICS | BOOKS | PRODUCTS | REVIEWS | ZONES | NEWS | HELP | COMPANY | RESOURCES

VISIT THE MANGA ZONE ON
DARKHORSE.COM
TO EXPLORE GREAT FEATURES LIKE:

- Exclusive content from editors on upcoming projects!
- Download exclusive desktops!
- Online previews and animations!
- Message Boards!
- Up-to-date information on the latest releases!
- Links to other cool manga sites.

Visit DARKHORSE.COM/MANGA for more details!

STOP!

THIS IS THE BACK OF THE BOOK!

This manga collection is translated into English, but arranged in right-to-left reading format to maintain the artwork's visual orientation as originally drawn and published in Japan. If you've never read comics this way before, take a look at the diagram below to give yourself an idea of how to go about it. Basically, you'll be starting in the upper right-hand corner, and will read each word balloon and panel moving right-to-left. It may take a little getting used to, but you should get the hang of it very quickly. Have fun!

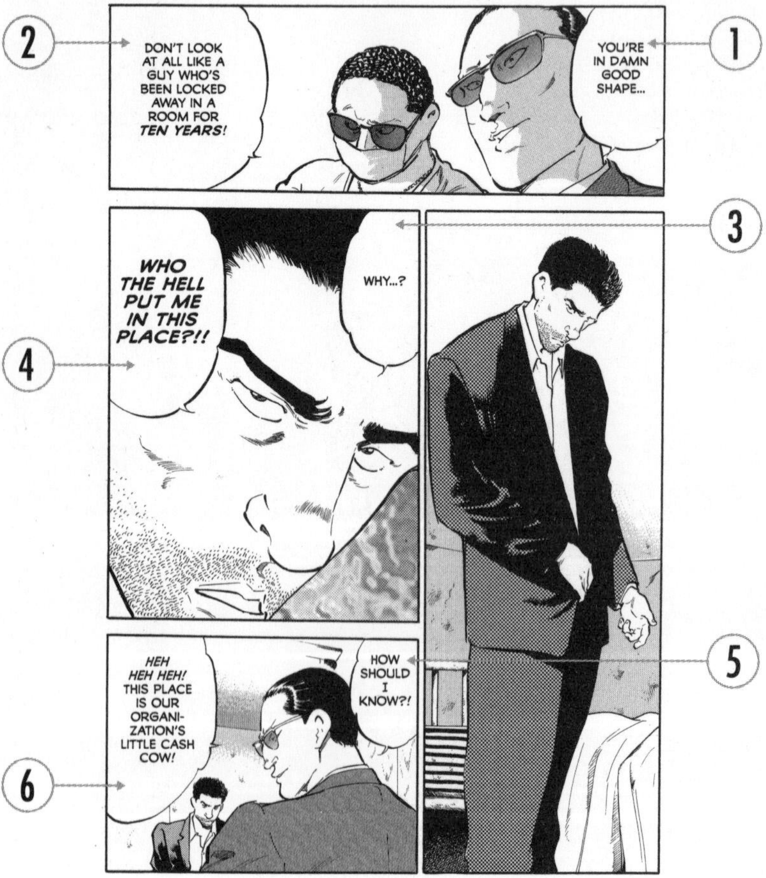
1
YOU'RE IN DAMN GOOD SHAPE...
2
DON'T LOOK AT ALL LIKE A GUY WHO'S BEEN LOCKED AWAY IN A ROOM FOR *TEN YEARS!*
3
WHY...?
4
WHO THE HELL PUT ME IN THIS PLACE?!!
5
HOW SHOULD I KNOW?!
6
HEH HEH HEH! THIS PLACE IS OUR ORGANI-ZATION'S LITTLE CASH COW!